The Dynamics *of* Intergroup Communication

Language
as SOCIAL
ACTION▶

Howard Giles,
General Editor

Vol. 8

PETER LANG
New York • Washington, D.C./Baltimore • Bern
Frankfurt am Main • Berlin • Brussels • Vienna • Oxford

The Dynamics *of* Intergroup Communication

EDITED BY
Howard Giles, Scott Reid, Jake Harwood

PETER LANG
New York • Washington, D.C./Baltimore • Bern
Frankfurt am Main • Berlin • Brussels • Vienna • Oxford

Library of Congress Cataloging-in-Publication Data
Giles, Howard.
The dynamics of intergroup communication /
Howard Giles, Scott Reid, Jake Harwood.
p. cm. — (Language as social action; v. 8)
Includes bibliographical references and index.
1. Interpersonal communication. 2. Intergroup relations.
3. Communication—Social aspects. 4. Group identity. 5. Social groups.
6. Intercultural communication. I. Reid, Scott.
II. Harwood, Jake. III. Title.
HM1166.G55   302.4—dc22   2009039366
ISBN 978-1-4331-0398-8 (hardcover)
ISBN 978-1-4331-0397-1 (paperback)
ISSN 1529-2436

Bibliographic information published by **Die Deutsche Nationalbibliothek.**
Die Deutsche Nationalbibliothek lists this publication in the "Deutsche
Nationalbibliografie"; detailed bibliographic data is available
on the Internet at http://dnb.d-nb.de/.

The paper in this book meets the guidelines for permanence and durability
of the Committee on Production Guidelines for Book Longevity
of the Council of Library Resources.

© 2010 Peter Lang Publishing, Inc., New York
29 Broadway, 18th floor, New York, NY 10006
www.peterlang.com

Printed in the United States of America

Table of Contents

Part Two: Intergroup Phenomena and Processes

Part Three: Contexts of Intergroup Communication

Part Four: Future Directions

CHAPTER ONE

Introducing the Dynamics of Intergroup Communication

HOWARD GILES, SCOTT A. REID & JAKE HARWOOD

What is intergroup communication? Imagine a family member introducing you to her future husband (Joe). Just by looking at Joe you will immediately figure out something about his sex (he's male), age (he looks very young), ethnicity (he looks Chinese), and perhaps other social categories. When he talks to you, you might gain additional information from his accent, his use of language, or even his nonverbal behaviors: perhaps his vocabulary suggests that he is educated, and his accent suggests that English is not his first language. As you start to respond to Joe, you are doing so based on numerous cues about groups that he belongs to in society—groups with which you have meaningful associations (young people are naïve; Asians are smart; non-native speakers have trouble understanding). Your communication with him is based on the groups that you see him as belonging to, and his communication with you is so influenced as well. In addition, communication actually shapes which groups you pay attention to in the particular context—saying certain things in certain ways makes people more or less aware of groups that you belong to. For example, if Joe made reference to his support for a Republican political candidate, your responses to him might suddenly shift from a focus on age or ethnicity to one on political differences or similarities between the two of you.

Now consider an alternate example. You have traveled into your nearest city to protest against a political leader whose views you disapprove of. The protest is met by a line of riot police with large plastic shields. As you move forward, two police officers drag one of the protestors out of the crowd, knock her to the ground, and beat her with their batons. The protestors start shouting at the police who respond by moving together to push you all backwards. The protestors (you included) push back against the police.

As illustrated by these examples, people often interact with one another based on groups that they belong to, rather than interacting purely as individuals. A focus on intergroup communication emphasizes the ways in which our communication with one another provides information about groups in society, and the ways in which information about groups and group memberships shapes communication. The chapters of this book provide a wide array of evidence suggesting that these intergroup processes pervade the communication we have with one another. It is in fact very rare that we communicate truly and solely as individuals; most of our communication is influenced at either a subtle or more obvious level by the groups to which we belong. As indicated by the first example, communication that is influenced by group memberships may sometimes be fairly innocuous. Indeed, one point of this book is to show that casual, everyday conversations can be influenced by group memberships in ways that we do not always think about. However, an additional goal of the book is to show that sometimes these same processes result in communication that is far from mundane. As illustrated in the second example, real and perceived differences between groups are the origins of much significant social strife and violence in our world—racism, war, terrorism, hate speech, riots, and lynchings are largely driven by one group's animosity towards another group. Therefore, as well as the innocuous, the book also includes rather more dramatic discussions of conflicts with life-or-death consequences, and the ways in which communication functions within such contexts. Our point is that both derive from similar processes. The mild anxiety you might feel communicating with someone from another ethnic group is related both theoretically and in practice to some of the much larger hatreds and conflicts that divide groups of people.

Let us now briefly dissect the notion of intergroup communication. What is a group? A group is a collection of people who have a perception of shared characteristics, interests, goals, history, or activity. Some groups can be very small (your Friday night poker game), but many are much larger (Americans, women). This book will primarily focus on the larger groups—ones with societal significance and recognition. You will read a lot about language groups (e.g., English and French speakers in Canada), gender, age, ethnic, and virtual groups, and some you may never have heard of hitherto (see for example, Chapter 2). You will also read a lot about how people *identify* with these groups as as well as the performative acts and communicative practices they creatively adopt in committing to different kinds of identities (e.g., see Chapters 2 & 19).

Groups only exist to the extent that people give them meaning. One way in which we make groups meaningful is by identifying with some groups (and not others)—by identifying we mean that you see yourself as a member of the group, you value that membership, and in a sense you view the group as a meaningful part of *who you are*. As a result, we have ingroups (groups we think we belong to) and outgroups (groups we do not think we belong to). Returning to the second example above, perhaps you went to the protest just as an individual with a personal opinion. However, once the conflict with the police began, chances are that you began to see yourself as having something in common with the other protestors (your "ingroup"), a sense of common fate, and you probably started to see a big divide between that ingroup and the police "outgroup" (see Chapters 5 & 6). Of course, sometimes other people may see us as being members of groups that we do not think we belong to, and we may actively resist such categorizations, or are forced to go along with them if the others have some power over us. A passer-by who is accidentally caught up in the protest may receive the same treatment from a police officer as a genuine protestor; in this case, the police would have mis-categorized that particular individual.

What is communication? In this book, communication is defined very broadly. As noted in the first example, a face-to-face discussion is clearly an act of communication. However, the field of communication covers the process of message exchange much more broadly. This book will consider intergroup communication in organizations (Chapters 17 & 18), in political contexts (Chapters 11 & 12), and in written forms (Chapter 7) as well as in traditional and new media (Chapters 16 & 17)—the portrayal of groups in television shows is intergroup communication, as is a racist posting on a blog. By the end of the book, we hope you will be convinced that the study of intergroup communication is fundamental to understanding our *interpersonal* relationships. We also hope that readers will come to understand how intergroup communication processes influence diverse modern civilizations' ability to exchange complex information and maintain organized social life. There are some phenomena that are arguably communicative that do not get much attention in this book. The use of cosmetics, hand gestures and facial expressions, dress, accessorizing, hairstyles, and body posture (see Chapter 2)—even architecture (see Chapter 7)—can all send messages about group memberships. Music is also beginning to receive attention as an intergroup communication phenomenon (Giles, Hajda, & Hamilton, 2009). Such issues, as well many others (e.g., marches, vigils, festivals, and artifacts), deserve more consideration, and might be deserving of their own chapters in future iterations of this book.

The remainder of this prologue provides some history of the research on intergroup relations that influences the authors featured in this book; this provides a backdrop to the chapters. Then, we outline the structure of the book and provide a taste of what is to come in the rest of this volume.

History

The history of work relevant to this book is long and illustrious, although at the same time limited by somewhat scant attention specifically to communication processes. The majority of early work of relevance comes from social psychology. As early as 1933, Katz and Braly examined perceptions of social groups by having people check boxes to report the characteristics of different nationalities and ethnicities. This was the first work to explicitly examine stereotypes of groups (see Chapters 4–6 & 8). Following WWII, various scholars attempted to explain the Holocaust and what features of human personality might have contributed to the extreme intergroup activities that occurred during that period. Adorno, Frenkel-Brunswik, Levinson, and Sanford (1950) developed the idea of the authoritarian personality, explaining negative intergroup attitudes as a function of stable personality traits such as excessive adherence to authority. Around the same time, other scholars were beginning to try to understand how to improve intergroup attitudes and stereotypes by increasing contact between groups (e.g., Allport, 1954).

The 1960s saw serious developments on at least two fronts. First, Sherif (1966) studied kids at summer camp and discovered that when resources are scarce, it is easy to incite conflict between groups. With colleagues, he developed a realistic conflict theory which emphasized the ways in which groups may come into conflict based on perceptions of win/lose scenarios whereby one group getting something means that the other group loses out. Sherif also found that having groups work cooperatively on tasks reduces conflict so long as both groups are able to contribute to the task at hand. Berkowitz (1962) developed a somewhat different approach, focusing on the idea that prejudice and discrimination are particularly likely under circumstances in which our attempts to meet goals are blocked. We get frustrated in such situations and "take it out" on a poor unsuspecting outgroup—a scapegoat.

In the late 1960s and early 1970s, a perspective emerged which was to have profound effects on intergroup social psychology and ultimately intergroup communication, namely, social identity theory (SIT; see for example, Chapters 2, 3, 8, 10, 14, 16, 18, 21, & 22). In the earliest work on this theory, Tajfel, Billig, Bundy, and Flament (1971) found that artificially created groups (e.g., the blue team and the green team) would display some intergroup discrimination, even though the groups were created in the laboratory and had no history or norms. For example, when asked to give rewards to one team or the other, members of the blue team would favor the blue team and would also limit rewards to the green team; this occurred even when the individuals distributing the rewards did not benefit personally from their actions. Tajfel's theory suggested that we have an inherent desire to view groups that we belong to in a positive way, and he posited that this is because our group memberships are an important part of *who we are.* Thus, *social identity* became defined as the aspects of the self that are made up of the groups that you belong to, and that are imbued with emotional and value significance. In the study of blue/green teams, by giving the blue team rewards and denying them to the green team, a blue team member could feel good about the blue team (because as a team they were different from and better than—had more rewards—the other group).

Social identity theory says that we categorize the social world, we identify groups that we belong to, and we seek ways to view those groups positively— including by finding ways of comparing our group positively relative to other groups (*we*'re smarter, funnier, cooler, faster, wealthier, etc., than *they* are). Tajfel claimed that these comparisons make us feel good about who we are by helping us feel good about the groups that we belong to. In simple terms, they provide us with self-esteem. This account of intergroup relations is grounded heavily in motivational concerns—people are motivated and desire to maintain a positive social identity, and their perceptions and relationships with members of their ingroups and outgroups are shaped by this desire (see Tajfel, 1978; Tajfel and Turner, 1979).

Our social identity is partly derived from the level of social status that our ingroups have. Some groups are clearly viewed more positively in society and have more status, wealth, and the like than others; indeed, power differentials are invoked repeatedly throughout this volume (e.g., see Chapters 4, 5, 10, 14, 16, & 18). This raises the question of how people cope when the groups they belong to are *not* high status, or that status is in some way threatened (see Chapters 13 & 20) . This question drives the second major part of social identity theory. How can you retain a positive social identity when you belong to a disadvantaged or negatively perceived group? Tajfel suggests a number of options (e.g., see Chapters 2 & 14; also Chapter 21 for an alternative theoretical position).

First, people can leave their groups in search of other more positive groups ("social mobility"). If you are an older person and you think that younger people are more valued in society (see Chapter 4), you can get plastic surgery or use hair dyes to appear younger (and hence get the rewards associated with that more positively viewed group). Second, you can engage in various creative perceptions of the group that you belong to ("social creativity"). For instance you can compare yourself with other groups on novel dimensions: Recent immigrants might acknowledge that they are low status (see Chapter 2), but maintain a positive ingroup perception as "hard working" or "family oriented." An alternative creative approach is to compare your group to a different target. For African Americans, it might sometimes be counterproductive to compare their group's status to Whites, but a comparison to Korean

Americans might yield more positive perceptions of the ingroup. Third, groups can engage in "social competition"—advocating, protesting, and fighting for more positive group conditions. The civil rights and feminist movements are great examples of this more proactive and group-based approach: Activists within those movements did not accept that the position of their groups was appropriate, and they fought (sometimes literally) to gain rights and status. Of course, this part of the theory highlights the dynamic nature of intergroup relations. Groups are not organized in some static arrangement that inevitably persists over time. Rather, groups may be struggling to gain a foothold on a metaphorical ladder, pushing to climb higher on that ladder, or grimly hanging on to the top rung and kicking anybody underneath.

Interestingly, although this work came from scholars in social psychology, Tajfel and his colleagues were clearly concerned with issues of language and communication from the very beginning (e.g., Bourhis, Giles, Leyens, & Tajfel, 1979; Bourhis, Giles, & Tajfel, 1973; Giles, 1978). Indeed, while work on SIT was progressing and yielded other theoretical advances (for example, see Chapters 15 and 17 for the SIT of intergroup contact, Chapter 16 for the SIT of media gratifications [and see also Reid, Giles, & Abrams, 2004], and Chapter 17 for the SIDE model), research was also being forged on the perceived status and strength of different language groups, and the ways in which members of those groups handled their relative group vitalities (e.g., Giles, Bourhis, & Taylor, 1977; see also Chapters 2, 10, & 16). Simultaneously, the first work on communication accommodation theory was emerging (see Gallois, Ogay, & Giles [2005] for an historical overview). This theory acknowledged more directly the role that group memberships play in influencing how people adjust their talk in social interaction with others. For instance, work from this perspective showed that people would emphasize group-related speech markers (accent, dialect, vocabulary) in situations that reflected group-related threat (Giles, 1979), and it also spawned further satellite models, including ethnolinguistic identity theory (Giles & Johnson, 1981) and the communicative predicament of aging model (see Chapter 4).

Later, Turner and colleagues (1987) developed self-categorization theory (SCT), a theory that builds on, and complements SIT (e.g., see Chapters 2, 3, 9, & 22). Turner's perspective aimed to explain the fundamental process that produces group behavior—when and why do people identify with some groups but not others, and how is it that group identification transforms social perception, judgment, emotions, and behaviors? In the example at the start of this chapter, there were lots of potential dimensions on which you might have compared yourself with your sister's fiancé (Joe). Aspects of your past experience and the context might all have been relevant. SCT describes which elements of experiences and social contexts are likely to lead you to use one social category or another; that is, the subjective salience of a group for an individual at any given time (see Chapters 3–5, 8, 12, 15, 17 &

22). Such would be apparent if someone is behaving in ways highly consistent with a stereotype of a particular group (e.g., your sister giggling about wedding dresses might make gender salient) as well as individual predispositions (e.g., if you speak Chinese and have been studying Chinese culture, then Joe's Chinese ethnicity might be particularly relevant to you).

Through the late 1970s and on, it's important to note that a perspective known as "social cognition" was developing in social psychology (Wyer & Srull, 1984). This approach emphasized the idea that we sometimes think about people in much the same way that we think about other objects (e.g., chairs, flowers, buildings). For instance, if I am trying to figure out what caused my girlfriend to break up with me, some of the processes I engage in might be the same as if I were trying to figure out what caused a window to break in my house. I'll try, for instance, to determine if it's something about the object (my ex-girlfriend was crazy; the window was made of cheap glass), or me (I said something mean to her; I just tried cleaning the window with hydrofluoric acid), or the situation (my girlfriend and I have both been stressed at school; the window got rattled by an earthquake). This approach extends to intergroup phenomena by investigating, for instance, whether explanations for events are driven by group stereotypes (e.g., when an outgroup member does something bad to me, I might be more likely to explain it as a function of their inherent negative tendencies, whereas from an ingroup member I may be more likely to see it as an "exception to the rule").

In recent years, the focus on intergroup processes in the field of communication has grown, as has the focus on language and communication issues in social psychology (see Chapter 8). For instance, as early as 1986, the first book about intergroup issues was published in the field of communication (Gudykunst, 1986). In the 1990s, the first special issue devoted to intergroup communication processes emerged (Clément, 1996) as did a substantial amount of work concerning the *linguistic intergroup bias* (for an overview, see Sutton & Douglas, 2008; see also Chapters 8–10 & 16). This bias occurs when people make very subtle decisions to use, say, an adjective versus a verb in describing the behaviors of ingroup and outgroup members; such language choices reflect attitudes in interesting ways, and can have important effects in terms of how readers/listeners perpetuate stereotypes. For example, (Chinese) Joe in our opening example may have told some anecdotes about his experiences in the United States, which we might then relate by saying that "Joe *talked* about his experiences at length" (thus disowning a stereotype) or embrace the stereotype by saying that "Joe is *inscrutable*."

Once we reached the new millennium, the International Communication Association developed an Intergroup Communication Interest Group, more special issues were published (e.g., Clément, 2007; Reid & Giles, 2005), and more interdisciplinary work began to mine the intersection of intergroup and language/communication processes (Robinson & Giles; 2001, Ruscher, 2001). The massive *International Encyclopedia of Communication Science* included a section titled "Intercultural and Intergroup Communication"—perhaps the first time a discipline-wide reference work had included intergroup communication as a key area (Giles & Watson, 2008). Finally, at least one new book published an edited series of chapters detailing the substantive development of our knowledge about intergroup communication processes (Harwood & Giles, 2005). Indeed, it is in response to this last book that the current was planned. Our goal here is to update the information in that previous book, to present a lot of the information in much more accessible and user-friendly form, and to stretch the boundaries of what was covered in that book by investigating new processes, new groups, and new applications of the important theory in the area. It is in this spirit that we now turn to a more detailed elaboration of the structure of the current book and the content of the areas that the chapters will cover.

The Current Book

Communicating Between Social Groups

The first section of the book examines specific social groups that are a chronic part of social interaction across all cultures. While it may be true that there are common-alities *across* different contexts of intergroup communication, there are also impor-tant ways in which each group, and hence each intergroup situation, is unique. Clearly, an array of possible dimensions is available for us to consider in terms of distinguishing between different intergroup settings (e.g., group vitality), and this is an exciting prospect for further conceptual and theoretical advances. Yet a cou-ple of dimensions that illustrate these distinctions are illustrated in Figure 1, and some of the groups featured in this book are located in the figure. The first dimen-sion is permeability—how easy is it for members of one group to move into anoth-er group? For instance, age groups are inherently permeable—we all move from one age group into another as a function of aging. However, that permeability is con-strained in interesting ways (see Chapters 5, 8, 12, 13, 18, & 19). We cannot move across massive age differences voluntarily—movement is constrained by time. The movement is also, for the most part, unidirectional—'
we get older, not younger. However, there are ways in which we individually may attempt to work around some of these constraints (e.g., and as mentioned earlier, using plastic surgery or Botox to look younger than you really are). In contrast, gen-der groups are considerably less permeable—people rarely move across gender boundaries. Still, even here certain levels of permeability exist. Transvestites can sometimes convincingly pass as members of the other sex, and sexual reassignment

surgeries are available and used. Permeability has important implications for inter-group relations—for instance, the "social mobility" option described earlier becomes less available as group boundaries become less permeable.

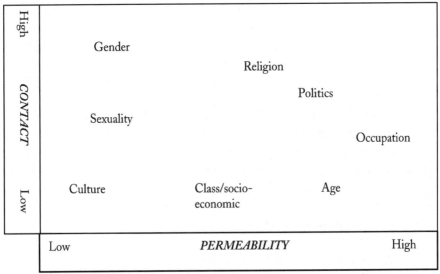

Figure 1. Intergroup Contexts in North America Arrayed (very approximately) on Dimensions of Contact and Permeability

The second dimension featured is contact (see Chapters 12 & 15–17): do groups have a lot of contact with one another or relatively little? Across most cultures, for instance, gender groups have a great deal of contact. Men and women require one another's presence at a minimum for reproductive purposes, and they have tradition-ally joined together to build families (see Chapter 22). On the other hand, it is often the case that ethnic groups are voluntarily or involuntarily segregated from one another and have little contact. For instance, Dixon and Durrheim (2003) show how in post-apartheid South Africa, Black and White beach-goers will tend to cluster in totally different areas of a public beach.

Of course, the precise placement of groups in this framework varies a lot based on the local situation. In some cultures, members of different religions, for instance, may mingle frequently, generally without even being aware of one another's religion. In such contexts, changing one's religion (re-categorization) is also probably rela-tively unremarkable. This is true, for instance, in contact between Christians of var-ious denominations, Jews, and probably other religious groups in North America. In other locations, religion may be a dominant and politically charged group mem-bership. For Hindus and Moslems in India, for instance, both contact and perme-ability may be considerably less likely. The placement of groups also varies based on the specific group. For instance, it is often the case that lower status groups have more contact with higher status groups than vice versa. Older people, for instance, have relatively more contact with young people than young people do with older people.

In addition to describing features of intergroup contexts, it is possible that the framework in Figure 1 also illustrates the extent to which relations between groups are characterized by conflict and hostility (see Chapters, 10, 11, 14, 15, 18, & 20). One might hypothesize, for instance, that the highest levels of intergroup *conflict* within a particular geographic region occur between groups characterized by low permeability and low contact.

As the discussion above has illustrated, it is helpful to understand how intergroup processes have been studied in a "one group at a time" manner, and this is done by the chapters in this section of the book. Verkuyten's examination of interethnic communication and identity gets the section under way. This chapter emphasizes the ways in which communication creates ethnic identity, treating identity in some ways as a "performance." Kalbfleisch then examines gender and communication, considering such phenomena as the connections between power differentials and language use in interaction between men and women.

Hummert examines intergroup processes surrounding age groups. Focusing particularly on the role of stereotyping and old age, her work clearly outlines the psychological and physical consequences that can accrue when negative assumptions based on age group memberships influence communication. Drury also takes on age as a topic, but with a focus on communication between adolescents and adults. This chapter emphasizes the ways in which stereotyping of adolescents is a major contributor to conflict between adolescents and adults in positions of authority, particularly the police.

The final two chapters in this section break somewhat new ground in terms of the groups they examine. Giles, Choi, and Dixon examine police-civilian interaction, outlining some of the processes by which police and civilians accommodate one another (or fail to) in communication. Their work includes, among other things, some direct recommendations for improving intergroup communication in this context. Klocek, Novoa, and Moghaddam's chapter focuses on religious groups. Despite the massive influence that religious conflicts have had in our world, these group memberships and conflicts based on them have been largely ignored in the previous intergroup communication literature, a deficit that this chapter should begin to erase. This chapter considers incredibly wide-ranging intersections between communication and religious life, such as the functions of very formal (sacred texts) and very informal (everyday talk about religion) communication.

Of course, no single book could examine in any detail every possible group dimension, emotional reaction (e.g., shame, fear, anger), or communicative variable and conglomeration that is invoked, concealed, or even actively avoided and silenced. And we would note that issues of class, caste, political affiliation, homelessness, and many others could have been addressed here with individual chapters. Each of us belongs to many different groups simultaneously as well drifts in and out of them throughout our lives, with certain groups gaining importance for us based on immediate situational factors as well as more long-standing dispositions. Some of those group memberships which have not yet been studied extensively may provide new insights for the field of intergroup communication. It is also worth mentioning at this point that some groups received more attention in our earlier book (Harwood & Giles, 2005). For instance, readers interested in issues of disability or sexuality should see the respective chapters in that book (see also Chapters 13 & 15).

Intergroup Phenomena and Processes

The next section of the book examines specific intergroup processes—concepts and phenomena that transcend specific groups. In this section, some of the processes that apply *across* the groups from the previous section should start to become apparent. The first chapter examines stereotyping. Drawing from both SIT and SCT, Reid and Anderson discuss the ways in which stereotypes reflect and instantiate group status positions through various linguistic devices like variations in linguistic abstraction and ethnophaulisms. The Sutton chapter focuses very specifically on language, emphasizing the ways in which language conveys information about groups, displays attitudes about groups, and is actively used to define groups. Clément, Shulman, and Rubenfeld discuss the large body of research on multilingualism and bilingualism, focusing particularly on the identity issues apparent in environments where two or more languages are widely spoken, and including work on second-language learning.

The next two chapters consider explicitly political issues. Ellis discusses the role of rational argument and debate in political conflicts, focusing on how deliberative communication is a crucial medium for mediating and solving conflicts. Myers and Stohl describe how communication may function to incite terrorism, as well as considering the nature of terrorist acts *as* communication to audiences of ingroup and outgroup members. Rintamaki and Brashers take the perspective of members of stigmatized groups, seeking to understand how subordinate groups in society use communication to manage stigmatized identities. Finally, Reicher considers the ways in which language and discourse can be used to structure views of both outgroup *and* ingroup, and the ways in which some forces in society may manipulate discourse so as to maintain control over how we view groups.

While each chapter in this section has its unique focus, as a set they should serve to illustrate that many concepts apply across specific intergroup contexts. For example, the content of stereotypes may vary across social groups; but the ways in which people use them to simplify judgments of other people, justify negative treatment of others, or to serve as communicative "short cuts" are fairly universal whether you are studying gender relations or intercultural conflict.

Contexts of Intergroup Communication

The book next moves to consider six important contexts in society. Each chapter in this section elaborates on how considering intergroup communication processes might help us understand what goes on in each of these contexts. The first five contexts (family, mass communication, new technology, organizations, and health) have been the subject of considerable communication research over the years, and these chapters emphasize how that research could be broadened to incorporate an intergroup perspective. In the family chapter, Soliz discusses how the family may constitute a "common ingroup" for people who otherwise differ (e.g., family members who are different ages, sexualities, etc.). In doing so, this chapter provides a clear indication of how intergroup processes can pervade even our most intimate relationships, and the ways in which intergroup phenomena can sometimes be used to overcome group differences. Mastro's chapter considers mass media and intergroup relations, focusing particularly on how specific portrayals of certain groups in the media (e.g., stereotypical portrayals) may affect consumers. Mastro also considers the ways in which contact with outgroup characters in the media may parallel "real world" contact. In their chapter on new technology, Walther and Carr take a critical eye to the idea that group memberships are dominant in on-line communication. They develop a perspective for understanding how and why our on-line communication may rely more (or less) on group memberships than off-line communication.

In the chapter on organizations, Peters, Morton, and Haslam address head on the issue of whether intergroup concerns are inherently barriers to effective communication. They present an innovative model suggesting that ignoring intergroup differences is futile, and so successful organizations will learn to work with, and even take advantage of, what may at first appear to be problematic divisions. Villagrán and Sparks consider many of the important identity issues that arise in health care. In particular, they consider identities relating to specific diseases, as well as identification as a patient (i.e., as someone who is sick). Their chapter extends beyond physical health issues to incorporate mental health, and more broadly to consider the role of stigma as an intergroup process in health care settings.

The final chapter of this section considers sport, a massively important cultural phenomenon, but one that has probably not received its fair share of scholarly attention. In this chapter, Haridakis discusses the ways in which fans identify with certain teams or with other fans, and discusses some of the consequences of that identification in terms of facilitating self-esteem on the one hand and aggressive acts on the other. Relating back to the Walther and Carr chapter, Haridakis also describes the role of Internet communication (e.g., online discussions) in reflecting and influencing team identifications.

Future Directions

The two chapters in the book's final section wrap up some of the key areas of discussion raised within the book and present some visions for the future. In the first of these, Taylor, King, and Usborne discuss the dominance of social identity theory within the area, and suggest that this dominance may not be entirely helpful. They suggest Jost's system justification approach as an alternative. This approach claims that some people are motivated to support the status quo and that the desire for a stable and predictable system can override the desire for personal or group-based change. They also address in depth the growing interest in implicit (unconscious) attitudes in social psychology and discuss the ways in which future communication research could more effectively integrate consideration of such attitudes. In a sense, this chapter is a call for a more diverse theoretical ecosystem in the field of intergroup communication. In the final chapter, Reid and colleagues elaborate on the continuing promise of the social identity approach. Specifically, they illustrate the potential for a merger between the social identity approach and the currently burgeoning area of evolutionary psychology. The chapter looks at how we can understand the evolutionary origins of various intergroup communication phenomena. Focusing particularly on communication accommodation and gossip, Reid and colleagues describe a variety of hypotheses that could be tested in order to understand more about where in the evolutionary process various intergroup issues might have emerged. Very finally, this volume closes with a uniquely comprehensive cumulative bibliography of works in, and related to, intergroup communication.

Conclusion

When we first planned this book, our goal was to generate a review of what we know about intergroup communication that was more accessible than our earlier volume (Harwood & Giles, 2005), as well as covering more ground. We have achieved this with chapters that investigate new intergroup contexts, present innovative models and typologies of intergroup communication, and provide critical review and synthesis of existing areas of work. As a result, we feel we have achieved our goal, and we appreciate the work of all the authors in pushing beyond a simple review and towards development of knowledge.

As we look to the future viability of the communication discipline, we see the consideration of intergroup processes as essential. Most of the world's population lives in contexts that are becoming increasingly multi-ethnic, multilingual, and international. Travel across national boundaries is becoming an everyday activity for many, and new technologies allow individuals to communicate easily and cheaply across such boundaries even if they stay home. Meanwhile, hostilities between ethnic, national, religious, and other groups do not appear to be decreasing and are on the rise in some sectors. These phenomena suggest that an understanding of how individuals communicate based on group memberships, and how communication creates and polices such boundaries, is essential academic terrain for the 21st century. We hope that this book provides a roadmap for that territory towards development of knowledge.

Part One

Communicating Between Social Groups

CHAPTER TWO

Ethnic Communication and Identity Performance

MAYKEL VERKUYTEN

In 1989, in France, the 'headscarf affair of Creil' attracted a lot of media attention and led to a political controversy involving the then Minister of Education Jospin, as well as the Supreme Court. The nationwide commotion was about the wearing of a headscarf ('hidjâb') in public schools by Muslim girls (see Chapter 7). It all started in September at the start of a new year at a public school when two Moroccan French and one Tunisian French girl, living in the city of Creil, refused to take off their headscarves during lessons.

In France, the state school is seen as one of the symbols of the victory of the state over the clergy. For those against headscarves, the neutrality of the school is related to core national values of universalism and equality. To them, the headscarf communicates the denial of individual freedom and enlightenment and is 'therefore' a threat to national identity. Wearing a headscarf represents fanaticism and a lack of willingness to integrate. In addition, feminist groups argued that the headscarf symbolizes the repression and assumed inferiority of women. To them, the headscarf obstructs emancipation and is incompatible with individual development and human rights.

Quite different symbolic meanings were involved for those in favor of wearing a headscarf in the classroom. To them, public schools symbolize equality of all ethnic groups and propagate freedom of expression. Pupils should not be forbidden to show their religion because this would go against these core national principles. Moreover, wearing a headscarf was seen to symbolize the identity and rights of Muslims, and the acceptance of minority groups in society. The acceptance of the headscarf was considered as a recognition of minority group identities which was seen as a necessary step for their integration. However, not all Muslims agreed and part of the disagreement was along ethno-national lines that in Europe typically divide, for example, Moroccan, Turkish and Pakistani Muslims who tend to have their own mosques and religious associations and organizations (Buijs & Rath, 2002).

This example clearly shows the importance of communication in ethno-religious group relations. The symbolic meanings were interpreted in different ways and as a symbol, the scarf was used for different purposes. This is not only the case in France but also in other countries, including Islamic ones, such as Iran, Turkey and Egypt. Throughout history, the headscarf and also the veil ('tchador') have been controversial and symbolic garments in identity and power struggles. For example, in Iran and Afghanistan the veil has been a symbol of national identity and independence in the fight against colonial oppression and westernization, where-as in Turkey, wearing a headscarf or veil is incompatible with the republican nation-alism initiated by Mustafa Kemal, better known as Atatürk.

Thus, the wearing of a headscarf is loaded with all kinds of symbolic, and high-ly contested, meanings. Different ethno-religious groups demand that their own identity can be expressed and is acknowledged, and identity expression typically has instrumental or political meanings. People are engaged in actions that mark and implicate their ethnic or religious identity. They perform behaviors relevant to the norms and values that are conventionally associated with a particular social identi-ty, and this identity performance can differ in relation to co-ethnics and to outgroup members (Klein, Spears, & Reicher, 2007).

In this chapter, ethnic identity performances will feature as a major form of intergroup communication. Subsequently, questions of ethnic identity confirmation and mobilization in relation to co-ethnics will be discussed. Then, identity perfor-mances oriented at outgroup members will also be considered. The concluding sec-tion examines the ways in which identity performance can shape people's sense of ethnic identity.

Identity Performance

In thinking about communication and ethnicity, we touch upon the 'identity' con-cept that has been given various definitions in the social sciences. For social psychol-ogists, collective identities have to do with people's sense of their group memberships. The emphasis is on the subjective aspects that are conceptualized in terms of, for example, cognitive centrality, importance and satisfaction. However, collective identities are not like private beliefs or convictions that, in principle, can be sustained without expression and social recognition. Social identities depend crucially on acknowledgment and acceptance by others (see Verkuyten, 2005). Anthropologists, for example, have shown how people use particular behaviors to form and negotiate their ethnic identity in everyday interactions, and discourse analysts have shown how social identities are accomplished in the ongoing exchange of talk. All this work indicates that social identities are sustainable to the extent that they are expressed and affirmed in acceptable practices. A Moroccan French Muslim identity, in any real sense, implies, for example, that one is able to claim desired images, positions, and self-understandings in a variety of contexts and especially in public spaces. And being a Muslim is often a more 'problematic' or accountable issue in public than in private life.

Identity performance can take a variety of forms and serve different purposes. Following Scheepers and colleagues (2003) who distinguish between two functions of ingroup bias, a distinction between an identity confirmation function and an instrumental function can be made (Klein et al., 2007). First, 'doing ethnicity' confirms one's ethnic identity by expressing the value of the group symbolically. Ethnic behaviors communicate one's distinctive social identity: it tells others who you are, to which group you belong and what this group membership means to you. The wearing, or not wearing, of a headscarf communicates what kind of Muslim you consider yourself to be and how you want to be seen and recognized by ingroup and outgroup members. Furthermore, the specific style of wearing a headscarf expresses subtle differences in meanings. Thus, identity performance can serve to value or affirm the group symbolically and thereby contributes to people's need for a distinctive and positive social identity (Tajfel & Turner, 1979).

The instrumental function refers to the achievement of collective goals related to the preservation or improvement of the standing of one's group. As argued by self-categorization theory (Turner, Hogg, Oakes, Reicher, & Wetherell, 1987), group behavior can promote group success by mobilizing members for collective actions. The wearing of a headscarf can become a political statement and the basis for group coordination and organization. It can be used to claim group rights and to enhance the standing of the Muslim community in, for example, Western Europe.

Obviously, the same behavior may sometimes serve both functions and identity confirmation is not entirely separate from practical outcomes. However, there can be a difference between the possibilities that ethnic minority groups have to publicly express and thereby consolidate their identity and the organization and mobilization of these groups for specific group projects. Furthermore, identity performance can differ in relation to ingroup and to outgroup members. In a study among Swedish-speaking Finns and the group of Sorbs in Germany, it is found that minority language is used in private and semi-official domains of their own ethnic minority group, whereas the majority language communicates national belonging and is preferred in official domains (Broermann, 2008; see also Chapter 10).

Ingroup Members

Identity Confirmation

People have a basic need to belong (Baumeister & Leary, 1995) and tend to act to secure acceptance as ingroup members. Being accepted as a full member of one's ethnic group implies demonstrations that communicate and authenticate membership. Depending on the criteria that define group membership, this is less or more difficult. Clay (2003) shows how African American youth use hip-hop culture, particularly rap music, to form and negotiate their black identity in everyday interactions with other African Americans. Ingroup acceptance as authentically black depends on one's ability to master the tools of hip-hop performance, that is the right language, clothes, posture, attitude and bodily gestures (see also Giles, Denes, Hamilton, & Hajda, 2009).

Another example comes from the anthropologist Herbert Gans (1979), who coined the term symbolic ethnicity to argue that processes of acculturation and assimilation among descendants of immigrants in the United States are often accompanied by a renewed interest in their ethnic identity. This interest is not intense enough to lead to ethnic institutions and organizations, but it does give rise to ethnic symbolism. This involves a nostalgic allegiance to the ethnic culture that is expressed in, for example, ethnic consumer goods, festivals and holidays. In a word, people who regard themselves as Irish Americans may have lost much of their Irishness but hold on to an Irish identity by celebrating St. Patrick's Day or frequenting an Irish bar.

Most people do not only belong to an ethnic group but also to a nation and these two categories often do not overlap. Rather, people define themselves as Irish or African American, Asian British or Turkish Dutch. Sometimes tensions between these two memberships exist making the public performance of ethnicity more or less contradictory to national belonging. For example, predominantly speaking an ethnic language can be considered a lack of commitment to the nation state, and speaking only the national language can be regarded as a form of disloyalty to one's ethnic community. However, ethnic identities do not always stand in tension with national belonging. This depends on the ways in which the ethnic and national groups are understood. Take the example of Mauritius, which is viewed as a strong candidate for 'truly successful polyethnic societies' (Eriksen, 1994). Mauritius is a small island in the south-western Indian Ocean and its cultural complexity is substantial. On a surface of 1,860 square kilometers, various ethnic groups live together (e.g. Hindus, Tamils, Telegus, Marathis, Muslims, Creoles, Whites, and Chinese), around fifteen languages are said to be spoken, and the four world religions rub shoulders. The central image of Mauritius is that of a diasporic nation, and the cultural politics of the state encourages the cultivation of 'ancestral cultures' (Eisenlohr, 2004). Mauritians are primarily conceived as subjects with origins elsewhere and ongoing commitments to authentic diasporic traditions. This means that the public performance of ethnic identities in ethnic holidays, religious festivals, and ancestral languages is one of the ways in which full membership in a Mauritian nation is claimed and demonstrated.

Ethnic identities are fundamentally shaped by social interactions and by practices and discourses about authenticity. Individuals negotiate their ethnic self-understandings in relation to ingroup members and by using various characteristics, such as language and cultural practices. Speaking and reading a particular language is often an important criterion for successful identity claims. Several studies have shown that a lack of ethnic language proficiency makes it difficult to feel fully accepted by co-ethnics. Chinese Canadian and Chinese Dutch people, for example, emphasize the lack of Chinese literacy as an important shortcoming, from not being able to carry on a conversation, to not being able to understand the news as the 'real' Chinese would (Belanger & Verkuyten, in press). They argue that they are and feel Chinese, but at the same time are not Chinese 'enough', or not 'really' Chinese because they lack critical attributes of Chinese culture and 'therefore' are not fully able to 'do' Chinese. Similarly, among South Moluccans living in the Netherlands, the ability to speak the Malay language is used to authenticate a Moluccan identity ('If you can't speak Malay, you're not a real Moluccan') (Verkuyten, 2005).

Identity Mobilization

Identity performance is not only about individuals because group members can also act together to secure the recognition of their shared social identity and to preserve and enhance the social standing of their group. Groups, for example, may emphasize language rights to ensure recognition and social power. In Mauritius, language has become central in ethnic claims because of its institutionalized link with 'ancestors and ancestral culture'. Eisenlohr (2004) shows how in the Hindustani community the rallying for Hindi in order to promote the 'Hindu cause' in Mauritius is made possible by identifying Hindi as the 'language of our ancestors'. This regardless of the fact that the immigrant ancestors were illiterate speakers and that the particular language version promoted was widely used in India only from the end of the 19th century.

Language is often a critical attribute that defines ethnic group membership and ethnic interests. The romantic equation of people, language and culture is widespread. Language is typically assumed to provide a natural basis for the existence of ethnicities and to play an important role in the mobilization of ethnic groups. In the European context, Krejci and Velimsky (1981), for example, discuss forty-seven ethnic groups that can be identified by their exclusive use of their own literary language. But language should not be equated with ethnicity or nationality. Linguists have estimated that there are some 6000 languages in the world, much more than the number of ethnic groups. Further, a linguistically distinct group does not have to have a strong sense of ethnicity. The Lazi of north-east Turkey have a fairly clear profile as a linguistic category because they speak a language (Lazuri) which is related to the Georgian languages of the Caukasus. However, the Lazi do not consider themselves on that account a separate people. They do not see themselves as any less Turkish than their (only) Turkish-speaking neighbors and feel no bonds with the Georgians who visit their region (Hann, 1997).

Furthermore, the same ethnic group can speak very different languages. An example is the Karen in Burma (Myanmar) who are involved in one of the longest 'civil wars' in the world which started more than 50 years ago. This group calls itself 'a people' but comprises members with mutually unintelligible languages of diverse cultural sub-groups (e.g., Sgaw, Pwo, and Pao). They also have different religions (e.g. Baptists, Buddhist, and animist) and are from various geographical locations. The stories about their common origin, the suppression by the Burmese government and cultural artifacts such as clothing form the basis and expression of a sense of peoplehood (Kuroiwa & Verkuyten, 2008). But these self-defining attributes are not self-evident, and establishing a singular pan-Karen identity and a sense of commitment among the different subgroups is a continuing challenge for Karen leaders.

Self-categorization theory (see Chapters 1 & 21) argues that a coherent shared social identity is the basis for group coordination and organization and that the elite plays a major role in this (Reicher & Hopkins, 2001). Different studies have examined, for example, how 'ethnic entrepreneurs' define, enunciate and enact identities for political purposes. In trying to mobilize co-ethnics, they communicate a particular understanding of what it means to be a member of their ethnic group and, in order to be persuasive, they construe themselves as typical and true group members. According to the Mauritian Constitution, the numerically relatively large group of Creoles, who are the former slaves of African origin, are not a separate community. Recently, there has been a movement for their official recognition lead by a Creole Catholic priest. Father Jocelyn Gregoire is an enigmatic priest with numerous followers who has independently, but with the approval of the local church authority, argued for the recognition of the Creoles in the Mauritian Constitution and the betterment of the Creoles' status through his movement the 'Federation des Creoles

Mauriciens'. By re-defining Creole identity from a one-sided victimhood position to a more confident and responsible self-understanding, as exemplified by himself, he tries to give the Creoles a new purpose and a new role in the Mauritian nation.

The Karen in Burma face a different challenge in mobilizing ingroup members. The Burmese government as well as some international organizations define the Karen as 'secessionists' and 'violent terrorists' who perpetuate the conflict only because of their stubbornness and for instrumental reasons. These kinds of negative labeling question the legitimacy of the goals and acts of an ethno-political movement and can easily hamper mobilization processes, because people can be reluctant to identify with a stigmatized social movement or group. Hence, it is crucial for the leaders to produce and communicate in narratives and symbols (e.g., Karen flag, anthem, Martyr Day) alternative understandings of the Karen insurgency. They do this in three ways (Kuroiwa & Verkuyten, 2008). First, their emphasis on the Karen's indigenousness positions them as 'freedom fighters' rather than terrorists (see Chapter 12): the Karen revolution is about getting back what was historically theirs. Second, and in contrast to the claimed dishonesty and aggressiveness of the Burmese, the Karen are presented as inherently simple, honest, tranquil and a peace-loving people. The Karen would be forced to act, and in a manner that goes against their moral nature. Third, the story of great endurance by their leaders creates an image of committed people fighting for a legitimate goal. The hardships and the duration of the conflicts become signs of the Karen's sincerity and commitment to the group and its cause.

Outgroup Members

Identity Confirmation

Orthodox groups such as the Amish or Hassidic Jews are very strongly ingroup oriented and not much concerned about criticism by out-groupers. In most cases, however, it is difficult to maintain a social identity without acknowledgment by relevant out-groups, and the intergroup sensitivity effect implies that people are more sensitive to outgroup than ingroup critics (Hornsey & Imani, 2004; see Chapter 9). In identity politics, not only are equal treatment and rights at stake, but also the social recognition and public affirmation of the value of a particular history, culture, or lifestyle. Disputes over group status find expression in issues such as the use of languages, the names of towns and cities, national anthems, and the wearing of particular clothes.

Social identity theory (Tajfel & Turner, 1979) argues that humans strive for a distinctive and positive social identity. Giles (e.g., Giles & Johnson, 1987) invoked this theory to explain the sociolinguistic phenomenon of language shifts. When ethnic identity is important for individuals, they may attempt to make themselves favorably distinct on dimensions such as language. They can adopt various strategies of so-called psycholinguistic distinctiveness, like accentuating their speech styles, switching to their ingroup language and using specific dialects. Language maintenance and speech divergence are useful strategies for achieving positive distinctiveness. In contrast, one's own language or dialect can contribute to a negative identity and be a source of shame. A slur on the language is a slur on the people which can lead to identity management strategies like individual mobility (see Chapter 1). The phenomenon of ethnic 'passing' implies not only a change in self-categorization but also a behavioral change that involves the purposeful expression of actions and practices that are normative of the 'new' identity and a suppression of old habits and behaviors.

Minority languages and identities are often considered to be of lesser value and the object of ridicule. Depending on the nature of the social structure, members of subordinate or low-status groups can adopt different collective strategies to achieve a distinctive and positive social identity. For example, group members can engage in identity performance to change the outgroup's stereotypes and treatment of their ethnic ingroup. The classic example is, of course, the 'black is beautiful' slogan, and other examples are situations were 'inferior' or 'substandard' languages or dialects are put forward as symbols of group pride. Another example is a Muslim woman living in the Netherlands who argues that on the streets, in the bus and in shops she deliberately and constantly smiles and puts on a friendly face in order to show that Muslims are not dangerous terrorists. A further example is Muslim girls who together with a headscarf have a dress style, cosmetics and speech style that communicate that Muslim women can also be modern.

A confirmation of ingroup identity can also be construed in opposition to the dominant group. On the individual level and following Goffman (1959), anthropologists talk about group memberships being *over-communication*. This means that the ethnic or racial identity is 'shown off' and indicated or claimed in almost all situations. A more positive example is the African American concept of 'race man' or 'race woman' which expresses that one's racial identity is the centrepiece of one's self-understanding and that one is devoted to the advancement of black people. There are also various examples of the communication of reactive or oppositional minority identities. This is the situation in which people emphasize their ethnic or racial identity and stress characteristics and actions as being self-defining that differ from those typically valued by the majority group (e.g., Ogbu, 1993). For example, when the importance of schooling and educational achievement is emphasized, one's behavior and attitude can communicate that educational success is useless in a white supremacist society. And when Moroccan Dutch young males are portrayed as being aggressive, violent and criminal, then it is exactly these anti-normative characteristics that they express in their gestures, spoken language, clothing and public behavior.

Identity (De)mobilization

Identity performance is not only about affirmation of one's ethnic group symbolically but also about group standing in society. Social identities direct group members toward a given collective goal and the "success of such projects also often demands collaboration or at least the lack of opposition by outgroup members" (Klein et al., 2007, p. 37).

Thus, the symbolic presentation of the Karen as a peace-loving, sincere and committed people is not only important for mobilizing co-ethnics, but also for demobilizing outgroup opposition. The possibility of support from, for example, international organizations, and for collaboration with foreign agencies and governments, crucially depends on the understandings held by these outgroups. Obtaining their support requires that the struggle is presented as legitimate and one's claims as reasonable. Internationally, for example, it is becoming increasingly difficult to ignore claims of so-called indigenous groups, because these relate to the dominant political and moral ideas about cultural and group rights. Like the Karen, these groups argue that they are '*a* people' rather than a population, and the United Nations draft declaration of the rights of indigenous peoples is premised on a rather reified and primordial notion of groups and cultures.

Collaboration and a lack of opposition are also necessary in order for a subgroup attribute to symbolize a superordinate or shared identity. For example, using a particular ethnic language as the *lingua franca* in everyday life is something else than presenting that language as the national one. Creole is the dominant vernacular of Mauritius. It is known and used on a daily basis by almost the entire population, regardless of ethnic background. Nevertheless, the official celebrations of the fifteenth anniversary of the independence of Mauritius from British rule on 12 March 1983 triggered a storm of protest. The reason was that leaders of the left government decided to sing at the celebrations in the capital the national anthem in Mauritian Creole instead of English. On the state-controlled television, the performance was announced as 'the national anthem sung in the national language'. The storm of protest that followed had immediate political consequences. The government coalition broke apart that same month, and the leftist political party was defeated in the ensuing general elections.

Language can also be a symbol of domination, and the survival of an ethnolinguistic minority strongly depends on how the majority uses its power and dominance. The dominant group frequently imposes its own language as the only legitimate one and adopts a policy of minority assimilation. In Turkey, for example, there are various national minorities that have been suppressed for centuries. In trying to create a nation state based on Turkish identity, the Kurds in particular have been the target of a longstanding assimilation policy. It was not until 2003 that the Kurdish people officially got the right to use Kurdish names, broadcast in their mother tongue, establish private language courses, and so forth. The long years of oppression and suppression of the Kurdish language and culture had not resulted in its disappearance. The low objective ethnolinguistic vitality—low group prestige, lack of institutional support, relatively low numbers—had not resulted in 'group death' (Giles & Johnson, 1987). Rather, their low ingroup vitality appears to have stirred the Kurds to mobilize collectively in order to reinforce their linguistic, cultural and political position. The negotiations about Turkey's forthcoming European Union membership have increased their possibilities of doing so.

From Identity Performance to Self-Understanding

Research in social psychology tends to emphasize that social action emanates from one's sense of identity. When people have a particular self-understanding they tend to act in ways that correspond to the behavioral norms associated with that identity. And coordinated group behavior is considered possible because different people define themselves in terms of the same social category. However, identity performance or the communication of ethnicity can also shape our feelings of ethnic identity. It is in interactions that societal relations, beliefs, norms and values are reproduced and changed, actualized or challenged. And it is in interactions that a sense of identity is formed. Social identities are communicated and negotiated in interactions and the outcomes of this can affect people's self-understandings. Identity performance elicit reactions from others and claims on, for example, ingroup authenticity can be questioned or rejected. A lack of confirmation makes it difficult to maintain a secure sense of identity. It is not easy to feel a proper member of one's ethnic group when language proficiency is an important ethnic marker and you do not speak the language. And for many Muslims, the communal aspects of rule-following ('orthopraxis'), and the public behavioural commitment to the rules of Islam, are important to feel a real Muslim.

People can also start to endorse and embrace particular social identities that are defined and performed by leaders or entrepreneurs of identity. The Huron Indians of Québec are today a respected Canadian 'tribe' known as the Wendat. They played a leading role in the Indian movement in the 1960s and 1970s. This is somewhat surprising because they were very much assimilated to the western way of life and had lost most of their original culture, such as their language, religion, and various traditions. When the anthropologist Roosens told fellow academics in Québec that he wanted to study the Hurons, he was advised not to, since they were no longer 'real Indians'. At the end of the 60s and the beginning of the 70s, ethnic leaders started to define authentic 'Huronness' in order to create a collective identity and political cohesion. But most of it was unrelated to the original traditions. Roosens (1989, p. 47) concluded that "when I compared the characteristics of this neo-Huron culture with the culture depicted in the historical records, most of the modern traits, virtually everything, were 'counterfeit': the folklore articles, the hair style, the moccasins, the 'Indian' parade costumes, the canoes, the pottery, the language, the music." Despite the invention of Huron culture, the leaders were very successful in establishing a sense of a distinctive and positive Huron identity among their followers. And the Huron have been quite successful politically in getting special rights based on their recognition as a Nation in a treaty with the British in 1760. This example shows that leaders can construct and perform ethnic identities in particular ways and influence others into adopting it as part of their self-understanding. The example also shows that social identities cannot be maintained without actions and practices that function as public expressions and markers.

Conclusion

Ethnic, racial or religious group membership is important to many people. It gives a sense of meaning and belonging, and it can be a source of pride. Social identities, however, are not 'simply' about subjective self-understandings but about the relationship between the individual and the environment. Social identity refers to the question of what someone is taken to be socially. It is about socially-defined and recognized distinctions and designations. Social psychological research often tends to forget or ignore this because the focus is on people's sense of identity that is measured along attitude-like dimensions of cognitive centrality and private regard. An emphasis on communication and identity performance allows us to go beyond this research and to recognize the importance of the level of social interaction for social identities (Verkuyten, 2005). It draws attention to the ways that people express their sense of identity and authenticate their group membership in identity-relevant behaviors but also to the ways that people reject and resist categorization by means of behaviors that are anti-normative. It also directs attention to actions and practices that value or affirm one's group symbolically and that preserve and enhance the standing of one's group. These are important and interesting issues for future research. This research could also systematically examine the relations between self-understandings and identity performance. For example, there may be tensions between identity assignments, or what people are socially taken to be, and the way they typically see and experience themselves. Furthermore, people belong to a large number of social categories that might overlap but also can have conflicting meanings (Verkuyten, 2005). This raises the question how a person balances the public expression of her religion (e.g., a headscarf) with national belonging to a highly secularized and traditionally Christian western country. This is not only a psychological task, but it can also lead to tensions between identity performance in relation to ingroup and to outgroup members.

People communicate their group membership and the identity of their group in many different ways and for different reasons. They want to belong and feel accepted; they want to have a distinctive and positive identity and they are concerned about ingroup interests and rights. There are different markers of identity and behavioral involvement is a clear expression of an identity. Ethnic identity is largely maintained through cultural practices, symbols, rituals and language. It is the 'doing' of ethnicity that validates individual identity claims, that consolidates ethnic group identities and that is instrumental in promoting group success. And the ways in which people communicate their ethnic identity depends on whether the performances are oriented at ingroup or outgroup members or at both at the same time. The wearing of a headscarf by the schoolgirls in Creil was oriented at both ingroup and outgroup members. It did not only affirm the value of their Muslim identity but was also considered a symbol of the backwardness of Islam, and it did not only serve to mobilize public support for religious rights but also triggered political opposition.

CHAPTER THREE

Gendered Language as a Dynamic Intergroup Process

PAMELA KALBFLEISCH

Army specialist Mickiela Montoya was standing silently in the back of a Manhattan classroom while a group of male Iraq war veterans spoke to a small audience about their experiences as soldiers. It was November 2006, and she had been back from Iraq for a year but was still too insecure to speak out in public. Anyway, the room was full of men, and Montoya had learned that a lot of men are not much interested in listening to military women.

"Nobody believes me when I say I'm a veteran," she said that day, tucking her long red hair behind her ears. "I was in Iraq getting bombed and shot at, but people won't even listen when I say I was at war. You know why? Because I'm a female". . . .

Not many people realize the extent to which the Iraq War represents a historic change for American women soldiers. More women have fought and died in Iraq than in all the wars since World War II put together. Over 206,000 have served in the Middle East since March 2003, most of them in Iraq; and over 600 have been wounded and 104 have died in Iraq alone, according to the Department of Defense. In Iraq, one in ten soldiers is a woman.

Yet the military—from the Pentagon to the troops on the ground—has been slow to recognize the service these women perform or even to see them as real soldiers. Rather, it is permeated with age-old stereotypes of women as passive sex objects who have no business fighting and cannot be relied upon in battle. As Montoya said about her time as a soldier, "The only thing the guys let you be if you're a girl in the military is a bitch, a ho, or a dyke. You're a bitch if you won't sleep with them, a ho if you even have one boyfriend, and a dyke if they don't like you. So you can't win" (Benedict, 2009, pp. 1–2).

The bitterness expressed by this female veteran is one of frustration with gender stereotypes and the primacy of being a female over being a solider or veteran. Her silence in a room full of men was, from her perspective, affected by both her stereotypes of men drawn from her experiences with military service and with life experience. When interviewed by a woman, Montoya speaks directly and harshly about her experiences during and after military service.

Montoya's experience is readily interpretable from an intergroup perspective. Salient group membership affects language choice; communication and deference to others differ sharply depending upon who is and who is not a member of the ingroup. In this case, membership in the group "female" was primary over membership in the group "veteran" or "soldier"—much to Montoya's frustration. Similarly, her choice not to speak at the meeting was affected by her stereotype that men did not value the experiences of a female veteran and were, therefore, not interested in hearing what she had to say. Despite this, the men gathered to listen to the veterans speak could have daughters serving in Iraq, wives serving in Iraq, or other female friends in military service. It is possible that there were, in fact, a variety of reasons why these men would have been interested in what she had to say about her experience. They also may not have viewed her primarily as a member of the group "female" but instead as a member of the group "veteran."

In other words, in order to predict what language is used by an interlocutor, more information is needed beyond the speaker's nominal gender. For example, from a self-categorization theory perspective (see Chapters 1 & 8), gender itself would not necessarily predict language use, so much as the psychological saliency of gender to the speaker. The physical maleness of an audience would be less important than the female speaker's beliefs about her male audience and the saliency of the outgroup "males" over the ingroup "patriots" from her point of view. From this perspective, gendered communication is based on the process of men and women communicating as a function of their subjective social identification with their gender as a social category.

The perception of the gender may be masculine, feminine, positive, negative, or comprise any number of attributes in the subjectively salient prototype for the gender group in question. Compare the valence and prototypical traits of categories like "rodeo queen," "farm wife," and "female professor." Further still, the features of these groups are not static but vary depending upon the context in which gender groups are being compared and the motives of those both within and external to the gender groups. For example, Williams and Giles (1978) considered strategies of social change for women and counter-strategies to resist this change by members who identified with the dominant male group. Among other points, their approach included a consideration of women who used social identity strategies to create positive images for women. For example, women seeking change could focus on producing positive references to women including messages pointing to the excellent features of being a woman, and by joining women's groups that were achieving social change.

When viewed through the lens of social identity theory (Tajfel & Turner, 1979), perceptions of military women as subgroups of bitches, hos, and dykes, could be actively changed by women and by men. These images are not and should not be viewed as fixed group assessments. Similarly the perception of military men as abusive brutes could also be actively changed by members both within and external to the group.

Language is a means through which group stereotypes can be embraced, changed, and resisted (see Chapters 8 & 9). Group members communicate with each other and with members of other groups through language, and in so doing, influence the content of stereotypes. Perceptions of male and female groups, salience of identification with these gender groups, and salience of identification with other groups (i.e., task, education, leisure) all have the potential to change. As such, predicting the actual language style that is used by men and women to enact major social change or to carry on routine conversation requires contemplation.

Researchers have found self-categorization theory (SCT: Turner, Hogg, Oakes, Reicher, & Wetherell, 1987) to be helpful in understanding and predicting the language used in intergroup communication. When using this theory to understand intergroup communication, gender salience must be considered. Gender salience is a "cognitive state wherein someone explicitly or implicitly self-defines as a member of their collective gender group" (Palomares, in press). For gender to be salient over other group memberships, three factors interact: 1) accessibility, the degree to which a person has a propensity to self-define using gender; 2) comparative fit, the extent to which differences between males and females are perceived to be greater than differences among gender groups; and 3) normative fit, the extent to which the pattern of differences between males and females correspond to social norms and expectations (see Oakes, 1987; Palomares, in press).

When gender is a salient social identity, social judgment and perceptions will be filtered through this gender identity (see Hogg & Reid, 2006; Palomares, in press). This occurs because people internalize (i.e., are depersonalized by) the salient gender prototype (Palomares, Reid, & Bradac, 2004; see also Chapter 17). Prototypes are fuzzy sets of attributes that are seen as best representing a category. Prototypes can be comprised of any kind of meaningful attribute; attitudes, beliefs, linguistic choices, and physical appearance, can all differentiate between males and females. Different social contexts and bases for social comparison between men and women will lead certain kinds of attributes to become psychologically salient (because of fit), and when salient, people will conform to the gender prototype (see Palomares, in press; Palomares et al., 2004). The prototype then predicts social judgment and behavior.

From an intergroup perspective, gendered language and gender group perception are dynamic, not static. Gender differences will not always be present, and those that do appear may present themselves in different ways and, hence, women and men will communicate based on their group affiliations. The dynamic that this intergroup communication takes on is variable, and gender differences may or may not be important. Most language research invoking an intergroup orientation to studying gender has been published in the last six years. The scholars Palomares, Reid, and their associates currently dominate the dynamic gender research paradigm. Consequently, key contributions by these researchers to understanding gendered language production and its implications are considered below.

Gendered Language Production

When considering gendered language production from SCT, gender differences may or may not be apparent depending on the salience of gender over other group memberships and the prototypes accessed for how men and women communicate. For example, Reid, Keerie, and Palomares (2003) found that under conditions of gender salience, women used more tentative language than men. Under low gender salient conditions in which a shared student identity was salient, women and men used moderate and indistinguishable levels of tentative language. Men used less tentative language in gender salient conditions than in low gender salient conditions, but this difference was not significant. In other words, Reid and associates found that tentative language that is more prototypically female was not used consistently by the women. Instead, women restricted their use of tentative language to a situation where gender was salient.

Bem's (1981) conceptualization of gender schemas can be related to the issue of gender identity accessibility. Gender schemas are predispositions of perceivers to process information in terms of cultural definitions of gender. With Bem's conceptualization, perceivers who are gender schematic will have a preference for culturally gender-consistent behavior. This model would predict that gender-schematic people are more likely than non-gender-schematic people to use gender-consistent language. However, SCT would predict that gender-schematicity is a component of category accessibility and that it should interact with social contexts that render gender more or less salient.

Indeed, Palomares (2004) examined gendered language use by women and men who were gender schematic or non-gender schematic, and who were placed in a context that made gender high or low in salience. He did not find differences in the language used by men and women overall nor in the language used by men and women who were gender schematic or non-gender schematic. What he did find was that gender schematics used traditional male and female gender-linked language when gender was salient, with gender-schematic females using traditional female-linked language, and gender-schematic males using traditional male-linked language. When gender was not salient and the group "student" was salient, Palomares found that gender-schematic men used female-gendered language and gender-schematic women used male-gendered language. Non-gender-schematics' language demonstrated minimal variation.

These findings are significant because gender differences in language use have been attributed previously to characteristic masculine and feminine communication styles. For example, Mulac and associates have found a set of linguistic features that characterize differences between men and women (see Table 1). For example, Mulac and associates' research shows that women are more likely to use intensifiers (*so*) and references to emotion (*happy*), whereas men are more likely to refer to quantity (*the engine is a 427*) and issue directives (*close the door*). In accord with the foregoing, these characteristic language features have been referred to as gendered-linked language (Mulac, 2006). One theoretical explanation is that gender-linked language originates from socialization into masculine and feminine cultures (see Mulac, Bradac, & Gibbons, 2001). Masculine and feminine communication, also called powerful and powerless communication, would be considered static and context-independent. In other words, males will typically use male language and females will typically use female language. Palomares et al. (2004) propose that prior inconsistencies in traditional gender-linked language differences noted in the research can be explained using SCT. For example, in the Palomares (2004) study, traditional gender-linked language was found for gender-schematic men and women depending on gender salience. It was not found for all men and women. This study provides evidence that gendered language is not static and that it is dynamic and dependent on gender identity.

Further work by Palomares (2008, 2009) provides evidence for the self-categorization explanation for gendered language use. As with Palomares (2004), these two studies used electronic mail as a context for the study of language and intergroup communication. Palomares (2008) found that women referenced emotion more than men when gender was salient, but this difference was not as large as when gender was not salient. Under conditions of gender salience women referenced more emotion in intergroup contexts than in intragroup contexts, and they referenced more emotion than men with gender salience in intergroup and intragroup settings. Palomares (2009) found the masculinity and femininity of electronic correspondence topics affected tentative language use in intergroup contexts. For masculine topics, women used more tentative language than men in intergroup contexts. In contrast for feminine topics, men were more tentative than women in intergroup contexts. Use of tentative language did not differ for women and men in intragroup contexts or with gender-neutral topics. For both Palomares (2008) and (2009), gender salience differentiated language use in the intergroup settings but not in the intragroup settings. That is, gendered language was affected by gender salience not simply the gender of the communicator.

Table 1. Language Features Differentiating the Genders.

Language	Example	Gender
References to quality	"6 ft., 4 in. tall"	Male
Judgmental adjectives	"good"	Male
Elliptical sentence	"Great picture."	Male
Directives	"Write that down."	Male
Locatives	"in the background"	Male
I reference	"I think. . ."	Male
Intensive adverbs	"really"	Female
References to emotions	"happy"	Female
Dependent clauses	"where the shadows are"	Female
Sentence-initial adverbials	"Actually, it is..."	Female
Mean length sentence	(relatively long sentences)	Predominately Female
Uncertainty verbs	"It seems to be. . ."	Female
Oppositions	"It's peaceful, yet active"	Female
Negations	"It's not a . . ."	Female
Hedges	"kind of"	Female
Questions	"What's that?"	Female
Personal pronouns	"we," "she"	Female/Male
Tag questions	"That's not right, is it?"	Female/Male
Fillers	"you know,"	Female/Male
Progressive verbs	"melting"	Female/Male
Justifiers	"It's not that, because"	Female/Male

Table adapted from Mulac (2006, p. 224.) Table information drawn from review of results from twenty-one studies in program of research.

Palomares and Lee (in press) went beyond electronic correspondence to investigate gendered language use with research participants using computer generated avatars of same and different sex from their own. Avatars are virtual representations of communicators and can have different genders, physical characteristics, and can be human or nonhuman. The appearance of an avatar is limited only by the skill of the person creating it, or the resources to have someone else make an avatar, or the capabilities of the computer hardware or software hosting the context for the avatar to communicate with other avatars and exist in a virtual environment. Avatars can communicate with text to other avatars, and depending on the virtual environment they can communicate orally using a computer generated voice. Communicators using avatars may or may not select avatars of the same gender and species.

For the Palomares and Lee study, research participants were paired with preselected male or female cartoon-character avatars. Research participants used these avatars to communicate using text with another avatar. For this study, gender salience for the research participants was not manipulated and no effects were apparent for intergroup versus intragroup communication. What is interesting about this study is that women used more references to emotion when using a feminine avatar versus a masculine avatar; women were more apologetic when their avatars were feminine rather than masculine; and women were more tentative when their avatars were feminine rather than masculine. Men did not differ significantly in their gender-linked language for references to emotion, apology, or tentativeness. This study may demonstrate that for women, language conforms to gendered language norms stimulated by the visual depiction of self as masculine or feminine.

An additional stance may provide further explanation for these results. The men in this study did not change their behavior based on the masculinity or femininity of the cartoon characters. It is possible they did not identify with either character or see the character as a representation of self. It is also possible that the women did not view the cartoon characters as visual depiction of themselves. The women, however, may have been accommodating their language style for their character based on their perception of how this character would interact. If traditionally raised with dolls, they may have had more experience animating external entities and developing perceptions of these doll characters as external entities with expected behaviors and communication. They may have also developed past relationships with these doll characters and accommodated their expected speech patterns.

Hajek, Abrams, and Murachver (2005) note that "accommodation can occur not only in response to the actual behavior of the speaker, but also to perceived or expected behaviors of the speaker" (p. 57). In an intergroup context, this would suggest that some of the changes by communicators are in accommodation to perceived or expected behaviors of others, not necessarily the actual behaviors (see Gallois, Ogay, & Giles, 2005). The female veteran's choice to remain silent in a room full of men is an example of a communication choice that accommodated expected behaviors. This is not to say that SCT and gender saliency are not evident from this veteran's account; it is to say that additional theoretical perspectives may further enrich explanation and prediction of language use.

Implications of Gendered Language Production

There are several explanations regarding how differences in perceptions of male and female communication impact the influence of speakers of differing genders. Primary among these are expectation states and role congruity theories as well as SCT. In a critical study, Reid, Palomares, Anderson, and Bondad-Brown (in press) further expanded our knowledge of gender and intergroup communication through examining the predictions yielded by these three theoretical perspectives. In this study, female and male participants listened to a recorded female speaker using tentative or assertive language to make a counter-attitudinal persuasive appeal. Research participants were told she was either a member of an all-female decision-making group or a college-educated decision-making group.

All three theories predict that women can be influential with men when they are represented by a shared identity in which case more assertive women will be more influential than tentative women. However, the three theories differ as to why this would be the case. Expectation states theory (Correll & Ridgeway, 2003) predicts that social influence is driven by people's expectations about group status relations. Specifically, assertive women should be perceived as more competent than tentative women when a college-educated identity is salient, and that the difference in perceived competence would account for the difference in influence. Role congruity theory (Eagly & Karau, 2002) predicts that when college education is salient, that prescriptive norms about female communality (i.e., that women are nuturing and friendly) should not be important, and that people should be influenced more by assertive than tentative women because of the greater perceived agency (i.e., confidence and power) of the assertive speaker. Finally, SCT contends that people should be more influenced by prototypical group members, and that when college education is salient, people will see themselves as more similar to the prototypically assertive than tentative speaker. When all three variables were compared (competence, agency, and similarity), it turned out that competence and similarity were the only viable mediators. Self-categorization and expectation states processes were additive contributions to explain social influence under shared identity salience.

Further, all three theories also predicted that when gender is made salient (by telling perceivers the female speaker is a member of an all-female decision-making group), the tentative speaker would influence men more than the assertive speaker. The prediction from expectation states theory is that perceptions of the female speaker's competence will mediate these effects. In essence, when gender is salient, the assertive speaker will be downgraded in perceived competence compared to the tentative speaker because she will be seen as violating the status order—when gender is salient, women are supposed to be deferential and tentative. From role congruity theory, it was predicted that this effect would be mediated by the degree to which the speaker was perceived to conform to the communal role. Finally, following a conjecture of Reid and Ng (1999), it was predicted that the greater influence of the tentative speaker would be driven by the increase in male collective self-esteem—men will feel good about their gender when they heard the tentative speaker, and this will confirm their status advantage over women. When all three variables were compared, only competence mediated the effect, and then only partially.

In sum, the results of this study provide more support for self-categorization and expectation states theories than for role congruity theory. In the college education context, men were more influenced by an assertive female speaker—as all three theories predicted. However, women were not influenced more by an assertive female speaker than a tentative speaker. Contrary to the predictions of all theories, the assertive female speaker was not less influential when gender was manipulated to be primary over education. Although support was found for expectation states theory for maintaining the status quo, Reid and his associates did not find the theory to explain mediating processes as well as SCT, nor the overall pattern of social influence.

Another intriguing, but unexplained aspect of the findings was (as found in other research) that tentative women were highly influential with men when gender was salient, whereas all three theories would only predict modest levels of influence. Reid and his associates conjecture that the influence of tentative women with men in conditions of high gender salience is due to their priming of mate selection processes. It may be the men who hear a tentative female speaker when gender is primed unconsciously consider her as a potential mate (see Chapter 22). Clearly from this test of three theories, the processes of intergroup communication among those with similar and different gender identity are intricate and are due our consideration as scholars and students of gender. Crucial studies such as tests of competing theoretical explanations of gendered language, social influence, intragroup and intergroup communication are needed to further our knowledge as a discipline of study. As such, this study by Reid and associates was important because it tested three competing explanations for predicting the implications of gendered language use.

Conclusion

Gender is one of the most obvious and not so obvious demarcations of group membership. Much has been written about women and men communicating across a panoply of venues. Physical sex differences that accompany the psychologically based gender distinctions constitute obvious gender distinctions and are often used for gender articulation. The very pervasiveness of gender information and research is related in part to its obviousness and ease of data collection. When respondents are asked to fill out questionnaires about almost any variable concerning human behavior, a request for demographic information specifying male or female is common. Research participants arriving for observational or experimental research are placed in dyads, groups, or other configurations, and their physical sex is either a part of the research design or it is minimally noted by the researchers studying human communication.

The research reviewed in this chapter is more thoughtful than a casual data collection of a dichotomous variable accompanying a primary research investigation. What we find is that gendered language and intergroup perceptions are not fixed states but are dynamic and changing. In many ways, the lines of research considered are empowering for female and male communicators seeking gender equity in intergroup communication especially where gender is salient.

What we need is more information about how these interaction processes work and how different theoretical perspectives can add to our understanding of gender and dynamic communication processes. In order to manipulate saliency, or focus on variables of interest, research participants generally are not exposed to the full spectrum of visual and language information that would be available in a typical intergroup situation that they would perceive and experience in actual interactions. As we move toward greater understanding of gender and intergroup dynamics, we need to include more sensory information for perceivers to process. This will more closely reflect actual ongoing intergroup interaction. For example, consider Reid et al.'s mate selection assumption where male attraction to a potential mate is aroused by a woman's tentative language in a gender salient condition. What happens when scent, physicality, and speaker attractiveness are added? Does the mate selection scenario become keyed with the tentative language, or is the sheer volume of sensory stimuli overwhelming mate selection, leading to some other physical or interactive process or fueling physical action?

While this example may appear extreme, consider that the account of the female veteran cited at the beginning of this chapter (Benedict, 2009) actually went on to discuss other outcomes. These included problems of female veterans returning to the United States being the victims of rape during their time in military, knowing of others who were raped, or otherwise feeling disempowered by male colleagues and superiors in the U.S. military. Is this mate selection gone too far (see Chapter 22)? Could language serve a role in mitigating gender violence in a situation, such as the military, where gender salience may primarily be operating over other social categories? What is the prototype activated when one thinks of military women deployed in a primarily male-dominated war? Can the dynamic nature of language help in empowering women in this situation or in avoiding sending mate selection signals in an atmosphere that may be highly physically charged?

A gendered language perspective that is dynamic and open to change can be empowering for both women and men in today's society. Whether fighting a war or negotiating everyday life, a gendered language that can change and that can also change others may be the key to a future world of equality and peace.

CHAPTER FOUR

Age Group Identity, Age Stereotypes, and Communication in a Life Span Context

MARY LEE HUMMERT

Recently my husband, son, daughter, and I were fortunate to spend three weeks traveling together in Swaziland and South Africa. My daughter had been working in Swaziland for several months, had traveled widely in her free time, and had a car. As a result even though my daughter is the baby of the family, she was "in charge." My husband and I found ourselves in a highly unusual position for parents: We were relegated to the back seat as our daughter, the driver, and our son, her co-pilot, assumed the positions in the front seat that had previously been ours on family trips. Not surprisingly, these moves also entailed changes in our communication regarding routes, stopping places, etc. To me, this switch in our normal driving positions was symbolic of the transitions that happen within families as its members age. It also made me aware of the life span transitions that each of us makes as we move from one age group to another over the course of our lives.

Age is one of the most common ways in which we define group membership. As a social category, however, age differs from some of the other group memberships considered in this book in that membership in an age group (young, middle-aged, older) is fluid rather than fixed. While it is difficult to pinpoint the exact age at which these transitions occur, people are generally aware of their current and past age group memberships as well as their future age group memberships. People also generally classify others as members of particular age groups, although they do not always do so accurately. In addition, age group memberships and transitions overlap with family roles (see Chapter 15): Children grow up and become parents; parents become grandparents. Often, as my story of our family trip illustrates, family transitions make age identities salient. As a result, it is not surprising that age group identities play a role in intergroup communication.

This chapter considers the research on how communication may serve to reinforce or minimize generational divisions, particularly the ways in which communication behaviors both reflect and activate age identities and age stereotypes. It begins by considering the research on age attitudes and stereotypes and presents a social identity theory perspective on why the older age group has received so much attention from scholars of age stereotyping and intergenerational communication (see Chapters 1 & 21). The chapter concludes with a consideration of a research agenda for future investigations of intergenerational communication as well as the benefits of bringing a developmental perspective to intergroup communication theory.

Age Attitudes and Stereotypes

The recognition of negative views about aging with their potential for bias against older people became the impetus for research on age attitudes and stereotypes. These investigations took one of two approaches, focusing on the evaluation of older persons in comparison to younger ones (i.e., age attitudes) or on beliefs about the characteristics of older persons and, albeit to a lesser extent, younger persons (i.e., age stereotypes; see Chapter 8). Results revealed that attitudes toward older people as a group were more negative than were attitudes toward young people, and that older people were believed to have more negative traits (e.g., weak, sick, forgetful, complaining) than were young people (for review, see Kite & Wagner, 2002). However, exceptions to this pattern also emerged: In some cases, older persons were not only judged as positively as younger persons, they were at times perceived more positively than young people and as having some positive traits (e.g., wisdom, experience) that young people did not.

These exceptions illustrated the complexity of age attitudes and stereotypes. For instance, while attitudes toward older people as a group were more negative than those toward young people as a group, attitudes toward older and younger people with similar characteristics were equivalent (Kite & Wagner, 2002). As another example, people appear to hold seemingly contradictory, positive and negative stereotypes of older persons (as well as of younger persons) in their social schemas (Hummert, Garstka, Shaner, & Strahm, 1994). Further, older individuals have more age stereotypes than do younger persons, suggesting that the complexity of age stereotypes increases across the lifespan (Hummert et al., 1994).

Examples of some of the positive and negative age stereotypes documented in this research are presented in Table 1. As shown, regardless of age, individuals have such negative stereotypes of older people as the Severely Impaired individual with numerous physical and cognitive problems, the lonely and sad Despondent, and the complaining and bitter Shrew/Curmudgeon. Likewise, they share positive stereotypes about a Perfect Grandparent, a hip and active Golden Ager, and the patriotic and proud John Wayne Conservative. Older individuals, however, have more refined and varied stereotype sets than do younger individuals. Examples in Table 1 include the Mildly Impaired person with some physical signs of aging, the stay-at-home Recluse, the liberal Activist, and the quiet, old-fashioned Small Town Neighbor. These differences in stereotypes between young and older people suggest that over the course of our life span, our age stereotypes expand and are modified based on our own experience of aging and our interactions with older and younger people (Hummert et al., 1994).

Table 1: Representative Positive and Negative Stereotypes and Traits of Older Adults as Reported by Older and Younger Participants (Hummert et al., 1994)

Negative Stereotypes Shared by Young & Older Participants	Negative Stereotypes Unique to Older Participants
Severely Impaired: Incoherent, Slow-Thinking, Senile, Inarticulate, Incompetent, Feeble, Forgetful	*Mildly Impaired:* Fragile, Dependent, Slow-Moving, Tired, Frustrated
Despondent: Depressed, Sad, Hopeless, Afraid, Neglected, Lonely	*Recluse:* Poor, Timid, Sedentary
Shrew/Curmudgeon: Complaining, Bitter, Ill-Tempered, Stubborn, Demanding, Prejudiced	*Self-Centered:* Inflexible, Stubborn, Humorless, Jealous, Miserly, Greedy, Nosy, Selfish
Positive Stereotypes Shared by Young & Older Participants	**Positive Stereotypes Unique to Older Participants**
Golden Ager: Lively, Sociable, Future-Oriented, Fun-Loving, Happy, Active, Interesting, Alert, Capable	*Activist:* Political, Sexual, Health-Conscious, Liberal
Perfect Grandparent: Kind, Loving, Family-Oriented, Generous, Understanding, Wise	*Small Town Neighbor:* Emotional, Frugal, Old-Fashioned, Quiet, Conservative
John Wayne Conservative: Patriotic, Proud, Determined, Retired, Religious, Nostalgic, Reminiscent	

Given that people have both positive and negative stereotypes, researchers have asked what characteristics of older people might trigger those stereotypes. Ryan and Capadano (1978), for example, showed that vocal age influenced perceptions, with listeners judging speakers with older-sounding voices more negatively than those who sounded younger. Hummert, Garstka, and Shaner (1997) found that facial cues to age were linked to positive and negative stereotypes of older people: Photographs of individuals who appeared to be in their sixties were more often associated with the positive stereotypes in Table 1, whereas photographs of those who appeared to be in their eighties or older were more likely to be associated with the negative stereotypes. Even so, the negative perceptions of the oldest-looking individuals were reduced, though not eliminated, when the individuals were shown smiling.

Why the Focus on Attitudes and Stereotypes of Old Age?

Social groups vary in status, and age groups are no exception (Harwood, Giles, & Ryan, 1995). Status is generally associated with access to money and power. Objective measures of social status (e.g., income) show that the middle-aged group has higher status than either the young or older age groups. Subjective assessments of group status confirm that middle-aged people are viewed as having higher social status than those in other age groups by adults of all ages (Garstka, Hummert, & Branscombe, 2005).

Because lower status groups have less access to resources and power, they can be characterized as marginalized. To the extent that lower status groups possess (or are believed to possess) undesirable characteristics, they can also be characterized as stigmatized. Therefore, although both young and older age groups have lower status than the middle-aged group and may be marginalized, the age attitude and stereotype research indicates that the older age group is more at risk for stigma than is the younger age group. In comparison to other low status groups, stigmatized groups are more likely to be the targets of bias and prejudice (see Chapter 13).

According to social identity theory (SIT; Tajfel & Turner, 1986), our awareness of the status associated with our group memberships carries implications for our self-esteem: It is easier to feel good about oneself if one is a member of a higher status social group. As a result, those in lower status groups are motivated to move to higher status groups if possible, a strategy that is termed social mobility within SIT (see Chapter 1). When moving to the higher status group is not possible (or at least not immediate), they may attempt to change the existing social structure to empower their group, a strategy termed social competition, or change the definition of "status" to advantage their group, a strategy termed social creativity. For example, young adults may use social creativity strategies such as adopting their own unique styles of dress to enhance their collective self-esteem or engage in collective action to improve youth-oriented benefits such as student aid. However, young adults are buffered from long-term negative effects of low group status by the normal aging process: Their movement into the higher status middle-aged group will be automatic.

This is not the case for older adults, for whom the normal aging process has not only resulted in movement from a high status group into a lower status group but also into a group at risk for stigma and its consequences. Without social mobility as an option, social creativity and social competition assume primacy as avenues to increase the status of their group and, in turn, improve their sense of self-esteem and avoid prejudice in the form of ageism. Recognition of the potential for ageism and the need to understand its bases stand behind the interest in exploring attitudes of and stereotypes of older people. These were also central to the development of models of intergenerational communication.

Models of Intergenerational Communication

Intergenerational communication constitutes both the ground for ageist behaviors and the means to counteract them, whether through social creativity or social competition strategies. Although the age attitude and stereotype research did not focus on communication between people in different age groups, its insights about the nature and content of age stereotypes became important influences on models of the intergenerational communication process. For instance, communication scholars recognized that many of the negative stereotype traits in Table 1 suggest that older people have diminished communication abilities: A person who is forgetful or slow-thinking might have problems in remembering or processing conversations (Hummert, Garstka, Ryan, & Bonnesen, 2004). Such beliefs carry implications for intergenerational communication.

Communicative Predicament of Aging Model

In 1986, Ryan, Giles, Bartolucci and Henwood provided a theoretical perspective on communication between older and younger people, which was named the communicative predicament of aging (CPA) model. That model has had a profound influence on the development of research on intergenerational communication— an influence which continues today. The model proposed in the article was built on the tenets of communication accommodation theory (Giles, Coupland, & Coupland, 1991), which provides an intergroup and social identity perspective on the communication process.

In brief, Ryan et al.'s (1986) CPA model illustrates a negative feedback loop in which the physical and vocal signs that an individual is "old" may activate a younger person's negative age stereotypes, including those regarding the communication abilities of older people. The younger person may then *accommodate* to the stereotypes by, for instance, speaking more slowly or more loudly, using a simpler vocabulary, etc., than he or she would with a peer. Such accommodations to stereotypes rather than the actual communication abilities of an older person have been identified as a particular style of talk termed patronizing or elderspeak, which, when carried to an extreme, has been likened to baby talk. The label *patronizing* captures the implicit message sent to older targets of this style of talk: You are less competent than I am, which is why I must speak to you as I might to a child. Though well-intentioned, such accommodations have the potential for negative relational and personal consequences for both the younger and older persons in the conversation by highlighting the intergroup nature of the interaction and, especially for the older individual, reinforcing an old age identity, negative age stereotypes and behaviors.

Age Stereotypes in Interaction Model

The age stereotypes in interaction model (ASI; Hummert et al., 2004) expanded the CPA model by incorporating the research on activation cues for stereotypes, multiple stereotypes, and age differences in the complexity of age stereotypes into a consideration of the intergenerational communication process. Communication accommodation theory provided the theoretical framework for this model as it had for the predicament of aging model.

The ASI model makes three additions to the CPA model. First, it acknowledges that whether an older person is negatively or positively stereotyped in a particular interaction will be influenced not only by that person's physical appearance or behaviors which make certain age identities and stereotypes salient but also by the context and the nature of the age stereotypes held by the other individual in the interaction. Based on the stereotype research that demonstrated that positive age stereotypes are less prominent in the age schemas of younger people than of older people, the model predicts that negative stereotyping is most likely to occur when a young adult encounters an older individual of advanced age in a setting such as a nursing home. Second, it adds a positive feedback loop involving the activation of positive age stereotypes and standard adult-to-adult communication between an older and younger individual. Third, it includes the potential for the contributions of an older adult to influence the nature of the feedback loop to the extent that those contributions reinforce positive or negative age stereotypes. Under the ASI model, then, the way in which the older person responds to patronizing or age-adapted talk could transform a negative feedback loop into a positive one by moving the conversational partner from negative to positive age stereotypes and a normal adult-to-adult communication style.

Research Supporting the CPA and ASI Models

Although a large body of research has demonstrated support for the processes represented in the CPA and ASI models (see Hummert et al., 2004, for a comprehensive review), only two representative studies are described here. Williams, Herman, Gajewski, and Wilson (2009) videotaped 80 nursing staff-resident interactions in an Alzheimer's care facility to examine whether patronizing talk or elderspeak was associated with residents' problem behaviors, such as vocal outbursts, aggression, wandering, and withdrawal. The investigators hoped to identify the parameters under which elderspeak might calm residents engaging in problem behaviors and those under which elderspeak might promote problem behaviors.

The nursing staff's communication and the residents' behaviors in each interaction were coded frame by frame. The staff's communication was analyzed for the psycholinguistic characteristics of patronizing communication or elderspeak versus normal adult talk. The residents' reactions to the staff's communication were categorized as either cooperative (i.e., engaging in the requested behavior) or resistive to care (RTC; i.e., refusing to engage in the requested behavior, shouting, pushing the staff away, etc.). Analysis revealed that residents were significantly more likely to engage in resistive behaviors after being addressed in elderspeak by the staff than when they were spoken to in normal adult tones. These results established a temporal relationship between elderspeak by staff and disruptive behaviors on the part of individuals with dementia, supporting the negative feedback loop of the CPA model. The authors noted that elderspeak predominated in nursing staff communication and speculated that residents may "respond with RTC to indicate their unmet need for less patronizing, adult communication" (p. 18).

The second study was an experiment that involved young, middle-aged, and older adult participants in two role-playing situations (Hummert, Shaner, Garstka, & Henry, 1998). In one situation, participants were asked to portray volunteers at a hospital who had become friends with an older patient. The patient was represented by a set of traits and a video photograph fitting either a positive or negative age stereotype. The patient had confided that she (or he) was experiencing some severe abdominal pains but was set to be released from the hospital and so had not told the hospital staff of these pains. The participants' task was to persuade the patient to tell the staff of the abdominal trouble. In the second situation, the participants were friends with an older neighbor facing a personal dilemma. The neighbor's only son was recently divorced but was marrying again almost immediately. The neighbor was torn between attending the wedding to support the son and staying away for fear of offending the son's children and former wife. The participants' task was to persuade the neighbor to attend the wedding. Again, the photograph and traits of the neighbor fit either a positive or negative age stereotype.

Analysis of the persuasive messages offered by the participants revealed three communication styles. The first two styles were patronizing in tone and told the older person what he or she should do, but varied in whether the speaker was highly controlling and cold (directive style) or highly caring and overly personal (overly nurturing style, much like secondary baby talk) in offering the advice. The third style, affirming, fit normal adult communication patterns. It was respectful and warm, but the speaker acknowledged the right of the older person to make his or her own decision. As predicted by the CPA model, when the patient and neighbor fit negative age stereotypes, they were more likely to receive patronizing messages. When they fit positive age stereotypes, they were more likely to receive affirming messages, as predicted by the ASI model. However, the positively stereotyped patient was less likely to receive affirming messages than the neighbor, illustrating how context can undermine positive stereotypes. Finally, young participants offered the highest number of patronizing messages, middle-aged participants fewer such messages, and older participants the lowest number.

These results support the predictions of the CPA and ASI models but also illustrate unique dynamics of age stereotypes and intergenerational communication from an intergroup theory perspective. Consider these specific findings: Regardless of whether the older hospital patient was portrayed in a stereotypically positive or negative way, the patient received more patronizing messages from participants than did the older neighbor. The strong link of a hospital with negative age stereotypes of older persons appeared to lead many participants to use it as a more accurate cue to appropriate communication with the patient than the patient's personal, positive characteristics. It was consistent with their chronological age for young and middle-aged participants to be more influenced by negative age stereotype cues than older participants and to communicate accordingly. After all, the older patient and neighbor in the experiment were members of an outgroup for the young and middle-aged participants. However, although older participants—presumably members of the patient's and neighbor's ingroup—were less influenced by the negative stereotypes than were the young and middle-aged participants, they were not immune to those effects and some delivered patronizing messages. Together, these results suggest that (a) negative age stereotypes are more powerful influences on communication with older persons than positive age stereotypes (b) whether that communication is *inter*generational or *intra*generational.

Two explanations for these results are plausible when we remind ourselves that people only become part of the older adult age group after traversing through the two younger groups. Thus, some older participants may also have viewed the negatively stereotyped patient and neighbor as members of an outgroup, perhaps because they did not accept "old age" as their age group identity but still viewed themselves as falling into a younger age group (Hummert, Garstka, O'Brien, Greenwald, & Mellott, 2002). In addition, age stereotypes are internalized early in life and though they become more complex with age, they do not necessarily become more positive. As a result, even older people who have an older age identity may be influenced by negative stereotypes in their judgments of and communication with ingroup members, becoming initiators of and co-participants in the negative feedback loops of the CPA and ASI models. As co-participants they are just as much at risk for the age-related declines associated with embracing negative age identities and stereotypes as an older person who has been the target of patronizing communication. These insights have led to increased interest in understanding the reciprocal relationships between communication, age identity, and age stereotypes, including the unconscious or automatic ways in which that relationship unfolds and how it may lead to self-stereotyping on the part of older persons.

The Reciprocal Relationship Between Communication, Age Identity, and Age Stereotypes

It is critical to remember that the CPA and ASI models are built on the premises of communication accommodation theory (Giles et al., 1991). That theory posits that individuals use stereotypes as heuristics to guide communication accommodations because they want to be effective communicators, not (as a general rule) because they wish to engage in biased behavior. This suggests that stereotypes may operate outside our conscious awareness to influence communication behavior. Taylor, King, and Usborne (see Chapter 21) have presented evidence that unconscious or implicit attitudes and stereotypes have the potential to influence intergroup communication, referencing several studies that have employed the Implicit Association Test or IAT (Greenwald, McGhee, & Schwartz, 1998) to measure these psychological phenomena. The IAT has also been used to examine the nature of implicit age attitudes, stereotypes, and identity across age groups as well as how those relate to intergenerational communication.

Differences in the age stereotypes of older, middle-aged and young adults were presented earlier which seem to indicate that attitudes and stereotypes about aging are developmental, that is, they change over the life span. Thus, from a developmental perspective, positive views of young people may be maintained into old age, even though from a social identity perspective, older people may be expected to have more negative views of young people than of their own age group.

Questionnaires that ask explicitly about attitudes toward other age groups typically find this ingroup bias. Similarly, when asked on questionnaires about their identification with specific chronological age groups, young and older people typically choose distinct age ranges even though younger people tend to pick slightly older ages and older people pick slightly younger ages than their chronological ages. These distinct age identities are consistent with a social identity perspective. However, from a developmental perspective, older individuals may retain a youthful inner age identity at an unconscious level even as they acknowledge when asked directly that they are members of an older age group.

To investigate these issues, Hummert et al. (2002) asked young and older participants to complete IAT tests assessing their implicit (i.e., unconscious or automatic) age attitudes (positive young versus positive old) and age identity (young versus old) as well as questionnaire measures of those constructs. They predicted that the IATs would be sensitive to developmental processes with older participants and younger participants being equally more positive in their attitudes toward young people than older people and both age groups showing evidence of an age identity that was more youthful than aged. In contrast, they predicted that the questionnaire measures would favor social motivation explanations consistent with social identity theory: (1) attitudes would reflect ingroup bias or alternatively social desirability effects with each age group endorsing more positive attitudes of the other age group than of their own; and (2) age identities would reflect the participants' chronological age groups. Results supported these hypotheses, demonstrating that unconscious and conscious processes have a role in intergenerational relations.

If older individuals have strong implicit attitudes and beliefs about aging—whether positive or negative—they may act unconsciously in ways consistent with those beliefs. Levy (2003) terms this *self-stereotyping* (see also Turner, Hogg, Oakes, Reicher, & Wetherell, 1987). Her research has shown that implicit activation of negative age stereotypes leads to poorer recall of older participants on memory tests, shakier handwriting, lower preference for life-extending interventions, and higher cardiovascular stress. In contrast, implicit activation of positive age stereotypes leads to better performance, greater preference for life-extending treatments, and lower cardiovascular stress.

O'Brien and Hummert (2006) found that an older implicit age identity can lead to age stereotypic behavior even for participants who are not technically "older adults." They asked three groups of participants in late middle age (50–62) to complete IAT and explicit measures of age identity and age stereotypes as well as a word recall task. One group served as the control, one group was told that that their memory performance would be compared to that of young adults, and the third that their performance would be compared to that of older adults. Two alternative hypotheses were tested: Stereotype threat (Steele & Aronson, 1995) which would predict poorer memory for those who thought they would be compared to young adults, and self-stereotyping which would predict poorer memory for those who thought they would be compared to older adults. Results supported the self-stereotyping hypothesis, with those in the old-comparison group recalling fewer words than those in the other two groups. Importantly, this finding applied only to those participants with an older implicit age identity (i.e., those who had begun unconsciously to think of themselves as getting older) but was unrelated to their chronological age identity as measured explicitly.

These studies are important in identifying unconscious and automatic processes which can play a role in intergenerational communication. Individuals of all ages share certain expectations about the characteristics of older persons. As the CPA and ASI models show, many aspects of a communication situation may make age and age-related beliefs salient. Those include not only the situation, context, and physical cues to age but also the communication behaviors of the people involved. Thus older adults may unconsciously "act their age" in the way they communicate, perhaps by engaging in painful self-disclosures or joking about a "senior moment" (Coupland, Coupland, Giles, Henwood, & Wiemann, 1988; Hummert et al., 2004). In turn, such communication styles may increase the salience of the intergroup context for younger adults. As a result, the younger individuals may unconsciously assume the need to use the accommodations of elderspeak in talking with older adults who communicate in these ways.

Conclusion

The theory and research reviewed in this chapter demonstrate the important role that intergenerational communication plays in maintaining the psychological and physical health of individuals as they age. The contexts in which intergenerational communication occurs in our daily lives are myriad: family, school, work, health care, entertainment, etc. This means that the opportunity for age stereotypes to affect our interactions abound. Yet as this research shows, we are often unaware of the subtle influences of stereotypes on our intergenerational interactions. Becoming more aware of the ways in which our own communication reflects and reinforces age stereotypes offers the primary avenue for improving the quality of our intergenerational communication.

This chapter has provided an overview of communication between age groups, with a primary focus on communication with older adults given the relative social status of young, middle-aged, and older individuals. However, young adults, particularly adolescents, are also at risk for negative stereotyping and unsatisfactory intergenerational communication and are becoming an increasing focus in intergenerational research (Williams & Nussbaum, 2001; see Chapter 5). To the extent that negative and positive stereotypes of adolescents apply, the CPA and ASI models could be usefully extended to encompass that age group.

As pointed out at the beginning of this chapter, age groups overlap with family roles. Recent research and theory have recognized that the family may serve as a meta-identity that can enable family members of varying ages to move beyond generational communication as intergroup to family communication as within group (Harwood, Raman, & Hewstone, 2006; see Chapter 15). Such research offers the promise of insights into ways to ensure more positive intergenerational interactions and the reinforcement of the positive feedback loop of the ASI model. For instance, to the extent that family members can focus on their common allegiance, they may move beyond viewing each other in terms of family role and age group stereotypes into interpersonal interactions that recognize their unique individual needs.

This chapter illustrates that developmental explanations can be useful in understanding the complexities of intergroup communication processes. A developmental perspective acknowledges explicitly that one's attitudes, beliefs, and, as a result, communication, not only are shaped by one's life experiences, but also serve to shape future experiences. Therefore, while this chapter has focused on the role of development in intergenerational communication, the developmental perspective also can provide insights into other forms of intergroup communication.

As my family travel experience illustrated at the beginning of this chapter, age identity is fluid but intimately related to relationships and communication. If we are fortunate to live long enough, each of us will have the experience of moving from youth to middle age to old age. Receiving respectful and supportive communication from others is important to each of us, regardless of age, but the research on intergenerational communication shows that it is critically important to maintaining the emotional and physical health of the most vulnerable members of our older population. Being sensitive to our own unconscious beliefs about aging can serve to minimize our stereotypical judgments of others and hopefully improve our communication across intergenerational boundaries, enabling us to approach such interactions as interpersonal rather than intergroup.

CHAPTER FIVE

Identity Dynamics in Adolescent-Adult Communication

JOHN DRURY

This chapter argues that adolescent and adult communications can fruitfully be conceptualized in terms of intergroup relations. While research and theory on both adolescence and intergroup relations is extensive, and adolescent communication is a research area that has grown in recent years, there has so far only been preliminary work to develop an intergroup perspective on adolescent communication (e.g., Fortman, 2003; Williams & Garrett, 2005). Herein, this is added to by suggesting how specific insights from the social identity approach to identity itself can take this area forward.

The chapter first provides an brief overview of current thinking in the field of adolescent research and theory. The focus here is on relations with non-family adults. While the nature of interactions with all adults also changes over the course of adolescence, relationships with non-family adults is a neglected topic requiring special attention in its own right. The general topic of family communication is dealt with elsewhere (see Chapter 15). Next, the chapter will examine how identity and group membership have been addressed in relation to adolescent communication and argue for the relevance of the social identity approach. After a review of existing intergroup analyses of adolescent-adult relations, an account is developed of the escalation of conflictual communication, using the example of adolescent-police interaction. By showing that there are issues of stereotyping and power involved (see Chapter 8), this account will provide a rationale for understanding adolescent-adult communication as a dynamic process. It will suggest that such a dynamic process can only adequately theorized with an equally dynamic model of the nature of identity. Although the emphasis here is largely on conflictual relations and communications, it is concluded that the field is potentially much broader than this.

The Nature and Construction of Adolescence

In terms of biological development, adolescence is identified with the onset of puberty and other physical changes taking place in the teenage years, such as accelerated growth. These bodily changes have obvious implications for the way that young people think about themselves, behave and relate to others—including both peers and adults (Coleman & Hendry, 1999). The social world around them also changes as young people reach the teenage years. Between the years 13–19, young people are treated increasingly like adults. They are granted more rights and have more responsibilities and have increasingly informal interactions with the institutions and representatives of the adult world. Secondary school relations are often more impersonal than those in the primary school: the institution is much bigger physically and hence more anonymous, and there will be different class teachers for different subjects rather than the same teacher who knows the pupil well. On reaching 13 years of age, young people (at least in the UK) have the legal right to enter the job market. Hence, as they progress through adolescence, young people get increasingly involved in work or may be claiming benefits, both resulting in more financial independence from their parents and hence more interactions with adults outside the family. In short, the number and quality of relations and hence communications with adults change during adolescence.

However, while there is agreement that 'adolescence' is a proper object of research, its precise nature is not easily pinned down. Even relying on biological indicators is problematic. For example, the age of onset of puberty has changed over the last 100 years (Thurlow, 2005). Social indicators are equally slippery. Socio-economic conditions have led to changes in the age at which young people become independent. The average age of economic self-reliance, leaving home, leaving full-time education and starting employment have all changed in just the last fifteen years (Coleman & Hendry, 1999).

If the nature of adolescence is disputable, then perceptions and constructions of adolescence might be a topic of investigation in their own right. Popular constructions of adolescence have varied over time. However, certain versions have been more persistent and influential than others. Griffin (1993) has detailed the development and ideological consequences of particular 'representations of youth' that have shaped theory and policy on adolescence. Thus the dominant biologistic 'storm and stress' model of adolescence as a sudden period of endogenous, hormone-fuelled turbulence has rationalized institutional policies in which 'youth is trouble' and therefore needs to be controlled by professional adults.

One of the arguments of this chapter is that both the objective features of adolescence (as a social-contextually defined age-stage of changing relations with the adult world) and its (controversial) representations feed into the relationships that adolescents have with non-family adults. The linchpin connecting the social relations and representations of adolescence with communication with the adult world is identity.

Identity and Group

The concept of identity has long been important in theorizing on adolescence. However, following the work of Erikson (1963), at least in psychology, adolescent identity has been conceptualized in individual terms. In this tradition, while contextual variability may be acknowledged, there is still argued to be a personal 'core' to identity, in the form of a representation of the individual self. Even where identity is understood as in some sense socially influenced or produced, the social is still understood narrowly in terms of interpersonal relations or one-way influence.

By contrast, other disciplines have conceptualized adolescent identity in collective and cultural terms as a property of youth groups or subcultures. Youth subcultures can provide an argot for young people to construct an identity distinct from both rival subcultures and the adult world. The creative use of language by adolescent subcultures in relation to their collective identity is illustrated by a recent special issue of *The International Journal of Bilingualism*. This included reports of studies of adolescents in a number of European countries, each group making creative use of features of ethnic minority language to define both their ethnic identity and their own autonomy as young people different from an older generation of their own ethnicity (e.g., Nortier & Dorleijn, 2008).

Studies of turn-taking and word-use in interpersonal communication also illustrate how identity is collectively struggled over and hence involves issues of power between young people and the adult world. Thus, in a study of girls' expressions of anger, Brown (1998) showed how, in the peer group setting, adolescents were able to appropriate (and subvert) the language of others in line with their own needs. Linguistic creativity was used by the girls to collectively problematize their middle class teachers' use of dominant definitions of femininity to interpret their experiences and behaviors. For example, what it meant to be a 'good girl' was challenged in the girls' accounts, where they defended their right to express emotions such as anger. (See also Rymes, 1995, for a study of adolescent linguistic usage in the service of classroom resistance.)

In summary, these studies of adolescent subcultural phenomena support the argument that their language use is constitutive of identity. These accounts also transcend classic psychological models of adolescence which conceptualize identity as essentially personal and individual. However, while these accounts of youth subculture also crucially suggest that adolescent identity exists in relation to that of other groups, they lack an explicit articulation of an intergroup social psychology. They imply relations between groups but largely do not theorize such relations, including their dynamics. We shall see, however, that the application of the social identity approach to intergroup aspects of adolescence in fact opens up the way for a more dynamic account of identity itself.

Adolescent-Adult Communication as Intergroup Interaction

In a recent review, Williams and Garrett (2005) suggested that, in many contexts, adolescents are defined and treated by others as a social group and hence often think of themselves as a group in relation to adults. More generally, they suggest, intergenerational communication can be regarded as intergroup communication—in terms of labels, boundaries, attributions, stereotypes, typicality and age salience. In this account, problems in communication between adolescents and the adult world can fruitfully be analysed as intergroup phenomena (Fortman, 2003; see also Chapter 5). This is an argument for extending some of the points in the literature on youth subcultures, such as the role of language in oppositional identity boundaries, to the broader field of adolescent-adult relations.

One way that adolescent-adult communication has been researched from an intergroup perspective is through the study of perceptions of communication between adolescents and other groups. Thus reviews of research based on communication accommodation theory (Fortman, 2003; Williams & Garrett, 2005) suggest that young people rate communication with older adults as less satisfactory than that with their same age peers, an effect which increases with the salience of the intergroup distinction. It is the failure to accommodate on the part of older adults (i.e., to move communicatively close to the other) that is suggested to be at the heart of this dissatisfactory communication. Research specifically on young people's evaluation of communication with non-family adults adds to this picture of negativity. Catan, Dennison, and Coleman's (1996) survey found that the number of young people describing experiences of bad communication with adults outside the family outweighed the number describing good experiences.

Adolescents' attribution of blame to the adult outgroup is reciprocated. Thus a study comparing the accounts of a number of different groups of professionals found that most participants had something to say about what they saw as adolescents' communication problems (Drury & Dennison, 2000). Among the professional groups studied, police officers and benefits officers were those most likely to say that young people lack adults' communication 'skills'. Police officers were found typically to conceptualize adolescents' communication skills in terms of motivation; young people are said not to want to communicate with them. Similarly, benefits officers referred not only to a lack of knowledge and experience, but also to young people's 'attitude' and lack of motivation (Drury & Dennison, 1999).

In contrast, 'good communication' between themselves and adolescents is often defined by professional groups in terms of disclosure from the adolescent. While police officers stressed their own willingness and ability to listen to the adolescent (Dennison & Drury, 1998), other research finds that police officers define effective communication simply as a one-way process: of them getting a message across to young people (Loader, 1996).

The social identity approach suggests that intergroup conflict is not inevitable but, rather, is a function of the particular nature of group identities and their specific relations (see Chapters 1 & 21). One of the dimensions along which groups relate to each other, and which may be a source of conflict, is power. The perceived illegitimate use of power by one group may in turn legitimize a conflictual response from the less powerful group. In line with the first of these points, Drury, Catan, Dennison, and Brody (1998) found that power was one of the main explanations offered by young people for their dissatisfactory communication with non-family adults. For example, adolescents often saw the power of police officers as a problematic issue in their communication with them. Similarly, in the case of communication with benefits officers, poorer adolescents were found to feel less positive about communicating with benefits officers than those better off; the former may be more likely to feel that they are at the mercy of individuals within the benefits system (Drury & Dennison, 1999).

A related explanation that adolescents gave for communication problems experienced with non-family adults was what they perceived as a lack of respect for the adolescent's point of view (Drury et al., 1998). In the case of police officers, it is often the style and demeanor of police officers (brusque, aggressive, impolite) rather than the content of contact (such as being arrested, charged or helped) that is the focus of young people's complaints (Hopkins, 1994; see also Chapter 6). As discussed above, police officers find adolescents hostile and uncommunicative. However, from the adolescent's point of view, one of the reasons for not wanting to communicate with the police—even when the adolescent is the victim rather than the alleged perpetrator of an offence—is that complaints will not be listened to or taken seriously (Loader, 1996). While adolescents may want greater dialogue with those in authority, they feel they cannot have the same kind of influence possessed by those in authority within such dialogue.

There is ambiguity in adults' accounts of the extent to which their own power plays a role in their communication with adolescents. For example, most benefit officers interviewed in the study by Drury and Dennison (1999) acknowledged that their own power was a potential obstacle to good communication with teenagers, but at the same time some also denied the importance of power. Similarly, Drury and Dennison (2000) found that police officers tended to gloss over the power difference when asked about it by stating that they treated the adolescent simply as an equal.

Dynamics of Identity: A Worked Example

In comparison to other age groups, adolescents are particularly likely to be in contact with the police, whether as victims or (perceived) perpetrators of crime. Research on adolescent interaction with the police has provided a number of insights into problematic and conflictual communication (e.g., Fielding, 1995; see Chapter 6). The example of this type of communication will be used to illustrate a dynamic social identity approach to adolescent-adult communication.

There is in popular culture a long-standing representation of adolescence as 'trouble', 'at risk', and 'anti-authority' (Griffin, 1993; Rymes, 1995). Features of this negative representation can easily be mobilized as explanations for the 'social problems' of adolescence, such as knife crime, gang culture and other kinds of activity that bring them to the attention of the police. However, as suggested at the beginning of this chapter, another way of viewing 'representations of youth' is as active ingredients in the interaction process itself. Culturally available constructions are drawn upon by those in power as a cognitive resource within interaction. In line with the discursive turn in social psychology, we also need to examine the social consequences of such constructions (Griffin, 1997).

In relation to police-adolescent communications, a useful starting point for unpacking this argument is Emler and Reicher's (1995) study of delinquency. Their analysis conceptualized delinquency as a group-level phenomenon whereby (some) young people define themselves (at least some of the time) in relation (i.e., in opposition) to the institutional order. Thus acts of delinquency are at once reflections of identity but also statements (of reputation) to others in the peer ingroup. Contained within this analysis, then, is the implication that adolescents are acutely aware of the power differential inherent in their relationships with adults in the institutional order, an order which they sometimes perceive fails to represent or protect them—i.e., lacks legitimacy. If communication of the (delinquent, anti-authority) identity to the peer ingroup is taking place, then it is implied that such identities might also be communicated to the relevant outgroup. Indeed, the presence of the relevant outgroup member—i.e., the police officer—can become a test of the veracity of the claimed identity to the peer ingroup audience.

Emler and Reicher's (1995) analysis took several features not only from the social identity approach in general, but from self-categorization theory (SCT; Turner, Hogg, Oakes, Reicher, & Wetherell, 1987) in particular. The social identity approach suggests that identity is multiple, that we have social (collective) identities as well as personal ones, and that these social identities correspond to our various group memberships. SCT adds that cognitive representations of the self take the form of self-categorizations, which are based both on our knowledge and motivations, and on real regularities in the social world. Seeing oneself as personally interchangeable with other ingroup members on some relevant dimension means sharing a definition of social reality with these others (see Chapters 1 & 21).

In this short definition, it is clear that the social identity approach offers a very specifically *social* account of identity processes, including reference to multiplicity, contextual variability, connectedness with others, and the constraints (and affordances) of real social relations. However, it is also necessary to be explicit that identity should be conceptualized not simply as a description of 'who I am' but as a model of proper and possible *action* in relation to others (Reicher 1996a). Only with such a conceptualization can we show how social identities are at the heart of dynamic (i.e., changing, conflictual) interaction. Thus, on the assumption that identities are in this way action oriented, and only because groups have the power to put their social identities into practice—to shape the social world in line with their conception of legitimacy—can such groups render their identity in the context within which others come to define themselves and act subsequently.

This insight into the mutually-defining properties of antagonistic social identities has been extensively applied to the domain of crowd behavior to explain the dynamics of conflict (e.g., Reicher 1996b). However, it is argued here that it also has potential for explaining features of police-adolescent antagonistic communication, for here too there may be the core conditions for the escalation of intergroup conflict: asymmetrical representations of the other, and unequal power. Hence, we suggest, concepts from this account of social identity can afford us some theoretical purchase into understanding the development of conflictual interaction between adolescents and police officers.

A commonly observed context for such interaction is the street corner gathering. We can suggest how such a gathering might come to be defined as a problem, and the psychological consequences of this for both sides. Thus, without knowing any personal details about the particular adolescents, police officers (along with other non-family adults) will have some idea 'who' they are interacting with on the basis of their definition of the other as a 'teenager' (e.g., as potentially 'trouble' and as 'uncommunicative'). This, and their knowledge of how they are seen by teenagers, will, in turn, influence their communication with that teenager.

As argued, representations do not simply 'drive' behavior, however, but can be used actively by participants. The discourse of inherent adolescent 'anti-authority', 'peer-group pressure' and 'storm and stress' have been found to feature as rationalizations and explanations in adults' accounts of their communication with adolescents (Drury & Dennison, 2000). Whether adolescent behavior is constructed as a function of biologically fixed repertoire or of supposedly indiscriminate malleability (Griffin, 1993), the social-psychological function is the same. It is to absolve the adults themselves of responsibility for poor communication, misunderstanding and conflict. Instead, they are rendered as merely the passive recipients of unreasonable hostility from adolescents. Whether deliberate or not, therefore, these kinds of representations of youth can operate as a self-serving attribution at the intergroup level.

Police officers' possibly 'defensive' initial reactions (e.g., firmness, formality) to a 'rowdy' adolescent gathering might feel to them as a passive response. But such a reaction might be perceived by the adolescents as a hostile act, an attempt to use institutional power to threaten their freedom to 'hang about' in the street (Loader, 1996). Since police officers have the ability to translate their perceptions into practice (through back up, threats of arrest, restraint and other physical acts), their understandings of the situation can operate as the context within which members of the adolescent gathering determine their own next move. Moreover, where police action is seen as illegitimate, the most readily available and apparently effective form of communication open to young people would seem to be defiance (Loader, 1996). Where the police action is also seen by the adolescent as 'indiscriminate' (rather than simply targeting one 'leading trouble-maker'), all members of the gathering may feel that such defiance is appropriate and necessary. Such defiant communications may be non-verbal as much as verbal, just as the teenagers may perceive disrespect, provocation and prejudice in the police officer's implicit 'attitude' as much as his words (Hopkins, 1994).

In terms of their representation of adolescents as 'trouble', it is rational for police officers encountering them to expect uncooperativeness or even outright aggression. Yet the point being made here is that police officers' representations of youth as hostile to authority may not simply reflect the given reality of tension and conflict in their relationship (Fielding, 1995; Southgate, 1986) but may also contribute to this relationship.

Looked at from the other perspective, where young people themselves bring to an interaction the expectation that police behavior will be illegitimately and indiscriminately hostile and disrespectful, this too can serve to produce the very antagonistic interaction expected, almost as a self-fulfilling prophesy (see Chapter 6).

Moreover, if supported by the peer group, the adolescents' hostile response to the perceived threat from the police could in turn serve to confirm police officers' initial expectations of hostility. Hence conflict escalates. The psychological outcome of this escalation could be that oppositional identities and reputations develop and are substantiated (Emler & Reicher, 1995): police generally come to be defined as 'pigs' (Hopkins, 1994) and the adolescents themselves as generally anti-authority. Thus, identities then are both condition and result of intergroup interaction.

In summary, then, with sufficient power, the identities (conceptualized as action in relation to the other) become the context within which this other acts. One of our opening arguments was that the (controversial) 'representations of youth', which are widely held by adults in authority, can feed into the communication process itself. In practice, the power differential means that adults in authority are able to define the context of interaction between themselves and adolescents using these representations as resources and explanations. Interaction between such adults and adolescents may, therefore, serve to instantiate or reinforce particular adolescent identities with their associated understandings and behavioral repertoires.

Conclusion

If, as has been argued, language is central to most intergroup relations, and adolescents and adults outside the family orient to each other at least some of the time as members of groups, then adolescent-adult communication can be analyzed using the same frameworks that have been applied to intergroup communications more broadly.

The nature of adolescence has been theorized along a number of dimensions, but one issue that comes up repeatedly is autonomy in relation to both the family and the wider adult world. One way that such adolescent autonomy might be achieved is through the affordances of the peer group. While (sociological) studies of youth subculture have embraced the notion of multiple (and conflicting) collective identities as a way of approaching adolescent communication, studies in this tradition have not theorized intergroup relations. The social identity approach in social psychology has only recently been applied to research on adolescence. It is not only the fact that adolescents see themselves and act a 'group' that points to the usefulness of a social identity approach, but the fact that adolescents are defined by others as a social category and have a whole set of culturally-defined group-level characteristics (stereotypic features) assigned to them.

From an intergroup perspective, and in line with social identity research in other domains, it is clear that issues of power affect the nature of communication (and the perception of that communication) between adolescents and non-family adults.

Non-family adults have the ability to impose their understanding on adolescents, sometimes by drawing upon particular (negative) representations of youth. These discourses of adolescence can feed into the communication process, and operate to justify (oppressive) adult practices towards young people. How adolescents define themselves and understand their social world is a function at least in part of their interaction with non-family adults. The power of adults, and young people's relationship to the discourses that they employ, can serve to construct and reinforce forms of identity for adolescents.

The social identity approach was developed to explain how groups attempt to change (or to maintain) their (unequal) relationships. Recent work on collective action suggests how identities can change, and are changed by, context. Using insights from this work, the example of police-adolescent interaction suggests how unequal relations of power and negative constructions of the other might (re)produce intergroup antagonism. This analysis has rested not only on the social identity theory of intergroup relations but also the social identity approach to identity (i.e., as social, multiple, and grounded in group relations). Further, the insight that identities are action oriented not simply descriptive has afforded some theoretical purchase on the dynamics of conflictual escalation in communication between adolescents and the police. The suggestion that one group's social identity can operate as the context for another (Reicher, 1996a) is a novel suggestion in this field, and hence one which offers to extend research and theory on adolescent communication in new and interesting ways.

This chapter has steered away from reviewing the substantial literature on family communication (see Chapter 15). But some of the points made here make at least intuitive sense of at least some within-family interaction. Parents may see the 'sullen', 'hostile' (non-) communicative responses of their adolescent offspring as a function of adolescence itself rather than a reflection of their personal identity. This in turn may shape their own reactions (e.g., 'it's just a phase') including the way they communicate back. The role of such intergroup representations in family interaction, as well as their role in all adolescent-adult communications, could usefully be the subject of future research. While most social-psychological analyses up to now have looked at these kinds of issues by studying (accounts of) perceptions (in the form of questionnaires and interviews; e.g., Drury & Dennison, 2000; Williams & Garrett, 2005), we could learn by borrowing from the methodologies of sociologists. Ethnographic studies and analyses of sound-track recordings of exchanges between adolescents and adults would add both validity and an essential longitudinal dimension to the research process.

Adolescents perceive family communication as more positive than that with non-family adults (Drury et al., 1998). One further reason for attempting in future research and theorizing some integration of research on adolescent communication with non-family adults with that within the family is that the analysis offered in the present chapter has focused almost exclusively on negative communications and conflict. Without neglecting structural impediments to 'good communication' between young people and adults, there are also theoretical and empirical grounds for examining the constructive role of adolescent-adult communication in the domains of identity, cognition and development (Drury et al., 1998).

CHAPTER SIX

Police-Civilian Encounters

HOWARD GILES, CHARLES W. CHOI & TRAVIS L. DIXON

In March 2009, an African American, Ryan Moats, was seen by a white police officer driving through a red light in Texas. Despite being followed with lights flashing, the car continued and ultimately stopped in a hospital parking lot. The officer was immediately on the offensive, drew his gun, and dismissed the driver's claim that he was driving quickly and safely to see his dying mother-in-law. "My first reaction was just to not react—just put my hands on the car," the man said in a TV interview. "Once he saw me get out, his attention came towards me, and that's when pretty much all the verbal abuse and everything came on." Despite the intervention of hospital staff corroborating the driver's story, Moats was cited after a prolonged engagement and thereby missed being at his relative's passing. Public indignation ensued as considerable media attention followed this videotaped event. The officer's chief condemned the action, ordered an internal investigation, rescinded the citation, and the officer subsequently apologized. This interaction doubtless had emotional consequences for Mr. Moats and his family at a time when they were already enduring distress. Furthermore, and via the media, the incident likely created and sustained negative views of the police by the public at large.

Yet as it happens, routine (rather than high-risk) traffic stops can be lethal for officers. It is the occasion when most police are killed on duty and the number in any year (from FBI data) is disquieting: up to 2004, 16,500 officers had been killed in the line of duty in America and, in the year 2004 alone, 1,530 were murdered. The officer in the above incident may have had this on his mind when communicating with this unknown, agitated violator. The drama of two California Highway Patrol officers killed—again in March 2009—in a routine traffic stop in Oakland is a recent shocking reminder of such incidents.

Studies show that most civilians have been involved in traffic stops—and it is typically this occasion when they meet law enforcement face-to-face. Civilians can feel intimidated and frightened when encountering officers, often fueled by societal stereotypes associated with them (see below and Chapter 8). In parallel, many officers can become suspicious and distrustful of civilians due to their frequent exposure to belligerent violators on the streets and in their homes. Clearly, police-civilian encounters can be "intergroup" par excellence. The intergroup essence of police work was captured, sadly, in this report from the Associated Press (04/23/04) when an officer was murdered in Pomona, California. The local chief remarked: "it's clear that the motive was to kill a police officer not this specific police officer." Indeed the badge, uniform, visible weaponry, and even hairstyle are likely to have engendered strong feelings of intergroup boundaries since childhood. Obviously, the intergroup divide is highly imbalanced vis-à-vis institutional power, as compliance with armed police directives is typically legally mandated. As gang violence (itself an intriguing intergroup arena) and active shooters in schools, malls, and the workplace become an increasing ingredient of our media diet, the relevance of scholarly research in this intergroup arena becomes all the more pressing.

Yet, police-civilian encounters have only recently featured in intergroup communication (Giles, 2002). This is surprising given that a large percentage of police work involves interacting with the public, with *communication* being regarded as "the central most important commodity that the officer has at his [or her] disposal" (Womack & Finley, 1986, p. 14). Nonetheless, we have here an intergroup context of police and civilian communication that we will argue is maintained and inflamed by a set of contributing factors, such as deep-rooted prejudices against the police and media depictions of police brutality. However, the position to be unfolded below is that there is a possibility of perturbing this problematic cycle of (sometimes mutual) mistrust through positive contact occasioned by particular patterns of accommodation.

We begin with a review of research into attitudes toward police officers and the possible social origins of them. The critical role of officer *communication* in molding public opinion and civilian trust is highlighted, particularly as manifest in police accommodations. However, we also argue that accommodative talk can be dysfunctional in certain settings and that self-protective *non*accommodation (which is typically misinterpreted and devalued by civilians) can, instead, be a rationally valued strategy for officers. We then turn our focus on the intra- and especially interracial dynamics of police-civilian encounters by recourse to behavioral studies on videotaped traffic stops. Out of this arises a new communicative perspective on ethnic profiling. The chapter concludes with ways of meeting the *bilateral* challenge of improving police-civilian relations.

Attitudes Toward Police

Research shows that those with negative attitudes towards the police (ATP) have often had (or heard that significant others have had) disturbing police contacts in the past and perceived the police as having verbally harassed them. As a result, civilians feel as though they have been unjustly treated by police officers and, thereafter, hold more negative opinions of this social category overall. Even though there is a significant difference between interactions that are police- versus civilian-initiated, relative to those who do not have frequent contact with police officers, those that do generally report more negative attitudes (Schuck, Rosenbaum, & Hawkins, 2008).

As above, the context in which many police-civilian interactions take place is often characterized by hostility and danger. Carr, Napolitano, and Keating (2007) found that when officers are working in lower socio-economic communities, they are often required to use more force and, at times, engage in actions that might be perceived by some as misconduct. While the use of extreme measures may be warranted to control a particular situation, this then creates negative feelings in community members toward law enforcement. This is especially so when police have to make split-second judgments about the need for lethal force in dangerous, ambiguous situations (White, Cohrs, & Göritz, 2008) and when the outcome is considered righteous yet ill-fated (e.g., a victim brandished a replica weapon) by an internal investigation (see Dailey, Reid, Anderson, & Giles, 2006).

Many investigations have pointed to the role of socio-demographic factors in predicting ATP. Older, female, urban, better educated, higher incomed, homeowners, and married respondents in lower crime neighborhoods consistently manifest more positive ATPs than their social opposites (e.g., Tyler & Huo, 2002). Ethnic perceptions of law enforcement in the United States have, in particular, received widespread empirical attention; Caucasians and Asians have the most favorable ATPs and trust in police, followed by Hispanics and Native Americans, and then African Americans (e.g., Taylor, Turner, Esbensen, & Winfree, 2001).

Again, few Americans have much direct and frequent contact with law enforcement officials. Ordinary citizens have little understanding of the reality of this unique occupation, let alone the roles of communication in it, and it is often through media representations where many citizens have their ATPs created (albeit sometimes unwittingly) for them. In the period 1949–1994, there were 225 individual, serialized, prime-time television shows on crime and law enforcement in the

USA (Perlmutter, 2000). According to cultivation and social reality media theories, Americans likely form an opinion of the police based on heavy consumption of police and law-related shows on television (e.g., Shrum, 2002). Some of the effects include the perception of high violence, exaggerated technological capabilities, a gross distortion of police access to background information, high success in solving crimes and making arrests, and the lack of realism for the repetitive nature of police work. These misguided depictions can influence the way in which real police officers are perceived and affect the relationship between them and civilians.

Police officers in the media, especially on television, are given a wide range of portrayals, many of which can depict law enforcement as a glamorous profession saving the public from wrong- and evil-doers. However, some commentators hold the position that the mainstream media in the USA seem, in general, to hold an anti-police bias, leading people ultimately to having somewhat ambivalent attitudes as revered yet despised (see Molloy & Giles, 2002). Interestingly, a within-profession survey conducted among Californian police agencies, reported that 94% conceded that they had an image problem (Oberle, 2004). This survey also pointed out that police agencies perceive that the public misunderstands law enforcement primarily due to the images portrayed by the media. Perlmutter (2000) argued that the media's images of police officers and crime help the public to create precarious and impractical expectations of their effectiveness while, at the same time, making the public more fearful and desirous of protections.

The Role of Communication

In sum, there are numerous studies addressing ATP cross-disciplinarily, although these have been conducted in very different locales over time, with varying methodologies and outcome measures and, somewhat inevitably, contrary findings. Given that the communicative concomitants of police-civilian interaction can facilitate or undermine the flow and outcome of such encounters, it is perhaps surprising that there are few studies dealing with language and communication factors associated with police-civilian relations (see Kidwell, 2009). In this vein though, Tyler and Huo (2002) found that support for and trust in the police were associated with how police treated civilians—particularly in terms of the perceived fairness and legitimacy of their actions—even when civilians acknowledged they were at fault. Moreover, these scholars reported that effective policing, regardless of the respondent's ethnicity, is that which is polite, respectful, sincere, and concerned with civil rights.

Creating such a social climate is challenging for officers as even ordinary law-abiding civilians are likely to perceive—and hence communicate with—police officers in terms of their social category membership rather than react to them interpersonally as idiosyncratic individuals, let alone as co-citizens. Developing this perspective further, social identity theory (see Chapters 1 & 21) would suggest that when police officers and civilians converse with each other and manage an interaction based on their social identities, they will differentiate from, rather than accommodate to, each other as a means of achieving a positive identity. Expanding upon this, self-categorization theory (see Chapter 1) focuses on how people socially identify themselves through a socio-cognitive process that highlights similarities and differences from a salient ingroup prototype. A person has many social identities that are each activated according to the social contexts they are seen to be in. Depending on how they categorize themselves and others, their attitudes and behaviors change according to the norms that satisfy the relationship between in- and outgroup members.

Furthermore, when the characteristics of a contextually-salient group prototype become prominent, the importance of individual characteristics diminishes. For example, if the group membership of civilian is made salient, individuals will categorize themselves as part of this particular group, and police officers will be excluded as outgroup members. The latter are usually judged and treated more harshly because of the negative bias toward outgroup members that ordinarily characterizes intergroup relations. Moreover, probably more than most other professions, officers communicate with "numerous people whose backgrounds, needs, points of view, and prejudices vary dramatically, moment to moment" (Thompson, 1983, p. 9); again, such interactions may be considered vividly "intergroup" as is well exemplified in police-adolescent interactions (see Chapter 4). Moreover, even when, by all objective indices, officers are actually transmitting accommodating messages, civilians who harbor prejudices toward the police may hear them as nonaccommodating anyway.

In complementary fashion, key aspects of police-civilian encounters can be understood from a communication accommodation theory perspective (CAT: see Giles, Willemyns, Gallois, & Anderson, 2007). This framework explores the ways in which individuals vary their communicative behavior to accommodate others given where they believe others to be, their motivations for so doing, and the social consequences arising. An accommodative climate is one in which conversational partners listen to one another, take the other's views into account, desire to understand their conversational partner's unique situation, and explain things in ways that "sit right" with their partner. An accommodative climate also features pleasantness, politeness, and respect and is predictably more positively perceived by the interactants involved (as well as third-party observers) than non-accommodative messages. In this way, accommodating police officers are construed as more competent and socially sensitive than their nonaccommodating counterparts (e.g., Myers, Giles, Reid, & Nabi, 2008).

Adopting this perspective in three studies in California, Giles et al. (2006) showed that the extent to which officers are perceived as accommodating is a more important predictor of ATP than some of the traditional socio-demographic factors outlined above. Interestingly too, when invited by open-ended questions to catalogue characteristics of policing they respected, wished improvement in, and had complaints about, in all three cases *communication* factors (e.g., officers' way of talking to civilians) assumed the premier position. In these studies, there was a strong correlation between perceiving how accommodating officers were and civilians' trust in them. As we know from Tyler's work exemplified above, garnering the public's trust is an important endeavor in police work. Indeed, to trust another is to expect that they will not exploit your own vulnerabilities and that they will also act in a cooperative manner (Tam, Hewstone, Kenworthy, & Cairns, 2009). Relatedly, trust is, of course, an important mediating factor in establishing peaceful and favorable relations between members of different groups. However, establishing mutual intergroup trust is obviously difficult, not least because the process of deciding whether to trust members of different outgroups can be cognitively and affectively taxing; dissimilar others may be perceived to be threatening and adhering to very different and troubling worldviews from one's own. And for some civilians, perceiving officers to be accommodating, let alone trustworthy, may not be an easily accessible cognition. This would be especially so given that police themselves can be negatively aroused and very uncertain about who they are dealing with, and what actions could transpire affecting their own safety.

Furthermore, we know from studies in England which have evaluated having police officers as part-time teachers and counselors in high-schools, that positive affect associated with any individual officer (typically out of uniform) will not usually generalize to the social category, that is, police officers *in general* (e.g., Hewstone, Hopkins, & Routh, 1992). Rather, these children will all-too-readily discount the officer's typicality to the group as a whole and or sub-type that person as a special kind of officer, unlike all others. If such school contact programs are going to successfully change attitudes toward the police, then friendly interpersonal relationships must indeed be fostered, yet not at the expense of construing the person as a typical member of the category, police officer. By this means, high schoolers' inclinations to discount or dismiss the individual and affable police officer as somehow an exception can be eliminated (see Brown & Hewstone, 2005; see Chapters 10, 12, 15, & 17).

With this in mind, and in a series of studies with grossly different histories of police-civilian conflict ranging from Russia, Turkey, Japan to the USA and Canada, studies have shown that the more police officers are seen to be communicatively accommodating, the more civilians are willing to report complying to their requests and demands (e.g., Barker et al., 2008). Importantly, in most cultures, officer accommodativeness did not lead directly to expressed compliance but, rather, worked through perceived trust as the intervening variable. Yet interestingly, in those cultures where law enforcement agencies are the arm of government (e.g., Zimbabwe, Bulgaria, Mongolia, and Armenia), trust did not predict compliance, but officer accommodativeness did, and directly so. In these contexts, where trust in the police (that is seen to be paid to fulfill governmental needs unhesitantly and aggressively) has not been historically apparent, the public might take even greater store by officers who are seen to be—perhaps unusually—accommodative.

All this notwithstanding, CAT acknowledges, with contextual caveats, that not all accommodative and nonaccommodative moves are borne out of positive and negative intentions, respectively (see Giles et al., 2007). With this in mind, so-called low-risk traffic stops are known, by police officers, as being amongst the most dangerous situations they can encounter with members of the public. More than not, FBI data show that 21% of traffic stop killings of officers occur at the very last moment; the felon is waiting for, and sometimes communicatively facilitating, the officer to feel overly comfortable. In other words, officers are often "on their guard" —even under seemingly the most mundane circumstances and necessarily for the entire duration of the encounter—and are trained to resist temptations towards complacency and, therefore, vulnerability. Accommodativeness (especially when violations of the law are on the cards) is, therefore, not a "natural" and entirely comfortable communicative strategy for officers.

Indeed, this is compounded further given that it is accommodative officers who are the ones most liable to be victims of lethal force in traffic stops; a finding known by most officers. In this regard, and from interviews with victims' peers and supervisors, slain officers are often described as "friendly to everyone, well-liked . . . and tend to look for 'good' in others" (Pinizzotto, Davis, & Miller, 1997, p. 12). Put another way, and paradoxically (and perhaps dialectically) so given prior focus on accommodative virtues, an officer who is invariably accommodating is most likely to become a dead one. Crafted in terms of incentives (i.e., risking death versus incurring negative public judgments), no wonder officers are seemingly nonaccommodative in so-called low-risk routine traffic stops. Many officers then may experience the tension of being pulled toward being accommodative in traffic stops and yet pushed toward more nonaccommodative stances.

All this suggests new vistas for future research, theory, and practice in the police-civilian domain. Communicative training for officers needs to be devised and evaluated so that an optimal balance occurs between officers' accommodative and nonaccommodative moves; perhaps partial accommodativeness is the answer, whereby an officer is alert and directive, but with associated politeness markers and a less distant nonverbal demeanor. Clearly, the study of police-community communication needs to pay due cognizance to the regional and cultural histories in which it is embedded, and future work needs to devise a multi-dimensional typology of such locales (e.g., as in media space and language devoted to disturbances, numbers of riots, deaths, and arrests). This would provide an important backdrop that inevitably will shape the communicative dynamics operating between law enforcement and the specific communities they serve. In addition, more sophisticated models of police-civilian interaction (besides the variables of officer accommodation, public trust, and reported compliance) need to be formulated. Among the panoply of additional antecedent, mediating and outcome factors that could be entered into such an equation would be: past contact experiences, intergroup anxiety, civilians' willingness to report certain crimes as well as the accommodative-nonaccommodativeness of *civilians'* own communicative patterns, too. And in the context of interracial encounters, it is to the latter's communicative stance that we will turn.

Police-Civilian Encounters: The Racial Factor

Many scholars and activists have investigated racial tensions between the Black community and the police following the videotaped police beating of Black motorist Rodney King and the riots that followed in Los Angeles. Subsequent racialized events in Cincinnati and elsewhere have raised serious questions about whether police actions contribute to racial tension (Lundman & Kaufman, 2003). While many Whites may perceive Black complaints about treatment by the police as exaggerations, many African Americans see police misconduct as real examples of the cost of being Black in America. Nonetheless, police resistance to accommodativeness might be accentuated when encountering members of a social category, such as ethnic minorities, that have more stigmatic associations with violent crime than others. In this regard, the statistics are rather stark: although African Americans account for only 12% of the U.S. population, 44% of all prisoners in the United States are from this racial category (Human Rights Watch Backgrounder, 2003; see also, Correll, Park, Judd, & Wittenbrink, 2002).

While the study of police-civilian relations has recently entered the intergroup communication arena, there are very few analyses of actual interactions between these social categories (see Cronin & Reicher, 2009). Dixon, Schell, Giles, and Drogos (2008) conducted a study to rectify this stark omission as it pertains to traffic stops as well as determine the role of race in police-civilian encounters. They had randomly sampled video recordings from police cars on traffic stops in Cincinnati content analyzed. As might have been predicted, the study showed that each party's accommodativeness was predicted by the other's level of it. Yet arguably of most interest in this context were key differences as a function of the officers' and drivers' races. First, African Americans experienced more intensive policing during the stop than Whites. For instance, the former were stopped 22% longer and they were about four times more likely to be searched for illegal items than Whites. Second, the communication quality of Whites was, on average, more positive than that of Black drivers; the latter were more nonaccommodating and were coded as less apologetic, cooperative, pleasant, respectful, and more belligerent than White drivers. Third, in same-race interactions, officers were coded as listening more carefully, more accepting of what drivers have to say, and gave the impression that they were interested in hearing drivers' accounts, relative to racially-intergroup interactions. In contrast, officers' communication behavior was less positive and less accommodating when the officer and driver constituted an interracial mix.

It is important to point out that there are many more White officers than Black officers in this police agency. Approximately two-thirds of all traffic stops of Black motorists are interracial interactions, while one-third of White motorist stops are interracial. In some respects, these difficulties in interracial communication may be a reflection of the level of racial tension in the community. However, interracial interactions are often strained even in the absence of any prejudice. In fact, non-prejudiced individuals can appear anxious, uncomfortable, and self-conscious in interracial interactions precisely because they are concerned about appearing prejudiced. Similarly, minorities who are interacting with majority group members may feel stress from concern that they are being judged on their race, not their behavior, and may have low expectations of a positive interaction that results in a less positive interaction and more social distancing.

In an as yet unpublished follow-up study selecting from a wider sample of video-taped traffic stops a year later by these same authors, there was strong evidence of an interaction between officer's and driver's race. More specifically, White officers engaged in more intensive policing (e.g., vehicle searches and longer stops) with African American drivers than the contrasting kind of intergroup encounter.

Towards a Communicative Perspective on Racial Profiling

The last set of findings do raise the specter of racial profiling. However, it is important to note that these findings do not provide direct evidence that police were, systematically, engaged in such biased actions. Indeed, racial profiling perceptions might not be based on overt behavioral responses to a situation but, rather, may be subtly communicatively constructed or negotiated by the interactants themselves. In this vein, consider the following alternative textualized model in light of the above findings and discussion.

Whites typically remain friendly and accommodative during traffic stops and, therefore, are less likely to encounter negative responses such as intensive policing.

White officers may encounter Black civilian non-accommodation, which the White officer misinterprets as a problematic and potentially threatening individual (especially given the group's disproportionate association with felonious crimes cited above) rather than a rational response by Black civilians to possibly many such invasive, humiliating, and aggravating stops in the past. This misinterpretation then leads to more acute nonaccommodations and self-protective policing by the White officer, which is then interpreted by the Black civilian as a prototypical White officer who is unfair. It could be that this perception then fuels Black drivers' experiences of being racially profiled, even though they may not be any more likely to be stopped than White drivers when driving in their neighborhood. Moreover, such experiences most likely contribute to African American support for police reform and resistance to increased police power.

In order to avoid these situations, White officers may need to consider whether extensive policing is appropriately or equally applied to both Blacks and Whites. In other words, White officers may be influenced by a biased slant on racial history that needs to be overcome and that might require them to be sensitive to why a Black, as opposed to a White, citizen might engage in nonaccommodating communication. In addition, an awareness of the historical legacy of mistreatment between the police department and the community might aid in White officers' perceptions of Black communication behaviors. Meanwhile, Black citizens need to be mindful of the extent to which their communicative behaviors might inflame the situation and might lead to more intensive policing. Clearly, this communicative model warrants empirical scrutiny and be of relevance to police relations with other social groups (such as adolescents, see Chapter 5).

Conclusion

Ironically, communication skills are given short shrift in police officer training. Approximately, 98% of such training in the USA is devoted to officer safety through acquiring arrest, control, defense, and weapon techniques. The extent to which the use of physical force could be avoided or attenuated if appropriate accommodative skills were used is an interesting empirical question. The importance of officer safety through training regarding the use of physical skills cannot be under estimated. However, our findings regarding the importance of officers' accommodative practices in easing police-civilian interactions suggest that far more attention should be directed at elaborating communication skills. In addition, if police-community relations are to improve, then intervention programs and training focused on mutual accommodation and trust need to be *bi*-lateral.

In this vein, civilians can benefit from understanding the complexities, tensions, challenges, and emotions involved in police work. This has been demonstrated by civilians being invited to take on the perspective and uniform/equipment of officers in simulated incidents with a confrontational (possibly dangerous) member of the public (Giles et al., 2007). Having undertaken this exercise (where many have witnessed themselves responding in a surprisingly aggressive, even lethal, manner themselves), participants as well as observers empathize more with police officers' dilemmas and, consequently, change their attitudes in a significantly positive direction. In addition, civilians need to be appraised of the potential consequences of aggressive, nonaccommodating, or distancing communication during interactions with police.

The more the intergroup divide dissipates, the more we can appreciate Sir Robert Peel's position at the head of this chapter and invoke more community-oriented policing programs. These involve ordinary citizens and community leaders meeting regularly with police officers to jointly define crime problems and set police priorities as a partnership (see Morash & Ford, 2002; Molloy & Giles, 2002). As a result, residents are encouraged to express directly their concerns and needs, and police officers are able to communicate directly with citizens who want to see change in their neighborhoods. An essential part of community-oriented policing is that citizens themselves take some real measure of responsibility for resolving the problems of their own community. However, and despite the optimism held out for communicative interventions, data suggest that very few (i.e., less than 13%) of Americans have even heard of or appreciate the meaning of community-oriented policing (Giles et al., 2006). In tandem, officers and their superiors currently differ in their willingness to embrace the philosophy of community-oriented policing. Hence, any widespread process of change will take some time and require patience. Hopefully, further research on the communicative dynamics of police civilian encounters will be a force to hasten policy implementations and avoid the kind of regrettable scenario of Ryan Moats that opened this chapter.

CHAPTER SEVEN

Communication Across Religions

JASON KLOCEK, CRISTINA NOVOA &
FATHALI M. MOGHADDAM

The suicide terrorist who shouts "Allah akbar!" as he is detonating a bomb, the Christian fundamentalist who condemns the followers of other faiths "to hell," the armed Jewish settler who fights to expand an illegal Jewish settlement in the West Bank, the Hindu fundamentalist who helps to burn down a mosque . . . we have become accustomed to daily media reports of such events (see Chapters 2 & 12). Less sensational and far less attended to are reports of peaceful dialogue between the members of different faiths.

Our disproportional focus on violence between religious groups is, in large part, explained by a number of cognitive processes (Kahneman & Tversky, 1973; Kunda, 1999). For example, the *availability heuristic* leads us to assume that how easily one can bring to mind events indicates their prevalence. Also, the *negativity bias* means that negative information has greater impact on our perceptions than does positive information. Because we can more easily bring to mind instances of violence rather than peaceful relations between religions, we neglect the countless situations in which inter-religious contact is peaceful and focus on instances of inter-religious conflict. In addition, the limited empirical research in this area has primarily studied religion as an ethnic marker, exploring relations between Israeli-Jews and Palestinians (Maoz & Ellis, 2008) and Protestants and Catholics in Northern Ireland (Hewstone et al., 2006), along with Muslim, namely Turkish, assimilation in the Netherlands (Verkuyten & Zaremba, 2005). This chapter, however, looks at communication across religions as more than interaction between two ethnic groups (see Chapter 2); it explores communication between people who at the time of communication identify primarily with their *religious* ingroup. Inter-religious communication deserves close attention because religion encompasses deep beliefs about death, the purpose of life, and other matters of the highest importance.

The Resilience of Communication Across Religions

Until the late twentieth century, the dominant view in the social sciences was that religion is an "epiphenomenal force in society, having no relevance in the modern era" (Fox, 2006, p. 537). Developed by Karl Marx, Max Weber and Emile Durkheim, modernization or secularization theory predicted that the influence of religion in the public sphere would decline, and that science would replace religion as a source of, and reference for, explanation and action. Trends in Western Europe have tended to endorse this view, with declining church attendance and secularization. The expectation was that communication between religions would become less influential and less central in social and political life everywhere.

Global events, particularly since the coming to power of Islamic fundamentalists in Iran in 1979 and the global rise of religious fundamentalism, have led to a serious reassessment of the "secularization thesis." Contemporary scholars now identify three distinct trends of secularization: institutional differentiation between the political and religious sphere, privatization of religious beliefs away from the public sphere, and a general decline in religious belief (Casanova, 1994). While a decline in belief may be occurring in Western Europe, other global trends suggest that religious beliefs still enter prominently into the public sphere. The increased political influence of conservative Christians in the United States, the unexpected growth of Protestant evangelicalism in Africa and Latin America, Islamic radicalization in numerous countries (including democracies such as Turkey and Indonesia), Hindu fundamentalism in India, and the political influence of Buddhism in Burma and other states, support the view that the world remains as "furiously religious as it ever was, and in some places more so than ever" (Berger, 1996/1997, p. 3). However, although religion continues to be influential, the social and political role of religion is in some respects transformed, and this has also changed communication between religions.

One unexpected consequence of modernization with implications for communication across religions has been a new religious pluralism, referring to a social and political phenomenon primarily concerned with the diverse social practices and institutions which bind individuals into groups through shared belief systems (Banchoff, 2007). The new context of religious pluralism means that there is more open competition between religions in social, cultural, political and even economic domains.

Religious belief systems and communities have become one option among many. A consequence has been that in order to survive and grow, religious communities have had to refine and articulate a more persuasive message, one that better matches the needs of twenty-first century populations. In this development, a more prominent role has been given to *sacred carriers* (Moghaddam, Harré, & Lee, 2008), means by which religious values, beliefs and practices are communicated. Examples of sacred carriers are the Christian cross and the Islamic veil.

Institutionally, religious pluralism means something like the establishment of a religious market (Berger, 2007). Religious communities must compete for the allegiance of followers. One of the most important tactics used by religious communities is to position themselves as both positive and distinct and particularly through differentiation come to occupy vacant spaces. Followers are more inclined to identity with religious communities when such a positive and distinct identity is achieved. (see Chapters 1 & 21).

Through what theoretical lens should we interpret communication between religions? Since our interpretation of communication across religions relies heavily on subjective identification, clearly intergroup theories that revolve around identity (see Moghaddam, Harré, & Lee, 2008) are particularly relevant to this discussion. Social identity theory (Tajfel & Turner, 1979) and terror management theory (Pyszczynski, Solomon, & Greenberg, 2004) both suggest that outgroup religions can pose threats, either because they can threaten ingroup identity, or because they can remind us of our mortality. System justification theory (Jost & Banaji, 1994) suggests that the adoption of a religious belief system can serve to support group-based inequalities ("We must tolerate our lower status and income, because we will be rewarded in heaven"; see Chapter 21). All three theories are associated with traditional experimental research methods, often laboratory studies conducted in an hour or so. An alternative approach is offered by positioning theory, which focuses on communication processes over longer time periods (Moghaddam, Harré, & Lee, 2008). Positioning theory is concerned with the ways in which the actions of individuals and groups are constrained to flow according to local normative systems, and with the social and psychological processes through which such local normative systems are collaboratively constructed and upheld. A *position* is the cluster of rights and duties that limit the range of social acts available to a person or group.

We regard religions as systems of beliefs that can be used to mobilize populations to more effectively engage in positioning in order to compete for resources. Communication between religions plays a central role in making such mobilization more effective, by increasing cohesion and conformity within the ingroup, by maintaining group boundaries, by defending and extending group territories, and by maintaining a competitive and often aggressive stand against competing religions.

In the remainder of this chapter, we explore how communication between religions occurs through verbal and written discourse as well as the "sacred" built environment.

Religion and Everyday Discourse

Shared Everyday Discourse

Because of the pervasive nature of religion in major societies, religious discourse has penetrated even the detailed aspects of everyday life. In many major societies, spoken language with religious roots is common, even among those who do not practice religion. Over time, some expressions with religious origins have lost their religious significance for most people. For example, goodbye in Spanish originated from the commendation "to God." Over time, the two words were joined, losing some of their spiritual connotations for most people, until today *adios* has become the standard farewell among most Spanish speakers. Perhaps a similar example in English is the expression "Thank goodness" from the more religiously charged "Thank God." Alternatively, the spiritual meaning of some idioms may have changed through use in many different secular contexts. This is reflected in numerous expressions involving the word "bless": "I give my blessing," "a blessing in disguise," "bless you," and many more.

The power of norms explains how language with religious roots becomes commonly used even in secular settings by non-believers. About 80 years of social psychological research (Moghaddam, 2005) indicates how individuals may conform to normative speech patterns even when these patterns conflict with their personal beliefs. *Khodâhâfez*, the Farsi farewell meaning "God keep you safe," is one example. This normative way of saying goodbye has trapped believers and non-believers alike into using an expression with religious roots. Similarly, in many Muslim countries with Arabic speaking and non-Arabic speaking populations, *Insha'Allah*, Arabic for "God willing," has become a standard way of ending utterances about the future. In English, the phrase "My prayers are with you" has become a standard means of expressing sympathy, whether one actually prays or not.

The influence of religion is not restricted to specific phrases. More broadly, religion influences a culture's view of the world, which is then reflected in other aspects of a language's structure. While living in Turkmenistan one of the authors recognized the frequent use of the conditional future ("I may go to the market this afternoon" as opposed to "I will go to the market this afternoon"). An older formula for expressing the conditional future required the use of *Nesip bolsa*, or the Turkmen equivalent of the Arabic *Insha'Allah*, before stating intended action. While this reference to the divine may be dropped in contemporary discourse, an emphasis on the future's unpredictability remains. Religious ideas underpin the Turkmen fatalist view of the future, even if the expression of this was dropped from everyday vocabulary. As with the previous examples, tradition has dictated certain speech patterns. Because of the pressure to conform to norms, people continue these patterns, which position others to respond with appropriate, religiously charged expressions of their own. At the same time, the religious faithful infuse everyday language with religious meanings and in this way use everyday expressions as sacred carriers.

Ingroup Religious Dialogue

Language with religious roots serves to position believers as part of an ingroup. Among practicing Christians, such language includes expressions like "We all have our crosses to bear" or indirect references to New Testament passages through phrases like "Love thy neighbor." Similarly, Jews reference acts of kindness as *mitzvoth*, an allusion to the Torah's 613 commandments and seven rabbinic commandments. Hindus and Buddhists discuss events with reference to karma and reincarnation in a way that is distinct from their popular meanings. Muslims use the term "kafer" (unbeliever) in a way that sharply sets ingroup members apart.

In each of the previous cases, the phrases' meanings are deciphered in particular ways that sets them apart from outgroups by adherents to the particular religion. When an individual chooses expressions serving as a sacred carrier—"We all have our crosses to bear," for example—it primes the listener to respond in a particular way. Most often, it positions the listener as a Christian with all the rights and duties ascribed to that position. Being in this position will impact the social meaning of the individual's actions, which will then position others as well. Religious speech at this level becomes self-replicating, strengthening individuals' religious identity and bolstering group cohesiveness.

Positioning in the Public Sphere Using Religious Speech

Religious speech can position a group as dominant in the public sphere. Competing groups accept or reject such positioning, by either challenging or supporting the public use of certain types of religious speech. Take for example the ongoing controversy over the use of "Merry Christmas" in the United States of America. Christians readily use this expression to not only express glad tidings and good will to members of their own faith during the Christmas season but also to non-Christians. However, is it appropriate for Christians to use this expression with non-Christians? Is it a simple expression of good cheer or a way of positioning their faith as superior?

In addition, is it culturally sensitive for government buildings to display signs

reading "Merry Christmas" or display crèches? Many argue that because most citizens of the United States, regardless of religious affiliation, celebrate the Christmas
holiday, such signs are appropriate. However, continued controversy demonstrates
that the boundary between religious expression and a public, communal holiday
remains unclear. Another example is the use of the Arabic greeting *Salaam Aleikum*
("The peace of Allah be upon you"). One author recalls an exchange in Syria where
a Syrian Christian community reprimanded a Catholic visitor from the United
States for using the above greeting. Although there is nothing theologically objectionable to a Christian expressing their desire for God "to be with" a fellow human
being, the use of the Arabic term *Salaam Aleikum* is objectionable to some Christians
because it positions Islam as dominant in the public sphere.

Written Communication and Religion

Written communication also serves to promote ingroup conformity as well as to
position the ingroup as different from and superior to outgroups. Three primary
forms are relevant to our analysis of inter-religious dialogue: sacred, interpretive and
discourse over praxis.

Sacred Texts

Sacred written communication refers to the central text or texts, such as the Gospels,
Qur'an or Hindu Vedas, or a collection of teachings, such as the Dhammapada, or
a book of laws, such as the Baha'i Kitáb-i-Aqdas, from which religious communities derive their primary understanding of the divine.

Attitudes among religious leaders towards giving the lay public access to sacred
texts vary across time and across religions. The leaders of all the major religions
began from a common position: the attempt to severely limit access to sacred texts,
particularly by preventing the translation of such texts into local languages. For
example, the translation of the Qur'an into the vernacular is still a problematic issue
in Islamic theology. The religious elite continue to argue that as the miraculous and
inimitable "recitation" of God's revelation to the prophet Muhammad, it should only
be recited in Arabic. At a second stage, typically following extended periods of internal conflict and violent persecution, the religious leaders of some major religions have
changed position and allowed the translation of sacred texts (such as the translation of the Bible from Latin to local languages), and then become active in their
propagation among the general public.

Although there are important similarities in the storylines of the major sacred
texts (in terms of how the world was created by God, heaven and hell, and so on),

each sacred text positions one community's authenticity over another's. For example, the Qur'an as "the final of a series of revelations by God" may permit Muslims to recognize the divine origins of both the Torah and Gospel, yet it also positions those sacred texts as tampered and falsified. In turn, Christians are as reluctant to identify the Qur'an as divine revelation as Jews are to see the Gospel as God's revealed word.

Interpretive Texts

A second form of written religious communication involves the interpretation of sacred texts. The Talmud, a record of rabbinic discussions pertaining to Jewish law, ethics, customs, and history, stands as a classic example. Interpretation amplifies the sacred texts of the faith, clarifying what ingroup membership involves in terms of thoughts and actions. Additional examples include, the *Hadith* in Islam, oral traditions related to the words and deeds of the prophet Muhammad, the *Zend*, interpretations of the sacred texts of Zoroastrianism known as the *Avesta*, and the *Sri Bhasya*, commentaries of Adi Shankara on the ten major *Upanishads*, the *Brahma Sutras* and the *Bhagavad Gita*.

Quite often the interpretive process results in a re-positioning of a religion against attacks from other faith traditions. Under such circumstances, it is critical that all adherents of a faith understand what makes them part of the community and what separates them from other groups. Examples here include the *Pauline epistles*, which make clear how the early Christians differed from Jews, and St. Irenaeus' *Against Heresies*, which defended Christianity against Gnosticism, a powerful threat in the 2nd century.

Discourse over Praxis

A final form of written communication between religions may be formal or informal exchanges between members of the faith tradition centered on practice, rather than only belief. This can occur at the elite leadership level, when officials exchange formal communiqués, between middle-range clerics in sermons or between the laity of a faith tradition. Each of these forms of communication tends to follow particular storylines, highlighting favored practices among ingroup members, distancing ingroup from outgroup(s).

Leadership-level written communication serves, similar to interpretive texts, to remind ingroup members of their identity, as well as demonstrate to outgroup members what keeps them distinct. For example, Papal encyclicals indicate high Papal priority for an issue at a given time, often clarifying the position of the Church on a certain issue, such as birth control and contraception or war and peace.

Middle-range communication often results through sermons by priests, mullahs, gurus and other clerics. These teachings may occur in places of worship at regular intervals or at significant life events (i.e., baptisms, marriages, funerals). Often times they are delivered from elevated architectural features, such as the pulpit or ambo but then posted online or printed in bulletins to be distributed throughout the community.

In conflict situations, such as in Northern Ireland, religious clerics may promote an end to violence through letters and writing. In 1986, Fr. Alex Reid wrote letters to Charles Haughey, then Fianna Fail leader and former taoiseach, and John Hume, leader of the Social Democratic and Labour Party, suggesting a partnership between the Nationalist parties of Northern Ireland and the Republic of Ireland. In addition, in his essay "A Pastoral Response to the Conflict in Northern Ireland," Fr. Reid emphasized the need to promote "a Christian presence in the midst of the conflict which could light and lead the way to peace by the power and after the example of the Good Shepherd who is always among us" (Little, 2007, p. 89). These writings clarified what he felt should be the proper Catholic attitude and actions during a time of armed conflict.

Finally, the laity may also distribute written communication between group members and to others of a different faith tradition. Religious communication is not confined to official representatives and leaders; it exists powerfully among the masses. The conflicts in the former Yugoslavia offer two examples. First, in the case of Croatia, the main Catholic weekly paper *Glas Koncila* (Voice of the Council) routinely positioned Catholicism as "the Church among the Croats," linking Catholicism in Croatia with one specific nationality. They went so far as to publish, in 1993, images of Croatian soldiers on a pilgrimage to the Holy Shrines of Krasno and Lourdes (Mojzes, 1994). This positioned Croatian forces as engaged in a holy war to defend their Catholic homeland. A second example is found in Bosnia, where Islamic publications highlight ancient and modern Muslim thinkers who stressed the unity of religions and political ideas, as well as the superiority of Islam over other religions (Mojzes, 1998). Both Catholic and Muslim publications depicted a zero-sum situation: the survival of one group depended on the elimination of another.

Religious Communication Through the Sacred Built Environment

The built environment has a powerful impact on human behavior (Kopec, 2006), and religions also communicate through the design of houses of worship, monuments, shrines, statues, and the like. Among the important functions of the sacred built environment, we focus on the following: territoriality and dominance of physical space, strategies to move people emotionally and physically, and the promotion of group conformity and cohesion through rituals associated with these spaces.

Territoriality

Historically, the three major monotheistic religions have communicated their power and territorial reach by building houses of worship that are large and impressive enough to dominate the physical landscape. By their sheer size and opulence, the grand cathedrals, mosques, and synagogues could position themselves as physically, socially, and spiritually dominant in cities, at least before the age of skyscrapers. Even today, the tradition continues of grand houses of worship being built as "landmarks"; for example, the three co-authors of this article live in Washington, D.C., where the construction of the United States National Cathedral began in the twentieth century and is being completed in a way to ensure that this building stands out.

Perhaps one of the best examples of religious communication through architecture is St. Peter's Basilica in Rome. As the largest building in Christianity, the Basilica imparts a message of power and influence. Its famous colonnade reaches far into St. Peter's piazza, symbolizing the Church embracing the earth. Through its sheer size and richness, it communicates power, at the very least over the material world. Power over the material world can be a religion's way of representing power over the spiritual world as well, thereby drawing followers.

Given the importance of territory, competition between religions is reflected in conflict over the right to build sacred buildings in certain spaces. A recent example of this comes from Granada, Spain, where the Muslim community succeeded in building the city's first mosque in over five centuries. City officials objected to planning proposals until opposition gradually subsided. The mosque was finally completed in 2003, twenty-two years after it was initially proposed.

Once erected, architecture spatially separates religions, marking off territory and people that belong to each. Mosque minarets and church bell towers, for example, are concrete symbols of a neighborhood's Muslim or Christian identity. Originally a dominant feature of any skyline, these architectural features extend a religion's territory as far as their calls to prayer can be heard. The peal of church bells or the *azan* issued by mosques strengthens a religion's presence in a given area, first by symbolizing a religion's ownership of an area, and second, by strengthening group cohesion through shared prayer.

Emotive Power of Sacred Space

In many cases, religions shape the built environment in particular ways in order to "move people," both emotionally and physically, and position them as tied to the faith. For example, each year millions of Muslims physically move to complete the

Haj pilgrimage to Mecca, sometimes travelling across continents. This physical movement is associated with emotional movement and closer social bonding with the ingroup—an experience also common to Christian pilgrimages, as reflected in Geoffrey Chaucer's (c. 1345–1400) *Canterbury Tales*, for example.

For the faithful gathered inside, the interior of a house of worship is moving, because it provides a wealth of features linking the space to the divine. Houses of worship are designed to "move" people in a very similar way to how art "moves" people, and often the best artists have been engaged in creating sacred buildings. Much like mosques, churches are typically built with a significant geographic orientation. Traditionally, churches have been built facing east, paralleling the individual's journey through life towards death and, ultimately, resurrection in Christ.

Other internal, formal architectural features and decorative arts further "move" those who enter, positioning the faithful as being in contact with the sacred. The prominence of Islamic calligraphy in mosque interiors is a visual reminder about the sacredness of the building. Because Qur'anic verses are incorporated into tiles and other decorations, the word of God is literally everywhere inside a mosque, positioning mosques and Islam in general as being connected to the divine. The interiors of mosques feature other reminders as well; the mihrab, a niche that indicates the direction of Mecca, acts as a compass pointing towards Islam's spiritual center and focusing prayers towards the sacred city. Similarly, the richness of decoration in Christian churches—including crosses, statues, artwork depicting biblical scenes and saints' lives, stained glass windows—position the faithful as witness to the sacred. These interior decorations provide instruction and invite contemplation and "emotional movement," helping those who enter grow in their faith. The faithful are moved to undertake *reflexive positioning*, by engaging in an internal dialogue, designed to strengthen their ties to the ingroup.

Promotion of Group Conformity and Cohesion

The sacred built environment also serves an important role in promoting conformity and cohesion within the religious ingroup. This point is best clarified by distinguishing between the interior spaces of houses of worship and the exterior sacred spaces used for rituals and pilgrimages.

Houses of worship create barriers that separate the sacred space inside from the outside world (and outside people). In mosques, these take the form of courtyards for *wuzu*, partial ablutions performed before entering. Similarly, churches feature a narthex, either a porch or an entrance area at the end of the nave separated from the interior by a screen or curtain. As in a mosque courtyard, the narthex represents a transitional space for purification. A common feature of the narthex is the baptismal font, which represents purification for Christians. Like ablutions courtyards, the narthex is not considered part of the church and was traditionally used by people not eligible for participation in the general congregation (penitents, catechumens). Not only do these features physically separate those who can participate from those who cannot, they communicate a message about the type of people housed in the building; people who have managed to enter have been purified and deemed worthy.

Inside houses of worship, formal rituals usually occur within the faith community. Examples include liturgies and sermons given by priests, mullahs or other clerics. These kinds of rituals instruct ingroup members on important aspects of the group's identity and promote unity. Within Catholicism, community members absorb important religious tenets by observing and participating in the seven Sacraments, religious rites in which God is believed to be uniquely present that include baptism, Holy Communion, and marriage. Interior sacred spaces are connected with external or "open" sacred spaces by "calls to prayer," as represented by the sound of church bells and the *azan* from mosques. Conventional rituals are comprised of performances, celebrations, and actions that are open to a broader audience.

One feature that these rituals share is their attractiveness to outsiders; regardless of faith, Indians and Nepalese enjoy the aesthetic appeal of Diwali's festival of lights. This attractiveness points to one of the functions of ritual in inter-religious communication. Certain rituals or performances can recruit new adherents to a religion or provide entertainment to those already initiated. More examples of these kinds of performances include medieval passion plays, re-enactments of important battles in Islam's history, and pilgrimages during the Middle Ages. Each of these rituals could provide enjoyment to participants (although pilgrimages often also involve suffering), regardless of their personal beliefs, and could win over new followers.

Conclusion

Historical evidence demonstrates that the major monotheistic religions have been tremendously successful in positioning themselves as essential in the lives of the faithful, as dominant in their territories, and as superior to competitor ideologies. In this sense, these religions have been efficient communicators, affecting ingroup conformity and obedience, distancing the ingroup from outgroups, and in some cases accumulating greater resources. Another indication of the effectiveness of communication across religions is that, despite the expectations of modernization theorists, the major religions have experienced decline in some regions (e.g., Western Europe), but are in some important respects experiencing growth globally. In this discussion, we did not have space to distinguish between communication and storylines involving traditional and fundamentalist religious movements, or non-violent and violent ones, but this should be a focus of future explorations.

Part Two

Intergroup Phenomena and Processes

CHAPTER EIGHT

Language, Social Identity, and Stereotyping

SCOTT A. REID & GRACE L. ANDERSON

In the United States, it is often remarked that Asians are mathematically gifted but bad drivers; that African Americans are athletic but aggressive; and that Jews are intelligent but stingy. By definition, these are stereotypes, characteristics (such as traits or values) that are perceived to be shared by members of social groups. While this is a useful definition, we will point to a number of ways in which it captures a mere fragment of the phenomenology of stereotyping. In this chapter, we will argue that a full understanding of stereotypes requires an appreciation of how linguistic manifestations of stereotypes shape and are shaped by social identity and intergroup relations. To date, most social psychological work has focused on social and cognitive processes underpinning stereotyping but with little attention to language (see Chapter 9). Research on language and stereotyping has focused largely on the ways in which stereotypes are expressed in language using short-range models but with little attention to large synthetic models. It is, therefore, our aim to illustrate how a more phenomenologically rich and general model of stereotyping can take our understanding further. We present a social identity model of language and stereotyping and use it to make novel predictions about stereotyping and linguistic abstraction, ethnophaulisms, code-words, and the narrative reproduction of stereotypes.

We begin by entertaining a thumb-nail sketch of the 88-year history of stereotyping theory and research to show why a broader synthetic model is desirable. At the outset, stereotyping was theorized with respect to its social context. Lippmann

(1922) viewed stereotypes as simplified, often fictional, yet culturally shared representations of social groups. In Lippmann's view, stereotypes are functional; they place a sense-making filter on social reality, and aid in the defense of our values. Despite this encouraging theoretical start, early research was typically descriptive. Most notably, Katz and Braly (1933) developed a trait checklist method for establishing stereotype content and consensus. This research, which catalogued people's endorsement of traits for ethnic groups, captured research attention for years. It was not until after Allport's (1954) watershed assessment that researchers turned their attention to the cognitive dimension of stereotyping. For Allport, stereotypes are rationalizations of intergroup relations that are intimately connected with prejudice. Still, it was not until the 1980s that researchers in the United States began to realize the potential of cognition for understanding stereotyping. When it arrived, the social-cognitive revolution (Fiske & Taylor, 1984) led to a new way of thinking about stereotypes. A first model characterized people as cognitive misers who used stereotypes to avoid the burden of complex individuating information. Later models viewed people as motivated tacticians who employ stereotypes in self-serving ways. While these models advanced our understanding, they were frequently and vehemently criticized for reducing stereotypes to non-social cognitive processes.

In Europe during the 1970s and '80s, however, research on social identity and intergroup relations blossomed. Eschewing individual cognitive theories, European researchers focused their attention on the ways in which psychology interacted with the context of intergroup relations. From this perspective, echoing Lippmann, and particularly Allport, Tajfel (1981) argued that a full understanding of stereotyping requires a theory that articulates individual cognitive processes with social functions. Tajfel proposed that stereotypes provide a *positive social identity* for ingroup members (e.g., the superior Arian race), *explanations* for distressing social events (e.g., evil terrorists hate Americans for their freedom), and *justifications* for actions committed or planned (e.g., the colonialist view that it is white man's burden to "civilize" savage nations). In a return to Lippmann's view, these functions were thought social in the sense that they capture normative visions of social reality that are *shared* within if not between groups.

Current research is at a point where social-cognitive processes have been united with the collective psychology of social identity (described below) in the form of self-categorization theory (Turner, Hogg, Oakes, Reicher, & Wetherell, 1987), and research attention has turned to understanding the role of language in stereotyping (see Fiedler, 2007; Kashima, Fiedler, & Freytag, 2008). When we consider the linguistic dimension to stereotypes, however, it becomes clear that they are rarely communicated as lists of traits. Rather, stereotypes are communicated through variations in linguistic abstraction (compare "John *enjoys* a drink" with "John *is an alcoholic*"), within ethnophaulisms (e.g., *towel head, asshole bandit*), are often explicit in rumor and conspiracy theories (e.g., *the Jews are avoiding the draft*), primed by code words (e.g., *welfare queen, inner city youth*), and communicated via mass media and interpersonally. Thus, stereotypes might have a coherent cognitive substrate, but linguistically they are highly variable.

Communicated stereotypes—even when implied—can have social consequences. On February 18, 2009 *The New York Post* published a cartoon of two police officers, one of whom had shot dead a chimpanzee. One officer remarks to the other: "They'll have to find someone else to write the next stimulus bill." While *The Post* defended the cartoon as a parody of a current events (the shooting of a chimp that had attacked a woman and the passage of an economic stimulus by Democrats), others thought it a racist attempt to depict Barack Obama as an ape and later picketed *The Post* headquarters. On September 30, 2005 the Danish newspaper *Jylland-Posten* published 12 cartoons, one of which depicted the Prophet Muhammad as a terrorist (see Chapter 2). The authors considered this pre-emption of a debate about religion and censorship (see Chapter 7), but Muslims considered it heretical and protested. These examples suggest that language is a dependent variable reflecting social relations and an independent variable affecting those relations (Giles & Johnson, 1981).

Our brief and incomplete history of stereotyping suggests that: (1) stereotypes are best understood with reference to strategic interests and intergroup relations; (2) stereotypes provide a normative frame of reference for behavior; (3) stereotypes imbue social information with clarity and meaning; (4) stereotypes are contained within and communicated through language; and (5) arguments over stereotypes affect (i.e., inflame or calm) intergroup relations. Stereotypes cannot be extracted from their social context, nor can they be extracted from communication.

We now outline and expand upon these points in the social identity approach to stereotyping (Oakes, Haslam, & Turner, 1994; Tajfel, 1981) and illustrate the ways in which language brings these psychological processes to life. In doing so, we will deduce several untested hypotheses. This view of stereotyping is depicted schematically in Figure 1.

The Social Identity Model of Stereotyping[1]

Following Tajfel (1981), we start with the intergroup social context. What we mean by social context is people's beliefs about the set of relevant group status positions (see the first two boxes Figure 1). Social identity theory (Tajfel & Turner, 1979) does an excellent job of characterizing the status strivings of people in groups and their concomitant attitudes and behaviors (see Chapters 1 & 21). It starts with the assumption that people are motivated to achieve a positive social identity. People

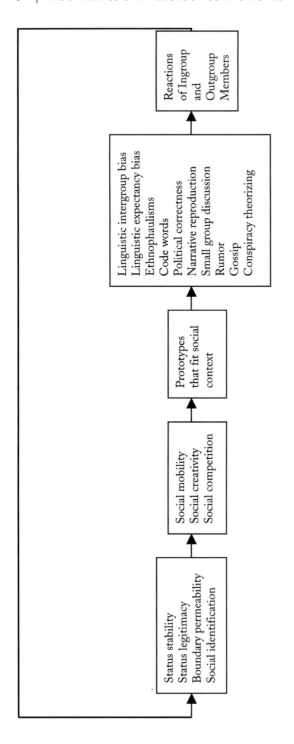

Figure 1: A Schematic Rendition of the Social Identity Model of Stereotype Transmission.
From this schematic, specific path diagrams can be derived. For example, when status stability, legitimacy, and group boundary permeability are low, and social identification is high, social competition will result. When social competition results, people will develop prototypes that provide positive ingroup descriptions and negative outgroup descriptions from social contextual data. Such prototypes will be rendered in the form of the LIB, a diminished LEB, negative and high complexity ethnophaulisms for subordinate groups, code words, and political correctness will be eschewed, particularly when communicating with ingroup members.

achieve positive social identity by searching for and constructing identities that are different from and better than other groups in the status hierarchy. Because people's striving for positive social identity depends upon the relative standing of social groups, people engage in an intergroup struggle to create a positive social identity for their group. There are three strategies that people use to pursue social identity enhancement. Which strategy people employ (social mobility, creativity, or competition) depends upon their beliefs about the status of their group relative to others. Namely, people view their ingroup's status position as being more or less *legitimate* (i.e., the status positions of groups are seen as more or less fair), more or less *stable* (i.e., more or less likely to prevail in the future), perceive the boundaries of groups as more or less *permeable* (i.e., some groups we can easily join, others will block membership), and possess a trait level of *identification* with their group (i.e., a person can have more or less commitment to their ingroup). Different combinations of these variables lead to the crystallization of one of three identity management strategies.

People pursue *social mobility*—a belief in the possibility of passing from one group into another—when they lack ingroup identification, perceive group boundaries to be permeable, and the status hierarchy as stable and legitimate. Social mobility explains linguistic assimilation with dominant groups, the endorsement of just world beliefs (e.g., people on welfare are lazy), and endorsement of the American dream.

People pursue *social competition*—a belief in the possibility of reversing the prevailing status hierarchy—when they identify highly with their group, view group boundaries as impermeable, and the status hierarchy as illegitimate and unstable. Social competition explains participation in linguistic revival movements, intergroup clashes, and terrorism (see Chapter 12).

People pursue *social creativity*—expressions of group solidarity that avoid direct comparison with a competing outgroup—when they possess the same views as those who are socially competitive, with the exception that the status hierarchy is viewed as highly stable. Socially creative people may wish to challenge the status quo, but they perceive any challenge as futile or worse. Social creativity explains why people search for lower status groups for social comparison, develop bi-dimensional status descriptions (e.g., we may be poor but we're friendly), and reject stigmatizing ingroup definitions (e.g., the slogan, black is beautiful).

In a nutshell, social identity theory characterizes groups in terms of their relative status; it predicts that people have beliefs about status relations, and those beliefs direct them toward one of three strategies for pursuing a positive social identity.

Social identity management strategies affect stereotypes. Socially mobile people, for example, achieve a positive identity by disowning their group and identifying with or joining another—we can therefore expect these people to endorse negative ingroup stereotypes. Socially competitive people, however, value their group and search for ways to improve its position. Consequently, socially competitive people will develop positive ingroup stereotypes, embrace stereotypes that justify their attempts at status enhancement, and disown negative stereotypes. Finally, socially creative people aim for a positive social identity while avoiding dominant outgroups. These people are likely to focus on stereotype content that is ingroup enhancing but not valued by an outgroup (e.g., we are nice, if not wealthy and sophisticated).

While social identity theory explains how intergroup relationships color stereotypes, it leaves important questions unanswered. Namely, what determines which group(s) we focus our stereotypical attention upon? How are stereotypes represented cognitively? This cognitive dimension to stereotypes is elaborated in self-categorization theory (Oakes et al., 1994; Turner et al., 1987).

Self-categorization theory describes the mechanism that explains social identity salience (i.e., what identity is activated when) and its link to social judgment and behavior as this volume well attests. The core argument is that social identities are activated when they make sense of patterns of social relationships. Cognitively, social identities are represented as ingroup defining prototypes that describe and prescribe appropriate behavior. The internalization of self-defining prototypes is the generative mechanism that explains self-stereotyping, conformity and social influence, social judgment, emotion, and the transmission of social norms.

Self-categorization theory assumes that people have multiple, independent self-images; we can define ourselves, for example, with respect to gender, occupation, age, ethnicity, and nationality. Information in the social environment is organized around fitting social identities. Three interacting variables determine fit. First, our biographical history, social values, and group loyalties make us more or less likely to (re)use categories—making some categories more or less *accessible* than others. Second, social stimuli (e.g., attributes of people like accents, skin color, and attitudes) cluster into patterns that we readily perceive as categories. We do this by cognitively accentuating the similarities of stimuli that we see as sharing attributes and at the same time accentuate differences between stimuli that fall into different categories. To state this differently, this stimulus-driven process—*comparative fit*—is a meaning-extracting device that clarifies group membership. Third, following *normative fit*, we are particularly likely to group people into categories on the basis of the consistency between the observed attributes of people and pre-established norms. We expect people to behave in accordance with norms, and when they do, we are all the more likely to attribute their behavior to their group membership.

Salient identities are cognitively represented as prototypes. A prototype is a representation of a category that best fits the distribution of information within a social context. For example, we might describe Americans as aggressive, militaristic, and patriotic in comparison to the French, but as brash, easy-going, and fun-loving in comparison to the British (see Haslam, Turner, Oakes, McGarty, & Hayes, 1992). The set of attributes that best fit is activated as a prototype. Ingroup defining prototypes are internalized as the basis for self-stereotyping, and for current purposes, linguistic manifestations of stereotypes.[2]

Self-categorization theory explains the cognitive reason for stereotyping and why people pursue any one social identity over another. Namely, people stereotype in ways that make best sense of their social environment, and they do so in ways that reflect the nature of intergroup relations and their prior identity commitments. When we see linguistic manifestations of stereotypes, we can be sure that they will more often than not accord with or be assimilated to salient prototypes. However, those prototypes will also be constrained by the nature of intergroup relations. People who are socially competitive, for example, will develop and communicate prototypes that make best sense of their social environment, while fulfilling status enhancing, sense making, and behavioral justification functions.[3]

We now consider how these contextual and social-cognitive processes described in social identity and self-categorization theories affect language use and intergroup relations.

Stereotypes and Linguistic Abstraction

Much attention has been directed at the ways in which language can be used to describe behaviors. According to the linguistic category model (Semin & Fiedler, 1988), language can describe behavior in four ways that vary in concreteness-abstractness (see Chapters 9 & 16). At the most concrete level, descriptive action verbs (e.g., punch, kiss) provide a direct account of an action. Interpretive action verbs (e.g., help, offend) provide both a description and interpretation of actions. State verbs (e.g., love, hate) describe behavior with reference to the internal psychological state of the actor. At the most abstract level, adjectives (e.g., honest, aggressive) describe actions with reference to an actor's traits. More abstract descriptions suggest that behaviors are stable attributes of people, situationally invariant, and repeatable. For example, one can say "Scott *exceeded* the speed limit" (a descriptive action verb), "Scott was *speeding*" (interpretive action verb), "Scott was *in a rush*" (state verb), or "Scott is *reckless*" (adjective). Compared to the less abstract descriptions, the adjective suggests that Scott speeds often, in many situations, and that this is attributable to his inherent recklessness.

People can vary linguistic abstraction to embrace some stereotypes but discount others. Confirming this, Maass, Salvi, Arcuri, and Semin (1989) discovered a

Linguistic Intergroup Bias (LIB): Socially desirable ingroup and undesirable out-group actions are described in more abstract language than undesirable ingroup and desirable outgroup actions. Thus, in the speeding example, middle-aged motorists might describe a teenager as "reckless," but discount their own or other middle-aged drivers' behavior as merely "exceeding the speed limit." This research suggests that the LIB is a linguistic path to stereotype perpetuation: positive ingroup and nega-tive outgroup actions are embraced by stable attributes expressed in abstract lan-guage, whereas negative ingroup and positive outgroup actions are discounted by situationally variable behaviors expressed in concrete language.

Maass, Ceccarelli, and Rudin (1996) proposed an explanation based "loosely" (p. 512) on social identity theory—that the LIB is driven by motivations to protect identity, and that it is more likely to be found under conditions of high than low identity threat. Consistent with this prediction, Maass et al. (1996) found that an insult from an outgroup (high threat) produced a stronger LIB than a condition where groups were asked to cooperate (low threat). While this is a sensible finding, we believe we can offer a more nuanced explanation using the social identity model. Starting with social identity theory, we already know that people are likely to use language to promote positive ingroup and negative outgroup images under social competition. Indeed, this is consistent with evidence that the LIB is robust when competing equal status groups are involved. However, researchers have yet to mea-sure components of social competition to predict variation in linguistic abstraction (i.e., social identification, the legitimacy and stability of status relations, and group boundary permeability). Thus, a simple and untested hypothesis is that the LIB should be most likely to manifest for people who are socially competitive, and it should increase with the intensity of intergroup competition. Further, and interest-ingly, we would expect the LIB to vary for people with different social beliefs. For example, those with social mobility beliefs should evidence a *reverse* LIB. Because socially mobile people deal with negative social identity by psychologically align-ing themselves with dominant outgroups, we can expect them to negatively stereo-type their ingroup and describe negative and stereotypic ingroup behaviors in abstract language.

While this evidence is consistent with Maass et al.'s identity protection hypoth-esis, other work shows that people do not always pursue the LIB; in fact, they typ-ically use abstract language to describe expectancy consistent behaviors (Maass, Milesi, Zabbini, & Stahlberg 1995)—a phenomenon labeled the Linguistic Expectancy Bias (LEB). Maass et al. (1996) tested for the LEB using northern and southern Italians.[4] Within Italy, there is agreement that northern Italians are mate-rialistic and intolerant but industrious and independent, whereas southern Italians are sexist and intrusive but warm and hospitable. Maass et al. (1996) proposed that because both groups have positive and negative stereotypes, it is possible to deduce competitive social identity and expectancy predictions. If the identity protection hypothesis is right, people will pursue the LIB—more abstract language for positive ingroup and negative outgroup behaviors than negative ingroup and positive outgroup behaviors. But, if the expectancy hypothesis is right, people will use abstract language to describe expectancy consistent behaviors independent of social desirability. The latter was the case, leading Maass et al. (1995) to conclude that expectancies, rather than social identity motivations, drive variation in linguistic abstraction.

Again, a more nuanced reading of the social identity model suggests the LEB will reflect social identity management strategies and prototypical images of groups. In fact, from the perspective of social identity theory, Maass et al.'s use of northern and southern Italian stereotypes is an example of social creativity (i.e., attempting to protect ingroup identity using a bi-dimensional stereotype). Indeed, there is evidence that social creativity characterizes many stereotypes. Scots, for example, are often viewed as poor but friendly people (i.e., low status/high solidarity), whereas the English have prestige, but are not so friendly (i.e., high status/low solidarity). In the United States, Californians are slow witted and gregarious, whereas those from New York are intellectual and impolite. The status/solidarity distinction is common, but the traits that make up the dimension vary from group to group. Stereotypes, therefore, are not so much expectations as reflections of social creativity and localized prototypes.

If this is the case, then we expect that variation in linguistic abstraction is contextually *variable* (like prototypes) rather than contextually *invariant* (like expectations). To make a specific prediction, we could depict a Californian being impolite to a shop assistant (i.e., *in*consistent with Californian prototype but consistent with the New York prototype). Were this behavior depicted in a context that compares Californians to New Yorkers, we would expect relatively concrete language to result because it is inconsistent with the prototype of Californians compared to New Yorkers (i.e., as predicted by both the expectancy hypothesis and self-categorization theory). However, were we to continue with the very same example but this time have the Californian being impolite to a British shop assistant, we would expect relatively abstract language to result because the Californian would now be viewed as an American in comparison to the Brit. As the context of comparison shifts, the Californian's behavior will be assimilated to the American prototype, which in comparison to the British, is likely to be stereotypically impolite. If this prediction were confirmed, it would be consistent with self-categorization theory but inconsistent with the expectancy hypothesis.

In general, rather than viewing the LEB as evidence that social identity motives do not drive variation in linguistic abstraction, we suggest that social identity management strategies manifest in prototypes that vary along status and solidarity dimensions, and that this social identity process accounts for the LEB in intergroup contexts.

Ethnophaulisms

Paki, towel-head, limey. These derisive ethnic slurs are ethnophaulisms, deriving from the Greek words meaning "ethnic group" and "to disparage." Ethnophaulisms in the United States have been investigated empirically by Mullen and colleagues (see Mullen, 2001). Ethnophaulisms can be classified into six mutually exclusive categories (physical traits, personal traits, personal names, food habits, group names, and other/miscellaneous); an ethnophaulism is considered more complex when it is categorized into a larger number of categories. Smaller, and less familiar groups have more negative and less complex ethnophaulisms. Historically, groups with less complex ethnophaulisms: had lower immigration quotas; were less likely to become naturalized United States citizens; had lower rates of intermarriage; and occupied more hazardous jobs. More negative ethnophaulisms are associated with greater ethnically segregated housing and increased rates of suicide. Ethnophaulisms do not just describe group status positions, they actively contribute to social exclusion and inequality.

Social identity theory has yet to be applied to ethnophaulisms. Nonetheless, some simple predictions can be made. We would expect that ethnophaulisms are particularly likely to crystallize and increase in negativity when groups come into contact under social competition. For example, Allen (1983) lists for Arabs: *aye-rab*, *dirty-arab*, and *sheik*. Recent years and the "war on terror" have added *camel jockey*, *towel head*, *rag head*, and *sand nigger*. By the same token, the valence and meaning of ethnophaulisms should dissipate when groups become allies. The term *limey*, for example, is a derisive American reference to British sailors' consumption of lime juice (to avoid scurvy). The term still exists but seems relatively benign.

Consistent with this line of reasoning, ethnophaulism complexity may reflect the degree of group contact and the degree to which higher status groups are aiming to maintain their status position. Smaller, more culturally dissimilar groups that occupy low status positions tend to live in ethnic enclaves and have little representation in the eyes of the wider culture. Such groups are, for example, unlikely to appear in the media. With this lack of contact, but pressure to maintain the status hierarchy, it is likely that ethnophaulisms focus on highly distinctive yet concrete aspects of group practices. Indeed, ethnophaulisms typically comprise of food preferences, physical traits, personal and group names. Mullen (2001) speculates that these concrete references are particularly effective ways of maintaining status hierarchies because they suggest that all members of a group are alike and should therefore be treated alike. This suggests that ethnophaulism valence reflects positions in the status hierarchy. A simple test would be to ask members of different ethnic groups to describe the status positions of each group. We would expect to find that the lower the status, the more negative the ethnophaulisms.

Further clues as to the role of ethnophaulisms in regulating status hierarchies are suggested by their distribution. While African Americans have referred to white slave owners as *cracker* (of the whip), *honkey* (possibly a vernacular reference to Eastern Europeans), and *peckerwood* (with connotations of loudness and intrusiveness), these references appear to be expressed rarely by members of other ethnic groups. Ethnophaulisms for lower status groups, however, seem to be widely shared across groups. It may be that ethnophaulisms are expressed more frequently by and about ethnic minorities because these groups are likely to be low in the status hierarchy, and therefore likely to make comparisons with other, similarly low status groups. More controversially, social competition or social creativity among subordinate groups may support and transmit ethnophaulisms that have origins in dominant group social competition. If true, we should find that ethnophaulisms for low status groups become more prevalent as the insecurity of a dominant group increases.

But ethnophaulisms do not just vary in terms of valence, they also vary in complexity. Ethnophaulism complexity probably reflects the entitativity ("groupness") of a group. As groups increase in status, they become more of a threat to the status position of higher status groups, and this will lead to the evolution of clearer, more differentiated prototypes. If ethnophaulisms are the control mechanism that we suspect, then ethnophaulism complexity will increase with the status strivings and entitativity of the group. Indeed, in the United States it is common to find that ethnic immigrant groups are initially all but invisible (low in entitativity), low in the status hierarchy, and attract simple and negative ethnophaulisms. As the group begins to improve its status position, it will also increase in entitativity, and attract more complex (and thus controlling) ethnophaulisms. Once a group achieves *stable* high status, we would expect ethnophaulisms to decrease in negativity and complexity.

Code Words

Stereotypes expressed as adjectives and ethnophaulisms are often disagreeable. In recent years, however, norms have arisen that proscribe against the expression of some stereotypes. While it is not kosher to express stereotypes about racial groups, women, or the blind, it is acceptable to express stereotypes about Nazis, the Ku Klux Klan, and pedophiles. Social movements that have raised the status of their group and persuaded the wider population that their group has been subject to unfair discrimination have been successful in changing language. Obvious examples are the civil rights and feminist movements. In contrast, groups which have lost social competition, or that are seen as having deserved low status, still face blatant discrimination.

Yet it would be a mistake to view stereotype expression as a simple matter of social convention. Expressions of prejudice can take subtle forms that evade social norms, such as racially tinged code words, words that render salient accessible (typically racial) categories. Consider this list: *quotas*; *welfare queen*; *inner city youth*. By using code words people (usually politicians) can evoke stereotypes, and at the same time avoid accusations of racism. Indeed, Hurwitz and Peffley (2005) found that people who endorsed negative stereotypes of African Americans were more in favor of imprisonment as a solution to crime prevention when the question contained reference to "violent *inner-city* criminals" than mere "violent criminals." Smith (1987) found that, compared with "*the poor*," "*people on welfare*" elicited less favorable attitudes towards assistance, were viewed more negatively, and as having too much influence on American life and politics. This research suggests that code words evoke stereotypes and that stereotypes, in turn, lead to intergroup status preserving reactions among those who are socially competitive.

There has been little research on code words. As of yet, it is unclear whether code words prime stereotypes directly, or visceral reactions like fear and anger. There is also no research on the effects of code word use on the endorsement of politicians. Presumably, there are circumstances where code words successfully produce stereotypes and support for politicians, and others where they backfire. Research suggests that people who have socially competitive views are most likely to be susceptible to code words; people who endorse social mobility or creativity may find code words offensive. Self-categorization theory would suggest, further, that code-words are most likely to be successful when they clearly differentiate between groups. Less fit-inducing code-words will be less likely to invoke stereotypes and will be less likely to be communicated to others or to have effects on intergroup relations.

The Narrative Reproduction of Stereotypes

Researchers have made use of the serial reproduction paradigm to test explanations for stereotype transmission. In this paradigm a story containing stereotype consistent (SC) and stereotype inconsistent (SI) information is presented to the first member of a communication chain, who is asked to memorize and then write down the story. Story reproductions are typically passed along a four- or five-person chain. This research has provided evidence for a stereotype consistency bias—SC information is more prevalent than SI information at the end of the communication chain. Research suggests a functional explanation. Clark and Kashima (2007) have shown that stereotypes pass along communication chains because they meet two social functions, the sharing of information and the regulation of social connections. Suggesting the information sharing function, Lyons and Kashima (2003) created stereotypes in the lab and found that people were more likely to pass SC information to a partner that they believed had partial rather than full knowledge of a stereotype. Suggesting a social connection function, the stereotype consistency bias was found when people believed they were passing stereotypical information to people who endorsed the stereotype, but a reverse bias when they believed their partners did not endorse the stereotype.

Clark and Kashima's account is consistent with the social identity model. However, the stories to be transmitted in this research are odd from an informational standpoint. They contain sizable quantities of SC and SI information (e.g., male characters display equal numbers of masculine and feminine behaviors), which would seem rare in real-world communication. This suggests that a major challenge for a communicator is to find a way to make sense of a bizarre story. From the perspective of self-categorization theory, these stories are low in normative fit. With a lack of normative fit, people may be particularly motivated to preserve their stereotypes, and one way to do this is to jettison SI for accessible SC information. More generally, for well-established and legitimated stereotypes, we would expect that the more normatively ill-fitting a story, the more likely that SC information will be communicated.

When stories are high in both normative and comparative fit (e.g., men act like men, women act like women, say, 95% of the time), we expect that people will reproduce relatively more SI information—in this case, high fit suggests stereotypes are shared, and that their communication would be redundant. Only novel SI information would be worth communicating, because that information is novel while SC information is not. Going further still, we would expect that this would be most likely to happen for highly accessible stereotypes. When stereotypes are not accessible (e.g., they are being constructed on the spot), we would then expect to find the opposite—in this case better normative and comparative fit will produce more SC communication. This would be likely, for example, when groups come into contact for the first time.

Conclusion

Stereotypes are linguistic tools that can be used to enhance ingroup status, prestige, and power. As such, social identity management strategies tell us when and why people embrace stereotypes. However, we cannot strategically invoke any stereotype—stereotypes must be psychologically meaningful, and this means that those stereotypes must conform to contextually fitting prototypes. Linguistic manifestations of stereotypes reflect contextually relevant prototypes, and when expressed, can maintain or challenge intergroup relations. The social identity model can be readily extended to understanding the transmission of stereotypes in small groups, normative constraints on free expression (e.g., political correctness and censorship), and the transmission of rumor, gossip, and conspiracy theorizing. We hope that our elaboration of the social identity model of stereotyping will serve as a synthetic model, and as a stimulus for further research on language and stereotyping.

Endnotes

1   It is not possible in the space we have to provide detailed treatments of social identity (Tajfel & Turner, 1979) and self-categorization theories (Turner et al., 1987), so we strongly encourage the reader to consult original sources. An accessible introduction can be found in Chapter 1 of this volume.

2   People are often confused by the distinction between a stereotype and a prototype. Within the framework of SCT, a prototype is a theoretical construct that is used to explain the phenomenon of stereotyping. Theoretical constructs and phenomena are often very different. Isobars—lines of equal atmospheric pressure—are used to predict the weather, but we would not confuse these lines with the phenomenon of weather.

3   It is important to note that we are presenting only one view on the relationship between social identity and self-categorization theories. It is also possible to use self-categorization theory to subsume many of the social structural arguments presented in social identity theory. For example, self-categorization as a group member will affect one's social identification with groups and perceptions of legitimacy.

4   It should be noted that linguistic expectancy effects occur in both interpersonal and intergroup contexts. We are obviously directing our attention at the latter. It is theoretically possible that social identity and self-categorization theories can account for interpersonal linguistic expectancy effects.

CHAPTER NINE

The Creative Power of Language in Social Cognition and Intergroup Relations

ROBBIE M. SUTTON

Intergroup relations would be impossible without language. Groups use language to form, organize, to attach and resist stigma, to conduct and to end conflicts with other groups. Nonetheless, in the study of intergroup relations, language has received much less attention than cognition.[1] Probably, it has not always been clear to researchers how language is more than necessary for intergroup relations. Of course, people need language to conduct intergroup relations, but they also need to breathe, eat, drink water, and many other things. No one would be satisfied with an explanation of an intergroup atrocity that invoked one of these merely necessary causes (e.g., "Oh, the problem was that everyone had drunk enough water").

In this chapter, we seek to examine whether language is more than a precondition for intergroup relations. Is language a causal force in its own right, with the power to create and change intergroup dynamics? If so, language must be able to affect, as well as reflect, the way that people think about groups. Thus, we review research that has been inspired by prevalent metaphors of the dynamic between language and cognition. First, language can be considered a *vessel* in which thoughts are encapsulated and transmitted from one mind to another. Second, language can be seen as a *lens* which focuses cognition on certain aspects of the world and away from others. Third, language can be seen as a *barometer* which reveals a communicator's cognition to the audience. We discuss the implications of each of these language-cognition dynamics for intergroup relations.

Language as a Vessel: Containing and Conveying Cognition

Of the three metaphors we consider in this chapter, this is perhaps the most immediately recognizable and has been dominant in the experimental study of language and intergroup relations (for reviews, see Fiedler, 2008; Maass, 1999; Wigboldus & Douglas, 2007). In this perspective, ideas about groups in the memory (*M*) of senders are transmitted through language (*L*) and implanted in the minds of recipients. In turn, recipients transmit these ideas to others, in *M-L-M-L* chains. Language is seen as essentially reproductive, in a process made possible by cooperative use of mutually understood symbols according to mutually understood rules.

Of course, the simplest possible way in which language can transmit ideas about groups is for senders to explicitly assert them: "those people are lazy and aggressive" (Sutton, Elder, Douglas, & Tarrant, 2008). However, the bald assertion of stereotypes has its disadvantages, as we shall see, and is by no means the only way in which stereotypes may be transmitted (see Chapter 8). For example, it is possible to transmit stereotypes of a group without referring to it. One can, instead, describe the behavior of individual group members in biased ways.

The Serial Transmission Paradigm: Biases in What Behaviors Are Described

One such bias is to describe more behaviors that are consistent, versus inconsistent, with stereotypes. Lyons and Kashima (2003) had participants relay a story which contained stereotype-consistent and inconsistent information about individual group members in serial communication chains. These chains are rather like the children's game sometimes called "Chinese whispers." As the original story is told to a recipient who in turn tells it to another recipient, and so on, it bears less and less resemblance to the original. Indeed, Lyons and Kashima found that by the time the story had reached the end of the chains, much of the stereotype-inconsistent information had disappeared, while significantly more of the stereotype-consistent information had survived.

Crucially, Lyons and Kashima (2003) found that this bias was stronger when communicators were led to believe that the stereotype was widely shared in their community. It appears that people tend to reproduce stereotype-consistent information because they think it is consistent with a shared world view, or a *common ground* and is therefore likely to be easily understood and accepted by recipients (Clark, 1996a). In contrast, information that is inconsistent with widely shared stereotypes is less likely to result in successful communication. Instead, communicators may anticipate receiving querulous, puzzled responses.

This suggests that senders tacitly view their language as a vessel: a means to transmit information in the context of a shared set of assumptions about the world. Ironically, they therefore withhold pieces of stereotype-inconsistent information, fearing that these would disrupt transmission. Apparently, how people think about language affects how they use language. This reflexivity gives language the power to do much more than transmit thought. The serial transmission paradigm illustrates why we can view cognition and language as "two sides of the same integral whole" (Fiedler, 2008, p. 45), capable of creating and modifying reality as well as reproducing it.

The Linguistic Intergroup Bias (LIB): Biases in How Behaviors Are Described

Whereas the study of serial transmission is concerned with biases in *what* behaviors are described, much research has been devoted to biases in *how* they are described. For example, a considerable body of research has examined how language may perpetuate and transmit prejudice in a process called the *linguistic intergroup bias* (LIB: Maass, 1999). Informed by the linguistic category model (LCM: Semin & Fiedler, 1988), the LIB assumes that behavioral events can be described at different levels, ranging from concrete verbs such as "hit" or "kissed" to adjectives such as "violent" and "affectionate." As language becomes more abstract, it conveys less about the situational context and the specific form of the behavior, implies longer duration, and conveys more about the characteristics of the person whose actions are described.

In the LIB, ingroup members' positive behaviors and outgroup members' negative behaviors are described in abstract terms, as if they reflected the underlying qualities of each group (see Chapters 8 & 16). In contrast, ingroup members' negative and outgroup members' positive behaviors are described in concrete terms, as if they were isolated events quite unrelated to how group members would normally behave. Therefore, even if an equal proportion of the positive and negative behaviors of each group were described, ingroup members' would be described more favorably. The LIB occurs in many intergroup contexts, in many countries, in several languages, and in naturally occurring settings as well as the laboratory. In part, the linguistic bias reflects the impact of stereotypical expectancies on the way people encode social information. Having encoded a negative behavior abstractly, perhaps because of ingroup bias, people are more likely to describe it in those terms.

The LIB is affected not just by how communicators have encoded events but also by their communication goals. For example, the LIB is heightened when communicators perceive an outgroup to be threatening, apparently because they are motivated to derogate it whilst bolstering the ingroup (Maass, 1999). Further research suggests that, under some circumstances, communication goals may turn out to reverse the LIB. For example, given a temporary motivation to describe an enemy in positive terms, communicators will use abstract language to describe their positive behavior and concrete language to describe their negative behavior, reversing the normal bias (for a review, see Wigboldus & Douglas, 2007). Thus, the LIB can be used strategically by communicators in order to create impressions of ingroup and outgroup members that diverge from their own perceptions. Far from merely replicating biased mental representations (although this is in itself an extremely important function), the LIB may be used to create new ones.

Facilitation and inhibition of behavior are regulated by different processes, as we see in the case of addiction. As many smokers may attest, being able to light a cigarette when one chooses does not guarantee that one is able *not* to light up. Similarly, communicators are able to use linguistic bias creatively but appear to have very limited power to inhibit bias when instructed to do so (Douglas & Sutton, 2008). As a result, even communicators with egalitarian intentions may be prone to the LIB and so contribute to intergroup bias unwittingly (Maass, 1999). The LIB appears to be a force both for creation and inertia in relations between groups.

Outside the Mind: Linking Biased Transmission to Intergroup Relations

Much of our social knowledge is based not on direct personal observation, but on information that has been communicated to us, for example in gossip or though the mass media. Thus, we rely on the vessel-like properties of language to faithfully convey information to us from people who have direct access to the facts. However, language is not a perfect vessel, because its use not only transmits but also transforms information. The transformation is directional rather than random, causing social information to converge upon prevailing stereotypes.

Not only is social information transformed by communication processes; it is also externalized. Every time we share information about ingroup and outgroup members, we place that information into the public sphere, where it can be received, remembered, and written down by others. In this sense, the biases in language that we have documented cause people to "upload" biased information into the public domain. Following Durkheim (1912/2001), it is even possible to think of stereotypes and prejudice as being represented there, freed by language from the local and fleeting character of thought but also enabled to influence the thoughts of many others (cf. Maass, 1999).

In sum, language changes social information and transcribes it from psychological to social media. Once made public, the information will impact on the psychological representations of many others. This continual interplay is deeply social-psychological, because communicators transform information in light of the stereotypes that they believe to be shared in the community and the effects they think their statements will have on others. The dynamics are complex and recursive, but each part of the process has been demonstrated in the relatively simple experiments we have reviewed. The A-causes-B structure of the social psychological experiment documents the operation of each cog in the machine. Only a body of experiments, considered together, comprises a model of the whole machine, that is to say, the process by which language, considered as a vessel for the transmission of information, shapes intergroup relations. Much the same thing is true of experiments that have been informed by our next metaphor. However the lens metaphor grants language a more obvious and immediate transformative power.

Language as a Lens: Focusing and Directing Cognition

This metaphor suggests that language has power—this has even been termed a "magic spell" (Stapel & Semin, 2007)—over cognition. This view of language was made famous by the anthropologist Benjamin Whorf (for a review see Fiedler, 2008). Human beings live in enormously complex, continually changing environments. In order to survive in such environments, they need to act in a co-ordinated, cooperative way. To do this, people need a shared focus, when required, on a discrete subset of goal-relevant objects and events. This is where language comes in. Like a lens, it directs the joint focus of senders' and recipients' attention, thought, and memory. In this sense, it constrains the reality that people experience.

The focusing, lens-like power of language is often obvious, as in "there's a car coming." At other times, however, it is more subtle. The masculine generic is an example relevant to our purposes. Here, linguistic convention in English has long had it that masculine terms such as "man," "his," and the collective noun "Man," can be used without reference to gender. Thus our examples are supposed to refer to "person," "his or her," and "Humanity," respectively. Nonetheless, Ng (1990) showed that participants who had been presented with these masculine generic terms did not encode them in this gender-neutral way. Rather, a subsequent memory test showed that they had encoded the masculine generic as referring to men *and not women*. This result suggests that male individuals will tend to be seen as the ones who contribute "manpower," who are responsible for the achievements of "Mankind," and so on (see Chapter 3).

Ng's (1990) findings are consistent with the lens rather than the vessel metaphor. Language is a vessel insofar as its symbols are used in accordance with rules of syntax and convention. According to these rules, we should think of people of both genders when the masculine generic is used. Nonetheless, we think of men. Probably, the masculine generic effect occurs partly because words like "man" and "his" are often used to refer only to males and so acquire an association with male referents that is carried over even into other contexts. Here is the power of the humble word to focus attention, memory and cognition, irrespective of the linguistic rules and conventions that are supposed to govern it.

Relations between other groups are also affected by this lens-like power of the word. Of particular importance are the words that people use to denote groups. Of course, some of these verbal labels are derogatory, as in "fag," whereas others are neutral or positive, as in "gay" (Carnaghi & Maass, 2008; see Chapter 13). In this respect, the labels are like vessels with which positive and negative attitudes to a group are communicated (see Chapter 9). As it turns out, the complexity of group labels is also very important (Leader, Mullen, & Rice, 2009; Mullen, Calogero, & Leader, 2007). Here, complexity is a property of a set of group labels rather than any single group label. Each label indicates a particular means of categorizing the group—for instance, according to its territory, language, or customs. A set of labels is simple if it tends to cluster within just one of these categories. It is complex if it is distributed across several categories, meaning that available group labels collectively indicate many facets of the group.

To illustrate, the Bari of central Africa are denoted by a simple set of two labels, *Bari* and *Bai*. This set is simple because both labels mean the same thing, "the others." In contrast, the Herero of southwestern Africa are denoted by a more complex set of two labels: *Herero*, meaning "to brandish a spear," and *Dimba*, which is "alluvial soil near a stream." This set is more complex because each label means something different and refers to different means of categorizing the group. *Herero* refers to one of the group's behaviors, and *Dimba* refers to where they are from (Mullen et al., 2007).

Across three archival studies in various ethnic settings, Mullen et al. (2007) studied how the complexity of these sets of labels affected intergroup relations. Their focus was on *ethnonyms*—the labels that a group used to describe itself. They found that higher complexity of ethnonyms was associated with lower levels of intergroup hostility (e.g., the incidence of warfare and intergroup killing, as recorded in academic tracts or official public records). In keeping with the lens metaphor, complex ethnonyms draw attention to the ingroup's many facets. If an ingroup's identity is multifaceted and complex, it is likely to be less susceptible to threat and capable of supporting nuanced relations with other groups (Mullen et al., 2007).

Extending this research, Leader et al. (2009) experimentally varied the complexity of the labels for an outgroup—all derogatory terms known as *ethnophaulisms* (see Chapter 8). Participants exposed only to simple sets of labels subsequently indicated the desire to socially exclude outgroup members (e.g., by restricting immigration and intermarriage). Those exposed to complex labels were more willing to include them. It is not yet clear what exactly drives this effect, but a reasonable guess is that simple sets of ethnophaulisms are consonant with a one-dimensional caricature of outgroup members. In contrast, complex sets of labels call attention to their three-dimensional, human character, making intergroup violence difficult to support or condone.

Intergroup relations may also be affected by another phenomenon consistent with the lens metaphor, namely, the saying-is-believing effect (e.g., Hausmann, Levine, & Higgins, 2008). This effect occurs when the act of describing persons or groups changes subsequent memory for them. For example, when you believe your audience does not like Group A, you are more likely to describe Group A in negative terms, and subsequently, to remember them more negatively. Impressively, the saying-is-believing effect tends to grow over time. Attributing negative traits to a group creates, in memory, an association between the group and those traits. If you have just made the negative comments, you will remember them clearly and realize that they contribute to your negative feelings about the group. If you made the comments some weeks ago, you are less likely to recall exactly what you said and why. Thus the negative mental associations seem attributable to the group itself, rather than what you have said about it.

The general point made by the saying-is-believing effect exemplifies the radical idea at the heart of the "lens" metaphor and is crucial for understanding the language-cognition interface: our language changes how we, as well as our audiences, think. These changes occur in parallel and indeed depend partly on each other, because the lens of language brings about a *joint* focus of attention, helping to create a reality that is shared by senders and receivers alike. In keeping with this idea, the saying-is-believing effect seems to work better when communicators believe their description has reached an audience and to work best when the audience is ingroup rather than outgroup (for reviews, see Fiedler, 2008; Hausmann et al., 2008; Holtgraves & Kashima, 2008).

Language as a Barometer: Revealing Cognitions

In this metaphor, the reflexive nature of the relationship between language and cognition comes to the fore. Language is now the object of cognition, serving as a cue that may reveal its users' thoughts, memories, and motives. For example, communicators who use hate terms such as "fag" signal that they are prejudiced (Carnaghi & Maass, 2008). Similarly, people who make explicit, negative statements about a group (e.g., "the British are a nation of binge drinkers") are likely to be seen to have malign intentions, especially if they do not belong to the group concerned (e.g.,

Sutton, Elder, & Douglas, 2006). If communicators use abstract language to describe a person's negative behavior and concrete language for their positive behavior, they are also seen as having negative attitudes and intentions (Douglas & Sutton, 2006); although it is not yet known whether this finding extends to cases in which groups, rather than people, are the topic of conversation.

These examples are grounds for hope that because it is a barometer, language can be employed in the fight against prejudice. Social authorities and motivated individuals can challenge, convert or sanction those who reveal their prejudices with language. Thus the linguistic barometer can be an invaluable aid in establishing and enforcing anti-prejudice norms. Further, motivated individuals may also refer to these norms in order to prevent using language that contributes to prejudice. For example, Sutton et al. (2006, Study 3) found that individuals were less willing to criticize outgroups than their own group. This was strongly related to the perception that criticism of outgroups is normatively unacceptable. It seems that people evaluate the potentially prejudiced things they might say, and perhaps anticipate how others would evaluate them. Hence they are more likely to show restraint.

That said, the barometric property of language is not all good news. For one thing, when people think that prejudice toward a group is normative, they may be encouraged to use hate terms, so winning kudos for adherence to the norm. Conversely, people may infer that prejudice is normative when they hear others using hate terms. In such cases, the barometer plays a vital role in a self-perpetuating cycle of prejudice. Similarly, members of groups that find themselves overtly criticized tend to view the criticism as a slur, a sign of prejudice. In research I am currently doing with colleagues, we are finding that this reading of criticism causes people to adopt a besieged, rather jingoistic form of attachment to their group that predisposes them to prejudice and intergroup hostility.[2]

Further, the barometric property of language can fuel adverse intergroup relations by changing the dynamics of self-presentation. For example, there is a stereotype in Western nations that compared to men, women are more fearful of crime. A woman who says that "I'm not afraid of crime" therefore risks the backlash that often accompanies violations of stereotypical expectancies (see Chapter 3). Fear of this backlash may cause women to express high levels of fear that do not necessarily reflect their private experience. In this way, a normative climate of fear becomes self-fulfilling. Women are controlled not only by the fear of crime, but the belief that they generally are, and should be, fearful. In this schema, the fear of crime is not only an "instrument" but also a "yardstick" of social control (Sutton & Farrall, 2008).

More pitfalls stem from the limitations of language as a barometer. Prejudiced attitudes are transmitted, but not reliably signified, by certain types of language use. The LIB and the selective transmission effects we have reviewed are examples of unwitting, covert, or implicit forms of transmission that are likely to go unnoticed. Because they are not noticed, they are unlikely to trigger appropriate responses. Instead, efforts are bound to center on aspects of their language that are obviously linked to prejudice, such as explicit criticisms of a group or the blatant use of hate terms. While the elimination of this type of language is strongly desirable and likely to benefit intergroup relations in many ways, a potential downside is that it becomes harder to identify and sanction those who are prejudiced. It may also be difficult to challenge ideologies that advocate prejudice and conflict when they are seldom voiced explicitly.

In contrast, implicit, gradual, and difficult to control biases are difficult for people to "read" barometrically, so may be left to degrade intergroup relations in their quiet way. As a result, minority groups may find themselves excluded from employment and many other opportunities, even though no-one goes on record with overtly prejudiced statements about them. Majority groups may be inclined to infer from the lack of blatantly prejudicial language in their community that prejudice is absent and so resist attempts to counteract it.

The flawed use of language as a barometer may lead to a paradox of liberalism (Sutton et al., 2008). Here, debate about prejudice and other overt modes of discourse with great diagnostic and transformative potential are all but eliminated from the public sphere. What remains are the insidious modes of communication that are better equipped to help prejudice grow and thrive than to stop it. Whether these really are perverse side-effects of the liberal agenda to reform intergroup language is a difficult empirical question which has not yet been fully answered, even if the scenario just outlined seems familiar (see also Leets & Giles, 1997).

Conclusion

We have seen that language does not merely reflect but also affects cognition, and that in its interplay with cognition language creates, as well as replicates, social information. One source of the creative power of language is the reflexivity of its use. That is, people's beliefs about language modify how they use i, and how they react to the language used by others. This causes them to transform information even as they attempt to transmit it. Another source of the power of language is the ability of words—its fundamental units—to direct and modify cognition independently of the rules that are supposed to govern their use. Further, language also has the potential to worsen or improve intergroup relations by acting as a barometric indicator of prejudice. When entrusted to interactions between reflexive, strategic, and promiscuously associative human minds, language seems unable to transmit information faithfully or to obey its own rules. Ironically, the imperfection of language grants it tremendous creative power.

Given that language has received relatively little attention in the study of inter-group relations, further research is likely to reveal that it has more tricks up its sleeve. For example, it is striking that no published empirical study has shown directly that stereotypes themselves are changed by the LIB or by the selective transmission bias. Dependent measures usually concern what is transmitted (e.g., Lyons & Kashima, 2003), or judgments about the individual group members whose behavior is described (see Maass, 1999). No study has taken explicit endorsement of a stereo-type of a group as the dependent measure. This should be a priority for future research and suggests a more general question: does language affect intergroup rela-tions principally by altering beliefs about groups or by other means?

In this vein, biases like the LIB may worsen intergroup relations in everyday life by biasing attention, rather than cumulatively changing the representation of groups. For example, by using abstract language for outgroup members' negative behavior, the communicator focuses attention on the traits and motivations that may have brought the behavior about. In contrast, by using concrete language for ingroup members' negative behavior, the communicator instead draws attention to situation-al forces which tend to exonerate the actor. Implicitly, joint attention and therefore joint action are focused on the outrages that are willfully and characteristically com-mitted by outgroup members but not ingroup members. This may lead to biases in punitive, vengeful, or group-protective behaviors. Here then is another priority for further research.

These questions highlight the ability of language to operate simultaneously in more than one mode—as both vessel and lens, in this case. Indeed, this is proba-bly how language normally functions: a verbal statement about a topic simultane-ously conveys information about a topic (like a vessel), focuses attention on it (like a lens), and also betrays information about the communicator (like a barometer). Thinking about the multiple functions of language opens up a range of important research questions, some of which we have already touched on. For example, can people infer from the group labels used by others whether prejudice and hostility toward outgroups are normative within their group? Similarly, can they detect whether an LIB is operating in their community and from that, infer whether prejudice is normative (cf. Douglas & Sutton, 2006; Holtgraves & Kashima, 2008)?

Considering the multiple functions of language also enables researchers to import insights from one line of research into another. To illustrate, the "vessel" metaphor tends to cast language as something that happens after cognition: beliefs about the topic and the communicative context shape the way that people transmit information. In contrast, the lens metaphor casts language as something that pre-cedes cognition—the idiomatic availability of group labels constrains the way that people can think about groups. The different temporal orders implied by the vessel and lens metaphors have shaped research on topics such as the LIB and group labels respectively, and it is possible to turn them on their heads. For example, researchers have already shown that audiences' responses to outgroups are improved by exposure to complex labels (Leader et al., 2009). Extrapolating backwards from this work, one can predict that individuals who mentally represent an outgroup in three-dimensional, sympathetic terms are more likely to use a complex set of labels when referring to it. In turn, those exposed to their language should be favorably influenced by it. If this works out, we would have an example of a transition from an "open loop," where language affects cognition, to a "closed loop" model, where language affects cognition, which in turn affects language, in a recurring and enduring social-psychological dynamic.

This kind of transition is crucial to understanding of the interplay between fleeting, situated micro-social processes and broader, more enduring features of the macro-social environment. More generally, we should not overlook the essential function of the day-to-day use of language for the survival of culture and society. There is an intuitive tendency to essentialize the social and cultural "status quo," to think of it as an entity that survives *de facto*. But, in fact, the status quo depends on perpetual enactment and renewal. Cultural ideas are continually passed on by the vessel of language. Objects and events of shared interest in the world are continually selected by the lens of language. The ideologies and values that hold us together are continually signaled by the barometer of language. If we were to use language in fundamentally different ways tomorrow, then our culture, society, and intergroup relations would be fundamentally different (Kashima, 2001). Thus, whether intergroup relations stay the same or change, we should look to the dynamic between language and cognition for an explanation. In this respect, language is not just *at* the heart, but *is* the beating heart, of intergroup relations.

Endnotes

1. At the time of writing (December 2008), a search of PsycINFO in which the terms "intergroup relations" and "cognition" are combined turns up more than four times as many papers (213) than does the combination of "intergroup relations" and "language" (48). Some of the research and ideas included in this chapter were facilitated by a grant from the Economic and Research Council (RES 000–22–2540).

2. This ongoing research is facilitated by a grant from the Economic and Social Research Council (RES 000–22–2540).

CHAPTER TEN

Bi- and Multilingualism Between Diversity and Globalization

RICHARD CLÉMENT, JESSICA SHULMAN &
SARA RUBENFELD

The Old Testament traces the origin of the multiplicity of languages to an incident that occurred in the land of Shinar in the early times of humanity. Upon noticing that the Sons of Men were building a tower which could reach to the sky, the Lord said:

> 'Look, they are one people, and they have all one language; and this is only the begin-
> ning of what they will do; nothing that they propose to do will now be impossible for
> them. Come, let us go down, and confuse their language there, so that they will not
> understand one another's speech.' So the Lord scattered them abroad from there over
> the face of all the earth, and they left off building the city. Therefore it was called Babel,
> because there the Lord confused the language of all the earth; and from there the Lord
> scattered them abroad over the face of all the earth (Genesis 11, 6–9).

It is interesting to note, as Laponce (2001) has, that this passage couples the existence of multiple languages with a scattering of the population across the earth.
Under his Law of Babel, Laponce further proposes that a sole language will eventually ensure communication in a network that is closed, heavily integrated and
extremely dense. These characteristics of what must have been the original Babel
are likely to be re-created in our modern world, thus entailing the demise of all languages but one. He also outlines circumstances under which linguistic diversity may
be preserved. In an attempt to deal with these opposing tendencies, we will, in what
follows, review some of the evidence pertaining to what bi- and multilingualism

mean from the point of view of intergroup relations. We will first be dealing with individual and social processes, arguing that these can only be understood in the context of world-wide forces and tendencies, thus returning us, in the end, to the issue of globalization.

What Is Bilingualism?

Merriam-Webster's online thesaurus defines *bilingualism* as "the ability to speak two languages: the frequent oral use of two languages" and *multilingual* as "of, containing, or expressed in several languages" and "using or able to use several languages." The simplicity of these definitions is, however, deceiving for numerous reasons. First, no distinction is made between individual bilingualism, that is, a person's competence in more than one language, and bilingualism as it may describe a collectivity such as a city or a nation. That distinction, as we will see, is in fact fundamental to understanding the relations between individuals and their milieu.

Second, defining bilingualism as characteristic of a community introduces, in itself, a number of questions. There are, arguably, 6000 languages distributed throughout 200 countries. Most countries would, therefore, be characterized by a state of relative bilingualism. Demographic considerations, including the number of speakers of distinct languages, however, are not necessarily sufficient for deeming a specific state or nation as bilingual.

For this to happen, languages must also be recognized and legitimately used. Take, for example, the matter of the distinction between a language and a dialect. Lyautey (1854–1934), a marshal of the French army, member of the French Academy, is said to have claimed that a language is a dialect that has an army, a navy and an air force. This notion introduces the issue of power hierarchies between the groups identified with specific languages. Groups must be powerful enough to have the state recognize their idiom as a language, implying, therefore, the obligation to support its acquisition, maintenance and use. Hence, the state-level degree of bilingualism is heavily dependent on the political and social climate in which groups evolve.

The third set of definitional problems is related to individual bilingualism or *bilinguality* (Hamers & Blanc, 2000). How fluent must one be in two languages to be declared bilingual? Here the answers vary widely. But more important in the context of this chapter, a strictly linguistic definition may not be appropriate.

Bilinguality

In most areas of the world, learning and using a language or languages other than one's own is a fundamental part of life. An early distinction, apparently without intergroup connotation, was made between simultaneous and successive bilingualism. In the first case, both languages are acquired simultaneously, whereas in the second case, the L2 is acquired later in life. Ronjat (1913) first observed the linguistic development (in French and German) of his son, Louis, from birth to age four, and concluded that infancy bilingualism is possible. Since then, numerous studies have been made of simultaneous bilingualism and generally support Ronjat's conclusions: children learning both languages together are able to differentiate each language at an early stage of their learning and are not disadvantaged in terms of language competence compared to their monolingual peers. Importantly, however, this state of 'balanced bilingualism' only evolves in the presence of contextual factors favoring the equal status of each language, their equal valuing by parents, the presence of a community for each language, as well as individual factors such as positive attitudes toward bilingualism in general, and members of the L2 group, in particular.

What affects successive bilingualism (the acquisition of a L2 after the L1 has been established) is similar to what influences simultaneous bilingualism. Empirical results stress the importance of factors including linguistic aptitude, learning strategies and personality factors such as extroversion. Gardner and Lambert (1972), however, proposed that motivation is an important factor determining L2 competence. They further showed that L2 motivation was closely linked to attitudes toward the L2 community and an interest in becoming similar to valued members of that group, a tendency which they referred to as 'integrativeness'. Originally a description of the Canadian situation, thirty years of research have shown that L2 motivation, anchored in intergroup attitudes, is a determining factor of L2 competence in varied settings worldwide.

In addition to attitudes, a more recent development has documented the importance of L2 confidence as a determinant of L2 behavior and competence. L2 confidence corresponds to the belief in being able to react adaptively to situations involving the use of a second language. It is related to positive self-ratings of competence and an absence of anxiety when using the second language (Clément, 1980). Its development can be traced to situations where contact with the L2 community is both frequent and pleasant (see Chapters 6, 10, 12, 15, & 17). Thus, while positive attitudes may orient the individual towards the L2 community, intercultural contact generates the confidence required for L2 interaction and, in so doing, promotes L2 competence as well as other aspects and consequences of L2 acquisition, as discussed below.

As should be clear from the foregoing discussion, the attitudinal context of bilingual development and L2 acquisition puts bilingualism at the intersection of individual and societal processes. In coining the concepts of additive and subtractive bilingualism, Lambert (1978) proposed that language learning outcomes are likely very different for members of majority and minority groups. Subtractive bilingualism refers to a situation where members of a minority group lose their first language as a result of learning a second one. Additive bilingualism, on the other hand, refers to situations where members of a majority group acquire the L2 without losing their L1.

The notion of relative group status was subsequently formalized by Giles, Bourhis, and Taylor (1977), under the concept of ethnolinguistic vitality, as "that which makes a group likely to behave as a distinctive and collective entity within the intergroup setting" (p. 308; see also Chapter 16). Ethnolinguistic vitality is defined along three dimensions. The first is demographic representation, which refers to the number of speakers composing a language group as well as their distribution throughout a territory. High numerical proportions and concentration have traditionally been used to weigh the importance of a language group. The two other dimensions may, however, have a drastic influence on the impact of demographics. Institutional control refers to the degree of control a group has over its own development through its commanding presence of political, social and religious institutions or more informally, through pressure groups. High institutional control can conceivably modulate and even thwart the effects of demographics when a small language group happens to control the institutions. In a similar vein, social status, corresponding to a language community's social prestige, actual and historical, may bias and even reverse the effects of demographics. Both institutional support and social status evoke the image of linguistically powerful and powerless minorities. For example, the 'English-only movement' in the United States has made English the only official language in those very states where Hispanic communities are most abundant. Although Hispanics show high demographic vitality in these states, their institutional power and linguistic status remain weak. Ethnolinguistic vitality, however, is far more than a purely descriptive concept. As will be shown, it is linked to a family of language phenomena and, in turn, to social and cognitive consequences to which we now turn.

Social and Cognitive Consequences

Emerging from the preceding discussion is the idea that positive benefits from L2 acquisition and usage will only be attained when the first language and culture are securely established within the individual (Clément, 1980; Hamers & Blanc, 2000). This presupposes a familial, educational, and social context which allows the development and transmission of the first language and culture (see Chapter 15). These conditions may be present for majority group members, but they may not characterize the situation of minority groups, immigrants, refugees, and sojourners. The relative status of the first and second language groups and the linguistic composition of the community are the main determinants of the linguistic and cultural outcomes of second language acquisition.

Specifically, there is an intimate link between communicative processes and individual identity. To the extent that the context brings about loss of the first language, it will also bring about a loss of the first cultural identity. Noels and Clément (1996) have shown this to be the case among minority group members but not among majority group members. More precisely, they compared minority and majority group members speaking either French or English as a first language. Buttressing the hegemony of English as a world-dominant language, Anglophone minorities seem to be little affected by their local (i.e., Canadian) status. Francophones, however, show profiles that immediately reflect their ethnolinguistic vitality. That is, minority Francophones show a gain in L2 identity at the expense of their L1 identity. Further jeopardizing their cultural integrity, their second language confidence was also related to increased psychosocial adaptation and well-being. It is interesting to note that while language programs may be intended to promote diversity, their effect may backfire in the case of minority groups. The systemic relationships between societal conditions, and language loss, therefore, risk bringing about results that are opposite to the intended goal of bilingualism programs.

Evolving beyond a strict dichotomous view of bilingual identity, recent research has opened the possibility that identities may become hybridized. Germain and Rose (2000) have observed that, especially among the younger generation of Montréal (Canada) residents, it is not uncommon for bilingual identities to emerge. Alternating from one language to the other then occurs frequently, and often within the same conversation. Bilingualism may, therefore, lead to the emergence of a bilingual identity through which individuals are capable of shifting between identities on the basis of a given context.

Still in the Canadian context, Dallaire (2003) commented on Francophones who 'live in English,' and suggested the emergence of a hybrid identity among those Francophones who have a sustained contact with Anglophones. In two further studies on this topic, Gaudet and Clément (in press) examined patterns of identity and communication among French-speaking Canadians living in Saskatchewan, a Western province where Francophones constitute only 2% of the population and where that percentage continues to diminish, largely due to exogamous marriages. Over half of the 'Fransaskois', as they are called, have a partner who is not French. That is to say that this group is in intimate and continuous contact with the other group and is, therefore, highly bilingual. As such, it is not surprising that 39% of the sample who self-identified as Fransaskois actually reported English as their mother tongue. Furthermore, both French- and English-language confidence contributed to psychological adjustment. Although Francophone and Anglophone identities were negatively correlated, English and French language confidence, as well as social support stemming from members of both linguistic groups, were positively correlated. So no matter the identity outcome, this highly bilingual group's life constantly straddles the two linguistic contexts, with positive outcomes for its health and its identification to both communities resulting from this hybridism. Their valued distinctiveness does not seem to reside with the exclusive identification to one group but rather with the ability to accrue more than one identity.

The cognitive consequences of bilingualism follow a similar pattern. It was originally thought that bilingualism would produce negative outcomes for cognitive functioning. A study by Peal and Lambert (1962), however, showed that the bilinguals scored higher than monolinguals on verbal and non-verbal intelligence tests and showed a more diversified intelligence structure. According to these authors, bilinguals have the ability to manipulate two symbolic systems and thus analyze semantic features in greater detail. Subsequent studies have resulted in the conclusion that bilinguals have greater meta-linguistic awareness and cognitive flexibility. They are, therefore, better able to distinguish the symbol from its specific meaning, which gives them an advantage in most school-based cognitive abilities. According to Hamers and Blanc's (2000) sociocultural interdependence hypothesis, however, positive cognitive outcomes will result only in situations where both the first and second languages are valued, buttressing the conclusion already reached regarding the social outcomes.

Attitudes, Prejudice and Discrimination

As exemplified above, much of the intergroup conjecture related to bilingualism hinges on the issue of harmonious intergroup relations. Fluency in another language emerges from positive intergroup contact *and* is presumed to entail a positive intergroup climate. But how does this actually happen?

Code-switching. Among the earliest forays in the field of the social psychology of language is the interest in the corollaries of code-switching. Code-switching corresponds to an individual's tendency to alternate from one code to another during the same interaction or across multiple interactions. The term 'code' is used here to designate either a language, a dialect or different styles of a language. The 'switching' coincides with speech turns, whereby one interlocutor changes code upon taking the floor during a conversation. Three strategies have been documented in this context: divergence, convergence and maintenance. Divergence entails reverting to one's first language when the conversation has been carried in L2. Conversely, convergence means switching to the language of the interlocutor. Finally, maintenance implies no switching at all. According to communication accommodation theory (CAT; Sachdev & Giles, 2004), the choice of a particular strategy is motivated by intergroup attitudes. In normal conversation, interlocutors would be expected to converge to facilitate communication. Positive attitudes, therefore, are related to convergence. Maintenance of a separate code and, more so, divergence are related to dislike or, even hostility. Being on the receiving end of this behavior is also significant. It signals to the interlocutor the positive or negative attitudes of the speaker.

From an intergroup perspective, bilingual code-switching is important because it is motivated by and conveys an individual's attitude toward the other language group. Understanding the phenomenon, however, also requires an awareness of the context in which it is situated. According to Sachdev and Bourhis (2001), the operation of CAT not only depends on individual predispositions but also on intergroup and sociolinguistic considerations. Given that switching is a socially meaningful act intended to enhance one's self-regard and distinctiveness, it is driven by the current ethnolinguistic vitality of the interlocutor's group. Linguistic convergence or divergence from a high ethnolinguistic vitality group has more important consequences than the same behavior with respect to a relatively lower vitality group.

Furthermore, norms and rules governing language choice may interact with ethnolinguistic vitality. In a series of studies conducted in Montreal, a bilingual Canadian city, Genesee and Bourhis (1988) showed that among the many combinations of French and English code-switching between a clerk and a client, the clerk converging to the client was always more favorably evaluated, testifying to the importance of situational norms. That is, no matter the relative vitality of the two languages, the client is always to be accommodated. In the same vein, in her ethnographic study of a bilingual neighborhood in Cape Town, McCormick (2002) found that the social and conversational norms governing informal interactions among neighbors and residents of the community influence the linguistic style and language choices of speakers. In this case, the norms dictate mixing and switching languages to enact identity profiles which show respect and demonstrate 'good-neighborliness'. Thus, norms may not always support solely the standard version of a language but rather a pattern of language usage that is socially functional.

The linguistic intergroup bias. If code-switching remains a powerful instrument of intergroup communication among bilinguals, other, more subtle processes are also at play. The role of verbal communication in the transmission of prejudice has received much theoretical attention, including the features of the linguistic intergroup bias (LIB; Maass, Salvi, Arcuri, & Semin, 1989). Yet few studies have examined the acquisition of an outgroup language as a factor in mitigating prejudicial speech. A study by Shulman and Clément (2008) assessed the extent to which subtle prejudicial beliefs are communicated within a bilingual context and investigated the role of ethnolinguistic identity and L2 confidence in the transmission of linguistic bias.

Accordingly, the LIB paradigm posits that the degree of language abstractness used to describe behaviors is related to intergroup appraisals (see Chapters 8, 9, &

16). The implications of choosing to describe a person using abstract rather than concrete terms (e.g., adjectives versus descriptive action verbs) involve ascribing temporal stability or enduring qualities to the person described, thus implying generalizability across situations.

In this study, the conditions under which minority Canadian Francophones use linguistic bias when communicating about the in- and outgroup (i.e., Canadian Anglophones) were investigated. The results reveal that, when describing the undesirable behaviors of outgroup Anglophones, Francophones were more likely to use subtly biased language than when describing the desirable behaviors of the outgroup. That is, Anglophone actors engaged in prosocial behaviors were given temporary, situation-bound descriptors, while their antisocial behaviors were more likely to be ascribed abstract terms, thereby implying temporal and cross-situational stability of those characteristics.

Importantly, this trend was detected only when participants' profiles of identification was taken into consideration; that is, the pattern demonstrating the LIB was only found among those with strong identification to the ingroup Francophones. In contrast, strong identification with the outgroup Anglophones and higher English-speaking confidence were both related to mitigation in the expression of prejudice toward the outgroup. Interestingly, however, these same factors appeared to promote linguistically biased speech toward members of the ingroup. In other words, a self-reported sense of affiliation with Anglophones was related to ingroup identity erosion and a greater tendency to speak disparagingly about members of one's own ethnolinguistic group.

Further, it was found that individuals who identify strongly as minority Francophones described both the undesirable *and* desirable behaviors of Anglophones using more abstract terms, meaning that all outgroup actions were assigned cross-situational and temporal stability, regardless of the valence of the behavior described. The actor-observer bias phenomenon, which suggests that individuals tend to explain the behaviors of others as a function of inner dispositions, while one's own actions tend to be guided by situational forces, offers one interpretation of this finding.

The relative power positions of the groups in contact may likewise play a role in influencing the attributions a perceiver makes about outgroup others. Accordingly, members of high-power groups are likely to be described in terms of stable dispositions, while low-power group members are more likely to receive situational attributions, regardless of the valence of the described behavior.

The investigation of the LIB within a sociolinguistic context characterized by an inherent disequilibrium in social power confirms its belonging to a family of phenomena related to ethnolinguistic erosion (e.g., Lambert, 1978). Over and above the development of positive social representations toward the L2 group, the consequences of L2 acquisition and confidence may also include a mitigation of prejudicial speech toward that group. The findings obtained in this study, therefore, expand upon previous research to include the linguistic aspects of prejudicial communication.

Intercultural mediation. The behavioral counterpart of prejudice is, of course, discrimination. Much of the research linking language and discrimination has been concerned with first language practices. However, an intergroup perspective supports the possibility that prejudice may be communicated between groups not sharing the same first language. Rubenfeld et al. (2007) explored how factors associated with the acquisition and use of an L2 contribute to the development of anti-discriminatory behaviors among minority group members.

The "cultural mediation measure" used in the study presents participants with scenarios, each describing a specific intergroup conflict, followed by potential meditational responses (e.g., I would mediate to reduce the tension; I would interrupt the conversation). Participants are then asked to indicate the extent to which they would endorse the provided meditational responses. Preliminary studies have documented involved and avoidant dimensions of the mediation measure. This suggests that when faced with intergroup conflict situations, responses tended to represent either some degree of active mediation in an effort to reduce the conflict or a tendency to avoid the conflict situation altogether.

A subsequent path analysis investigated the influence of aspects of L2 acquisition on the use of involved or avoidant mediation behaviors. Contrary to expectations, identifying with the L2 community did not play a significant role in influencing intercultural mediation. Rather, greater identification with the L2 community, stemming from confidence in the L2 and contact with its group members, only led to more positive representations of that community. Identification with an L2 group, therefore, appears to have affective consequences in the form of more xenophilic attitudes about the L2 group, but it does not result in a willingness to employ behavioral interventions when witnessing intercultural conflicts.

In contrast, identification with one's own ethnic group was shown to be a necessary precursor to a willingness to become involved as a mediator. These results suggest that venturing into intercultural conflict situations require the assurance or existence of a strong first language identity. Minorities who risk assimilation to the dominant culture may be hesitant to involve themselves in unfamiliar conflict situations if their own identity is vulnerable. These results support a conjecture extending social aspects of L2 acquisition to the development of anti-prejudicial attitudes and anti-discriminatory behaviors in that they provide insight into the processes and mechanisms underlying positive intergroup relations in a multilingual context.

Bilingualism and Society

In view of the current state of knowledge on the outcomes of acquiring and using a second language, as reviewed above, we now revisit our initial statement on the link between bilingualism and its societal context. Returning to the notion that a language is a dialect with an army, a navy and an air force, the inherent role of the state in creating an environment that either is, or is not, likely to foster bilingualism again becomes salient. Language planning has been the political and administrative instrument used to promote and protect languages according to predetermined societal options. Accordingly, the state may determine the goals of language education, the medium of interaction with government agencies, tribunals and schools, and the relative visibility of different languages in public and commercial signs—namely, the linguistic landscape.

Undoubtedly, high-vitality majority groups, which control the institutions, will define language policies that are likely to serve their own ends. That does not, however, necessarily imply that the laws and policies would always be aimed at the eradication of minority groups. Indeed there is a wide variety of approaches to multilingual situations guided by an equally wide variety of ideologies. Bourhis, el-Geledi, and Sachdev (2007) suggest that these varied ideologies can be described along a continuum including four categories varying in the extent to which they guarantee the dominance of the majority and survival of the minority language.

At one extreme, the pluralism ideology implies that all citizens should adopt public values linked to the maintenance of law and order, including the responsibility to learn the languages of other groups represented in the society. In this context, the state also protects individual liberties such as the right of minorities to transmit and use their own language. This implies that it is willing to financially support social diversity among its citizens.

The civic ideology, in comparison, is more conservative. It also proposes a tolerance of diversity, but, unlike pluralism, it does not actively support the development and thriving of minority groups. Minorities are free to form associations and promote cultural and linguistic activities but at their own cost. This subjects minority linguistic groups to the natural forces of the linguistic market, which largely favor the dominant group.

Still further to the right, the assimilation ideology implies that language minorities will abandon their own language and culture in favor of the dominant group's characteristics. This may occur naturally or be enforced through laws and regulations. Finally, the 'ethnist' ideology not only promotes assimilation but, at the same time, limits the extent to which members of minority groups will eventually be able to participate fully in society. In those states, full citizenship is reserved to a specific subset of the population.

This ideology continuum is molded by historical, political and economic processes which may involve any combination of leadership-directed change and grassroots movements. Ideological orientations may vary under the influence of a powerful majority struggling with its public, national, and international image, or, equally well under the pressure from cohesive and persistent minorities claiming their rights. In turn, ideologies and their consequent policies will influence expectations of both majority and minority groups regarding what is the most acceptable mode of acculturation for both groups (cf. Bourhis et al., 2007). A harmonious situation would exist to the extent that these expectations are shared by minority group members and the mainstream community. For example, under a pluralist ideology shared by all groups, it would be expected that minority groups would be welcomed in a community's mainstream while, at the same time, protecting its own language and culture. This would result in a harmonious situation. It may, however, be that expectations are not shared, such as when a minority group aspires to integration into the mainstream under a pluralist ideology which is not shared by the majority group operating under an assimilation ideology. In those cases, intergroup conflict is probable, likely at the expense of the minority group's language and culture.

Conclusion

Bilingualism is undoubtedly a matter that far exceeds the context of a language classroom. The introductory references to the Shinar 'incident' and to Laponce's (2001) 'Law of Babel,' indeed direct one's thinking to the notion that language and bilingualism are as much intergroup experiences as they are individual phenomena. It is in fact intimate connection between the two planes of reality (i.e., the individual and the group) which makes language an instrument of communication *par excellence*. Such a link also entails, as has been shown, a direct impact of the intergroup situation on the acquisition and usage of languages, and specifically, languages other than that which was first learned. Depleted ethnolinguistic vitality is a central feature explaining the demise of languages, and, consequently, the accelerated growth in importance of some at the expense of others. The ultimate consequence is a dominant world-wide language, most probably, English.

The relatively straightforward scenario forecasting the hegemony of English is, however, moderated by factors or tendencies which interfere with a simple power analysis. According to social identity theory (SIT, see Chapters 1 & 21), individuals strive for distinctiveness along valued dimensions. Furthermore, according to communication accommodation theory, language may very well be one of those valued dimensions. This would implicitly provide the impetus for the conservation and protection of minority languages. However, this would only occur to the extent that current beliefs and values held by the group promote these characteristics. If, indeed, members of a minority group would rather accept beliefs and values disparaging their own language and culture, as Chapter 21 suggests, then these elements would not be part of their valued distinctiveness, providing little momentum to preserve the language.

The crux of the matter, as described above, are prevailing ideologies and understanding their emergence as well as the ways in which they come to be shared. The dimensions which nourish ethnolinguistic vitality are interpreted within an ideological context which modulates their meaning. Neither social status nor institutional representation means anything unless a language is recognized as part of a valued identity, and this may pose a challenge to current formulations of SIT. Among problematic questions would be: How does the quest for a distinctive and valued identity relate to the objective characteristics of the community? How do social representations of these characteristics factor into group allegiance? And, finally, what determines the social representation of languages?

Arguably, current trends in language erosion play against linguistic diversity. There are, however, powerful countercurrents anchored in world-wide movements promoting diversity. The Universal Declaration of Human Rights, for example, guarantees to all humans the right to be different, that is, not only the tolerance of difference, but the protection and promotion of that which is different. Skutnabb-Kangas and Phillipson (2008) have recently argued that the failure of states to protect minority languages could, in the current legislative context, be interpreted as a crime against humanity. Simply put, language and culture are valid, legitimate, and necessary constructs in defining one's identity, both as an individual and as a member of a group. Systemic efforts which neglect or disparage the language rights of *all* citizens are akin to a serious attack on human dignity and integrity.

CHAPTER ELEVEN

Democratic Argument and Deliberation Between Ethnopolitically Divided Groups

Donald G. Ellis

Argument and verbal contest are important to a democracy. The process of deliberation, which is so central to democratic political processes, requires respect for disagreement and the use of dialogue and communication to transcend social and intellectual borders. In fact, engaged participation in democratic culture necessitates a healthy regard for argument and contestatory discourse (see Chapter 12). Public conversation designed to solve problems and based on principles of communication and rationality is naturally community building and inclusive. Such engaged argument helps participants in a conflict to work through issues from different points of view and to do more than simply accept or tolerate diversity. This perspective on argument and problem-solving between conflict groups has its roots in deliberative democracy and its communication expectations. But most of the literature on deliberative democracy focuses on existing democracies and their efforts to create public spaces for discussion. This chapter extends the principles of argument and deliberation to ethnopolitically divided groups and draws on the traditions of intergroup communication (Harwood & Giles, 2005) to show how argument and deliberation can accommodate the very difficult and intractable identity conflicts that have arisen in the last century (Coleman, 2003; Ellis, 2005).

Intractable Intergroup Conflict

Intractable conflicts are deeply rooted political conflicts where religion and ethnicity are usually implicated (see Chapter 2). They are typically referred to as ethnopolitical conflicts. Unlike traditional wars between states, ethnopolitical conflicts are often between groups within a state. Common examples are Israelis and Palestinians, Protestants and Catholics in Northern Ireland, Hutus and Tutsis in Rwanda, Sunni and Shia in Iraq, Singhalese and Tamil in Sri Lanka, Blacks and Whites in South Africa, Bosnians and Serbs within Bosnia-Herzegovina, and others. These conflicts have at least two things in common, the most important of which is identity. Each group is mobilized into a group identity based on religion, culture, language, or nationality. Some inequality of distribution of goods and resources is the other common characteristic of intractable ethnopolitical conflicts. One group is perceived as receiving more benefits and resources than the other, and when this inequality correlates with identity—such as one ethnic group is deprived of resources available to the other—then the opportunity for conflict is particularly potent.

Such conflicts are particularly intense and unrelenting. They are contrasted with more "realistic" conflicts that do not involve the existential issues of identity, conflicts over material resources. Identity conflicts are persistent and difficult to resolve. They are not very amenable to compromises and tradeoffs because they involve claims of group and religious rights. These conflicts fuel wars, terrorism, and geopolitical struggles (see Chapter 12). They wrestle with issues of self-definition, historical narrative, and group rights. Since World War II, the availability of mass produced cheap weapons have allowed these conflicts to flourish and provided the means for increased violence and human suffering.

Ethnopolitical conflicts go through stages of peace and war, tension and relaxation, as well as periods of more or less active conflict resolution. But ultimately, the two sides must talk to one another. They must negotiate to resolve political issues and transform attitudes and relationships with the "other." Moreover, stable solutions require democratic structures and relationships. The conflicting parties must move toward relationships based on fairness, equality, and inclusion. There are three themes that inform this chapter and its approach to argument and deliberation between ethnopolitically divided groups. The first is the centrality of democratic theory; the second is deliberative communication based on the fact that contestation is natural and desirable to democratic solutions to problems; the third is the importance of negotiation and argument. Each undergirds a communication approach to managing these divided groups, and each is considered briefly below.

Democracy and Ethnopolitical Conflicts

There is near universal agreement that *democracy* is a desirable political system. The idea that laws and policies are rooted in the consent of those they affect is rarely challenged as anything but a minimum condition of the politically legitimate state. And of all the defining features of democracy (Dahl, 1998) such as elections, association-al rights, freedom of expression, etc., the matter of deliberation or deliberative communication is most fundamental. At its core, democratic processes require the engagement and management of divergent discourses. It is communication that is responsible for coordinating differences among groups. This perspective on com-munication emerges from a pragmatist tradition (Russill, 2006) which takes an action orientation in terms of the usefulness of communication in responding to the problems of a democratic community that is trying to manage differences. Communication is essentially the management of incommensurability and is the tool of democratic processes working toward acceptable and morally legitimate social control.

Conflicting groups must have access to proper information in order to solve problems. This is particularly important with respect to necessary institutions for conflict resolution. Institutions remain important for handling deep-rooted conflicts by providing accountable social frameworks. These frameworks have a degree of legitimacy and inclusiveness that assists with the conflict resolution process. But more importantly, democratic processes allow for the norms of negotiation, com-promise, and cooperation to have a pacifying effect on the behavior of deeply divid-ed groups. It is true that if not handled correctly, democratic politics can inflame ethnopolitical passions rather than restrain them. Majoritarian politics can help one group dominate another. In fact, it is important to underscore that not all forms of intergroup contact improve the image of the other and break down stereotypes and antagonistic intergroup attitudes (see Chapters 6, 10, 12, 15, & 17). Forbes (2004), for example, explains how intergroup contact can *increase* stereotypes and unpro-ductive attitudes. One strength of deliberative democratic theory, as it relates to intergroup conflict, is that it draws attention to the pragmatics of problem-solving based on sources of realistic conflict. Stereotypes are part of the private sphere of life and thus an artifact of conflict and not the source of realistic conflict (see Chapter 8).

In my own work with Israelis and Palestinians (see Ellis, 2005; Ellis & Maoz, 2007; Maoz & Ellis, 2008) they have stereotypes about one another to be sure. But their conflict is rooted in realistic political grievances. Contact between them is designed to promote conflict resolution, and a democratic framework is most amenable to the values of negotiation and inclusiveness. A democratic framework is not based on ideological convictions but on pragmatic argument. This emphasis on complex democratic processes—based on meaningful competition, inclusive participation, and civil liberties—is designed not simply to pose an ideal but to address complex problems that are deep-rooted and prolonged. Intractable ethnop-olitical conflicts stipulate a focus on more fundamental issues. In the next section, we focus more on what it means for communication to be deliberatively democratic.

Deliberative Communication

Deliberative communication emerges from the literature on deliberative democracy and is rooted in the advantages that accrue from reciprocity. As Gutmann and Thompson (2004) explain, "The basic premise of reciprocity is that citizens owe one another justifications for their institutions, laws, and public policies that collectively bind them" (p. 133). This means that justice and the legitimate acceptance of social and political constraints on a group must emerge from a process where all parties have had ample opportunity to engage in mutual reason-giving. From reciprocity flows respect for the other. Gutmann and Thompson (2004) also refer to publicity and accountability as essential conditions of deliberative democracy. That is, discussion and decision-making must be public to ensure justifiability and that those who make decisions on behalf of others must be accountable. Binding decisions lose moral legitimacy to the extent that they have been made in a manner unavailable to the public, or by individuals who are not accountable to their constituencies.

What is particularly important about deliberative democracy from a communication perspective is its ability to transform the perspective of the individual. Election-centered and direct democratic processes value the individual but focus primarily on the opportunity to participate. Deliberative processes draw on communication in the form of discussion and argument with the aim to change the motivations and opinions of individuals. The deliberative process contributes to a changing sense of self and identity because participants are immersed in a social system that manufactures new ways to think about problems and orient toward others. This deliberative social system moves people out of their parochial interests and contributes to a broader sense of *community mindedness* as well as providing new information that clarifies and informs opinions.

Deliberation and Ethnopolitically Divided Groups

Deliberation is typically associated with rational communication in democratic societies. And rationality is often criticized as an unrealistic demand on decision makers. Moreover, deliberation is sometimes even considered inappropriate for deeply divided groups because they are incapable of such discourse. But deliberation does not seek rationality in the strongest sense of the term. Deliberation is not a process of rationality but one of "error reduction" (Bohman, 2007; Sunstein, 2004). The interactive effects of deliberation between divided groups make the participants less susceptible to errors and biases. This is why framing effects discussed below are not enduring but susceptible to change as a result of exposure to alternatives (see Chapter 16). Frame change and adjustment are even more likely when exposed to radically different identity perspectives. Interaction among like-minded people, who have similar identities, has a reinforcing affect, so it is the presence of different identities and perspectives—e.g., ethnopolitically divided groups— that is most important for reducing error and resulting in positive deliberative effects. Deliberation among the like-minded encourages distortions in the form of enclave polarization (Sunstein, 2004) or the exaggeration of existing beliefs and attitudes. The force of deliberation, on the other hand, is actualized in situations of intergroup conflict because such situations are the epistemic base of deliberation. Deliberation is not very effective amongst groups that think alike because there is no room for cognitive movement.

Deliberation between deeply divided groups helps reduce error because of the distributed nature of knowledge. Different identity groups represent information, values, and world views and deliberation is most suited to improve the lot of the least well off and balance the consequences of unfair advantages of others. In the same way that persuasive arguments theory holds that groups converge on opinions because members are exposed to new arguments, deliberation between divergent groups increases the pool of knowledge and information. And discussion during deliberation of particular facts (e.g., who did what to whom and when) is less effective than directly confronting the identity premises that undergird facts. For this reason, deliberation must include the engagement of different group narratives, feelings, and emotions. It is deliberation that forms the basis for improving the lot of the least well off. Those who have most to gain from deliberation are the participants from groups who are most divergent, especially when one group is disadvantaged with respect to some power asymmetry. They gain the opportunity to engage other perspectives.

One of my principal claims in this chapter is that deliberative communication, which is oriented toward controlled discussion and problem-solving, can improve relations between conflicting ethnopolitical groups. This is as opposed to dialogic strategies, which claim that deeper cultural and psychological engagement is necessary to transform relationships. Deliberative processes seek agreement at lower levels of abstraction that are, in Sunstein's (1999) terms, "incompletely theorized," but solve practical problems and establish a foundation for deeper agreement to emerge. Deliberative discourse seeks a public space by which groups can confront one another on a problem and produce binding results, results that have attendant psychological and attitudinal benefits as well as practical and political benefits. Below are qualities of deliberative communication that characterize the deliberative context. They are not exhaustive but related to the benefits of deliberation and the process of managing conflict between groups.

One of the problems posed by anyone making decisions is how to *process* information. In other words, even with the best information one could gather it is never exactly obvious how to use the information. This is because problems are complex and humans are often limited. This is the problem of *bounded rationality* termed by Simon (1983). Very simply, deliberation increases the odds of making better choices because individuals can step beyond the boundaries of their own abilities and interact with others. They can participate in the intelligence of others and have their own intelligence stimulated in new ways. Moreover, conflicting groups are often motivated to deceive the other. They withhold information, motivations, and manipulate information for strategic reasons. This is because there are usually incentives to misrepresent information and gain advantage. But deliberative discussion improves the availability and clarity of information. Even if I believe that someone has strong reasons to manipulate me, it sharpens the consideration of my own information. And the opportunity to see things from the other's perspective is improved by deliberation.

This is related to the problem of bounded rationality because my own information and experiences limit the extent to which I can conceive of things in any other way. Numerous studies point to the value and effectiveness of communicative contact where members of conflicting groups transcend their limits and find new ways to solve problems with former enemies (see Hertz-Lazarowitz & Eden, 2002). Wittes (2005), in her analysis of negotiations between Israelis and Palestinians, stated that "the small teams who met repeatedly over months in Oslo built a common language and a common view of their task that enabled them to overcome obstacles" (pp. 140–141). This is recognition of the multiplicative effects that deliberative discussion has on the available intelligence applied to problems. Even though the Oslo Accords later stagnated, the early deliberation laid the groundwork for what would be new diplomacy between the Israelis and the Palestinians.

The "engagement with others" is one of the strengths of the deliberative process. This is one way that deliberators "participate in the intelligence of others" and reach beyond the boundaries of their own rationality. For instance, *deliberative communication forces a particular form of justification*. In other words, the presence of others makes relying purely on "self interest" difficult, if not impossible. At its core, deliberative communication is based on disagreement, but more importantly "skilled disagreement." There is much to skilled disagreement—e.g. task focus, knowledgeable use of reasoning and evidence, perspective taking, etc.,—but these details are not my concern here. There is a presupposition toward justifying claims by logical means. This implies a treatment of issues with respect to advantages and disadvantages in search of novel and acceptable solutions. There is more to this than the familiar call for reasoned discourse reminiscent of high school civics. Deliberation, in particular, is a process of moving from personal opinion to group judgment. It helps conflicting groups progress from the constrictions of selfish interests to choices based on the inclusion of others.

One criticism of deliberation is that it is elitist and that minority or disadvantaged groups must rely on passions. But passions (symbolic passions) are certainly within the traditions of deliberative communication and may still be analyzed rhetorically as substantive and matched with reason. Moreover, as Gutmann and Thompson (1996) explain, the argument that rational deliberative discourse favors an established order lacks historical perspective, and "most of the force of radical criticism of society in the past has relied on rationalist challenges to the status quo" (p. 134). Even the telling of a personal story or narrative (Bar-On, 2000) can be part of the deliberative process as a step toward reaching consensus on difficult issues. Moreover, narrative structures are certainly subject to argumentative analysis.

Deliberating groups by their very definition assume that the exchange of information and reasons among group members is beneficial. The assumption is that distorted or misleading information can be "corrected" and that there is something to be gained by the assembly effect of the group. Sunstein (2004) has written incisively about deliberative judgments of groups and reports that deliberation does reduce variance; that is, group members converge after talking together. Moreover, group members increase their confidence in judgments following deliberation. Group confidence is high regardless of decision quality. These findings have important implications for deliberating groups that are experiencing intergroup conflict, even though most of the data cited by Sunstein derives from more uniformly organized groups. Cognitive convergence and commitment to decisions are essential goals of conflict management between groups in conflict. Additionally, deliberating groups increase decision accuracy. Individuals with correct and knowledgeable answers speak with credibility and are thus more convincing. Groups tend to gravitate toward convincing members.

In some cases, a group can reach an agreement, and it requires little of the group members with respect to implementation or compliance. It is more likely that a collective decision will benefit from a group commitment to the decision. Deliberative communication improves participation and increases *cohesive consensus*. A collective decision following deliberation has the psychological benefit of commitment by group members because of the nature of the communication. The process of subjecting communication to stricter argumentative criteria and exceeding the boundaries of one's own rationality prompt proposals that are more "public" in nature; that is, they represent the attitudes and opinions of the participants and they are more committed to the results. Simply the opportunity to speak and "have a say" increases support for the outcome of discussion. Moreover, deliberative communication draws theoretical sustenance from democratic communication which emphasizes processes rather than outcomes. People in mature polities are accepting of political decisions even if they do not agree with them, because they accept the process as adequate or fair. The principles of deliberative communication have substantial legitimacy since they are grounded in those individuals most affected by the outcome. As Manin (1987) makes clear, the source of legitimacy in decisions is not the will of the majority but the outcome of the idea formation process. The sense of liberty and respect that groups benefit from comes from a process of research, discussion of alternatives, and the social exchange of reasons and arguments.

Argument in Divided Groups

In a recent article, Pettigrew (2008) explained how there has been an renewed interest in contact theory and matters related to how interaction between conflicting groups either exacerbates or ameliorates group prejudices and problems. Contact theory is the well accepted, even commonplace, idea that participants in group conflict are more likely to accept one another following structured communicative contact. One of the points made by Pettigrew is that there is a need to specify the processes of intergroup contact most associated with desired effects. In other words, there is a need for increased attention to various communication processes that facilitate contact effects. There are numerous intergroup contact communication processes and many associated with deliberation such as willingness to compromise, understanding the other's position, equality, fairness, publicity, empathy, willingness to compromise, and others. But *argument* is probably the most basic deliberative communication process (see Ellis & Maoz, 2002, 2007), as well as characteristic of any intergroup contact designed to confront differences. There is much to be said about argument in this context, but below I focus on two things, namely, the importance of argument in political polarization and how argument is effective during discussion and negotiation.

Argument and Political Polarization

Argument and deliberation are essential to democratic processes and the problem-solving that must characterize divided societies. More specifically, actual confrontive interaction is required at some point. In fact, contestatory discourse, where conversation crosses cultural, national, and political borders, should be considered a social value. Neisser (2006) uses the term "disagreement failure" to describe the situation where violence, human rights violations, and suffering are allowed to flourish because of the persistence of disagreements. Anytime issues are not brought to the surface and in-depth intergroup conversation has not taken place, then there is disagreement failure.

The process of avoiding disagreement failure involves contestatory engagement in all its forms. In other words, deliberative communication is both dialogic and strategic. This is especially true of intergroup contact between ethnopolitically divided groups. *Dialogue* is typically associated with ethical processes, orientation toward others and genuine concern for their interests, and personal authenticity. Dialogue makes personal and group transformations possible. Dialogue is often perceived as a normative ideal but difficult to achieve and even naïve by some. True deliberation must account for, and incorporate, the natural processes of strategy and manipulation attempts. *Strategy* is counter to dialogue in that it is concerned with calculated goal orientation. Strategy is oriented toward personal interests and instrumental effectiveness. These two are often conceived of as polar opposites and adherents of one approach typically ignore the other. But deliberation can grapple with both dialogic and strategic orientations to communication and, thereby, improve on purely dialogic approaches. In fact, the inclusion of strategic forms of communication is particularly important for deeply divided groups, because the goals of conflict resolution require both; that is, achieving the delicate balance of one's own goals in conjunction with the others' goals. With no orientation toward others there is no communication, but the self is also definitionally implicated in all communication. Hence, dialogue and strategy are interdependent and both part of the mutual understanding that can only be achieved through deliberation.

My goal is not to elaborate on strategy and communication (see White, 2008) as these are Habermasian issues and taken up elsewhere (Habermas, 1984). But deliberation involves dialogue and strategy in a truly interdependent manner, because of the communicative consequences if representatives of deeply divided groups choose one or the other. If both groups choose to be only strategic, then they negotiate to an acceptable exchange of advantages and disadvantages. This results in the typical standoff that may "contain," "manage," or "control" conflict but not solve it or transform it. On the other hand, if both parties are dialogic they may achieve social support and therapeutic change but make little progress toward problem resolution. If one party is strategic and the other is dialogic then a powerful asymmetry exists between the two usually to the dialogic party's disadvantage as well as ethical challenges. Yet, one of the problems with the dialogue-strategy distinctions is that the two are not so easily separable. Strategy assumes some aspects of intersubjectivity and mutuality, and dialogue can be instrumental.

Deliberative discourse is the medium that joins dialogue and strategy, and argument is the vehicle that produces reason and mutuality. The purpose of deliberative discourse between deeply divided parties is to reconstruct outcomes that are facilitative of change. And this always requires "communicative rationality" or justification and validity claims. Burkhalter, Gastil, and Kelshaw's (2002) treatment of deliberative discourse is rooted in issues of argument defined as information, careful weighing, ranges of solutions, and evaluative criteria. A goal of managing intergroup conflicts is to move from strategic communication that is bargaining in nature to a mode of communication that is more argument based. When groups first confront one another, they try to exert ideological or resource power over the other in order to limit options in favor of your own group. Communication is based on preferences and interests and outcomes might be compromised with no change in preferences or interests. But argument-based deliberation rests on validity claims subject to good reasoning. The outcomes should be reasoned consensus that plays a role in changing interests and preferences.

Reframing and Argument

Reframing is the essence of argument-based deliberation. Most any conflict resolution specialist will explain that reframing an issue is one of the most effective ways to begin the path to transformation and resolution. Thus, Israelis exert military control over Palestinians and invoke a "security" frame. Israelis "explain" and "justify" what they do as their right to protect themselves. The security frame provides a strong version of reality for Israelis and is a naturalized category of understanding that is so entrenched in the cultural mindset of Israelis that it underscores the intractability of the conflict. But if the issue is reframed into a "human rights" issue, then it is at least possible to alter the Israeli mindset. The "human rights" frame raises the level of generality so issues from both sides are considered. The issue is reframed and at least increases the chances that the communicative environment will move from adversarial in nature to reflective and integrative. Framing involves the organization of information; it is an effort to make sense. This sense-making includes relevant events and associated ideas. The frame channels meaning in a particular direction. Frames define problems and underlying social and political issues, including considerations relevant to the issue. Accordingly, a security frame would include existential threats and the permissibility of violence. A human rights frame challenges the security frame and directs attention to basic freedoms and humanitarian considerations for everyone.

Conclusion

Deliberation is the purposeful establishment of new meaning over time. Deliberation is political argumentation that evolves over time to form new associations between concepts. The idea of associations is important to frames. It relies on the premise that messages are constructed in such a way that some ideas are included—and others are not. Hence, a security frame strengthens the associations between violence, survival, and the right to protect oneself. These ideas are framed together and they help establish associations between concepts that can be either helpful or not.

Framing is part of the deliberation process because frames of understanding ("security" or "human rights") vie for discursive dominance; the frames compete for a version of reality. Changing, altering, or merging frames is the stuff of deliberation. Argument is essentially competing frames. And conflict occurs when one group questions or challenges the validity of another group's competing frame. The fact that frames in ethnopolitical conflict rely on identity positions underscores the importance of these issues in a deliberative process.

There remains no better way to resolve difficult conflicts than equal communicators using the deliberative process. True, the process is normative and difficult to achieve. Some consider deliberation so idealistic as to be naïve. But given the power of media and intergroup dynamics to distort messages, the cooperative search for solutions to problems becomes even more important. Argument, the basic tool of deliberation, clearly helps members of different conflicting groups acquire new information and introduces them to new ways of thinking about possible solutions. This stimulates a reformulation of interests. The conflict between ethnopolitical groups is typically intractable and intense. But by entering into the deliberative process perceptions and preferences change, and this is a step toward the identity change that is typically a prerequisite for ameliorating such intergroup conflicts. Future research should take on the demanding role of identifying the communication processes that will provide the relevant body of empirical evidence for understanding and controlling the deliberative process. Clearly, arguments and their frames should be part of this empirical agenda.

CHAPTER TWELVE

Terrorism, Identity, and Group Boundaries

PAUL D. MYERS & MICHAEL STOHL

Senator Barack Obama in his campaign for the White House promised to remove troops from harm's way in Iraq if he became president and to redirect America's fight against terrorism to those who had actually attacked the United States on September 11, 2001. As soon as he took office, he declared he would increase troop levels in Afghanistan to counter threats to the homeland. And shortly thereafter senior officials in the United States, while continuing to identify terrorism as a major threat to the security of the United States, ceased using the phrase "War on Terror." In November 2008, terrorists in Mumbai, India, killed more than 150 people in the Taj Mahal Palace and Tower hotel, and, in March 2009, two terrorist attacks left soldiers and a police officer dead in Northern Ireland. As these incidents reveal, terrorism remains high on the global agenda.

This chapter considers the intersection of terrorism and intergroup communication. Of note is that few have examined terrorism processes through the lens of intergroup relations and social identity. One exception, Sparks (2005), describes how social identities were created through the September 11 terrorism experience and how mass communications representations of terrorism impacted these identities. Her analysis focuses on the role of the audience as victim and how identities helped victims to cope with the aftermath of the attack. In this chapter, we will consider how the acts of terrorism impact relations within and among groups and consider not only how these processes affect the victims and audience of terrorism but the perpetrators as well.

We begin by examining the concept of terrorism and then proceed to consider how "political identities" are defined, how salient these identities are in particular contexts and conditions to ingroups and outgroups (and often how interdependent these identities are), and how these vary globally and historically across political conflicts. We then examine the impact of terrorist acts on political polarizations, what it communicates to ingroups and outgroups, and how this shapes conflict processes such as attracting supporters to the cause, alienating others, and altering the roles of moderates. We explore how language mobilizes supporters and creates identities and how leaders exploit identities, and discuss potential dampening devices as demonstrated through successful post-conflict situations.

Terrorism and Identity

Terrorism is communicatively constituted violence and is a tactic that is often employed in the context of identity-based and/ or defined conflicts. It is important to understand what we mean by that statement. First we must distinguish terrorism from violence. For an act of violence to be considered *terrorism* it has to communicate a message. Schmid (2009) has catalogued more than 200 definitions of terrorism used in the social science and policy literature. Many of the definitional conflicts are centered around the "legitimacy" of the perpetrator (state or insurgent; legal or illegal) and the standing of the victim (combatant or non-combatant, innocent or culpable). However, when one sorts through the definitions, we find that the key words which distinguish terrorism from violence in almost all the definitions, despite their variety, are *purposeful, violence, fear, victim,* and *audience.* Incorporating these elements, we may define terrorism as "The purposeful act or threat of the act of violence to create fear and/or compliant behavior in a victim and/or audience of the act or threat." It is intentional that this definition does not distinguish among perpetrators who are ingroups and outgroups, state or non-state actors, or legitimate or illegitimate wielders of violence. Rather, it focuses upon the act or threat of the act of violence and the victim and audience to whom it is directed (see Stohl, 2006, for further discussion of the implications). It is crucial to understand that the victims of the violent act must be distinguished from the multiple targets of the act, i.e., the audience(s) of that violence.

When we examine terrorism we are cognizant that the actions are *denoted by three key elements* which correspond quite directly to those enumerated by Walter (1969). *First,* threatened or perpetrated violence is directed at some victim. *Second,* the violent actor intends for violence to induce terror in witnesses (mediated or unmediated) who are generally distinct from the victim—the victim is instrumental. *Third,* the violent actor (an insurgent group or the state itself) intends or expects that the terrorized witnesses will effectuate a desired outcome, either directly (in which case the witness is the target) or indirectly (in which case the witnesses and the target are distinct—the witness is also instrumental). The process of political terrorism may thus be characterized as consisting of three component parts: the act or threat of violence, the emotional reaction to such an act or threat, and the social effects resultant from the acts and reaction.

While the specific initiation of the process of terrorism arises for a number of quite different specific purposes, which are dependent upon the position of both the agents and the targets of terror, what distinguishes terrorism from other acts of violence are its instrumentality and its targets. First, it distinguishes direct from indirect victims. Second, it is crucial to understand, whether we are examining insurgent or state terrorism, how the multiple audiences of the terror react is perhaps more important than the act itself and the instrumental victims who are direct casualties. Clearly then, terrorists are primarily interested in communicating with the audience—not the victims.

The act or threat of violence is but the first step. The victims are instrumental. This may be clearly seen in the French misunderstanding of the Algerian situation of the 1950s.

> The French thought that when the FLN [National Liberation Front of Algeria] planted a bomb in a public bus, it was in order to blow up the bus; whereas the real FLN purpose in planting the bomb was not to blow up the bus, but to lure authorities into reacting by arresting all the non-Europeans in the area as suspects. (Fromkin, 1975, p. 694)

The victims of the terrorist act were the relatively limited number of passengers and bystanders in the area of the bombing. The targets of the bombing were many and varied. The French *colons* (the French and other Europeans who had migrated to Algeria since 1948 when France declared Algeria a part of France) in Algeria perceived the attack as aimed at them, became fearful, and demanded greater protection and an increase in security measures. Many also began to question the ability of the French government to provide that most basic of governmental services—security. Some formed vigilante groups to engage in activity that they perceived the government as unwilling to perform or incapable of performing. A campaign of terror aimed at the native Algerian population was then initiated. These actions, of course, only further undermined the legitimacy and authority of the French regime. The Algerian population, having been singled out by the government as an outgroup distinct from the "normal" French and having become the object of terror by the *colons*, began to question the legitimacy of the regime and became more receptive to the message of the FLN. In addition to these two primary targets, the population and government of Metropolitan France began to see the Algerian colony and the *colons* not only as an economic, military, and political liability, but as "not French." Debates then ensued as to why Frenchmen ought to be potential victims because of these *colons* in Algeria, and a way out of the dilemma was sought. The initial reaction of increased force, while providing a temporary halt to the Algerian revolution, in the end created severe strains within Metropolitan France, including the overthrow of the Fourth Republic, and led to the granting of independence to Algeria. While it is impossible to know if Algerian independence, given the global movement against colonialism that began after World War II may not have eventuated with far fewer deaths in a few years time through non-violent political challenges, it is reasonable to conclude, based on the historical record, that as a result of the campaign of terror and the reaction of the French government and the *colons*, that victory came to the FLN more from the divisions they caused within the French polity than from military actions. As Pontecorvo's 1965 film *Battle of Algiers* so vividly captures, while the French defeated the FLN militarily within Algiers, their misunderstanding of the impact of these military actions on both the Algerians and the people of France resulted in the alienation of both the ingroup and the outgroup and the collapse of support for the French polity.

Boundaries and Identity

As this example illustrates, in the context of political conflict that leads to terrorism, the most important ingroup/outgroup division centers around the key political idea of the nation and the key political entity of the state. This is because it is the political organization within which the political life of the nation and its authority to distribute benefits is located. In the oft-cited work of Anderson (1983), he suggests that the nation "is imagined because the members of even the smallest nation will never know most of their fellow-members, meet them, or even hear of them, yet in the minds of each lives the image of their communion" (p. 6). These "nations" share a commonly held language, culture, history, and geographic location and, therefore, a sense of who is a "member" of the nation—and who is not. Thus, in the case of the terrorism of the FLN, the FLN employed their violence to both rally their community to the "imagined" community of pre-colonial Algeria (an Algerian state had never existed, the territory previously had been a province of the Ottoman Empire and before that an area of much instability and struggles for power amongst rival kingdoms) and to distinguish that community from the French State and the French colonials. The misguided French counter-terrorism reaction, which worked to separate the communities for security reasons, helped to reinforce the FLN message establishing the boundaries between the groups. The vigilante actions of the *colons* served to create a boundary between France, the state inhabited by

Frenchmen, and the French colony inhabited by Algerians and colonials who, by their actions, made themselves in the eyes of the French, not French. As we shall see, the issue of managing and attempting to resolve terrorist threats based on these imagined communities often creates divisions within ingroups.

Throughout history, political ideologies have been a major contributor to acts of terrorism. Political terrorism in the contemporary period most often arises within states when groups challenge the inclusion or exclusion within the nation of particular ethnic groups or ethno-religious communities (themselves most often the foundation of the idea of a "nation"); see Chapters 2 & 7. On other occasions, conflicts arise due to the unequal benefits or costs of the nations (groups) within the society, what may be referred to as objective or realistic conflicts. These realistic conflicts involve disputes over power, wealth or territory, whereas symbolic or "subjective" conflicts include attempts to establish positively valued distinctiveness.

We should also note that while many consider that terrorism is primarily a weapon of the weak, it is most often and most destructively employed by the strong—the most powerful of which is quite often the state itself. States have employed terrorism, such as the "Regime of Terror" instituted by Robespierre and his colleagues following the French Revolution, from which the term terrorism entered the English language, to solidify their control over territory, to terrorize potential opponents, to mobilize the peasants to transform the agricultural sector into collective farms as in "the Great Terror" in the Soviet Union of the 1930s or to intimidate the ruling party hierarchy and eliminate the threat of capitalism to the society in the Cultural Revolution in China in the 1960s (see Stohl, 2006, for further analysis and additional examples). Political terrorism also occurs across state boundaries when groups target groups (nations) that are considered to be supporting the "other" in the context of their struggle. It is also the case that terrorism has been employed by those who seek not only to challenge existing rule within states, but also those who seek to expand existing political boundaries. Some of these acts hark back to either real or imagined communities that precede the establishment of nations, such as Christendom, the Holy Roman Empire or the Muslim Caliphate.

In stable nations with clear political boundaries, nations are contained within a recognized state that allocates resources and is charged with the maintenance and security of the "nation-state's" boundaries. The occurrence of terrorism may threaten, and, or be perceived to threaten the imagined community of the nation-state. It may also serve to reinforce ingroup/outgroup conceptions. Thus, in the wake of 9/11, public officials and the Ad Council, a public service organization, created an advertising campaign called "I am an American" due to concerns that some Americans might react by distinguishing between "real Americans" (presumably Caucasian, Christian Anglo Saxons) and "other Americans" (presumably people of color, non-Christians, etc). These 60-second broadcasts featured dozens of

Americans of all ages, colors, religious communities and classes who proudly proclaimed "I am an American." The advertisement concluded with the phrase *E pluribus Unum* (Out of many one), one of the core and recognizable political myths of the American nation.

In similar fashion, on September 13, 2001, the French newspaper *Le Monde* declared, "*Nous sommes tous Américains! Nous sommes tous New-Yorkais* . . . (We are all Americans, We are all New Yorkers)" and continued "How can we not feel, in fact, as in the gravest moments of our history, deeply attached to this people and this country, the USA, we are so close and to whom we owe the freedom, and therefore our solidarity." In short, the boundaries between the attackers and the audience that identified with the United States were made distinct and a clear division between the ingroup and outgroup established in the minds of that audience sympathetic to the U.S. victims.

However, in addition to the American audience and those who supported the U.S. government whom Osama bin Laden later identified as the enemy, the message of fear was also directed to other audiences who were energized by the audacious and horrific violence, death and destruction of that day. The attacks became a message of violence to the ingroup within whom the terrorists sought to create a sense of belonging and support, a message that said we will attack our/your enemies on your behalf and promise future retribution.

The creation of political identities and the establishment of group boundaries may serve both positive and negative forces. Simply put, in the political context, such identities are positive when they support the establishment and maintenance of the political state and potentially negative when they challenge (particularly with violence and terrorism) the existing boundaries of inclusion and exclusion. Numerous national, international and scholarly reports in the past decade have cited the claims for recognition and equality by diverse groups as amongst the biggest factors that threaten international stability. This recognition and sense of legitimacy include that of ethnicity, religion, and language.

In the current decade, much of the focus on terrorism and identity has been concerned with that of the Muslim community (see Chapter 7). One common denominator that runs through the recent movement of Muslims from Western nations to fight in Chechnya, Iraq, Afghanistan, Palestine, or Kashmir has been a sense of shared identity with Muslims who are seen as suffering from domination. Many younger Muslims in Europe, who are second or third generation immigrants, struggle to find their own identity between that of their host nation and that of their Muslim heritage. It is often the case that that these individuals become radicalized not from directly experiencing domination or desperation but more from the need for a sense of identity. They move through a process whereby their identity becomes less connected with their old identity and more with like-minded individuals who share a similar ideology.

In this context, Alimi (2006) argues that political groups can become radicalized by processes *within*, *outside*, and *between* the groups involved. Some individuals find that the goals and agenda of the political ingroup do not match those of their own and go on to create a new group (e.g., Arafat's Tanzim, which emerged out of Hamas). Others find that threats or opportunities arise from outside the group to enable its formation. New groups also emerge from friction between the ingroup and an outgroup (e.g., Tanzim's limited violence against Israel led to the shooting of troops and then escalated to include attacks on settlers). It is also important to note that some Muslims who travelled to countries such as Afghanistan decided not to fight after finding members of the Ummah (the Muslim "community of believers") warring amongst themselves, thus challenging the existence of this new shared identity that they sought. These young Muslims then returned to their host nations and challenged others' decisions to offer their assistance to insurgencies because they would not find the ingroup identity for which they were searching.

Terrorism, Language, and Identity

For Muslims who have struggled to assimilate into European host cultures, classical Qur'anic Arabic has become central to their sense of unity and a distinct identity (Marranci, 2007). This use of language has transcended ethnic and national affiliations to empower Muslim religious identity as a form of resistance against assimilation into the existing, often secular, state. Ambiguity of texts provides opportunity for both political and religious leaders and activists to assert religious-based justifications for not only the ingroup identity but also "acceptable" behaviors towards non-believers and apostates. In the case of Muslim extremists, the Jihad as described in the Koran is interpreted as allowing violence in order to defend and preserve Allah's will and particular religiously inspired political goals such as the overthrow of regimes, the elimination of the state of Israel, the expulsion of non-believers (and the U.S. military presence) from Saudi Arabia amongst others (see Esposito, 2002).

The use of language can be a powerful predictor of whether a group will address grievances with political action or whether they will turn to violence. In documents seized from groups that eventually turned to violence, Smith (2008) found that the language is generally higher in ingroup affiliation imagery and focuses on the desire to maintain friendly relations within the group. Thus, a Hamas leader states "It is our natural right to defend our kinsmen, our people, our citizens" (p. 70). In contrast, language is typically low in external affiliation imagery that stresses the desire to establish friendly relations with others as illustrated by the appeal of the

Palestinian Central Council, "The Council . . . addresses its appeal to all peace loving nations. . . ." (p. 70). This mentality as evidenced in the group's writing leads to greater cohesiveness and tight-knit loyal group ingroups that eventually turn to violence. In contrast, groups who remain focused on political solutions use language that is more inclusive of outgroup members.

This contrast in language use is especially evident when groups eventually shun the non-violent political process. In general, non-violent groups who are pursuing peaceful processes tend to blur the line between the ingroup and outgroup in an attempt to bring as many supporters into their group as possible, even outgroup members (Smith, 2004). In contrast, violent groups are more likely to show higher levels of ingroup affiliation and show distinct boundaries of the ingroup in order to show distinction from outgroup members.

Further support for action against others can be garnered through the choice of language to dehumanize others and promote ingroup ideals in order to protect the group's image. The "other" is seen as evil, alien, and inhuman. In contrast, the ingroup is portrayed as heroes, innocents, and united in their struggle. The ingroup is also portrayed as having the support of the divine, such that Americans fighting in Iraq according to President George W. Bush have the blessings of God while Al Qaeda explains they fight with the will of Allah. Furthermore, the ingroup is also often reminded of historical victimization as a means of reducing collective guilt, such as Israelis being reminded of the Holocaust (Wohl & Branscombe, 2008). Most importantly, the dehumanization of the outgroup reduces inhibitions to violence against them (for further implications with respect to state terrorism, see Stohl, 2006).

In the case of nations who are fighting violent groups, it is usual to find loyalty-inducing dichotomies of "us-versus-them" and "my-country-right-or-wrong." Recently, this language was evoked by President Bush in the declared "War on Terror." During the 1990s, similar phrases were evident both while and after Kosovo Albanian Muslims waged war against the Serbian State in a struggle for independence. After the 2006 referendum that declared Kosovo as a part of Serbia, nationalist papers called on past religious discourses and described Kosovo attackers as "local perpetrators" instead of insurgents or guerrillas to demonstrate a unified nationalist identity (Erjavec & Volcic, 2007).

Terrorist groups often frame their actions (or receive support by frames provided by journalists and even scholars) to justify their behavior. In Chechnya, fighters argued they were engaged in a war of freedom, not terrorism. During the *intifada*, the Palestinians successfully framed the conflict as one of *injustice and defiance* which dominated the Israeli preferred frame of *law and order* among international journalists outside the United States (Wolfsfeld, 1997). Broadcasting by supportive media outlets may further support a group's acts of violence (see Chapter 16).

Al-Manar, Hizbullah's television station, has justified the killing of victims as being the will of Allah, removing any responsibility from the assailants by explaining that if Allah had wanted the victims to live, they would have been prevented from finding themselves in that situation (Schbley, 2004).

Terrorism and Boundary Maintenance

As indicated above, the main actors involved in the conflict will include the state and a range of actors that vary in their depth of support for the terrorist group. This assistance can range from the legal (e.g., peaceful protests) to the gray (e.g., providing material support) to the illegal (e.g., actual violent acts). While not all this support is needed for violent acts to be carried out, an organization will not be able to survive for an extended period of time without the full range of help. Some of the most important supporters for a group may be those who may not wish to be directly involved in any violence or terrorism but who identify with the ingroup and support their strategic goals. These moderates include those who disagree with violent means but are still sympathetic to the cause and vote for political wings associated with the group (such as the IRA's Sinn Fein or ETA's Batasuna, the Basque nationalist political organization) or those who help with materials such as the provision of safe-houses or funding.

Frequently, terrorist groups or insurgents first seek support from within the ingroup community through actions considered legal, such as charitable contributions. Over time, the community support may move to other forms of assistance such as providing safe havens and the passing of messages. For those who continue to eschew violence, philanthropy can be a demonstration of passive support. While moderates, who may shun violence, are beneficial to the terrorist group, they also come with costs. Terrorist groups may be constrained from conducting more extreme forms of violence or risk losing their support.

Groups who are genuinely seeking to address political, economic, or social grievances, however, have to weigh the level of support they receive from a community for their actions, such as vigilantism, with political concessions they are willing to make in any peace process. In the case of Northern Ireland, the IRA had to "balance" the level of violence they employed and their need for support. The group had to maintain the support of those who were not only willing to use extreme violence to attack British and Protestant outgroups and were angered when such means were not employed but also moderate Northern Ireland republicans and non-violent Republic of Ireland supporters. These latter supporters of the legal political party Sinn Fein (officially not linked to the IRA) would not support excessive violence (or anything beyond the threat of violence).

Whereas terrorist groups in the first half of the 20th century were forced to rely primarily on local communities in the geographic spaces within which they were operating, globalization, and its concomitant ease of travel, transfer of money, materiel, moral, and manpower support from external sources including individuals, charities, or even nation-states, enables groups to garner support and operate outside the immediate geographical area in which they identify.

While acts of terrorism are typically perpetrated with the intent of terrorizing a third party, groups also use terrorism and its threat as a means of cementing support within the ingroup and to remove both ingroup dissenters and non-conformist elements. This applies to the state apparatus itself or the terrorist group and the relationship between the group and the community it purports to represent. This was demonstrated by both Stalin's purges within the ruling communist party in the Soviet Union in the 1930s and Mao's purges within the Chinese communist party in the 1950s and 60s to insure the conformity of the members of the ruling regime. During the period of what was often referred to as "The Troubles" in Northern Ireland (1969–1998), the IRA's success depended largely on support from disadvantaged working-class republicans. To maintain this support, the IRA not only attacked symbols of British occupation, such as soldiers and police, but they also protected republican communities from "anti-social" elements. These groups, as defined by the IRA, consisted of two groups, criminals and "disloyal Catholics," some of whom may have been thought to have informed on the IRA to the British. As part of this process, criminals who were not sanctioned by the group to carry out illegal activities could expect a beating or have their knee-caps shot or drilled through. Those seen as dissenters and non-conformists could expect similar punishments or even death as the group maintained a homogeneous and loyal support base. The IRA also shaved the heads of Catholic women who dated Protestant men or British soldiers to identify them as crossing the boundary out of the ingroup.

Responding to Terrorism: Managing Ingroup/Outgroup Boundaries

As has been repeatedly demonstrated with conflicts in Afghanistan, and more recently with the war in Iraq, a nation-state's overwhelming military power does not necessarily ensure an easy and decisive victory. Instead, what has proved effective has been the increased permeability of group boundaries such that local communities, who traditionally may have been antagonistic, are brought into a more inclusive "ingroup." This not only brings an increased sense of legitimacy to the ingroup, but it also starves support to those seen as the outgroup. In Peru, the state was able to defeat the Sendero Luminoso (SL, or Shining Path) and the Movimiento

Revolucionario Tupac Amaru (MRTA) through the establishment and cooperation of rural *rondas campesinas* (self-defense committees).

Similar results were achieved in Iraq, where the insurgency relied on its perceived legitimacy by Sunni Arabs. To increase the legitimacy of the Shia dominated Iraqi regime and its U.S. military backing, the U.S. fostered what were designated as "Sunni Awakening" groups. These organizations, composed of members of local populations, were supported with weapons and training to not only protect their own communities but also to fight Al Qaeda in Iraq (a Sunni group). The result was to align the U.S. military with the ingroup while challenging the legitimacy of Al Qaeda in Iraq. The terrorist group's legitimacy was further undermined by televised confessions of former members that described their brutality and targeting of other Muslims. A similar, albeit less successful, strategy had been attempted after the Oslo agreement to reduce hostilities in the Palestinian-Israeli conflict. In this instance, groups were brought together with the goal of sharing a sense of togetherness and empathy (Schulz, 2000). After the agreement, joint security patrols and economic cooperation were promoted.

To ensure that as many people can come to the negotiating table as possible, those directly involved in the conflict need to refrain from classifying the actors in simplified dichotomous terms as either legitimate or illegitimate, ingroup or outgroup (see Chapter 11). Such terminology was used by President George W. Bush when he asserted "you're either with us or against us." With such simplified categorizations, the outgroup is perceived as homogenous and all of its members are automatically labeled as terrorists. Rather, it is necessary to acknowledge a range of opposition, in short, outgroup heterogeneity, to avoid combining actors who nonviolently pursue group goals together with those that employ violence and terror. We may argue further that a distinction must be made between radicals and extremists. While an individual's life may have been radically changed through a belief (e.g., a life changed through a spiritual conversion), this does not mean they will either support or employ violence and terror. Thus, by acknowledging a multiplicity of identities, an appropriate response can be initiated.

Traditional efforts to reduce the violence of intergroup conflict and encourage acceptance of diversity and pluralism rely on developing shared visions of the future for both ingroups and outgroups. Hargie, Dickson, Mallett, and Stringer (2008) found increased attraction of the outgroup and weakening of ingroup identification could be achieved between Protestant and Catholic children in Northern Ireland with increased intergroup contact arising from desegregating schools and participation in after-school activities (see also, Chapters 6, 10, 15, & 17). Recognizing the rise of extremist Muslim ideologies in Europe after 9/11, as demonstrated by attacks in the UK and Spain, other European nations have also attempted to create a shared vision of their societies. This has been based on input from within the

Muslim community from civic and religious leaders, community organizations, the media, and citizens. Engagement with moderates in this instance has included the support of moderate Imams and leaders, recognition of Islamic organizations (and the delegitimization of those considered extremist), increased intergroup contact between leaders and organizations, assistance to mosques and Islamic schools, the sponsorship of domestic travelling road-shows promoting moderate ideology, and international cultural exchanges (O'Duffy, 2008).

Though there have been exceptions, such as the publication of controversial cartoons of Mohammed in the Danish press that were later reprinted in much of Europe, in general and particularly since the reactions to the publication of the Danish cartoons, the media has promoted a more inclusive view. The press has presented a greater number of positive stories about Muslims within Europe in an attempt to "humanize the Muslim community." In these stories similarities between Muslims and the society they live in, such as their shared values of getting a good education, hard work, respect for elders, and even their love of sports are highlighted with the intent of reducing the perceived social distance between groups.

Efforts have also been made from within communities who consider themselves part of the ingroup to prevent segments of their group feeling disfranchised. In the battle against extremist Islamic ideology, initiatives have also been launched from within U.S. Muslim communities. Even though Muslims in the U.S. do not feel as isolated from the predominant culture as much as they do in Europe, some still see their role as involving conflict prevention and resolution (Huda, 2006). Some groups have taken a proactive stance by positioning themselves within the political infrastructure of the country. Others have promoted anti-extremist ideology through grass-roots campaigns. Similar strategies have been recommended for Southeast Asia, where delegitimization is needed of Muslim radical ideology that promotes violence against an "American-Zionist crusade" (Ramakrishna, 2005). In addition to some of the strategies described previously, the teaching of progressive mullahs and intellectuals in the media, mosques, and universities is encouraged.

Conclusion

In this chapter, we have explored how terrorism affects the dynamics of intergroup relations through its "clarification" of boundaries between and among groups, and have provided examples of intergroup conflict such as the Algerian War of Independence, the Northern Ireland "Troubles," the attack by Al Qaeda on September 11 and the subsequent wars in Iraq and Afghanistan, and the Israeli-Palestinian conflict. Very few of our examples have been drawn from research by scholars of intergroup communication.

However, we believe that there are many insights that future research built upon these current explorations, which draw upon the theoretical contributions of intergroup communication, could further illuminate. Terrorism through its extreme nature forces individuals to confront group identities and to determine their salience in deciding if actions are acceptable or unacceptable in the context of political struggle. Terrorism, because of its violence and instrumental victims, often polarizes political struggles and communities, and as we have seen creates a set of conflicting messages to ingroups and outgroups who are the audiences of the violent acts. The language employed by groups to describe themselves and their enemies as well as mobilize supporters is another instrument for polarization and the establishment of ingroup and outgroup identity. These polar identities, hardened by violence and victimization, become the target of conflict management struggles. Not only do leaders have to end the violence, but they have to create new shared visions and potentially new shared identities which transcend the existing ingroup and outgroups to moderate the conflict and isolate those who would endanger the future by continued violence. This shared language of hope and future that transcends the violence of past cleavages is almost always necessary if long-term success rather than a brief cease-fire is to be achieved (see Chapter 11). As many of these examples have shown, the research community has begun to uncover the dynamic processes that underlie the cleavages between ingroups and outgroups and how terrorism serves to exacerbate these cleavages.

Yet, much more needs to be done to better understand both the differential power and scope of the message of terrorism actions as well as the accompanying verbal messages and to comprehend how they are transmitted and received. But even more work needs to be undertaken which examines the form, content and transmission of messages which transcend these cleavages and speak to both ingroups and outgroups and which can overcome the legacies of violence amongst communities so aptly expressed by Israeli prime Minister Golda Meir at a press conference in London in 1969: "When peace comes we will perhaps in time be able to forgive the Arabs for killing our sons, but it will be harder for us to forgive them for having forced us to kill their sons" (Syrkin, 1973, p. 242).

CHAPTER THIRTEEN

Stigma and Intergroup Communication

LANCE S. RINTAMAKI & DALE E. BRASHERS

In societies across the world, people are stigmatized for a variety of reasons (e.g., age, race or ethnicity, gender, sexual identity, religion, physical or mental illnesses, and so on). The study of stigmatized identities provides some of the most dramatic and compelling work in the field of intergroup communication, as it examines how and why people are devalued, shunned, and persecuted. Throughout the HIV epidemic, for example, people have experienced stigma—partly because the disease has been associated with homosexuality, drug use, and contagious and life-threatening illness. Ryan White was 12 years old when he was diagnosed with the illness. He experienced stigma when parents of other children acted to prevent him from attending his elementary school, from which he eventually was expelled. This became a very big controversy, and Ryan quickly became a public face of the illness.

Although considerable effort has gone into understanding what motivates stigma, why it is perpetuated, and how it is expressed, far less research has considered how those who are stigmatized manage their social interactions. The research that does exist suggests that stigmatized people are not passive victims of their social circumstances; rather, they are mindful and strategic during interactions with others. Stigmatized people evaluate others with a critical eye, always watchful for potential enemies or valued allies. They actively work to shield and protect themselves, and are often found striving to educate others and disarm the stigma afflicting their group. In Ryan White's case, he had support from celebrities (including singers Elton John and Michael Jackson, and talk show host Phil Donahue) that brought national attention to the challenges he faced. He became a spokesperson for those stigmatized by the illness, and his name became associated with the federal government's funding for health care for individuals living with HIV (The Ryan White Care Act) after he died in 1990.

In this chapter, we draw from a range of disciplines, including intergroup communication, that converge on the study of stigma and social interaction to present the extant research on these phenomena and to propose an organizational system for conceptualizing the distinct components and processes of stigma communication. In doing so, we also underscore just how well suited those working in communication are to advancing the study of social stigma and conducting research that has the potential to improve the lives of those suffering from its deleterious effects. We begin by defining stigma, and continue to explore four foundations for understanding interactions between those who stigmatize and those who are stigmatized (i.e., the cognitive processes and the behavioral performance of stigmatizers and the stigmatized). Finally, we provide some insight on promising directions for future research on stigma and communication.

Defining Stigma

It is useful first to establish a working definition for stigma, to better understand its implications for communication. Research on stigma has a long history in many academic fields, but the foundations of most modern research in the area trace back to sociologist Irving Goffman's (1963) seminal book. By compiling his observations and musing about prejudice, discrimination, and identity politics, Goffman conceptualized stigma as the possession of a "deeply discrediting" trait or attribute that spoils a person's positive identity within his or her social community (p. 3). From his perspective, the designated trait promotes ridicule, ostracism, and social distancing towards those who possess it. Since this watershed event in the study of stigma, researchers have critiqued, tested, and further developed Goffman's ideas about stigma and what it entails. It is a credit to Goffman's insight, however, that his definition is still the touchstone that most contemporary stigma researchers reference as the foundation for their own work.

It is worth noting that current stigma researchers often extend Goffman's original definition or underscore specific, underlying assumptions of this definition in three specific ways. First, contemporary stigma research focuses not just on the cognitive responses people have towards those who possess a stigmatizing trait but also on the need for social consensus on the negative value of that trait (Crocker, Major, & Steele, 1998). From this perspective, stigma is not necessarily about the stigmatized attribute or the person who bears it; rather, it stems from the social environment and the convergence of context and circumstances that lead people to devalue both a particular characteristic and those who possess it. Because stigma is dependent on social consensus, something that may have once been the norm may now be stigmatized and vice versa, such as women wearing pants or men wearing earrings. At different points in time and across different cultures, each may have been considered normal behavior or seen as breaking social norms. When social norms pertaining to appropriate role performance are violated, such behaviors are likely to be seen as deviant traits and stigmatized accordingly.

Second, multiple stigma researchers have noted that people need not necessarily possess the negatively valued trait to be stigmatized for it (e.g., Herek, 1999). Instead, they need only be perceived to possess it. For instance, if people think you are gay, you may experience homophobic stigma and discrimination, *regardless* of your sexual orientation.

Third, stigma researchers now explicitly define stigma as affecting not only the individual bearer of a negative trait but also the individuals and groups with which he or she is associated (e.g., Abrams & Giles, 2004). Although Goffman (1963) referred to this kind of stigma-by-association as courtesy stigma, he kept it conceptually separate from his original definition. As an illustration of this aspect of stigma, a nurse practitioner who coordinates an HIV clinic once shared with the authors an event during which she was dropping off her daughter at a junior Girl Scouts meeting. At these meetings, the kids regularly bring snacks to share with the group. As her daughter scampered off to join her friends, the nurse practitioner overheard another parent tell other children not to accept any snacks from the nurse practitioner's daughter. The reason the parent gave for this prohibition was "'because her mom works with *those people.*" Although stigma directed at people with HIV is not uncommon, this event was not targeting a person living with the disease or even a person who provides health care for people with the disease. Instead, it was directed at the *child* of a health care provider who works with people living with the disease.

Each of these additions to Goffman's original definition has use for refining our understanding of stigma's many nuances. By integrating these ideas, we define stigma in this chapter as negative attitudes held about individuals who are perceived to possess a trait deemed negative by the community at large as well as those with whom these individuals are associated. We use this definition as the foundation for understanding how stigmatizers and the stigmatized think as well as how their thoughts translate into action. Specifically, we propose a four-tiered system for understanding the role of stigma in social interaction, which involves (a) the cognitive processes of stigmatizers, (b) the behavioral performance of stigmatizers, (c) the cognitive processes of the stigmatized, and (d) the behavioral performance of the stigmatized.

Cognitive Processes of Stigmatizers

To understand stigma's role in shaping social interaction, it is important to further dissect the cognitive processes that precede behavior. In the mind of a stigmatizer, far more than negative attitudes are at work. Indeed, there appear to be multiple innate and unavoidable cognitive processes in the mind of a stigmatizer that, once understood, help illuminate the purpose and strategies inherent to behaviors directed towards stigmatized individuals.

Categorization

At the core of these cognitive processes lies the basic human need to organize and categorize ourselves and those around us. Much of the self-concept is derived from social group memberships (e.g., Tajfel & Turner, 1986). In essence, people incorporate the values, norms, and behaviors of the groups to which they see themselves belonging. People also place considerable importance on these group memberships, as they help to define who they are, particularly when they compare themselves to others. For these reasons, people identify not only to which social groups they belong but also to which social groups others belong. This process also helps define the individual as similar to or different from (or better or worse than) members of other groups. As a result, whether they are aware of it or not, people are perpetually engaged in this categorization process, which includes determining who belongs to valued and devalued (stigmatized) groups.

Group Protection

One reason people perpetually categorize themselves and others may, in fact, be a hard-wired survival mechanism. As social beings, humans evolved to survive through communal living (Cottrell & Neuberg, 2005). Being able to identify and positively interact with members of one's own group grants access to the benefits and resources of that group. Being able to identify and protect against threats to one's group similarly is essential to survival (Neuberg, Smith, & Asher, 2000). Such threats can be categorized as being instrumental (physical) and symbolic (social) in nature (e.g., LePoire, 1994). Instrumental threats hold the potential to undermine the physical health and well-being of a group or individual. For instance, the ways in which people stigmatizes people living with contagious or dangerous diseases, such as tuberculosis or HIV, share similarities with how people stigmatize ax murders. Each is seen as a threat that jeopardizes the physical safety and well-being of society and the individuals who comprise it. Symbolic threats, on the other hand, potentially undermine the moral foundations or cultural underpinnings of a group or individual. For this reason, those who pose symbolic threats to a group, such as those who challenge or reject the group's mores and ideals, may face no less severe treatment than those who pose physical threats (see Chapter 14). For instance, those who question a religion's tenets, a community's laws, or society's norms threaten the cultural cohesion that helps define these groups. When such cultural bonds are corrupted, the group is weakened or may even cease to be. As such, categorization and social stigma may have evolved as survival strategies through which groups protect themselves by identifying and marshalling defenses against those who might threaten physical or social contamination of groups and their members (Brown, Macintyre, & Trujillo, 2003).

Master Status

Given the evolutionary importance of categorization and stigmatization (see Chapter 22), perhaps it should be unsurprising how salient stigmatized traits can become once an individual is identified as possessing them. In fact, once people categorize an individual as possessing a stigmatized trait, people may view this trait as the most defining feature of that individual (Link & Phelan, 2001). When this *identity engulfment* (Goffman, 1963) or *master status* (e.g., Frable, Blackstone, & Scherbaum, 1990) occurs, others will filter and interpret all of the individual's behaviors through a stigmatizing lens and will consider that individual as a stigmatized person first and foremost, regardless of other qualities that he or she may possess. For instance, a student in one of the author's classes recently described developing a variety of negative views about Muslims, largely as a product of where she grew up and the predominate disdain she learned from her family, friends, religious leaders, and members of the larger community. As fate would have it, when she came to college, her first roommate was a Muslim woman. Despite her roommate's friendliness, eagerness to connect with her on a personal level, and excellent habits at keeping their room tidy, the student described always prefacing in her mind the word "Muslim" when interacting with her roommate and making sense of her roommate's actions. In her mind, she saw her roommate as "Muslim" first and foremost, no matter what her roommate was doing or saying. Within two weeks from the start of school, the student feigned a personal excuse and managed to get reassigned to another residence hall with a different (non-Muslim) roommate.

Behavioral Performance of Stigmatizers

How do these cognitive processes affect how a person performs during social interaction? Although possessing stigmatizing attitudes does not necessitate acting on them, people do tend to express their attitudes in some way during social interactions, often resulting in either avoidance or discriminatory behavior. The expression of stigma can serve to bolster self-esteem, which helps explain the forms such expressions often take (e.g., mocking or putting down others as being less valuable or inferior to one's self). In addition, however, the expression of stigma often serves the social function of group protection and perpetuation described in the preceding section, which may also explain the forms stigma takes.

Social Sanctions

Sometimes the expression of stigma serves to police a group's cultural boundaries (e.g., Lewis & Sherman, 2003). For instance, we may tease or ridicule our friends when they act foolishly, reflect badly on us, or do things the group finds unacceptable; religious leaders chastise those who fail to uphold their faith's moral teachings; communities punish those who break laws. It is through these social sanctions against those who violate the group's rules and norms that group members may hope to reform stigmatized individuals and bring them back into the fold. Alternatively, they may also use such sanctions as a means of making an example for other members of the group and demonstrating the consequences of stepping out of line. If, however, stigmatized individuals are perceived as unredeemable (e.g., possessing unchangeable traits, such as belonging to a denigrated racial group or suffering from an incurable, communicable disease), they may be ostracized, isolated, or even killed as a means of expelling them from the larger community (e.g., Cottrell & Neuberg, 2005).

The ways in which these social sanctions are delivered can be conceptualized as occurring at both micro- and macro-social levels. At the micro-social level, people often express stigma through their interpersonal behavior. Examples of such interpersonal expressions include people refusing to touch or shake hands with the stigmatized, staring them down, and openly ridiculing or mocking them for their stigmatized trait. If the stigmatized trait is not readily apparent but instead must be made public (e.g., sexual orientation, mental illness), such revelations can result in the dissolution of former social ties. Such social distancing may occur not only in relationships with strangers or acquaintances but with friends and family as well. Social distancing may also occur in the workplace and community, including denial or termination of employment and housing. People on whom the stigmatized may depend for their health and well-being may provide poor quality of care or refuse to provide service altogether. Those on whom stigmatized people depend for the protection of their civil rights may turn a blind eye to discriminatory practices or even target stigmatized people for persecution. In its extreme forms, hostile expression of stigma has even take the form of physical violence, as with the highly publicized case of Matthew Shepard. A college student at the University of Wyoming, Shepard was robbed, beaten, tied to a fence in a remote area in sub-zero temperatures, and left to die by two men who witnesses say targeted Sheppard because he was gay. Matthew Shepard subsequently died as a result of the injuries he sustained in the attack.

At the macro-social level, the expression of stigma may take multiple forms, such as media campaigns that underscore the social evaluation of stigmatized people or social policies that restrict the rights of stigmatized people. Historical examples of such macro-level expressions in the United States include the denial of voting rights for women and racial minorities, internment of Americans of Japanese ancestry during World War II, prominent media portrayals of people with mental illnesses as dangerous or incapacitated, and the proposal of laws that would publicly identify and deport people infected with the Human Immunodeficiency Virus. Each of these examples is systemic in nature, operating on large scales and permeating the institutional fabric of the country.

The relationship between these micro- and macro-social levels may be cyclical, such that pervasive discrimination at the interpersonal level may lead to the introduction and public support of social polices that impair the lives of stigmatized people. In turn, the presence and enforcement of such policies subsequently may promote and instigate active ridicule, distancing, and hostile expressions of stigma at the interpersonal level against stigmatized people. Through this cyclical process, the values that underscore the social stigma are perpetuated and reinforced. As such, once this cycle has begun, it can prove difficult to undermine.

Cognitive Processes of the Stigmatized

Given the range of ways in which stigma is expressed at both the micro- and macro-social levels, one cannot help but imagine all that must go through the minds of stigmatized people who must endure such treatment. How do they make sense of the negative social consensus surrounding their stigmatized trait? How do they evaluate and make sense of expressions of stigma directed (either implicitly or explicitly) at themselves? What impact does being stigmatized have on the human psyche? The answers to these questions help explain how and why people respond to their stigmatized status and the choices they make when navigating the tricky social mine field stigma places around them.

Social Identity Development

Literature in counseling and developmental psychology provides insight into the psyche of people belonging to stigmatized and disenfranchised social groups. Within these traditions, researchers have worked to describe identity development and social interaction among various stigmatized groups, including members of racial and ethnic groups, women, gays and lesbians, older adults, and people with disabilities (for a review, see Howard, 2000; and other relevant chapters in this volume). Each resulting group model specifically addresses the ways in which people reflect on and manage social stigma, including how this may change over time. These theories specifically suggest that stigmatized people often go through stages during which they accept and internalize society's negative evaluation of them. Such shame involves the negative emotions, sense of self-inadequacy, and feelings of responsibility for one's failure to meet society's standards. In this context, shame is interchangeable with self-stigmatization, and reflects internalization and self-acceptance of society's devaluation of oneself (e.g., Kaufman, 1996). As a result of such internalized stigma, stigmatized people are at increased risk for poor self-esteem (Crocker et al., 1998; Goffman, 1963; Jones et al., 1984). The poor self-esteem experienced by those who internalize society's negative evaluations can then segue into depression, which is often exacerbated by the amount of stigmatization the individual experiences (Crandall & Coleman, 1992), illustrating how those who deal with greater amounts of negative social interaction are also at greater psychological risk. Depression has been found to increase people's hopelessness, demoralization, and impulsiveness (e.g., Angelino & Treisman, 2001), which, in turn, has been linked to risky behaviors such as substance abuse (e.g., Crum, Brown, Liang, & Eaton, 2001). In addition, diminished social networks and subsequent lack of support often reported by stigmatized people can impair their ability to find meaning in their lives. As a result, stigma reduces the sources of meaning that people depend on to make sense of their lived experiences by eliminating or reducing their social ties which, therefore, influences suicidal behavior (Starace & Sherr, 1998).

This same body of research suggests that stigmatized people also may transition out of these earlier stages, moving away from accepting and internalizing social stigma to rejecting it and denouncing the pejorative stance others may take towards them. Those who do move through these stages may be unburdened by the shame and depression described above, as well as adopt defensive dispositions against those who would stigmatize them. The relationships between these identify trajectories and subsequent communication have not been well researched, but the implications are considerable.

Attributional Ambiguity

Regardless of stigmatized individuals' orientation to social stigma, they also engage in the processes of self- and other-categorization. They identify who is in their group and must suffer their shared fate as well as who belongs to the other, dominant groups that are prone to dole out abuse. In addition to this initial categorization process, stigmatized people also engage in a second categorization, in which they carefully scan members of dominant groups to determine who might be a threat, as well as who might be a supportive ally and safe haven against abuse (Frable et al., 1990). Because they are aware that others may actively work to conceal their prejudicial attitudes (e.g., Crocker & Major, 1989), stigmatized people may be particularly alert for the more subtle and indirect clues that belie others' true attitudes (Frable et al., 1990; Goffman, 1963). This heightened sensitivity to potential signals of bias has consequences for how stigmatized people assess and evaluate their interactions with others. Specifically, stigmatized people are prone to struggle over the meaning of ambiguous cues and, ultimately, tend to interpret such cues as products of stigma and discrimination, even when other explanations are equally viable.

Many people living with HIV, for example, are not able or willing to respond as Ryan White did. They may fail to disclose to others, in order to protect themselves from possible discrimination. For example, people with HIV have reported being especially on guard with people on whom they must depend, such as health care providers. The authors know one person who described being particularly wary when meeting new care providers, such as when he first attends a new clinic. If a healthcare provider seems terse or abrupt during these initial encounters, he admits to assuming the provider dislikes him because he has HIV. What is more, this same man has explained how he is aware that other factors may explain these events, such as the provider having a headache, being short on time, or having a bad day. Despite these possibilities, he tends to "err on the side of caution" by assuming the worst in these situations. As he explains it, if he later discovers his interpretations are wrong, he will lower his guard. If, however, he is right, his defenses are already up and ready for some form of attack (such as mistreatment or disdain from the provider). By his own admission, he likely misinterprets others' actions on occasion, but from his perspective, his excessive caution is far better than being caught unaware by someone who holds a bias against him.

Behavioral Performance of the Stigmatized

Understanding the cognitive processes of stigmatized people provides insight not only on how they may interpret others' behaviors but how they might strategically communicate given their stigmatized status. Although the research in this area is less developed than that on their cognitive processes (and far less than research on the cognitive and behavioral processes of stigmatizers), considerable evidence demonstrates that people prefer to feel good about themselves and work to avoid negative affect and self-evaluations (Abrams & Hogg, 1988); therefore, stigmatized people are likely to respond to stigma and stigmatizing encounters in ways that would protect their self-esteem. This is an area that is especially relevant for communication researchers, Indeed, people belonging to stigmatized social groups are "not passive, powerless individuals; rather, they are strategists, expert managers, and negotiators who play active (although not always successful) roles" in managing social interaction (Herman, 1993, p. 324). It is reasonable, then, to assume that stigmatized people thoughtfully interact with others in ways to attempt to mitigate the impact of both potential and enacted stigma (although these efforts may be more or less successful). Far more research is needed in this area to best understand how stigmatized people strategically interact with others; however, current research on these phenomena focuses on four key areas: (1) disclosure and concealment, (2) social networking, (3) advocacy, and (4) stereotype threat.

For some, that which leads others to stigmatize them is visible or well known (e.g., disfigurement, racial group membership). For others, however, their stigmatizing attribute is not readily apparent, which leaves them with the dilemma of disclosing or concealing their stigmatized condition (e.g., Goffman, 1963). Self-disclosure of one's stigmatized status is something that entails many risks, including being ostracized and shunned by strangers, friends, and family alike. As such, concealment offers anonymity and reprieve from persecution. On the other hand, a price may be paid for concealment, as it can prevent people from networking and accessing the social benefits of relationships with other stigmatized people or resources that are beneficial or necessary for maintaining their health and well-being. For instance, people with stigmatized diseases may avoid treatment for fear of other people learning of their conditions.

Considerable research by communication scholars has explored the processes by which the stigmatized navigate these decisions. Despite the risks, people often intentionally reveal their stigmatized status to others. For instance, we know that stigmatized people may choose to disclose their status out of a need for assistance, cathartic release, loyalty, or honesty (e.g., Derlega, Lovejoy, & Winstead, 1998). For some, hiding their stigmatized condition becomes a source of stress in and of itself. The act of disclosing that information to others is akin to lancing a boil, excising the pent-up anxiety caused from keeping their stigmatized status a secret. For instance, some people have reported experiencing great strain from hiding their sexual orientation from their family, but the act of finally sharing that information, though sometimes painful, also can bring a tremendous sense of relief. In other circumstances, people will choose to disclose their stigmatized status to those who they think may help them, as well as out of a need to educate others about their stigmatized condition.

The choices stigmatized people make about concealment and disclosure appear related to the social networks they maintain. Those who conceal their stigmatized status may maintain social ties similar to their non-stigmatized peers, as their stigmatized attribute is unknown to their network and may not overtly interfere with their social relationships. Stigmatized people also may maintain secret social networks beyond their primary network that include other members of their stigmatized group. By keeping these networks apart, stigmatized people may benefit from relating to other stigmatized people, while shielding their other relationships from the potential damage incurred by revealing their stigmatized status. Some people find ways in which to integrate their social networks, such as by interacting with people in the larger community who are comfortable with or indifferent to their stigmatized condition, while openly relating to others from their stigmatized group. Finally, some stigmatized people maintain social networks comprised primarily or solely of other stigmatized people. This may be a conscious and intentional choice for some, whereas others may be forced out of their original social networks after people discover their stigmatized trait, leaving them with little option than to rebuild their networks with those who share their plight (for review, see Howard, 2000).

Research in intergroup communication and developmental psychology suggests that stigmatized people may band together not only for social support but as a form of activism and means of educating and addressing society (e.g., Brashers, Haas, Neidig, & Rintamaki, 2002; Howard, 2000). By banding together, stigmatized people may gain greater visibility and social capital, with which they may actively confront the larger social system and seek to bring about change that may improve the plight of their group. Such has been the case for people living with HIV and their grassroots organizing, which changed the ways in which the broader society understood the disease and those living with it. Specifically, AIDS activists directly influenced governmental policy and funding for HIV research, galvanized general education campaigns about the disease, and pressured the pharmaceutical industry to develop and provide greater access to life-saving medications for those living with HIV.

Finally, the heightened awareness stigmatized people possess around non-stigmatized people can extend to an acute awareness of negative stereotypes that may exist about the stigmatized group. In particular, stigmatized people may be concerned with either dispelling such stereotypes altogether or, perhaps, demonstrating that they do not always apply (such as when they do not apply to oneself). Subsequently, stigmatized people may go to great lengths to refute such stereotypes through educational efforts or through performance (for review, see Crocker et al., 1998). For instance, some women report working hard to conceal emotional upset when made aware of stereotypes that describe them as emotionally unstable or easily unbalanced.

Conclusion

Research in the area of stigma communication has progressed in a variety of ways during the past four and a half decades, evolving to include nuanced perspectives on what constitutes social stigma, how cognitive processes inform and predict behavioral processes, and the social levels at which such stigma communication can occur. Although there are many potential avenues by which scholars can expand upon this body of work, we propose two key areas that require additional investigation. First, we suggest efforts first focus on better identifying the links between stigmatized identity development and communicative outcomes, such as self-disclosure, self-advocacy, and social activism. To date, research in counseling psychology has hinted at these links, but communication scholars are best equipped to fully uncover these relationships. Second, we suggest considerable effort be focused on determining how allies can best communicate their support to people belonging to stigmatized groups. In particular, determining how this may be accomplished in socially subtle or savvy ways could be of particular value in contexts such as medicine. Mindful that patients with stigmatized conditions (e.g., sexually transmitted, contagious, or mental illnesses) may be extremely sensitive to subtle cues of bias, sometimes leading them to misinterpret innocent events as negative, health care providers often ask the authors what, exactly, they can do to disarm their patients anxiety. Currently, the extant literature on stigma communication does little to answer these questions.

Stigma communication remains one of the most compelling areas of intergroup communication research. The area has evolved considerably over the short span of a few decades, providing insights on how and why people stigmatize. These efforts have revealed the strategic nature of stigma as well as how stigmatized people manage their denigrated social status. By exploring the links between identity development and communication, along with strategies for self-presenting as a supportive ally, intergroup scholars will propel this area of research forward in ways that not only pique academic interest but also serve to improve the lives of stigmatized people.

CHAPTER FOURTEEN

The Mobilizing of Intergroup Hatred

STEPHEN REICHER

There is a tale, both depressing and depressingly familiar, according to which we are doomed to hate others. The tale is told in various ways, with the cause put in different places, but what all variants have in common is that hatred is part of the human condition, that it is unavoidable, that we can regret it but that we cannot reverse it. Sometimes, the cause is located in our psychology, in a 'natural tendency' to misperceive to denigrate, even to dehumanize members of other groups, such that all people will always be at odds with all outgroups (e.g., Allport, 1954). At other times, the cause lies in our culture, and in some cultures more than others. For instance, the Japanese slaughter of Chinese people, culminating in the indescribable brutality of the 'rape' of Nanking has been ascribed to the militaristic, hierarchical and disciplinarian character of Japanese society (Chang, 1998). Or else, Goldhagen (1996) has explained the Nazi holocaust as deriving from a longstanding anti-Semitism which inhered—and continues to inhere—in German culture. In this case, particular groups will always be at odds with other groups, albeit (in certain cases) some groups more than others

At yet other times, hatred is explained through history. Contemporary antagonisms simply perpetuate ancient hatreds. They are the manifestation of a longstanding pattern which we are increasingly locked into. Israelis will always hate Palestinians. Serbs will always hate Croats and Bosnians and Kosovars. What happened in the Battle of Kosovo in 1389 is still happening today. Here, particular groups will always be at odds with particular others. But although the hatred is more specific, it is no less inevitable.

There is, of course, much to be said about these various approaches—far too much for the space I have here. So I shall limit myself to three comments. The first is that all of them either suggest a reality that has never occurred or else misrepresents the realities that have occurred. While there are all too many incidents of mass hatred, and while they command our attention when they do appear, it is nonetheless true that such incidents are extremely rare in relationship to the number and variety of intergroup encounters within our world. For instance less than 1% of multiethnic societies in Africa result in ethnic conflict (Mann, 2005). Equally, no single group is violent towards more than a very small proportion of the others it encounters and is violent towards a given other more than a small proportion of the time. There is an analogy here with explanations of individual aggression. Even the worst of aggressors spends but a small amount of time in being aggressive, hence an explanation that refers to inherent tendencies of whatever sort does not help us understand when, where and in response to what offences actually occur.

Mann (2005), referring specifically to the Balkan conflicts, refers to the notion that they derive from ancient hatreds spanning the centuries, as "nonsense" (p. 19), but his scathing judgement can be applied more generally. Equally, Mann's argument that supposedly historical parallels are in fact anachronistic myths created for the purposes of the present also has a broader resonance. Thus, far from the Battle of Kosovo revealing a continuous process of ethnic antagonism over more than 600 years, it was actually a case of two multi-ethnic forces confronting each other in the cause of dynastic advancement. Only in the 19th century did Serb nationalists reconstrue events as Serbs versus Kosovars.

This observation points towards our second comment, and also one of Mann's own contentions. That is, where one finds intergroup antagonisms one generally also finds political actors mobilizing those antagonisms in the service of political interests. I will have more to say about the nature of these interests in the next section. For now, I simply want to stress that the term 'mobilization' is critical here, since it underscores the conclusion that hatred does not occur spontaneously but, rather, is the result of careful communication and agitation. Hatred involves agency. What is more, agency is not restricted to those doing the mobilizing. It also extends to those who are mobilized. 'The people' are not passive dupes of Machiavellian elites. While their motives may be different to those of elites, they do have their own reasons. For all involved, then, hateful acts are knowing acts. As Todorov (2004) puts it, reprising the humanism of Montaigne and Rousseau, evil acts "are the fruits of our freedom, of our ability to choose at every point between various courses of action" (p. 26).

Third, then, explanations which suggest the inevitability of intergroup violence effectively exonerate the perpetrators (see Reicher & Haslam, 2006). For they deny that people make choices, that they are responsible for those choices and that they need to be held accountable for those choices. Far from violence being an error, a mistake, a result of some fateful flaw in our psychological or social make-up, it is deliberate, and it is committed because actors consider that it is to their advantage. The old forensic adage of *cui bono* (who benefits?) applies as much to acts of hate as to any other act.

To summarize all three comments, we need to move from seeing hatred as determined despite anything we can do towards a recognition that hatred is a product of what we choose to do. Hatred does not 'just happen', hatred is broadcast and promoted and embraced. To quote Sontag from her introduction to Hatzfeld's collection of interviews with Rwandan killers: "Our obligation, and it is an obligation, is to take in what human beings are capable of doing to one another, not spontaneously (crimes of this order are never spontaneous) but when mobilized to think of other human beings... as not human beings at all, and when organized for and directed to the task of slaughter" (2005, pp. vii-viii). Accordingly, there are three issues that we need to consider: *first*, why do people seek to propagate messages of hatred?; *second*, why do people endorse messages of hatred?; *third*, how is hatred most effectively advocated. In the next section, we shall briefly address the two 'why?' questions before devoting the rest of the chapter to examining the ways in which hate messages are structured.

Why Hate Is Propagated

Why do elites use the channels of communication at their disposal to generate hatred? Why, for instance, did the Hutu regime in Rwanda use Radio Mille Collines (also known as 'Radio Machete') to broadcast a constant stream of diatribes against the Tutsi population—the 'infiltrators', the 'cockroaches'. Why did they call upon the Hutu population, to take up arms against Tutsis, to "look at their small noses and then break them."[1] The obvious place to look for an answer lies in the struggles between groups for political power, and indeed Mann, having enumerated multiple reasons for ethnic cleansing, argues that the circumstances most likely to produce such an outcome are where more than one ethnic group seeks to rule over one and the same territory. Even so, he acknowledges that hatred against outgroups is often bound up with violence against ingroups, and indeed that sometimes there are more ingroup than outgroup victims. This is the phenomenon of ingroup policing, and it certainly applies to Rwanda where the Hutu moderates were the first victims of the genocide and where anyone who refused to kill was at risk of death themselves. For Mann, though, the primary cause still lies at the intergroup level, and intra-group violence is primarily a means of coercing everyone to join in the attack on ethnic or other foes. In many cases, though, intra-group power struggles may assume the primary role, and invoking outgroup demons may be a means to winning these struggles.

To illustrate this point, consider two mirror image antagonisms that dominated and spanned the course of the 20th century: the hatred of communism, particularly Soviet communism, in the United States and the hatred of capitalism, particularly American capitalism, in the Soviet Union. Certainly, the two were locked into a very real struggle for power. But at the same time, there were points where the spectre of the other was invoked for domestic reasons. Thus, the so-called 'red-scare' of the 1920s was a means of crushing labor organization in the USA (see Murray, 1955). American civilization was said to be teetering on the brink the power of communism, both internationally and domestically was vastly over-estimated, and anyone who advocated Labour rights or progressive causes was deemed to be siding with the enemy. This was summarized in a popular ditty of the time:

> *You believe in votes for women? Yah! the Bolsheviki do.*
> *And shorter hours? And land reforms? They're Bolshevistic too...*
> *Bolshevik! Veek! Veek!*
> *A reformer is a freak!*
> *But here's a name to stop him, for it's like a lightning streak*
> (cited in Murray, 1955, p. 169).

The Soviet terror of the 1930s employed the same logic (see Getty & Naumov, 2002). Drawing upon sensibilities that were developed during the civil war of 1918-21, Stalin propagated the idea that the country was besieged by fascist enemies and enemy conspiracies. Anyone who opposed or even questioned his leadership over the Party was a fascist conspirator. Indeed the logic became so extreme that anyone who, on being accused of some treachery, denied the accusations was ipso facto guilty since they were implying that the Party could be fallible. What is more, mere acknowledgment of guilt was still insufficient. The accused had to thank the Party for pointing out the error of his or her ways and to work enthusiastically to root out others. The only option was to join the terror. But, as Overy (2004) points out, 'terror' is our analytic term. The process was only possible because, at the time, it was posed as a *defence* against an *enemy* terror.

As these examples demonstrate, the invocation of outgroup enemies in order to bolster ingroup policing occurs on at least two levels. The one has to do with marginalizing rival elites. At the very least, the mere act of invoking a dangerous foe is to accuse one's rivals of not being aware of or concerned about a threat to the ingroup. More seriously (as in the Soviet case), rivals can be accused of abetting, colluding with or even being part of the enemy (see Reicher, Hopkins, Levine, & Rath, 2006). Thus Carter (1995) documents the 'politics of rage' in the career of George

Wallace, three times governor of Alabama. In his infamous inauguration speech of January 14th, 1963, Wallace draws on the sense that the desegregation policies of an 'ungodly' federal government were destroying all that was good in American society. He ratcheted up the sense of racial fear by invoking the recent massacre of Belgian colonists in the Congo. Then he delivered lines that are still remembered:

> In the name of the greatest people that have ever trod this earth, I draw the line in the dust and toss the gauntlet before the feet of tyranny... and I say... segregation now... segregation tomorrow... segregation forever. (cited in Carter, 1995, p. 11)

Seven years, when Wallace was again standing for the governorship, one of his aides privately explained the campaign strategy to a reporter: "Promise them the moon and holler 'Nigger'" (p. 392). Whenever his campaign faltered the spectre of racial threat—and the accusation that his opponent, Albert Brewer, was neglecting the threat—was stepped up. So, when, following George Wallace's loss in the first primary, a journalist asked his brother, Gerald Wallace "what are you going to do now?" Gerald smiled and replied confidently "we'll just throw the niggers around his [Brewer's] neck" (p. 392).

The second level at which ingroup policing operates is the populace in general. There is nothing novel in this assertion. Indeed it is commonplace to recognize that foreign wars and the repression of domestic dissent go together. To use one of many possible examples, as the troopship *Canberra* returned victoriously to port after the Falklands war, it sported a banner that read "call off the rail strike or we'll call an air strike."[2] It was a theme that Margaret Thatcher enlarged upon shortly afterwards in a speech at Cheltenham racecourse on July 3rd, 1982. The union leaders and union members supporting strike action "misunderstood the new mood of the nation". They, like the Argentinians, were acting against Britain. They were using their "undoubted power for what?—to delay Britain's recovery, which all our people long to see."[3]

However, it is not just that a generic outgroup is used to impose generic discipline on the ingroup, it can also be the case that the specific nature of the outgroup is used to say what ingroup members must not (and therefore must) be and do. In Thatcher's terms, Argentinians are bullies, coercive Trades Union leaders are unBritish, and the British stand up to bullies. Peukert (1988) provides a similar analysis of the way in which anti-Semitism functioned in everyday life under the Third Reich. Why, he asks, were Jews elevated to the position of the demonic other when they were few in number, limited in power, and so hard to identify? Well, he argues, the lack of an outside threat tells us that we need to see anti-Semitism as a tool aimed inside the majority community, and the indeterminate nature of Jewishness is precisely what made it such a powerful tool. It meant that anyone who departed from the rigid, hierarchical and militaristic norms of Nazi society became suspect of being a 'community alien' with all the terrible consequences that flowed from such a definition.

Let us move on to the second question of motive, which by now may seem more obscure than before. If elites use outgroup hate to secure ingroup power—to eliminate rivals and to subjugate populations—why on earth should any population be influenced by messages of hate and embrace hatred as their own? Let us start by dismissing one retort—that people embrace nothing but are simply too cowed and too terrified to do anything but comply with what they are told. Even in the most repressive of regimes—Nazi Germany is an example – surveillance was limited and noncompliance (as opposed to active opposition) was always possible. Browning (1992), for instance, shows that even amongst the murder squads that shot Jewish populations before the death camps were built, soldiers could refuse to kill. And while their careers might not thrive, they did not put themselves in danger.

In recent years, the tide has turned against another popular explanation: that people kill more from inattention than from hate, especially in our modern mechanized world. According to this view, perpetrators focus on the technicalities of mass murder—on following orders, on bureaucratic administration, on making sure that the trains to the death camps run on time (e.g., Arendt, 1963). But closer inspection of the perpetrators reveals that they knew very well what they were doing, that they believed in what they were doing, that they even celebrated it.

For instance, Adolf Eichmann has often been portrayed as the typical insignificant bureaucrat, with the difference that he organized the Nazi murder machine. But, as Cesarani (2004) documents, he was actually a creative and conscientious Nazi. He actually challenged Himmler when he felt the latter was not being strict enough in deporting the Jewish population. And when, after the war, he was interviewed in Argentina by a Nazi journalist, he declared that "my innermost being refuses to say that we did something wrong" and that if the Nazis had managed to murder the entire Jewish population of 10 million: "then I would be satisfied. I would say 'All right. We have exterminated an enemy,'" (Cesarani, 2004, p. 219).

Eichmann fits into Mann's category of ideological killers. This is but one of nine bases for killing identified by Mann (2005). People kill, or condone the killing by others, for reasons that span from career advancement to gaining the approval of their peers to straightforward material gain. Certainly many Germans benefited by getting the jobs vacated by Jews or else from buying Jewish property that was sold cheaply in sales all around Germany. Yet the ideological motive has a certain primacy since, even if people do advance their careers through murder or else get peer approval or material gain, still, it is hard to kill if one knows that one's actions are wrong.

Mann suggests that the principal ideological motive is to justify killing as self-defence. There is much to this, as we shall see, but in one sense Mann's claim is potentially misleading. People are able to support acts of hate precisely because they are not for their personal gain or defence but because they are for the group. What is more, they are not necessarily acting in defence of life and limb, but more in defence of the existence of the group as a group with a distinctive culture, values, and 'way of life' (see Carter, 1995). Consequently, if we want to find the bases of ideological hatred we must look to group rather than individual level processes.

Groups, it is often argued, subvert human rationality and agency. When perfectly sensible individuals become part of a group, they lose their ability to make sound judgements and to control their behavior. Cognition gives way to emotion and that is why people do such extreme things in groups (see Le Bon [1895] for the classic expression of this view). Recent research in the social identity tradition (for a review see Reicher, Spears & Haslam, in press; see Chapters 1 & 21) suggests precisely the opposite. As group members we shift from looking at ourselves in terms of what makes us unique as individuals (personal identity) to what makes our group unique compared to others (social identity). Rather than losing control over behavior, control shifts to collective beliefs, norms and values. Along with this cognitive shift, there is a second transformation—a transformation towards intimacy.

To the extent that people define themselves at the group level, then fellow ingroup members stop being 'other' and become an extension of the self: they share one's perspectives; they share one's priorities; their fate is part of one's own fate. This is reflected in a series of behavioral shifts (for summaries, see Reicher & Haslam, 2009): one is more likely to agree with, to respect and trust ingroup members. One is more likely to support and help them. One is more likely to concur with them in choosing leaders. As a consequence of all this, group members are able to align their actions and work together. They become empowered and hence are able to pursue their goals more effectively.

Putting all this together, groups both give people a clear perspective on the world and a means of transforming social reality in line with their perspective—what John Drury and myself term 'collective self-objectification'. In other words, far from removing agency, groups turn people into agents. As group members, people can create history rather than adapt to a history made by others. In a phrase, groups make people *social* beings. It is this which goes a long way towards explaining why people are so passionate about their groups and about group action. Conversely, it is this which explains why people react so strongly when their groups are seen to be in danger. Life and limb may not be in danger, but one's survival as a social being is.

So often, groups and group psychology are seen as the problem and as the source of hatred. Clearly, people can do terrible things in groups. However even where this happens, it is generally the consequence of actual or anticipated group failure. When failure looms, people can become callous and brutal towards those they blame for their woes. People also become more authoritarian, more willing to allow others to make decisions for them, more willing to accept extreme social measures; in short, more willing to accede to tyranny (for psychological evidence, see Reicher & Haslam, 2006; for historical examples, see Hobsbawm, 1995). For my purposes here, however, the key point is that, where people consider their groups to be endangered, they will be strongly—passionately—motivated to destroy the danger.

It follows from the analysis that, even if the motives for hatred may differ somewhat between elites and masses, there is a convergent concern with danger to the group's way of life. I have already referred to George Wallace, and this is a message Wallace learned young when he was outflanked by Seymore Trammell in a 1952 election. Trammell's campaign literature always featured the words: "I will dare defend against all forces calculated to destroy our Southern way of life" (Carter, 1995, p. 98). Wallace himself noted: "I started off talking about schools and highways and prisons and taxes—and I couldn't make them listen... then I began talking about niggers—and they stomped the floor" (p. 109).

It also follows from this analysis that successful hate communication will take a particular form, identifying particular groups as a threat to one's own group and to the survival of the group culture. That is, although I have spent quite some time on the 'why' of hate messages, I have also gone quite some way towards addressing the 'how'—the nature of the messages themselves. However, it remains necessary to examine the form of hate communication rather more precisely.

How Hate Is Propagated

How is it that Eichmann could face up to the Holocaust and conclude that he did nothing wrong (besides not being thorough enough)? How is it, more generally, that people can justify and sometimes glorify mass murder—often portraying themselves as victims? There is a common pattern, often found at the sites of the worst killings wherever and whenever they occur. It involves four steps. Nonetheless, these can be divided into two pairs, in each of which one step involves the definition of 'us' and the other involves the definition of 'them'. Significantly, I shall suggest, the primary term in each case involves ingroup rather than outgroup definition.

Steps 1 and 2: Defining 'Us' and Excluding 'Them'

Before 'we' can be endangered, there needs to be a 'we' to be put in danger. This may be a logically trivial point, but it is far from socially insignificant. The categories through which we define ourselves and others are always constructs. Far from times where 'danger' is less an assault on an established 'us' than part of the process of constituting us.

When Argentinians first landed on South Georgia and then on the main Falkland Isles themselves, the nature of the phenomenon (and of the categories involved) was far from self-evident. Was it a matter of predatory traders?; of struggles over oil rights in the South Atlantic?; or of national sovereignty? Thatcher's political genius was in using the Falklands to reassert the primacy of national categories and then use them as a prism through which to frame subsequent domestic struggles. Equally, when planes hit the Twin Towers it was unclear whether this was an attack on financial capital, on New York or on the nation. Like Thatcher, the political success of Bush (and his advisors) was to make of 9/11 an attack on America and thereby to mobilize the nation behind his response.

To constitute categories, then, is to define a zone of inclusion. It is to say who is touched by an event, and in what way. It is to say whose fates are intertwined. And, as I detailed, in the previous section, it is also to say who we can rely upon, who can rely upon us and, hence, who will be implicated in a system of mutual trust and support. But, by the same token, constituting categories is to constitute exclusions. It is to say who is not of us, and hence who we will exclude from the embrace and support of the group.

A while ago, Mark Levine and I designed some studies in which Manchester United football fans saw someone—alternatively wearing a United shirt, a Liverpool shirt (Liverpool being the perennial rivals) or an unbranded red t-shirt—fall over and hurt themselves. When we made our participants think of themselves in terms of team, they only helped the actor in the United shirt (see Chapter 20). When we made them think of themselves as football fans they helped the actor in a Manchester and a Liverpool shirt but not the t-shirt. The group boundary varied but helping was each time coterminous with this boundary (Levine, Prosser, Edwards, & Reicher, 2005). More recently, a colleague, Nick Hopkins, has run an (as yet) unpublished study in which a young Chinese woman wearing a Scotland football shirt is seen to stumble and drop a load of pencils that she is carrying. When the Scottish participants were led to define their national identity in ethnic terms, her face signalled that she was outside the group and they provided little help. When participants were led to define Scottishness in terms of commitment, her shirt defined her as within the group and many more pencils were picked up. Again, how we define 'us' defines who is 'them' and hence who is outside the circle of support.

Now consider a more consequential example. In his *ABC of National Socialism*, Geobbels asks "What is the first Commandment of every National Socialist?" and he answers "Love Germany above all else and your ethnic comrade [*Volksgenosse*] as yourself" (quoted in Koonz, 2003, p. 7). At one level, this is an attractive call to solidarity. But, of course, it defines Germanness and hence solidarity in ethnic terms. Jews are outside the circle. They are denied the positive consequences of ingroup inclusion. But, as we know, they were ultimately denied far more, and to understand this we need to consider the next pair of steps to glorifying hatred.

Steps 3 and 4: Ingroup Virtue and Outgroup Threat

I need say little about outgroup threat, having already referred to it in the previous section. Mann is but one of many who recognizes the role played by claims that 'they' are a danger to 'us'. Muslims endanger Hindu civilization. Tutsis endanger Hutus. Jews endanger an Aryan Germany. Even the imagery has much in common. The other is characteristically portrayed as vermin—as cockroaches or maggots or rats. The image is significant not for being animal, but for being pollution: something that defiles and destroys the pure essence of the ingroup. As Hitler wrote of Jews in *Mein Kampf*: "he is and remains the typical parasite... wherever he appears the host people dies out" (1980, p. 277). The point I want to make here, though, is that outgroup threat works in tandem with a more neglected twin—ingroup virtue.

Koonz (2003) provides a compelling analysis of what she calls "the Nazi conscience." Her point is that, repugnant though it might seem from the outside, one can only understand how Nazism worked on the inside by understanding it as a moral project. Between 1933 and 1939, Hitler hardly ever mentioned the Jews. He spent his time insisting on the 'cleanliness' of his National Socialist Germany. Some at the time took this as a sign of his diminishing racism. They missed the point catastrophically. Ingroup virtue provided the grounds for the destruction of the outgroup. For if 'we' are the sum of all good and 'they' are a threat to our existence, then to destroy the outgroup becomes an act of preserving virtue. Moreover, those who actually carry out the onerous task of killing become the most virtuous amongst us. It is precisely this logic which allowed Himmler, speaking to a group of SS Guards in Poznan in 1943, to praise those involved in implementing the final solution: "to have stuck it out and at the same time... to have remained decent fellows. This is a page of glory in our history" (Rees, 2005, p. 226).

The significance of 'ingroup virtue' in the propagation of hate is all the greater because it is harder to spot its danger. For instance, we generally applaud the value of tolerance (though who wants to be 'tolerated'?), but in recent studies, Nick Hopkins, Wendy van Rijswik and I have shown that people are more likely to see illiberal outsiders as beyond the pale when reminded that they themselves belong to a tolerant group. Whether we use for our example revolutionary France (Scurr, 2006), revolutionary Russia (Overy, 2004), fascist Germany (Koonz, 2003), or recent experience in the UK and the USA, to claim a monopoly of virtue and to see the world in Manichean terms of good and evil is profoundly dangerous. What Carter says of Wallace's words could be said of virtually any rhetoric of hate: they offer victory over a dangerous foe combined with the "balm of righteousness"

(1995, p. 109)—a truly toxic combination.

Conclusion

In this chapter, I have argued that analysis needs to focus on hatred as a process of mobilization, and I have sought to address both why hatred is mobilized and how it is mobilized. The core of my argument is that the worst of acts become possible when they can be represented as the best of acts. This is a complex ideological construction or set of constructions. Their exact details, the nature of the relevant elements and the interaction between them are all open to further investigation. In particular, the role of ingroup virtue and its interaction with outgroup threat is an important area of research. What is not in doubt, though, is that these constructions are both made and endorsed by people, and therefore people must take responsibility for them. Hatred, that is, is an act of choice.

But to say this is not to deny that there are circumstances that make it easier to choose hate or to avoid the consequences of one's actions. Nor is to deny that people may fail to see how the small and seemingly innocent choices they make may combine to create catastrophic consequences. None of the steps I have described is necessarily dangerous on its own. Some, in isolation, can be quite benign. However, by making quite explicit where they lead together—and especially by inducing people to pay more attention to how groups define themselves—perhaps we can make it a little harder to follow the path to its bloody end.

Endnotes

1 See http://www.enotes.com/genocide-encyclopedia/radio-television-libre-mille-collines
2 Footage can be found at
   http://video.google.co.uk/videosearch?q=canberra+falklands&hl=en&emb=0&aq=f#
3 The full transcript is at
   http://www.margaretthatcher.org/speeches/displaydocument.asp?docid=104989

Part Three

Contexts of Intergroup Communication

CHAPTER FIFTEEN

Family as an Intergroup Domain

JORDAN SOLIZ

Scholarly definitions of family highlight members' collective history, shared sense of commitment and group affiliation. As such, our family operates as an important social group for which we identify, forming many of our attitudes, values and beliefs. As a collective "ingroup," familial identity can be at the heart of interfamilial conflict (e.g., Capulets and Montagues) and interfamilial comparison as we are inherently biased toward those families who share similar values, practices, and backgrounds. Yet, whereas our families can function as a collective identity, they also exist in social context in which individual social identities can influence perceptions and interactions with others (Harwood, Soliz, & Lin, 2006). This raises questions about the interplay between social identity and family functioning. How does the age difference between family members influence grandparent-grandchild relationships? How do individuals in interracial/ethnic and interfaith unions manage the divergent histories and/or beliefs associated with their respective heritages? How do heteronormative attitudes affect the way parents interact with their gay or lesbian child? Likewise, the manner in which families come together (e.g., formative processes) also reflect circumstances in which individuals may identify only with specific family members or a cluster of family members. For instance, individuals in stepfamilies and in-law relationships are, by their very nature, relationships that emerge from the union of two distinct family groups. Whereas these relationships may be satisfying and harmonious, they may also be characterized by distinctions of ingroups and outgroups in a family (e.g., family-of-origin vs. "new" family).

At its core, intergroup theorizing concerns "us" vs. "them" categorization and comparisons (see Chapters 1 & 21). The family, which is typically considered a homogenous, highly interpersonal context, may actually be influenced by *intergroup* dynamics. An intergroup perspective on family relationships does not imply that some families are "more intergroup" than other families. Rather, through this lens, we recognize the role of social categorization and group affiliation in differentiating positive and negative family relationships. Research on families employing intergroup theorizing is still in its infancy. Thus, the objective of this chapter is to emphasize the benefits of this perspective by discussing the theoretical attributes of a shared family identity as well as highlighting how this perspective is useful for understanding specific family relationships. The chapter concludes with a discussion of how family communication serves as a context for intergroup contact and, hence, may hold promise for positive change in attitudes toward others (see Chapters 6, 10, 12, this chapter, & 17).

The Common Ingroup Identity Model and Shared Family Identity

Group salience, as defined by Harwood, Raman, and Hewstone (2006) is "an individual's awareness of group memberships and respective group differences in an intergroup encounter" (p. 182). Typically, group salience is negatively associated with attitudes and overall quality of contact in intergroup interactions. Conversely, identifying and recognizing a common ingroup can reduce and possibly eliminate the negative consequences of outgroup categorization. For instance, fans of rival sports teams (see Chapter 20) may come together to support a national team (e.g., Olympic and World Cup teams). More significantly, political and ethnic strife may be reduced or eliminated when groups come together for the purpose of national unity. This represents the major tenet of the common ingroup identity model (Gaertner et al., 2000), which stipulates that the negative aspects of intergroup comparison "can be reduced by factors that transform participants' representations of memberships from two groups to one, more inclusive group" (p. 133).

This model is useful for understanding the family as an intergroup domain as it suggests that common familial identity is central to transcending difference and positive family functioning. Banker and Gaertner (1998) first applied this model to research on stepfamily harmony, where they found that more positive contact between stepfamily members was associated with a common familial identity which, in turn, was related to stepfamily harmony. In the family context, this common ingroup can be conceptualized as a perception of *shared family identity* (Soliz & Harwood, 2006) in which intergroup distinctions are minimized. This model does not suggest that difference disappears. Rather, the common ingroup of family supersedes the differences. As such, perceiving a common ingroup is theoretically related to more positive perceptions of the interaction or relationship. For instance, Soliz, Thorson, and Rittenour (2009) found that perceptions of racial/ethnic difference were negatively related to a shared family identity and relational satisfaction in multiracial/ethnic families. Scholars and practitioners have argued for a systems-level perspective on understanding families. Although this is informative, it is important to understand how family members manage intergroup distinctions individually as the influence of divergent social categorization may not be consistent across all family relationships. Thus, shared family identity is a conceptualization at the dyadic level (i.e., between individual family members).

Recent intergroup scholarship has recognized that contact is more complex than whether or not it is simply positive or negative. To speak to this complexity, we must attend to the communication that both influences and reflects affiliation and distinction (Harwood, Giles, & Palomares, 2005). In addressing difference within a family, Galvin (2006) discusses the internal boundary management practices families enact to "maintain their internal sense of family-ness" (p. 11). The remainder of the chapter highlights various family types or relationships that represent differences that emerge from distinct social identities or formative processes with a particular emphasis on the communicative dynamics in these families. There are two important points to consider in this discussion. First, not all of the information is a result of intergroup theorizing on families, although the research certainly attends to intergroup issues. Second, and perhaps more importantly, the family types or relationships highlighted in this discussion are by no means inherently negative. Rather, the purpose is to recognize the interplay between the role of social categorization and family communication.

Intergroup Dynamics in the Family: Social Identity

Intergroup relations may emerge when divergent social identities influence perception of and/or interactions with others, oftentimes resulting in more negative experiences when group differences are apparent. However, as Harwood et al. (2005) point out, "not all individuals have to perceive an interaction through an intergroup lens in order for intergroup communication to occur" (p. 3). In other words, divergent social identity may not always be evident or important in interactions. Hence, within a family dyad, we are interested in how perceptions—by one or both family members—of divergent social identities are reflected in or shaping family communication.

Age Identity

One of the most important social identities for many is age (see Chapters 3 & 4). Age does not refer simply to chronological years but rather to the socially constructed age groups to which we identify or are categorized by others (e.g., teenager, middle-aged, older adult). Age-group distinctions are a significant social concern given the general negative attitudes toward older adults. Interestingly, whereas negative attitudes toward older adults (i.e., 65+ years) and intergenerational interactions are held by younger adults, many have fairly positive perceptions of relationships with their grandparents who, by definition, are older adults (Williams & Harwood, 2004). Attempting to understand this perceptual contradiction spawned some of the early work employing an intergroup perspective on families. Soliz and Harwood (2006) found support for the hypothesized relationship put forth in the common ingroup identity model in that age salience—an outgroup distinction—was negatively associated with grandchildren's perceptions of a shared family identity with a grandparent.

Building off Banker and Gaertner's (1998) study on the role of quality of contact in engendering a sense of familial solidarity, research guided by intergroup theorizing and communication accommodation theory (Harwood et al., 2006) has linked accommodative communication (e.g., self-disclosure, supportive communication, compliments) to more positive perceptions of the relationship such as quality of contact, relational satisfaction, or shared family identity. Further, the presence of nonaccommodative behaviors (e.g., patronizing communication, complaining) as well as age-based cues (e.g., physical health) were found to be associated with age salience (Harwood, Hewstone, Paolini, & Voci, 2005; Soliz & Harwood, 2006). Thus, more person-centered communication is associated with perceptions of an inclusive, family orientation. Conversely, nonaccommodation is associated with more negative evaluations which may trigger group-based distinctions such as age salience. Therefore, shared family identity is more evident in grandparents who partake in personalized behaviors and are involved in satisfying relationships with their grandchildren. However, grandparents who are nonaccommodative or have physical/mental impairments associated with older age are more likely to be perceived in terms of their age than the familial connection.

In addition to further demonstrating the link between contact or, more specifically, communication and group-based categorization, research on grandparent-grandchild relationships has also shown how other components of intergroup theorizing may enhance our understanding of family dynamics. For instance, Allport (1954) proposed that institutional support of contact between groups is important in creating a cooperative, positive interaction. For positive contact to occur, social norms permit or encourage the collaboration of individuals from different groups toward a goal of positive outcomes or reconciliation. Obviously, like much of the work on intergroup theorizing, these conditions were brought up in thinking about contact between strangers rather than in personal relationships. However, in the family context, institutional support can be thought as family encouragement of contact. As evidenced in recent work (Soliz & Harwood, 2006), parental encouragement of grandparent-grandchild contact was a significant predictor of shared family identity. This finding suggests that alleviating barriers associated with age-based distinctions is, in part, contingent on the support a grandchild receives from other family members in maintaining a relationship with the grandparent. Intergroup theorizing has also positioned communication anxiety as an important factor to consider given its prevalence in intergroup interactions (Brown & Hewstone, 2005). As demonstrated in the grandparent-grandchild relationships, communication anxiety is negatively associated with more personalized communication (e.g., self-disclosure) and overall quality of contact (Harwood, Hewstone et al., 2005).

Sexual Identity

Sexual identity is an extremely important aspect of self that lies at the center of much of today's public discourse. Likewise, it is a sense of self that, for many, carries with it the potential negative effects of heteronormativity and the prejudicial attitudes of others (see Chapter 13). Thus, it is not surprising that family relationships between lesbians or gay men and family-of-origin members may be tainted, at times, by negative experiences (Peplau & Beals, 2004). Difficulties that do emerge can be attributed to the intergroup nature of these relationships. Disclosing sexual identity is, at its core, a social identity process in that an individual is communicating an identity that is different from other family members. Further, many of the negative response by family members can be traced to perceptions of sexual identity outgroups, such as negative attitudes toward gays and lesbians in general and/or heteronormative expectations of family members. These attitudes are oftentimes an extension of a family member's social identity such as religion or political affiliation. In fact, interactions may be characterized by a heightened sense of communication anxiety stemming from an awareness of group difference. This anxiety may be a reflection of either negative attitudes or a reflection of communication uncertainty in that family members may want to "say the right thing" or avoid certain topics. Thus, anxiety may not be driven solely by negative attitudes but by the desire to create a harmonious interaction. Regardless, the presence of intergroup anxiety reflects an intergroup recognition on the part of the family member.

Obviously, not all of the experiences for these family relationships are destined for difficulty, and understanding the interplay between intergroup factors and communication may help differentiate positive and negative family relationships and overall functioning. For instance, Soliz, Ribarsky, Marko Harrigan, and Tye-Williams (in press) found that, while negative attitudes toward gays and lesbians predicted higher levels of communication anxiety between family members with different sexual identities, respectful accommodation (i.e., taking an individual's opinions into account in conversations) and reciprocal self-disclosure reduced this anxiety. This suggests that more personalized communication lessens effects of outgroup distinctions. Conversely, avoiding topics such as religion, relationships, and politics increased communication anxiety. Intuitively, one might think that avoiding topics would reduce anxiety. However, intergroup anxiety is associated with recognition of social group differences. If topics that are part of the public discourse are intentionally avoided in interactions, then there is an awareness of this group difference in the interactions. Overall, more person-centered communication and lessened anxiety were associated with more satisfying family relationships.

An additional benefit of intergroup theorizing on these families is that it may help explain why individuals can have satisfying relationships with a gay or lesbian family member yet still hold fairly negative views toward homosexuality. Although individuals may identify with distinct social groups, this difference may not always be salient either because a common ingroup such as shared family identity is transcending these differences, or individuals do not perceive their family member as typical or representative of gays or lesbians in their opinion. Theoretically, this would allow a parent who holds negative views toward gays or lesbians to still view their child in a positive manner because they view them as an *atypical* member of the outgroup (i.e., "My son is not like other gay men") or the family identity trumps the divergent sexual identity. Although this may be beneficial for the immediate family relationship, there are obvious negative consequences to this in that positive experiences in these family relationships may not always generalize to more positive perceptions of gay men and lesbians in general. Employing an intergroup perspective to focusing on the relational maintenance between gay men and lesbians and their families-of-origin complements the majority of the research on families and sexual identity which has focused on disclosure of sexual identity, parental reactions, couple relational maintenance, and gay and lesbian-headed households (Peplau & Beals, 2004).

Race/Ethnic Identity

Intergroup scholars have devoted much of their attention to understanding racial/ethnic identity and interracial/ethnic conflict (see Chapter 2). Whereas some of the extreme outcomes of intergroup conflict (e.g., violence) may not be present in personal relationships with individuals from different racial/ethnic groups, these relationships are still characterized by intergroup dynamics as is evident in experiences of couples and children in these multiracial/ethnic families. Similar to grandparent-grandchild relationships and communication between family members with different sexual identities, differences within interracial/ethnic families are not always at the forefront and by no means are these families overly challenged. However, we should not ignore the influence of the divergent values, attitudes, and histories associated with the racial/ethnic identity as well as the monoracial/ethnic social norms. Soliz (2008) summarizes some of the family communication practices highlighted in the research and theorizing on these families, and there are clear representations of the intergroup dynamics. For instance, couples often mention that, while they perceive themselves in terms of a common family identity, recognition of racial/ethnic differences and any consequential tensions may be triggered by some external event, such as a family member making a racial comment or a controversial current event. In these circumstances, couples rely on relational maintenance strategies such as directly addressing the issue to put it to rest. Other couples may have a mutual understanding that the best way to manage these circumstances is to avoid open discussion as talking about it may agitate or prolong any tension. Whereas these represent different approaches, they both indicate that couple communication is, at times, a method for managing difference associated with racial/ethnic identity. Of course, families do not simply wait for an external influence before appreciating the intergroup nature of the family. Family rituals, stories, and other internal family discourses center on engendering a sense of familial identity and, for many families, also recognizing the separate racial/ethnic identities that constitute the family. An additional influential factor in relational solidarity is the support (or lack thereof) couples receive from the rest of the family which is indicative of Allport's (1954) emphasis on the role of institutional support in positive intergroup relations.

For multiracial/ethnic individuals, identity is a complex aspect of self. Family communication plays a role in the identity of multiracial/ethnic children as a socializing agent, a method by which individuals convey identity to those in and outside of the family, and a strategy for managing perceived differences between oneself and other family members. In Soliz, et al. (2009) study on multiracial/ethnic individuals' family relationships, personal communication as indicated by self-disclosure and supportive communication was associated with relational satisfaction and/or a greater sense of shared family identity. The study also highlights important communicative practices in these families that are not as important in monoracial/ethnic families. For instance, findings suggest that identity accommodation, defined as "*communicatively* recognizing and affirming the multiracial/ethnic heritage of family members" (p. 8), is an important aspect of satisfying relationships and reducing a sense of racial/ethnic difference. For the latter outcome, it appears that directly acknowledging the complex and divergent racial/ethnic backgrounds of family members in an affirmative manner actually reduces the sense of group difference in the family. As with the family types covered thus far, multiracial/ethnic families are becoming more common. Hence, scholars and family practitioners would be served well by equipping themselves with a theoretical lens accounting for individual, familial, and societal factors surrounding race/ethnicity.

Similarly, as concern for physical and cultural similarity has lessened in desires of parents adopting a child, international and transracial adoption are becoming more common. As such, a unique aspect of these families is how the cultural and racial/ethnic identity of the child and parents are incorporated into the larger family identity. As Galvin (2003) points out, socializing messages from parents to children about identity, narratives that focus on a child's heritage, family labels that incorporate the varying background of family members, and legitimizing the family to challenges or questions from extended family or friends (e.g., "Is she your *real* daughter?") are examples of communication processes somewhat unique to these families. Hence, the intergroup nature of these family experiences does not imply a negative or uncomfortable relationship. Rather, it sheds light on the fact that recognizing similarities and difference can be, and often is, a central function of family communication.

Religious Identity

Following similar trends as multiracial/ethnic families, interfaith families are becoming more common. Research on these families suggests that interfaith relationships are more turbulent than other relationships especially when it comes to issues associated with faith such as religious identity of the family members and disapproval from extended family members (see Chapter 7). Although there is minimal research on how religious difference is communicatively managed, religious orientation offers some insight. Religious orientation accounts for the commitment and salience of one's faith, importance of religious social networks, and tolerance for other perspectives. Thus, it is not surprising that religious orientation in interfaith couples is linked to the nature of marital conflict, relational satisfaction, and dependence on the social network for relational maintenance (Hughes & Dickson, 2005). The manner in which religious differences affect family interactions and relationships is an area ripe for research. In addition to different faiths, families may also have to manage different levels of religious commitment. Although family members may identify with the same religion, the strength of this identity and its role in the self-concept of individual family members may differ, creating similar tensions as we would expect in interfaith families.

Age, sexual identity, race/ethnicity, and religion are by no means the only significant types of identity that can influence family interactions and relationships. For instance, political affiliation, socioeconomic status or "blue" vs. "white" collar professions, and (dis)ability are but a few of the additional aspects of self that often permeate family functioning. As demonstrated in this discussion, intergroup theorizing provides a framework for understanding the interplay between social influences and family interactions.

Intergroup Dynamics in the Family: Formative Processes

Banker and Gaertner's (1998) study on stepfamily harmony highlighted the idea that families are an ever-changing entity oftentimes augmented by formative processes, and it is through interactions that family and individual identities are created and maintained after the introduction of new family members (Galvin, 2006). The following discussion highlights intergroup dynamics and family identity emerging from formative process of joining two distinct family groups: stepfamilies and in-law relationships.

In discussing potential barriers to stepfamily development, Braithwaite, Olson, Golish, Soukup, and Turman (2001) highlight factors that reflect the ingroup versus outgroup nature of some stepfamilies such as feelings of loyalty or affiliation to the family-of-origin, minimal shared experiences or histories with new family members, and uncertainty as to the new family identity. Evident in stepfamily development is how everyday communication serves as a barometer of familial solidarity. For instance, the choice to use the label "step-sister" as opposed to "sister" is a way of explicitly demarcating family inclusion or exclusion. Similar to other research on ingroup identity, personalized communication and feelings of equality in family interactions characterize stronger perceptions of family solidarity whereas destructive conflict and/or avoidance of interaction are indicative of a less cohesive group. One of the more notable implications of stepfamily development research is that stepfamilies are not "all or nothing." The new versus old (i.e., outgroup versus ingroup) identity is typically in a state of flux. Although it may stabilize for some individuals in relatively constant perceptions of either family solidarity or separateness, it may also change over the relationship's life course. Thus, stepfamily solidarity (i.e., ingroup identity) is reflected in or shaped by the communication practices of the family members.

Similar to stepfamilies, barriers to satisfying in-law relationships are a reflection of family-of-origin versus "new family" categorization and comparison. In fact, perceptions of ingroup identity have been shown to be an important characteristic of positive in-law relationships. For instance, Morr-Serewicz, Hosmer,

Ballard, and Griffin (2008) demonstrated how self-disclosure predicts ingroup identity which, in turn, is associated with relational satisfaction. In addition to communication associated with perceptions of shared family identity such as self-disclosure, supportive communication and sharing experiences, Rittenour and Soliz (2009) identified those nonaccommodative behaviors that may accentuate familial boundaries or a sense of exclusion for the child-in-law such as in-laws failing to explain family rituals, not taking into account religious or political views of family-of-origin, or not including them in family story-telling. Likewise, there are behaviors that dissuade children-in-law from even wanting to affiliate with the spouse's family. These include overly personal disclosures, complaining, and negative personality disposition that is reflected in everyday talk. These studies also highlight the importance of understanding how aspects of the family system (e.g., spouse's support of in-law contact, in-laws' relationships with grandchildren) can promote or hinder a sense of affiliation. Finally, a sense of shared family identity in in-law relationships is associated with willingness to allocate personal and financial resources to caring for in-laws and/or maintaining relationships even in cases when the legal "connection" is absent (e.g., a daughter-in-law maintaining a relationship with her mother-in-law following the death of the spouse, siblings-in-law still interacting as "family" following a divorce).

Family Communication and Outgroup Attitudes

Family communication is central to the formation of identity and corresponding attitudes. Typically, we think of this in terms of the socializing process of younger family members in that attitudes are intergenerationally transmitted. However, intergroup theorizing sensitizes us to another manner in which family communication influences our attitudes toward others. At the heart of the intergroup tradition is not only understanding the dynamics of intergroup relations and conflict but also in identifying conditions of intergroup contact that can improve intergroup attitudes (Allport, 1954; Pettigrew, 1998; see Chapter 8). Given that intergroup interactions occur in our families, intergroup contact may be associated with our attitudes toward certain groups. In fact, frequent contact with members of an outgroup may exist only in family interactions. For many younger adults, for instance, the most frequent contact with older adults is in the family (Williams & Harwood, 2004). Considering that society is relatively segregated, sustained contact with individuals from different groups is limited. With the changing nature of families (e.g., interracial/ethnic families), it is likely that families may be a context where individuals have contact and relationships with members of various outgroups. Thus, it is where intergroup contact and potential changes in outgroup attitudes may occur. Support for this has been found in recent research as more positive contact in grandparent-grandchild relationships is associated with more positive attitudes toward older adults and aging (Harwood et al., 2005: Soliz & Harwood, 2006). Likewise, Soliz, Ribarsky, Harrigan & Tye-Williams (in press) found that person-centered communication on the part of both family members was associated with improved attitudes toward homosexuality in general in families with divergent sexual identities.

One of the complex aspects of intergroup contact is that, in order for positive contact to result in a positive change in outgroup attitudes, individuals have to perceive each other as typical and representative of their respective social groups (i.e., group identity should be salient: Brown & Hewstone, 2005). If I have fairly negative views of a specific religious group, positive interactions with an individual from that religious group may improve my attitudes toward that group overall *if* I believe the individual is truly representative of the religion. If this is not the case, then I am likely to dismiss this positive experience as atypical and, thus, my attitudes are not changed. Traditionally, intergroup contact has been investigated within the context of non-personal relationships where group salience is typically negatively associated with positive contact. However, Pettigrew (1998) suggests that it is within personal relationships that we may find great promise for reducing group-based prejudice. Because individuals typically have some type of personal relationship with members of an outgroup, they are able to experience positive interactions with outgroup members without the same level of negative effects of a contact between strangers (e.g., high levels of intergroup anxiety, constrained communication).

Families provide a context for this more personal relationship. Testing Brown and Hewstone's (2005) contact hypothesis, Soliz and Harwood (2006) demonstrated an association between grandparent-grandchild contact and attitudes toward older adults is present when age salience is high. In other words, the grandchild has to perceive their grandparent as an older adult, not just a family member. If age identity is not salient, this generalization is less likely to occur and this would explain circumstances where families may have positive relationships with family members who belong to different social groups yet still hold negative views toward that group. For instance, a son-in-law may be of a different faith than his wife's family. Even though the parents have an extremely positive relationship with the son-in-law, they may still hold negative views toward his faith because his religious identity is not salient in their interactions or they do not see him as representative of the religious group. The same process holds true for in-laws and stepfamilies: can contact with a member of the step- or in-law family generalize to perceptions of the step-families or in-laws as a whole? This is perhaps one of the greatest benefits of an intergroup theorizing in that it further positions communication in the family as central to shaping our perceptions of others.

Conclusion

The purpose of this chapter was to position intergroup theorizing as a "lens" for understanding family relationships (see Figure 1). To summarize, our outgroup attitudes likely influence the initial recognition of group-based differences, communication with family members, and overall relational satisfaction. Obviously, the effect of this influence is dependent on the valence of the attitudes (i.e., positive or negative). Yet, as the relationship progresses, the nature of the communication between family members influences and can be affected by this awareness of group-based differences and/or relational satisfaction. As an example, we can extend the previous discussion on sexual identity in the family. The relationship between a father and his gay son is influenced by his attitudes toward gay men, especially if the father perceives his son as a "typical" gay man (i.e., the son enacts behaviors that fit the father's stereotypes). If these attitudes are negative, the quality of the relationship is contingent on whether or not the communication reflects a more personal or intergroup orientation. If the father and son are communicating as "individuals" with minimal awareness or influence of the different sexual identities, then relational satisfaction is likely to be high as any negative consequences of intergroup salience (e.g., intergroup anxiety) is minimized. Conversely, interactions that reflect group-based differences (e.g., direct disclosures of disapproval, avoidance of controversial topics, conflict related to sexual identity) are likely associated with less relational satisfaction.

Given the importance of both familial relationships and social identities in our lives, it is likely that interactions between the father and son lie between these two extremes. At times, communication may reflect an intrafamilial relationship (i.e., father-son) while being influenced by intergroup dynamics at other times (i.e., interactions between individuals with divergent sexual identities). As depicted in Figure 1, family relationships also have the potential to change outgroup attitudes. Thus, if the father and son have a positive relationship and the father recognizes the sexual identity of his child, it is likely that his negative attitudes toward gay men will improve. The process also applies to families formed through the union of two distinct family groups as the outgroup, in this case, represents perceptions of the "new" family (e.g., in-laws or stepfamily members; see Rittenour & Soliz, 2009).

Families are one of the most important social groups in an individual's life and scholars have realized long ago that families are complex, dynamic entities. Understanding families requires theorizing that can draw attention to this complexity and, more importantly, provide a conceptual framework for understanding that communication and identity are embedded in family functioning. Although not the only theoretical framework that can serve this function, this chapter has highlighted the utility of an intergroup perspective on families. First, this perspective draws our attention to the fact that personal relationships such as those in families are not immune from the, some would argue, innate process of categorizing our world into social ingroups and outgroups. Second, it highlights the fact that macro-social influences such as social identity and the corresponding attitudes toward different groups are at play in our family relationships. Third, it positions communication as central to understanding how shared family identity is created and maintained. Finally, intergroup contact theorizing further places family as a context where attitudes toward others are created, maintained, or changed. Whereas family is typically thought of as a collective identity, it is also a context in which difference exists. Given the significance of family in our lives, intergroup scholars should turn their attention toward families to understand how affiliation and difference operate in our daily lives and personal relationships. Likewise, family scholars who hope to broaden our understanding of family functioning should consider intergroup theorizing as a "lens" to their inquiries.

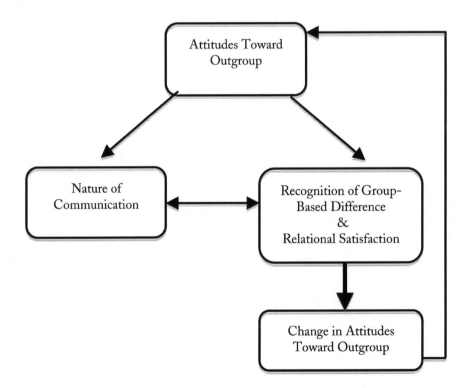

Figure 1: Intergroup Dynamics of Family Communication

CHAPTER SIXTEEN

Intergroup Communication in the Context of Traditional Media

DANA MASTRO

" . . . there were no Latin people on *Star Trek* . . . this was proof that they weren't planning to have us around for the future."

JOHN LEGUIZAMO, U.S. ACTOR AND COMEDIAN

It is probably safe to say that when John Leguizamo offered the above remark, his primary intent was to provide a humorous critique of the portrayal of Latinos on television (or lack thereof). What he additionally succeeded in highlighting with this commentary is the fundamental role of media representations in intergroup processes. From the practices of the institutions that produce the messages to the consumption patterns of the individuals that choose them, mass media are enmeshed in the fabric of real-world intergroup dynamics. Yet, despite the relatively conspicuous link between mass media offerings and real world intergroup outcomes, researchers have only recently begun to apply the assumptions from intergroup theories to issues pertaining to media production, use, and effects. The present chapter highlights this work, focusing specifically on research addressing intergroup processes associated with traditional media (e.g., television, newspaper, magazines, etc.).

Intergroup Messages in Traditional Media

Content analytic research documenting media depictions of groups has long revealed that mainstream media offerings (particularly in the U.S.) provide little in the way of diverse or equitable characterizations of racial/ethnic minorities and other non-dominant groups (Harwood & Anderson, 2002; Mastro, 2009). Media portrayals are meaningful as both the quantity and quality of depictions communicate messages to consumers about the relative strength and standing of different groups in society as well as the legitimacy of prevailing intergroup dynamics. Further, the form of language used (i.e., concrete to abstract) in reference to different groups subtly maintains and transmits expectations and beliefs about these groups, typically supporting intergroup comparisons that favor dominant groups (Maass, Corvino, & Arcuri, 1994). Thus, the mere existence of different groups in the media coupled with the manner in which they are verbally and visually characterized lets each play a role in defining groups' status in relation to others across different intergroup contexts (Abrams, Eveland, & Giles, 2003; Harwood & Roy, 2005).

Group Vitality and Media Messages

From a group vitality perspective, media exposure contributes to the development of (oftentimes subjective) perceptions about groups which then become a part of societal belief systems regarding groups' efficacy, power, privilege, value, support, and sustainability (Abrams, Eveland, & Giles, 2003). As Harwood and Roy (2005, p. 194) assert, " . . . the content of media represents important turf and identity battles between particular groups. It is clear that media content reflects group status and vitality (via the presence and nature of portrayals), conveys societal values concerning diversity (via the offerings available focused on specific groups), and serves as a barometer of intergroup relations." Of course a variety of factors (both individual and group based) are likely to influence media-related intergroup outcomes; nonetheless, the overarching representations identified through systematic assessments of media content can hardly be ignored.

Quantitative content analyses examining overt representations of different groups in the media indicate that non-dominant groups have been consistently underrepresented compared to their proportions of the real world population (Harwood & Anderson, 2002; Mastro, 2009). In particular, whereas African Americans and White Americans are presented on primetime television at rates that meet or exceed their proportions of the U.S. population, the same cannot be said of Asian Americans, Latinos, Native Americans, women, children, or older adults (although exceptions exist for some groups in certain genres and times of day).

When the nature of these roles is considered, distinct pictures emerge for each group. In terms of White males, they enjoy an assortment of roles representing a wide range of characters and portrayals. In addition, they are more likely than their on-air counterparts to be seen in prestigious or authoritative positions. For White women, although they have often been portrayed in secondary and dependent roles, the nature of these characterizations appears to be changing for the better. Among African Americans, representations vary considerably based on the type of media. On primetime entertainment programs the images are generally evenhanded. The same cannot be said for depictions in the news. Here, African Americans (particularly males) are disproportionately presented as criminals and likely to be portrayed in need of restraint (with control produced at the hands of White police officers; see also Chapter 6).

When it comes to other groups, much less is known. Older adult characters are presented in a more unflattering manner than younger characters (Harwood & Anderson, 2002; see Chapter 4). Latinos are depicted in a relatively limited set of roles, often revolving around themes of subservience, laziness, criminality, sexuality, or intellectual ineptitude—a set of features generally characteristic of both men and women (Mastro, 2009). The few Asian Americans that are seen in the media are most often found as minor and non-recurring roles but in high status positions. Native Americans, if portrayed, are likely to be presented as spiritual, as social problems, or as warriors (Fryberg, 2003).

Irrespective of the intentionality or veracity of these portrayals, they carry meaning to audience members about the features and values associated with different groups. Moreover, they help to define norms of treatment associated with different groups across contexts. Accordingly, these representations (alongside real world experiences) assist in defining and reinforcing societal norms about groups and group-based interactions. But, such overt characterizations are not the only intergroup messages conveyed by mass media content. Implicit messages also are transmitted by the type of language used in reference to different groups.

Linguistic Intergroup Bias and Media Messages

According to assumptions rooted in models of linguistic intergroup bias (see Chapters 5, 8, & 9), variations in language abstraction can be utilized, whether or not consciously, to support group-based identity needs (Maass, Corvino, & Arcuri, 1994). Specifically, because abstract statements are inherently perceived by consumers to be more dispositional, stable, and generalizable, messages communicated in this manner are seen to offer trait-based information about the target that is difficult to verify while simultaneously resistant to disconfirmation. On the other hand, concrete statements are naturally interpreted to be situational (i.e., context-specific) and verifiable. Consequently, as language in the media shifts from abstract to concrete, subject-specific informativeness is diminished and situation-specific informativeness is enhanced, allowing for the subtle transmission and maintenance of stereotypes, generally in support of dominant groups. Accordingly, highly generalized, abstract language would be expected to be used in reference to the positive behaviors and characteristics associated with dominant/majority groups as well as in reference to the negative behaviors and characteristics associated with non-dominant/minority groups (provoking internal/dispositional attributions among consumers). Alternatively, concrete language would be expected to be associated with negative majority group behaviors and positive minority group behaviors (yielding external/situational attributions).

The small number of content analytic studies on broadcasting and print media that have investigated these patterns have established preliminary substantiation for the existence of such group-based linguistic distortions in media messages. When it comes to reports of topics ranging from soccer games (national versus outgroup team; see Chapter 20) to issues such as domestic interethnic conflict (Jewish versus non-Jewish; see Chapters 2 & 11) to international war (Gulf War: 'allied' versus Iraqi forces), the evidence cautiously suggests that media producers and journalists shift their language to maintain the identity needs of the dominant group (Maass, Corvino, & Arcuri, 1994); however, these patterns are not entirely consistent across media types and content. Nonetheless, they point to the potential for media messages to subtly and even unconsciously contribute to partisan real world intergroup dynamics.

When considering the increasing concentration in ownership of traditional media outlets and the lack of diversity among media producers and newsmakers, it is not surprising that these linguistic patterns would serve to retain dominant/majority conceptions about group characteristics and social positions (Maass, Corvino, & Arcuri, 1994). Media ownership and management are inherently tied to issues associated with the quantity and quality of group-based media offerings (Harwood & Roy, 2005) and news editing practices (Bell, 1984). Accordingly, disparities in the control of media content raise concerns about the nature of the characterizations likely to be offered. This is not to say, however, that consumers mindlessly absorb the messages provided in mass media. Instead, research suggests that consumers select and avoid media content (to the degree possible) in order to negotiate identity needs.

Media Selection and Avoidance

Researchers applying aspects of the social identity approach to media contexts have found that consumers utilize media, television in particular, in an effort to manage their group identity needs. According to social identity theory (see Chapters 1 & 21), individuals' self-concept is derived, in part, from the group memberships to which they belong. Depending on the salience of the particular group membership and the importance of the group to one's self-concept, it can be used in group-based comparisons to provide a comparative advantage for the ingroup; thereby securing positive social identity and maintaining self-esteem. As such, the selection of comparative dimensions is not arbitrary. Rather, individuals are motivated to select dimensions which maximize differences in favor of the ingroup, then preserve their favorable distinctiveness by constantly maximizing beneficial group-based differences. To these ends, the potential for mass media to play a role in this process is highly conceivable. Compared with real world intergroup contexts, mass media offerings are more easily manipulated to meet identity needs, particularly for dominant group members. For these groups, numerous media options are available which provide a basis for auspicious intergroup comparisons. Among non-dominant groups, interactions with media are likely to require increased consideration.

Among the notable contributions of the social identity framework in the context of media, is the research applying its assumption to understanding usage patterns. This research has consistently revealed that *group identification*, beyond more idiosyncratic accounts of media use, meaningfully impacts on viewers' television choices. Specifically, as audience members' group identification increases (e.g., age identification, ethnic identification, etc.) so, too, do preferences for programs that positively feature ingroup characters (Harwood, 1999a, b). Moreover, this relationship appears to be reciprocal in that the selection of programs depicting ingroup characters reinforces group identification (Harwood, 1999a). Thus, by revealing group identification to be a driving force in the selection process, this research builds on longstanding findings (e.g., uses and gratifications, selective exposure, and the like) which demonstrate that consumers prefer characters that are similar to themselves.

Needless to say, the ability to actually locate favorable ingroup portrayals can be a challenge for some groups (as evidenced by the content analytic research addressed previously). For these groups (e.g., racial/ethnic minorities), identity needs are managed via selection *and* avoidance of media messages (Abrams & Giles, 2007). What's more, these choices are predictive of group vitality perceptions, such as social standing and relative power (see Chapter 10). As would be expected, when programming is selected to meet group identity needs, perceptions of group vitality are enhanced. Alternatively, when programming is deliberately avoided to preserve group identity, perceptions of vitality are diminished.

These vitality-based effects should not be altogether surprising given that the decision to choose or reject media content is an active process (although these decisions can become automatic over time). They gain increasing importance, however, when considered from the standpoint of who benefits and who loses as a result of this process. From this perspective, it is clear that dominant groups are advantaged over non-dominant groups when it comes to traditional media (e.g., television), as favorable images are abundant and the need for avoidance to protect identity needs is virtually (although not entirely) nonexistent. For non-dominant consumers, on the other hand, this process is likely to induce awareness of their group's marginalized status and standing in society, producing unfavorable effects on vitality perceptions (Abrams & Giles, 2007). The implication here is that alongside developing differences in media usage patterns, dominant and non-dominant groups may form entirely different responses to media messages.

Minority Group Responses to Mainstream Media Offerings

In addition to its influence on patterns of media use, group membership also affects interpretations of and effects associated with traditional media. Here again, the role of ingroup identification cannot be overstated. As identification with a group increases so, too, does the motivation to protect the status and interests of the group. Accordingly, it is the degree of group identification that determines responses to intergroup media messages. A group membership that holds little or no value for the consumer is not likely to encourage a reaction, regardless of the quality of the image or the ability to generate favorable intergroup comparisons. Alternatively, for media consumers who have a strong sense of affiliation with their ingroup, exposure is more likely to provoke intergroup responses. Among marginalized groups, this may mean actively managing identity threats stemming from negative characterizations in mainstream media fare. For majority groups, exposure is likely to produce stereotypical judgments of outgroup members and more advantageous evaluations of ingroup members. In other words, the messages offered in mainstream media may, for some, facilitate intergroup comparisons in favor of self. For others, these same images may be harmful to social identity, requiring more thoughtful selection of media content and necessitating strategic efforts to maintain self-concept. In this regard, the nature of media messages of social groups becomes a critical feature in the process.

As a result of the threat to group identity posed by exposure to negative media images of one's ingroup, minority consumers may employ a number of social creativity strategies to improve or at least psychologically manage intergroup status (Harwood & Roy, 2005). This goes beyond merely controlling media profiles (e.g., selection/avoidance) and, additionally, considers how different groups process and respond to media messages (Fujioka, 2005a,b). Further, it takes into account how ingroup identification impacts on these practices—thus underscoring the truly group-based nature of such processes, beyond individual preferences (Harwood & Roy, 2005). It is important to note, however, that although such responses are typically associated with non-dominant/minority groups, it is reasonable to suggest that dominant groups would also utilize these tactics when their status is threatened.

Still, research generally suggests that threats to identity resulting from exposure to mass media primarily affect oppressed groups (Fujioka, 2005a, b). In the main, this work has revealed that minority audience members are critical of the unfavorable manner in which they are commonly featured in traditional, mainstream media and, indeed, see these depictions as damaging to group identity and intergroup status. Not surprisingly then, when exposed to mainstream media offerings minority group members are more likely than majority groups to judge these messages to be inaccurate and negative. These conflicting interpretations (between dominant and non-dominant groups) plainly reflect the influence of intergroup dynamics on the ways that consumers understand media messages. Among marginalized groups, challenging the legitimacy of messages aids in protecting the group. For majority group consumers, accepting the message maintains dominance and preserves the status quo. What is important to note is that these divergent construals of media messages are likely to stem from differences in cognitive processing. Negative media messages about one's ingroup are likely to provoke arousal. This arousal then increases attention to the message, generating increased scrutiny and encouraging retention of the message. Thus, the group-based characteristics of the consumer trigger differential processing strategies that lead to distinct intergroup interpretations of media messages.

Because of the inherent need to enhance one's self-concept by way of favorable intergroup comparisons, minority consumers may even reinterpret media messages in an attempt to support their social identity. When this is the case, rather than criticizing or rejecting the content, audience members may focus on different aspects of the message, different dimensions within that social identity, or different social identities altogether. Although these assertions have yet to be empirically tested, media and social identity theorists contend that such strategies are conceivable and even likely when the need to preserve or improve intergroup standing emerges. For example, American Indian consumers confronted with negative, stereotypical ingroup characterizations in the film *Pocahontas* may reject the film in its entirety. Alternatively, they might: (a) emphasize messages of interracial collaboration in the film; (b) focus on alternate and favorable ingroup characterizations in the film, such as nurturing; or (d) select another salient social identity depicted in the film, perhaps gender.

Despite attempts to mitigate the potentially detrimental effects of consuming negative media images of one's ingroup, research demonstrates that exposure can, nonetheless, damage the self-concept and esteem of minority group audiences. For example, in her research examining the impact of exposure to Native American mascots on Native American consumers, Fryberg (2003) found evidence that viewing these images (e.g., Chief Wahoo) negatively impacted audience members' esteem and beliefs regarding community efficacy.

Majority Group Responses to Mainstream Media Offerings

When considering contemporary portrayals of social groups in traditional media (particularly news and primetime television), it becomes clear that this environment provides dominant groups a uniquely advantageous opportunity to engage in ingroup favoring social comparisons. Decades of experimental investigations on media priming and socialization support this contention, although not explicitly tested as intergroup designs (for review, see Mastro, 2009). This work demonstrates that exposure to the unfavorable depictions of non-dominant groups in the media can influence dominant group members' evaluations of the outgroup's competence, socioeconomic status, group status, social roles, and their general attributes. In other words, the bulk of this research has focused on the extent to which media exposure promotes outcomes such as stereotyping, prejudice, and discrimination—all issues of intergroup dynamics. Despite this obvious association, only a small number of studies have considered the assumptions from intergroup theories in application to media effects. Most prominent within this area of inquiry is the research utilizing social identity theory, although studies assessing the influence of media exposure on consumers' linguistic intergroup bias also have begun to emerge.

Social Identity-Based Effects

When applied to the effects of exposure to mainstream media (beyond the selection of content, addressed previously), the social identity framework (including social identity theory and self-categorization theory; see Chapter 1) provides a conceptual model for understanding how media use may contribute to stereotyping and discrimination by promoting biased intergroup comparisons. That said, it should not be presumed that this framework's tenets apply only to dominant group members. Instead, these theories provide insights into which subgroups of consumers are more likely to engage in intergroup behaviors and what features of media content may provoke these outcomes (Harwood & Roy, 2005).

Experimental tests of these models' assumptions in the context of television have met with relatively consistent support in application to majority group (e.g., White) exposure to minority group representations (e.g., Latino). Among majority groups, exposure to stereotypical media representations of minorities appears to encourage race-based social comparisons, which advantage the ingroup and serve identity needs, particularly among consumers who are high in racial identification (Mastro, 2003). That is, viewing unfavorable depictions of minorities in the media can provoke negative, stereotypical responses among White consumers (often highly race-identified Whites), which, in turn, may bolster self-concept by offering a comparison that privileges their dominant group.

Further, when the features of media content, such as message ambiguity, obfuscate the threat of appearing racist (i.e., aversive racism), the potential for intergroup bias is enhanced (Mastro, Behm-Morawitz, & Kopacz, 2008). Certainly, discriminatory responses to media content emerge based on exposure to overtly negative depictions of outgroup members, however, such outcomes appear to manifest even more so when the media content offers protection from appearing racially biased. Simply put, White consumers' intergroup responses to media, particularly among those highly identified with their race, appear to be more pronounced when the content of the message offers sufficient ambiguity for the response to be deemed unrelated to race. This ability to privilege one's ingroup through advantageous comparisons with a mediated outgroup promotes social identity and esteem maintenance (although not consistently so), while simultaneously protecting viewers' egalitarian self-concept.

Linguistic Intergroup Bias as an Effect of Media Exposure

Alongside prompting the overt intergroup responses noted above, media exposure also has been linked to more nuanced group-based outcomes. Research examining the effects of television consumption on linguistic ingroup biases in describing minority groups (Gorham, 2006) reveals that the consumption of high quantities of television news (which disproportionately features African Americans as criminals) predicts the use of abstract language when describing outgroup (African American) suspects (signifying dispositional attributions) and the use of more concrete language when characterizing ingroup (White) suspects (indicative of situational attributions). These subtle language distortions in response to media exposure, Gorham (2006) suggests, demonstrate that biased processing favoring one's ingroup occurs without the conscious knowledge of the consumer. Further, these results highlight the media's role in perpetuating unfavorable intergroup relations through its persistent reliance on negative depictions of racial/ethnic and other non-dominant groups.

Factors That Diminish or Enhance Unfavorable Intergroup Outcomes

To this point, little has been said about the insights that intergroup frameworks provide into the features of media content and consumers that may discourage negative intergroup dynamics and even promote more favorable group-based outcomes. In fact, these theories identify a number of important aspects of media and intergroup processes that may positively affect intergroup dynamics, including: (a) identification with superordinate group memberships; (b) exposure to prototypical and accommodating messages and; (c) intergroup contact (both real and mediated).

Superordinate Group Membership

Given the ability of the media to activate specific dimensions of social identity that govern how we judge the social environment, it is reasonable to assume that cuing more inclusive group categories can reduce intergroup bias. The underlying assumption here is that "by inducing people to identify with a larger social category, former out-group members can be recast as belonging to the larger in-group, thereby increasing the tendency to regard them more favorably" (Richardson, 2005, p. 506). To test this assertion, Richardson experimentally manipulated the framing of editorial newspaper responses to a U.S. Supreme Court ruling in an affirmative action case, such that the inclusiveness of the frame varied (e.g., superordinate identity, subgroup identity). His results offer support for social identity based predictions regarding superordinate group membership and demonstrate the media's role in influencing group salience. In particular, White participants who read the article framed around an inclusive social category revealed more positive affect toward African Americans. Framing of the news story did not, however, influence support for affirmative action. Despite this inconsistency, the present study aids in elucidating the intergroup processes that may underlie framing effects (see Chapter 11) and points to the potential for media messages to improve intergroup attitudes. Research utilizing self-categorization theory additionally advances our understanding of this association by further explicating the cognitive processes that may produce more favorable intergroup outcomes.

Prototypicality and Accommodation

From the perspective of self-categorization theory, the process of categorization informs person perception through the development of prototypes of group membership (see Chapter 8). These prototypes are sets of characteristics considered emblematic of the group, serving as the point of reference when evaluating self and other. This prototype-based processing depersonalizes social perceptions so that individuals are no longer considered in terms of their unique features and are, instead, assessed in terms of their embodiment of the group prototype. When evaluating others, the more prototypical the target-individual is along the salient category the more positive the evaluation, irrespective of whether the target is an ingroup or an outgroup member (Mastro, Tamborini, & Hullett, 2005). In other words, the more similar an ingroup or outgroup member is to the relevant characteristic of the perceiver's ingroup, the more favorable the evaluation.

Although traditionally applied to intergroup contexts, this process has been found to operate in much the same manner based on exposure to the media, influencing race-related attitudes and judgments. Indeed, findings from Mastro et al.'s (2005) investigation of the effects of celebrity prototypicality on White consumers' liking of White and African American celebrities revealed that the greater the similarity of media personalities to the ingroup (White) prototype (along a primed, group-based attribute), the greater the social attraction (see Chapter 17); with prototypicality affecting perceptions of both ingroup (White) and outgroup (African American) celebrities in a similar manner. Simply put, the "closer" the character to the ingroup prototype, the more favorably the target is evaluated, regardless of ingroup or outgroup status.

Although not conceptualized from a self-categorization perspective, additional support for this relationship can be gleaned from work applying a media accommodation framework. From this perspective, Coover (2001) posits that White viewers' preferences for certain media representations of race (over others) can be explained as a reflection of the extent to which these depictions affirm White norms. Indeed, her findings suggest that the greater the conformity to White social identity in intergroup interactions among characters, the more positive the audience members' appraisal of the media content.

Taken together, this research suggests that media depictions of race/ethnicity that conform to dominant value systems, preserve White identity, and encourage racial harmony elicit the most favorable outgroup evaluations among dominant group consumers (Coover, 2001; Mastro et al., 2005). Such messages even appear to promote outgroup social attraction, although not consistently. The subtext of these findings, however, is that messages which represent dissenting views, positions, traits, behaviors and the like, have the potential to promote stereotyping and a variety of unfavorable intergroup outcomes. Nevertheless, these results speak to the media's ability to play a meaningful role in improving intergroup relations. Further insights into the link between media and prosocial intergroup outcomes are offered by work applying assumptions from intergroup contact theory.

Real World and Parasocial Contact

Intergroup contact theory holds that contact can be an effective mechanism for the development of more favorable attitudes toward outgroups. In particular, this framework stipulates that positive intergroup contact can lead to constructive changes in attitudes and behaviors toward outgroup members. For such outcomes to emerge, the intergroup contact setting must meet several conditions, including shared goals, equal status between interactants, and support for cooperative interaction. If these specifications are not satisfied, the contact experience may not produce positive results. Notably, because emotional as well as socio-political influences can hinder optimal intergroup encounters in real world contexts, the potential for media messages to intervene in a positive manner becomes increasingly consequential (Ortiz & Harwood, 2007). As such, the assumptions of this theory have been applied to media exposure in a number of ways.

Initial applications of the theory explored how real world intergroup contact may moderate the effects of exposure. Consistently, this research has found that media messages have the most pronounced impact when real world contact is lacking. In particular, exposure to unflattering media characterizations of outgroup members produces the most negative intergroup outcomes when consumers have no favorable real world contact experiences to consider when forming judgments (Mastro, Behm-Morawitz, & Ortiz, 2007). The counterpoint to these results is that positive real world contact experiences can minimize or even eliminate the negative intergroup effects of exposure to unfavorable stereotypes in the media.

Recently, contact theory has been extended to include interactions involving media characters themselves. The belief underlying this parasocial contact hypothesis is that through mediated contact with outgroup members, viewers can develop relationships that serve to improve viewers' attitudes toward the outgroup (Schiappa, Gregg, & Hewes, 2005). Specifically, this parasocial interaction refers to the relationships that individuals develop with media characters/personalities. Over time, the perception of shared experiences with the character produces an affective attachment which can lead to attitude changes paralleling those in real world intergroup interactions. However, for parasocial contact effects to generalize to the entire outgroup, the character must be perceived to be representative of the group. That is, if the character is not seen as typical of the group, then the positive effects of the mediated, intergroup contact situation will not be applied to the outgroup as a whole. Ultimately, then, the parasocial contact hypothesis stipulates that exposure to even a single, outgroup television character can lead to improved attitudes toward the outgroup among viewers. However, this character must be appealing enough to encourage the development of a parasocial relationship and sufficiently archetypal to generalize to the outgroup as a whole (see Chapters 6, 10, 12, 15, & 17).

In a final approach to mediated contact, Ortiz and Harwood (2007) test the assertion that consumers can acquire positive intergroup attitudes and behaviors from exposure to television depictions in which ingroup characters (with whom viewers are highly identified) engage in constructive interactions with outgroup members. Unlike parasocial contact, which emphasizes exposure to outgroup members, mediated contact assumes that identification with ingroup characters can be equally important in improving intergroup attitudes, given the depiction of appropriate intergroup behaviors. Their results offer some support for this association.

Identification with ingroup characters involved in optimal contact encounters with outgroup members was, in certain cases, predictive of more positive attitudes toward outgroup members and less social distance.

Altogether, the work applying contact theory to mass media reveals that both real and mediated intergroup experiences play a role in determining the effects of exposure. In both cases, quality contact is of import. When real world contact is considered in the context of media exposure, it is clear that the effects of exposure to negative messages can be mitigated by constructive experiences with outgroup members in society. In terms of mediated contact, exposure to positive characterizations of outgroups as well as favorable intergroup interactions involving one's ingroup, each can effectively engender positive intergroup outcomes.

Conclusion

The evidence offered in this chapter suggests that intergroup theories have far-reaching implications for media researchers that complement and extend Turner's (1991) discussion of social identity theory and social influence. First, it is clear that the types of messages about social groups offered by traditional media play a part in both the selection and avoidance of mass media offerings which, in turn, influence perceptions of group value, status, and support. Second, exposure (whether incidental or intended) contributes to the production of collective group definitions and shared social identities which then shape intergroup dynamics. Third, exposure plays a prominent role in the activation of particular dimensions of group identity, which trigger the perceptual frames that govern how consumers see the social environment. Thus, once a social identity becomes salient, group norms impact social behaviors in a manner consistent with relevant intergroup and identity-based demands. Finally, the particular features of media content, in visually and verbally characterizing social groups and intergroup interactions, serve as a catalyst for the accentuation or abatement of biased intergroup outcomes.

From this intergroup perspective, it is easy to see how media messages can play a fundamental part in determining not only: (a) *that* people are exposed to the same information and perspectives on which to base their group-based categorizations and, (b) precisely *which* information they collectively share but also, (c) *why* they respond in a particular manner. Given this, the importance of programmatic research directed at increasing our understanding of the prosocial and antisocial effects of media on intergroup outcomes becomes unmistakable. Such work would not only shed light on the potential for media messages to provoke unanticipated, adverse intergroup responses but may also provide a resource for redressing these effects and even promoting more favorable group based interactions in society.

CHAPTER SEVENTEEN

Internet Interaction and Intergroup Dynamics

JOSEPH B. WALTHER & CALEB T. CARR

The Internet enables people to communicate in a variety of new ways. People exchange messages by email, group discussion channels, dyadic chats, through status messages or wall postings in social network sites, text messages on mobile phones, or via blogs and micro-blogs. The Internet also allows users to find, form, and maintain groups and virtual communities who share concerns, situations, or interests; who provide advice to one another about problems, professors, or products; who play online games with friends or strangers. Accompanying this array of applications have been changes in the way we communicate relative to more traditional communication modes. Online, we may communicate with people about whom we have no personal knowledge other than the interests or tasks we share with them. Most often, online, we send text to one another, without the physical appearance and vocal cues that otherwise convey part of what we mean and reveal part of who we are.

These differences between computer-mediated communication (CMC) and face-to-face interaction have potent psychological and social consequences. Early research on CMC suggested that the absence of nonverbal cues significantly hampers our ability to relate to one another when we communicate, particularly with people with whom no interpersonal relationship previously existed. However, more sophisticated understandings have arisen, suggesting that under a number of circumstances CMC offers very potent identification dynamics, and that CMC often invokes intergroup identifications, in a manner similar to ways reflected throughout this book. In fact, some theorists have claimed that when communicating online, identifying with others as members of a social group is the dominant form of relating: When communication partners are visually anonymous to one another, they use ingroup/outgroup distinctions to affiliate, rather than the individual and interpersonal dynamics that accompany face-to-face interaction. This form of identification—intergroup identification—affects *who* we like as well as *how* we like others, how social influence takes place, and the basis on which trust and accommodation occur.

This chapter discusses how and when intergroup dynamics affect CMC. We review theoretical frameworks that explain how CMC triggers different identification processes, and research which has illuminated how this works, and some limitations. We will review research on virtual teams to explore variations in the connection between intergroup processes and CMC effects. As we gain more precise understandings of when an intergroup approach works well and when other processes appear to come into play, we can make theoretical and practical suggestions of how to harness CMC most effectively to improve communication in some very important settings.

Impressions in CMC: Interpersonal or Intergroup

Online or offline, people may develop perceptions of others via the development of *interpersonal* impressions or via *impersonal*, group-based identities. When we meet others, our first impressions tend to form based on stereotypes involving the social categories people seem to represent: young or old, black or white, students or teachers or business people, etc. (see Chapter 8). If and when stereotyped impressions are proven incorrect or we discover that more refined impressions are needed to interact effectively with others, we reassess or seek to develop impressions further (Fiske & Neuberg, 1990). We progress beyond cultural stereotypes to develop more individuated impressions of others—how smart, funny, conservative, or attractive the individual is—and what the person's interpersonal demeanor is, such as friendly or unfriendly, casual or formal, etc. Face-to-face, it is not hard to discern individuals' personalities by observing their physical appearances, vocal characteristics, and the behaviors they exhibit through rapid and reciprocal interactions with us. CMC, however, makes the apprehension of individual characteristics more effortful and time-consuming than it is face-to-face. CMC users must focus on others' subtle language choices, message content, and message timing to build mental pictures of individuals they meet online. Building impressions this way takes time and effort in order to gather signals, sort them out, and construct impressions of individual partners. It is even more difficult if the channel is asynchronous (where messages are posted only every so often, such as an online discussion board, rather than a "real-time" chat) and/or when there are numerous individuals who are not terribly distinctive in what they write (for review, see Walther, 1996).

One consequence of the lack of immediate individuating cues in many CMC environs is that there is a heightened focus on the cultural and social categories and groups to which other users seem to belong. Focusing on users' social identities, rather than individual characteristics, provides users a path of lesser effort, given the decoding efforts and patience that interpersonal impression formation would demand.

The tendency to apprehend other online communicators in terms of their social groups is further promoted because in many cases interpersonal impressions of others online are unnecessary: A sense of other users' memberships in certain social groups is all one really needs in order to chat, play, gather advice, or make a decision in an online forum. For instance, when seeking advice online about how to cope with a chronic illness, CMC users seem to be less attuned to the particular demeanor or even the medical credentials that a discussion board message poster conveys. What matters more in accepting or rejecting another person's opinion is whether the message poster seems similar to the reader. The quality that makes the message poster credible is not what kind of individual person she is, but whether she, too, is a patient (see Chapter 19), presumably with the kinds of experiences that are attributable to that group of people with which discussion board readers have identified themselves (Wang, Walther, Pingree, & Hawkins, 2008). These two factors—that interpersonal cues are more effortful to discern, and that social identifications frequently suffice for effective online communication—go hand-in-hand, to help make many CMC interactions reflect the kinds of social dynamics that follow intergroup dynamics as discussed in this book.

For example, a friend who knows you are a *Star Wars* aficionado sends you the link, http://groups.google.com/group/alt.startrek.vs.starwars/topics/, where you peruse the Usenet newsgroup, "alt.startrek.vs.starwars". You notice among the screen names who posted comments, "StarWarsFan" and "StarTrekFan." Knowing nothing about the individuals behind the screen names, you would tend to perceive "StarWarsFan" as more like yourself, and you would likely have a greater attraction to that user. This prediction is the result of several things. First, you do not know any identifying, individuating information about either typist behind the screen names. As a result, your interactions are guided by social categorization (their affiliations with the two different fan factions) to draw you to the one who is identified as belonging to the same social group as yourself. Second, this dynamic occurred because the social categories were made salient by the discussion group's name and theme.

The SIDE Model of CMC

One of the most influential theoretical frameworks to incorporate intergroup dynamics in the study of CMC is the social identification model of deindividuation (SIDE; Spears & Lea, 1992). The model focuses on two factors that make CMC different from traditional communication: visual anonymity and the salience of a social identity. When we use CMC we are usually not within sight of the people to whom we are writing. The visual anonymity of communicators to one another produces *depersonalization* and *deindividuation* (Reicher, Spears, & Postmes, 1995). *Depersonalization* refers to not being able to discern that other people are uniquely different from one another, which can happen when people cannot see their partners and their apparent idiosyncrasies. It leads people to treat one another as though they are similar, even interchangeable, group members (Lea, Spears, & de Groot, 2001). *Deindividuation,* which also results from visual anonymity, is a temporary loss of self-awareness or a state in which people lose a sense of their own uniqueness. Deindividuation leads people to identify with others along the dimensions of small-scale social groups or large-scale social categories to which they belong. This brings up the second factor in the SIDE model: a salient social identity, meaning that a social group to which an individual feels some belonging is particularly apparent. Group salience can be activated by situational features, noticing the common characteristics of a group of people, detecting some threat to a group to which one belongs, or by someone's assignment of members to a group. Deindividuation, depersonalization, and social identification can also occur offline in some cases, such as when someone is thinking about an abstract group of people—one's fellow students at ABC University, for instance, or psychology majors, or British people. But acting toward people on the basis of group identities should happen less when there is active face-to-face interaction that reveals individual differences in attire, physical features, and mannerisms that remind a perceiver that his audience is composed of different people. In CMC the medium hides these features. Therefore users are deindividuated, and they rely on their identification with some group that is apparent to them to relate to others (Spears & Lea, 1992).

Laboratory experiments designed to test the SIDE model have developed a variety of interesting ways to raise or lower social identification in CMC environments, as well as to affect whether subjects experience depersonalized or individuated impressions of their partners. Most of these experiments use synchronous (real-time) computer-mediated chat with small, unacquainted groups in relatively brief encounters. Although there are a number of variations, a typical study involves experimental procedures like these: First, researchers gave each half of their experimental CMC groups different instructions before their online discussion. To stimulate greater social identification, instructions may frequently use the word "group," emphasize unity, and encourage participants to look for ways in which their group is unique. The other set of instructions encourages individual identification rather than social identification. They repeat the word, "individuals," stress diversity, and prompt participants to look for differences among members (Spears & Lea, 1992).

Second, in order to raise the level of deindividuation/depersonalization, researchers prevent half the groups from seeing their partners by placing visual barriers between the members or by having them communicate online from different rooms. In the other groups, to maximize perception of the different people involved, researchers have group members meet in the same room with no barriers between them, or, if participants are in different rooms, show participants' pictures to one another while they communicate. Social identification is typically highest both when members have been given the group-oriented version of instructions and cannot see others during their CMC chat.

SIDE Effects

What are the effects of CMC when it is involves visual anonymity and a salient group identity? When people interact in this manner, there is a certain kind of attraction they experience. People like one another on the basis of *social attraction*, which is conceptually different than *interpersonal attraction* (see for review Lea et al., 2001). Social attraction refers to a person's liking for a group as a whole, and abstractly—without reflection about individuals who comprise it—to all its members. Interpersonal attraction, on the other hand, refers to the level of affection an individual group member experiences with regard to each individual partner. Social attraction is also subject to systematic biases: As we identify with a group, we like the group and its members without considering how much we like member A, member B, or member C. In contrast, interpersonal attraction is thought of, from this perspective, as idiosyncratic: We like some people and dislike others based on their individual features. As CMC blocks interpersonal perceptions and reinforces one's sense of belonging to a group, SIDE argues, CMC promotes social attraction.

Social identification, depersonalization, and social attraction also lead CMC users' opinions and judgments to be more susceptible to influence by their online group than they would be when these factors are not as strong. As Lee (2006) demonstrated, when a CMC group member has acquired no information about the unique characteristics that would differentiate her online partners, she feels greater similarity to them—even when the partners' opinions on a controversial topic are objectively quite different from her own. Moreover, when the group is deindividuated in this manner, a member is more likely to conform to the majority's position. In contrast, when a CMC group member is provided information about her partners' different college majors, ages, hobbies, favorite TV shows and music, it has a similar effect to seeing their pictures in other studies: She individuates, feels less similarity to the members overall, and is less likely to change her position on the topic to match the other members'. Depersonalization leads people to feel like part of a CMC group and leads them to conform more strongly to the group norms, as reflected by a consensus of others' opinions. When we perceive others as distinctive individual people, some who we like more and others who we like less, the apparent consensus of other group members is less influential on an individual.

CMC users' susceptibility to groups' norms is also reflected in how they reciprocate their groups' subtle language variations and in how they evaluate partners' writing. In an important study that looked at actual discussion groups on the Internet, rather than experimental groups in a laboratory, Sassenberg (2002) found that groups with stronger social identification reflected certain linguistic behaviors more closely within their conversations, than did Internet groups with lower social identification. Sassenberg identified two types of online discussion groups on an Internet chat system: "common identity" and "common bond" groups. *Common identity* groups gather based on members' common interest in some topic, such as a particular hobby or software system. *Common bond* groups gather based on interpersonal interests. They are composed of friends who like each other as individuals (some of whom know each other offline) and simply use the Internet to chat together about whatever topic comes to mind. In Sassenberg's research, common identity group members experienced greater social attraction than interpersonal attraction. Analysis of their chat comments revealed that participants in common identity groups also showed more similarity to one another in terms of the use of emoticons, acronyms, and other certain phrases than did the members' common bond groups (whose social attraction levels were lower as well).

Another field study also revealed the development and reflection of language norms in CMC groups. Postmes, Spears, and Lea (2000) analyzed the language that students in a statistics course produced in an online discussion of the course. They found that subgroups naturally developed over time, based initially on when people were online to chat with one another. The more that these subgroups used their computer lab to chat, the more insular and unique they became with respect to different patterns of language that they used. In some groups there was more slang, humor, or personal disclosure than in others. Some groups used more affectionate language, while others were more formal. The patterns were more uniform within respective groups than they were when looking across them. Although the research did not discuss why any particular group developed the character that it did, the fact that differences arose from group to group shows how CMC may reinforce distinctive, "locally-defined" identities, not just amplify a broader social group or category (such as a certain type of person or student) which is often the focus of other studies.

In these ways, the SIDE model shows how CMC users relate to each other through impersonal but collegial relations in groups. Not seeing and not knowing each other as individuals enhances a certain kind of liking, social attraction, which makes people more attuned to their partners' opinions and online behaviors such as language. The model helps explain how the absence of nonverbal appearance cues in CMC does not really make people unable to relate to each other, as some have argued. Rather, as Lee (2006) has said, CMC can actually accentuate rather than attenuate social influence, and it can foster one's connection to others through non-interpersonal interaction.

Inconsistencies and Revisions

Although the SIDE model has significant utility in explaining group relations online, the research has also experienced setbacks. The disappointments, at times, suggest alternative interpretations that warrant new perspectives and additional research. For instance, following from its roots in social identity theory (see Chapters 1 & 21), SIDE theorists have suggested that the effects of CMC should be most pronounced when there is both an ingroup and outgroup. CMC users' suspicion that there are people different than themselves encroaching on their group may take several forms: simply being told that other groups are lurking in the research lab or on the Internet, or the presence of another group's members in an online group discussion, should do it. Both approaches, in fact, were predicted to magnify social attraction to the ingroup as well as raise negative responses toward outgroups in various research studies. As reasonable as this seems, the research specifically examining ingroup/outgroup dynamics in CMC has produced inconsistent results. Experiments have been conducted that led CMC users to believe that some of their online partners were from different countries, from rival universities, or in other ways represented social categories that differed from the primary subjects themselves. However, these studies have not generally produced the kinds of negative reactions to alleged outgroup members that a social identity approach predicts (e.g., Lea et al., 2001; Postmes, Spears, & Lea, 2002). Only by increasing CMC users' focus on participants being male versus female (Postmes & Spears, 2002) have ingroup/outgroup effects resulted in significant differences in behavior.

Other researchers have pointed to these studies' failure to generate ingroup/outgroup effects to mean something more positive: that visually anonymous CMC groups comprised of members from distinctive subgroups relate to the group as a whole and do not experience ingroup/outgroup discrimination among members. It may be as though they relate to all participants as "members of my CMC group," losing sight of the notion that members might represent different social groups or categories (Amichai-Hamburger & McKenna, 2006). This possibility is intriguing, and it deserves further study since the SIDE experiments in which visually anonymous CMC groups achieved the strongest identification effects were generally not composed of real subgroups rather than fictitious ones. It remains unclear if these effects occur when participants truly represent offline subgroups that differ strongly or exhibit prejudice to one another. We will return to this possibility later in this chapter.

Another problem with SIDE has arisen, as a recent study found that when a single member acts unexpectedly in a CMC group, social identification turns out to be rather fragile, and its influence almost disappears when evaluating the unusual member. This experiment (Wang, Walther, & Hancock, 2009) created 4-person teams comprised of two sub-groups based on members' horoscope signs. Initially, members identified more strongly with their ingroup than with outgroup members. The experimenters prompted one participant in each group to act especially friendly or unfriendly towards the other team members. Friendly individuals were consistently liked by all, regardless of whether they were ingroup or outgroup members with respect to other participants. For unfriendly-acting confederates, likewise, being in the same subgroup with another person did not spare them being disliked by their partner. Although the groups met all the conditions that SIDE enumerates for social identification to occur (visual anonymity and salient group identities), the interpersonal actions of one member who violated norms, positively or negatively, overpowered intergroup dynamics. Future research is needed with subgroups who have stronger identities than simply based on astrological signs. Otherwise, in the numerous online settings where interpersonal impressions are unneeded, unavailable, or inefficient, the SIDE model continues to provide insight into the nature of attraction and influence that CMC can promote.

Intergroup Dynamics in Distributed Virtual Teams

There is other research about CMC that also illuminates intergroup phenomena. A growing body of research examines how CMC interacts with the placement of group members in different geographic locations. Some of these studies reveal how intergroup dynamics in CMC increase conflict, and how alternative geographic/intergroup arrangements reduce it.

Location, Location, Location

In our increasingly global society, a great deal of organizational work is conducted by "virtual teams," that is, people in different locations who work together primarily through CMC. Mortensen and Hinds (2001) approached the subject with somewhat pessimistic predictions. They drew on older perspectives about the supposed negative effects of technology, as well as on studies showing how diversity within groups promotes interpersonal conflict, to predict that three characteristics of virtual teams increase conflict and reduce performance quality: greater use of CMC, more demographic diversity, and increased geographic distribution of members were all expected to have negative effects. They gathered data from members of actual corporate teams whose members resided in different countries and connected online. Contrary to their predictions, all three factors correlated with *lower* levels of interpersonal conflict and *higher* levels of group performance. The researchers concluded that perhaps the fewer things that members of a virtual team have in common, the more its members unite *through communication about their work*. In fact, Mortensen and Hinds (2001) also found that virtual team members' levels of group identification also corresponded to lower conflict and improved performance. The researchers suggested that group identification may be the antidote to the problems we would otherwise expect to result from geographic distribution and mediated communication.

Another study on virtual teams provides more insight about the relationship of geographical dispersion and its effects on group identification. Polzer, Crisp, Jarvenpaa, and Kim (2006) focused on different levels of "configural dispersion," or the degree to which members of a virtual group are located across different geographic places. They were interested in the ways that configural dispersion affects the perception of potential outgroups, how these perceptions affect group conflict. Drawing on participants at several colleges, Polzer et al. formed a variety of six-member groups, with different configurations of the groups' members: six members in one location; six members but with three residing in one location and three in another; six members divided into three subgroups of two members in each location; and six members spread entirely among six different locations. All groups completed several tasks over seven weeks using the Internet.

The researchers had predicted that groups whose members all resided in one place would experience little conflict—they were all ingroup members—and they indeed found conflict to be lowest in this configuration. In contrast, members of groups that were divided into two geographic subgroups were expected to perceive their remote half as an outgroup, based on their different location, and to trust and like them less than their closer colleagues. As expected, research found a high degree of conflict in such groups.

What of a group split among three dispersed subgroups? Would members experience greater conflict, being more likely to feel outnumbered by the other factions? Such was not the case. Three-part groups experienced *less* conflict than two-part groups. Finally, teams that were completely dispersed across six locations experienced even less conflict than the other, partially-distributed teams. Even though they had the most remote locations and each member had more potential outgroup members, completely distributed teams got along fairly well.

There are several interpretations available to explain these findings. It may simply be that as subgroups get smaller, they experience less conflict. But why? Gaertner and Dovidio's (2000) *common ingroup identity model* argues that the more integrated members from disparate groups become, the less they experience each other as ingroup/outgroup members. The relatively low conflict in the completely distributed teams suggest that subgroup identities became so diffused, members came to identify with others as a unitary group instead of multiple factions.

Another interpretation observes that different people behave in different ways in virtual groups, and when group identifications grow more diffused across numerous locations, members begin to focus on factors other than group identities in order to understand the actions of their virtual partners. When virtual group members in some places behave in ways that are similar to members at different locations, or partners at the same location act in different ways than one another, characterizing people based on their subgroups makes less sense. People look for situational factors that account for others' behaviors, rather than assume that remote partners acted the way they did because of who they are (Bazarova & Walther, 2009). In such cases, group identifications no longer provide an efficient way to understand people's actions. It is possible that members become motivated to look for individual and interpersonal characteristics to help make sense of others and modify their group-based perceptions.

Hybrid Identifications in CMC Groups

Researchers are beginning to ask if group identifications and interpersonal perceptions can operate in complementary ways (see Harwood, Giles, & Palomares, 2005), and some CMC research has shown they can. For example, Walther (1997) had British/American student groups work on class papers via the Internet in either long-term or short-term associations. These different time frames are known to trigger favorable different interpersonal behaviors and evaluations: Long-term partners tend to ask and answer personal questions, and like partners more, whereas short-term affiliations prompt more efficiency and task-orientation. Before the long- or short-term virtual groups began to work, they were given instructions designed to increase social identification or individual orientation, just as earlier SIDE studies had done (by emphasizing unanimity and group uniqueness or stressing diversity and individuality, respectively). Results showed that *long-term groups* who were primed for *group identification* experienced the most positive outcomes. They liked each other more, interpersonally, and made greater efforts on their projects. They even rated their partners as being more physically attractive (despite never having seem them) than did groups in the short-term or individually orientated conditions. This example provides an interesting look at the intersection of social identification and interpersonal effects and how they may blend in CMC. People can learn about each other individually, and come to value intragroup diversity through collaborative online tasks.

Applying CMC to Intergroup Relations and Prejudice

It is with this potential in mind—the merger of intergroup and interpersonal dynamics in CMC groups—that current research is attempting to discover how CMC can help members of different ethnic groups learn to work together and cohere, in ways that may be difficult or impossible to do without CMC (Walther, in press). Amichai-Hamburger and McKenna (2006) have suggested an "Internet contact hypothesis." The traditional "contact hypothesis" (Allport, 1954) is a much-studied intergroup approach to reducing prejudice between social groups (see Chapters 6, 10, 12, 13, & 15). To put it simply, when people from one social group have meaningful communicative contact with a member from a group against which they are prejudiced, they learn about the other person as an individual, come to like the individual, release stereotypes, and eventually reduce prejudice against that person's social group as a whole. The Internet, argue Amichai-Hamburger and McKenna (2006), allows individuals from disparate groups such as Israeli Jews and Palestinians, who are segregated or avoid each other at risk of harm, to communicate with one another without travel and without danger (see Chapter 11).

A blending of intergroup and interpersonal factors may be particularly important in this context. The contact hypothesis originally suggested that intergroup contact should foster *personal* impressions and *individual* attraction among those who are involved in contact (for review, see Hewstone & Brown, 1986). Therefore, social identification dynamics that lead participants to identify only with a group, and not its individual members, may be little help. On the other hand, using CMC to foster exclusively interpersonal relations might be equally as disappointing. Hewstone and Brown (1986) argue that for contact to reduce prejudice, participants must remain aware that their interpersonal acquaintance is also a member of the outgroup. Conceptualizations and methods need to explore how CMC can be used to bring people into collaborative communication that fosters a positive ingroup experience *as well as* the gradual development of favorable interpersonal relations among different members. As the research on virtual teams suggests, factors related to the number and locations of subgroups have the ability to reduce distrustful ingroup/outgroup distinctions. With time and collaboration, and with multiple locations, a common identity as a group can emerge among diverse members of a CMC group, just as interpersonal relations among members may develop, with the potential to diminish antagonism to the various outgroups they represent.

Conclusion

This chapter has explored the way that characteristics of CMC accentuate intergroup dynamics. The Internet provides useful discussion spaces that benefit from users' encountering each other on the basis of their common characteristics or concerns. Coupling these contexts with certain attributes of CMC—the lack of nonverbal cues in CMC that would otherwise make apparent users' individual differences—there are many occasions when CMC interaction can be best understood from the perspective of group and subgroup identifications. As the SIDE model explains, there are certain psychological responses to visual anonymity and salient group identity. Depersonalization and deindividuation lead CMC users to seek some basis from which to apprehend online partners, and when a particular group identity fits the situation, social identification results. Social identification increases social attraction, social influence effects on users' opinions, and their adherence to observable group norms such as language use. Although SIDE research is less conclusive with respect to subgroup identification dynamics, organizational studies of virtual teams are beginning to show different intergroup effects when group members are dispersed among different geographical locations. There seems to be some tendency for groups with two remote halves to behave along ingroup/outgroup lines, but as configural dispersion increases the spread of group members across more locations, greater superordinate group identification ensues, or interpersonal perceptions arise, or both. Future research needs to continue to explore these social and interpersonal dynamics, and particularly their intersections. CMC holds promise to reduce prejudice by providing electronic contact and by providing a vehicle for virtual groups of potential adversaries to develop positive relationships within a context of intergroup diversity.

Future research should also examine new technologies from an intergroup versus interpersonal perspective. When a visually anonymous group member acts differently than expected, do partners "Google" the person to try to learn more about him as an individual, to figure out why he acts as he does? Does access to a group partner's picture on Facebook break down social identification toward that individual? Toward the whole group? Or do people relate to their Facebook "friends" on the basis of social attraction, since they are unlikely to really know all 300+ of them at an individual level? Facebook also indicates in what groups (such as college- or city-based social networks) an individual belongs. Do new CMC technologies trigger both interpersonal and group-based impressions, when both kinds of information are made salient? As these questions reflect, intergroup dynamics continue to provide interesting insights and counterpoints to developing CMC systems and offer great potential tools with which to understand new CMC technologies as they develop.

CHAPTER EIGHTEEN

Communication Silos and Social Identity Complexity in Organizations

KIM PETERS, THOMAS MORTON &
S. ALEXANDER HASLAM

Organizational success depends, to a large degree, on employees having the right information at the right time. The wrong information—or the right information at the wrong time—can be disastrous, leading to poor decisions, ineffective leadership, failed negotiations, low morale and underperformance. Accordingly, communication lies at the heart of organizational functioning: get it right, and the organization prospers; get it wrong, and it founders. However, the very nature of organizations means that getting communication right is far from easy. All organizations share two characteristics that distinguish them from many other social groups: (a) internal differentiation and (b) a purposive nature (Haslam, 2001). People within organizations work in different departments, teams, areas, sections, regions; and yet they also have (or should have) a common purpose.

It is widely acknowledged that the first characteristic of organizations (their internal differentiation) impacts critically on their achievement of the second (their purpose). To effectively coordinate their joint efforts towards some organizational goal, employees in different groups need to have a *mutual understanding* of who will contribute to that goal, in what way, at what time, and for what purpose (Clark, 1996b). Communication is the vehicle through which employees establish this mutual understanding. At the same time, however, the internal differentiation of an organization will structure how communication flows through it. This is because communicators who perceive that they share a group membership tend to *move towards* each other, and so *hear* each other more clearly than communicators who perceive that they belong to different groups. This is the so-called 'silo problem' whereby communication is only observed to be effective, and information is only found to flow freely, *within* particular organizational units (for an overview of literature that demonstrates the impact of organizational group boundaries on communication effectiveness, see Haslam, 2001).

In light of the above points, a key task for any organization is to manage and structure employees' perceptions of internal differentiation in ways that facilitate, rather than impede, communication. In the present chapter, we discuss the two contrasting approaches for this task that contemporary organizational literature typically presents: the *superordination* (or *recategorization*) approach and the *individuation* (or *decategorization*) approach. Where the first approach recommends creating a bigger silo, the second recommends getting rid of silos altogether. We suggest that, in their raw form, both these approaches are likely to be of limited utility because they ignore the group-based realities that provide much of the structure and meaning to organizational life. Silos may be a source of problems, but their existence is rarely arbitrary and, when used to good effect, they can be a vital source of organizational sustenance.

In an attempt to define an alternative solution to the silo problem, this chapter outlines an approach that is based both on the ASPIRe model of diversity management (Haslam, Eggins, & Reynolds, 2003) and on dual-identity models of conflict management (Hornsey & Hogg, 2000). Unlike the above approaches, this solution acknowledges and engages with the multi-level complexities that arise in the context of a diverse and changing workforce in order to facilitate the construction of the higher-order organizational identities upon which effective communication (and hence organizational functioning) depends.

Internal Differentiation Shapes Organizational Communication

As noted above, an organization's internal structure can facilitate or inhibit effective communication. The notion that group memberships (and organization silos) can be an important basis for relating (and communicating) to others is central to the social identity perspective (incorporating both social identity theory, Tajfel & Turner, 1979; and self-categorization theory; Turner, 1982; Turner, Hogg, Oakes, Reicher, & Wetherell, 1987). This perspective (see Chapters 1 & 21) argues that group memberships are an important aspect of a person's sense of identity so that alongside knowledge of one's unique personal attributes and qualities (personal identity), the self-concept also includes knowledge both of one's group memberships (social identities) and of the attributes typically associated with those group memberships (i.e., group-based norms, values and ideals).

These social identity-based relationships have a significant bearing on communication effectiveness because group memberships are a source both of shared knowledge and shared perspective. When we belong to a particular organizational team, for example, we are likely not only to be aware of the expertise of the other team members (allowing us to better take each other's perspective in designing and interpreting messages), but also tend to look out on the world from the same team-based vantage point (increasing our motivation to actually do so). This means that when an organization's internal structure leads employees to perceive that they share a social identity with another person (i.e., that they are in the same identity-based 'silo'), the transfer of meaning should be facilitated. As a corollary, though, when differentiation leads employees to perceive that they have different social identities (i.e., that they are in different 'silos'), the transfer of meaning is liable to be compromised.

Hypotheses of this form have received a great deal of empirical support (for a review, see Haslam, 2001). In one example, Mackie, Worth, and Asuncion (1990) demonstrated that people are more likely to be persuaded by an ingroup member than by an outgroup member—even when the content of their arguments is identical—because people pay closer attention to messages from ingroup sources. More recently, Hornsey (2005) showed that common group membership makes it easier for people to 'hear' difficult criticism. This is because ingroups (but not outgroups) are assumed to have your best interests at heart (to be doing this 'for your own good'); in contrast, outgroups are thought to come from a position of ignorance (after all, what would *they* know?); see Chapter 9.

Such findings highlight the point that influence depends on much more than simply *what* someone has to say (i.e., the content of communication). Instead, to be persuasive, it is necessary to attract people's attention in the first place and the ability to attract others' attention (or, more specifically, to have them attend *sympathetically*) is contingent on identity-based relationships. Moreover, having attracted someone's attention, the *motivations* that are imputed to the communicative act are critical to its interpretation. The social identity perspective thus suggests that one of the most important barriers to effective organizational communication is likely to be the salience of internal organizational divisions. For this reason, the social identity perspective leads us to assert that, at core, issues of organizational communication relate primarily to questions of *social identity management*. That is, how we manage organizational identities will have a critical bearing upon the dynamics of organizational communication: its form, its flow, its effectiveness.

Managing Identities to Manage Communication: Traditional Approaches

The argument that managing employees' social identities is key to achieving effective organizational communication (as well as purposeful, co-ordinated organizational behavior) is by no means new. Moreover, in seeking to translate the insights of the social identity approach into practice, researchers have identified a number of practical strategies that managers and practitioners might employ. As suggested above, these strategies tend to take one of two forms: recommending either (a) removing the possibility of group-based silo-ing by encouraging employees to interact on the basis of a shared superordinate identity, or (b) downplaying social identities altogether and encouraging people to interact as independent individuals. Before moving on, it is worth considering the rationale and utility of each of these approaches in more detail.

Invoking Inclusive Identities: The Superordination Approach and Its Problems

The social identity perspective recognizes that self-definition is often stable over time. Amongst other things, this stability is a product of constancy in structural features of the world that bear upon identity salience and in the history of social experience that people bring into any given context (Oakes, Haslam, & Turner, 1994). Nevertheless, self-definition is not inherently stable but rather flexible and context-dependent. This implies that although employees may encounter communication difficulties when they interact with others solely in terms of distinct lower-level social identities (e.g., as members of different teams), these difficulties may diminish should communication come to be informed by higher-level, more inclusive, group memberships. Thus, to the extent that employees who define themselves as members of different teams are encouraged, and motivated, to *recategorize* themselves in terms of a single inclusive identity (e.g., as members of the same organization), they may be able to overcome barriers to communication because the new shared identity provides a shared framework for perception and interaction.

Many organizational researchers have made precisely this point, drawing in particular on Gaertner and Dovidio's (2000) *common ingroup identity model*. This suggests a number of relatively simple solutions to problems of sub-optimal organizational communication. Most obviously, those in positions of power may want to strategically emphasize shared identities in order to promote a spirit of mutual co-operation amongst their subordinates. Indeed, simply referring to others in the organization as 'us' rather than 'them' may make it easier for people to engage constructively with those others and more willing to communicate productively, because 'we' signals the existence of a sense of shared identity between relevant parties. Illustrative of this point, research by Hornsey, Trembath, and Gunthorpe (2004) found that people's defensiveness in the face of criticism of their group was reduced when the critic signaled that they shared an identity with them by using inclusive language.

Nevertheless, most practitioners would probably agree that the long-term solution to organizational problems involves more than using the word 'we' as often as possible. One reason for this is that shared social identity is itself likely to play a role in determining whether such appeals succeed or fail. Illustrative of this point, Gómez, Dovidio, Huici, Gaertner, and Cuadrado (2008) found that students from different schools were more willing to act in terms of their shared student identity (rather than specific school-based identities), when this shared identity was invoked by someone from their own school (i.e., their ingroup). Under these conditions, 96% of the participants reported that they personally viewed students from their own school and from some other school in terms of a single inclusive identity. Yet when exactly the same claim was made by a student from another school acceptance of the message dropped to 44%.

As such findings demonstrate, the effectiveness of invoking shared identities is dependent on the audience being willing to accept the speaker's claims to being 'one of us'. If collective language is used to engage an audience that does not perceive a collective that includes them, then this strategy is likely to fail—or even backfire as people re-assert the boundaries that are being crossed. In order to mobilize people towards some common goal, it is therefore important that appeals to shared identity are experienced (or at least have the potential to be experienced) as authentic and grounded in some underlying material reality. In short, to be effective, the language of 'us' needs to be more than just rhetorical flourish. A key challenge for leaders, then, is not simply to 'talk the talk' of inclusive identity but to 'walk the walk' by providing a framework for translating language into both structure and practice.

However, in seeking to achieve this end, it is important to recognize that the complexity of organizational life means that there are likely to be diverging perspectives on the importance and meaning of different organizational identities. We term this divergence *identity asymmetry*. Identity asymmetry can take at least two forms. First, different subgroups within a social structure may have very different ideas about what constitutes 'us'—so that there is asymmetry in identity meaning. For teachers, administrators and students the meaning of the 'us' that is invoked in relation to the school in which they work is likely to be very different. Second and relatedly, within the same organization, people are likely differ in their ideas about which identities matter to them—so that there is asymmetry in identity importance or salience. Critically, such asymmetries make people differentially responsive to the idea that there is a single 'us'.

Asymmetries of meaning are particularly likely to be accentuated by status-based differentiation within the organization. Groups in a position of power routinely assume that their qualities are representative of the organization as a whole (Mummendey & Wenzel, 1999). They see themselves at the center of the organization and are likely to construe the organization in ways that affirm their own leadership. Amongst other things, this means that members of higher-status groups are typically motivated to construe the organization in terms of an inclusive superordinate identity for which—and to which—they speak (e.g., Saguy, Dovidio, & Pratto, 2008). Conversely, low-status groups are likely to be more aware of their differences from other groups, and of their distance from the organizational centre. As a result, lower-level subgroup identities are likely to be more important for their members and to provide the basis for what they say and what they hear.

For example, in a hospital context, O'Brien and colleagues (2004) found that senior nurses (a higher status group) were more likely than ancillary staff (a lower status group) to define themselves, and engage with the organization, in terms of relatively inclusive identities (i.e., as employees of 'Hospital X'). The ancillary staff instead preferred to define themselves in terms of their sub-group identities—for instance, as porters or caterers. Amongst other reasons, this could be because their low status within the organization meant that an inclusive organizational identity was less likely to furnish them with a positive sense of self (Tajfel & Turner, 1979) or because their relatively low status meant that they did not feel entitled to claim an inclusive identity when communicating with a higher status audience (in this case, the researchers). As a result of such factors, employees' communicative agendas and the identity platforms from which these are delivered are likely to differ significantly depending on the position of their ingroup within the organizational hierarchy.

Asymmetries of importance are also likely to become more prevalent as organizations undergo change. Change, of course, is a pervasive feature of modern organizations and arises both directly from attempts to manipulate their formal structure (e.g., through restructuring and mergers), and indirectly from changes in the world outside the organization (e.g., increasing diversity, globalization). Whatever its source, change increases the likelihood that employees will have different understandings of the organization's internal differentiation, leading them to draw on different identities during interactions with other organizational members.

For example, the increasing diversity of contemporary workplaces means that many employees who enter organizations will have highly salient minority identities. When members of minority groups raise issues related to their minority identity (e.g., as women), employees from majority groups may react negatively to this reference to identity-based differences that they do not see; minority employees may in turn feel offended by these reactions. Similar dynamics are likely to arise in the context of organizational mergers. Employees from acquired organizations may still find meaning in pre-merger identities—identities that are likely to be ignored by members of the acquiring organization. Indeed, here the perception amongst members of lower-status pre-merger groups that their collective interests are not being represented in the process of organizational change can lead them to disengage with the new organization and to reassert pre-existing organizational identities (Terry & O'Brien, 2001).

Finally, it is notable that in recent decades many organizations have moved away from strongly formalized internal structures towards ones that are flatter and more flexible (e.g., Veenstra, Haslam & Reynolds, 2004). As Veenstra and colleagues observe, the dynamism that accompanies the absence of a formal organizational structure (such as the tendency for employees to work in self-organizing, temporary teams) may increase the likelihood that employees will form asymmetrical representations of the organization and its objectives. In particular, without a consensual representation of the organizational structure to anchor employees' understandings, they are free to impose their own idiosyncratic viewpoints on it.

As the above discussion reveals, the structure of employees' social identities within contemporary organizations is both complex and nuanced. Thus, rather than employees' identities being clearly defined and static, they are likely to be 'fuzzy', fluid and negotiable. As we have seen, this fact increases the likelihood that different groups of employees will have different understandings of the organization's social landscape and that there will be significant asymmetries in the meaning and importance of the identities they draw on. Significantly too, these various complexities militate against attempts to unilaterally impose a sense of shared identity from the top down. Indeed, such attempts are likely to encounter significant resistance and 'backlash'—processes which contribute significantly to the observed communication failures that are partly responsible for the fact that very few top-down restructurings and mergers succeed. A key point here, then, is that before attempting to mobilize a single shared organizational identity, it is important to first take account of the alternative social identities that might be meaningful for members of the organization.

Expunging Social Identities: The Individuation Approach and Its Problems

If it is the case that the complexities of contemporary organizational identities undermine attempts to facilitate communication by invoking inclusive identities, then one obvious alternative solution would be to forsake groups altogether, encouraging employees to interact simply on an interpersonal basis (see also Chapter 17). The logic here is that expunging social identities should allow the organization to side-step issues of identity asymmetry and thereby avoid the difficulties associated with attempting to communicate across unrecognized, or unshared, identity boundaries.

The roots of this philosophy can be traced back to Frederick Taylor's (1911) seminal *Principles of Scientific Management*, which was highly distrustful of engagement with collectives and recommended that managers instead pursue individualized relationships with those they manage. Over the course of the last century, the appeal of this solution has increased quite dramatically and, indeed, this is responsible for many of the flexible working practices that we remarked upon above. It is reflected, for example, both in employment arrangements (e.g., out-sourcing, individualized contracts, casualization), and in space management strategies that transcend traditional organizational affiliations and boundaries (e.g., flexible space, tele-working, hot-desking).

All these changes have implications for the ways in which employees communicate with each other. Specifically, contemporary organizations have witnessed a shift from personalized, face-to-face communication toward more anonymous forms of communication (e.g., e-mail, bulletin boards). Many commentators have asserted that these developments serve to break down identity- and status-based boundaries and, thereby, facilitate freer and smoother communication (see Chapter 17). Indeed, according to this analysis, the modern information age is characterized by near-utopian ease of communication. As the brochure for the 2008 Annual Global Conference of HR professionals put it:

> Rapid advances in communications technology are helping create a world without boundaries. This presents . . . even greater opportunities for organizations, as employees and customers are becoming more connected and more mobile.

Research suggests, however, that such enthusiasm may be misplaced. Indeed, against the idea that anonymous, individualized communication media are drivers of social leveling, evidence suggests that they often *increase* the salience of social identities and reinforce traditional group-based structures and divisions (for a discussion, see Postmes, Spears, & Lea, 1998). For without the individualizing cues of face-to-face communication, it appears that people are more (rather than less) likely to draw on available social cues when interpreting the communicative behavior of others in virtual environments—cues that are revealed both in the topics about which they communicate and the communicative styles they adopt when doing so. Thus, rather than erasing boundaries, anonymous communication may amplify group memberships as the relevant basis of self-definition among employees.

Moreover, even in the absence of cues to participants' social identities, organizational interactions are unlikely ever to be fully individualized. One reason for this is that communication between people inevitably creates new social identities from the 'bottom up'. In a recent demonstration of this point, Millward, Haslam, and Postmes (2007) explored the intersection between physical and social structures in a large international organization that was moving from a traditional strategy of assigning employees desks to one of hot-desking whereby they occupied desks on a first-come-first-served basis. During this transition, the researchers randomly assigned employees to fixed desks or to hot-desks. Not surprisingly, the different physical structures supported different communication behaviors. Hence, while employees who were assigned to fixed desks (and as a result were in close proximity to the other members of their work team) prioritized face-to-face conversation, those who were assigned to hot-desks (and were not in close proximity to their team mates) prioritized electronic communication.

Of particular interest, these different communication behaviors supported different patterns of identification. Fixed desk employees who prioritized face-to-face communication, and hence communicating with those in close physical proximity, were relatively more identified with their work team than were hot-desk employees. In contrast, hot-desk employees who prioritized electronic communication, and hence could equally easily communicate with any of the organization's employees, were relatively more identified with their organization than were fixed desk employees. Therefore, what differed between employees who communicated in more and less anonymous ways was *which part* of the organization they identified with, not *whether* they identified.

The above discussion suggests that organizational identities are, to a large degree, *organic*. Thus even where they are repressed from the top down (in ways suggested by Taylor, 1911), they will still tend to grow from the bottom up. In particular, fertilized by communication, they grow to fill the space between people and to surmount any obstacles that try to constrain them artificially.

Why is this so? A simple answer is that social identities are both a product, and an underpinning, of our fundamental sociality as a species. Organizations themselves are testament to this and to its productive potential (Haslam, 2001). Indeed, if social identity is what makes group behavior possible (Turner, 1982), then the very idea of organization without social identity is a logical impossibility. A key point that emerges from this discussion, then, is that rather than seeking to expunge social identities, the way forward for organizations is to find better ways of working *with* them. For, were it possible to achieve (which is questionable), the sublimation of social identity would herald not the apotheosis of organizational life, but its end.

ASPIRe-ing to Improve Organizational Communication

The above discussion suggests that it is not possible to overcome the barriers that social identities present to effective communication simply by invoking inclusive identities or by repressing group-based identities. In communication, as in agriculture, the problems of siloing cannot be addressed either by putting everything into the same silo or by pulling the silo down. Rather than pursuing a strategy of social identity extinction, we thus suggest that the way forward is to recognize, and engage with, the complexities and asymmetries of social identities in organizations. This philosophy is one proposed by a number of researchers working with the social identity tradition who have attempted to devise practical solutions to issues of diversity and conflict management (e.g., Hornsey & Hogg, 2000). A unifying theme of these approaches is that they all see social identities not as an inherent obstacle but as a platform for progress.

Our focus here is on the particular solution proposed by the ASPIRe model (whose acronym signals the underlying objective of *A*ctualizing *S*ocial and *P*ersonal *I*dentity *Re*sources; Haslam et al., 2003). As represented schematically in Figure 1, this model proposes a series of structured activities whose goal is first to identify the social identities that matter to people in organizations and then to use these as a basis for the development of a superordinate organizational identity within which lower-level identities are recognized and instantiated. Rather than seeking to impose a superordinate identity from the top down (through superordination), the goal of the ASPIRe model is to build one organically from the ground up. In this way, the ambition is to build *authentic* consensual identities that allow employees to harness the beneficial aspects of groups (turning employees towards each other) while avoiding the detrimental consequences of asymmetric identities.

Importantly, this strategy builds upon two valuable insights that emerge from previous work (as reviewed above). First, it acknowledges that where employees authentically identify with a higher-order organizational identity (e.g., as a member of the organization), communication should be facilitated. Second, it recognizes that communication processes are themselves central to identity development—so that opportunities to interact in terms of a particular group membership facilitate the development and internalization of that identity.

As Figure 1 suggests, within the ASPIRe model these ideas are a basis for four stages of structured communication. Centrally, this process requires employees to engage in dialogue about organizational identities that forms a basis for shared understanding both of the different identities that they consider important in their working life and of the meanings that they imbue them with (see also Chapter 11).

First, *AIRing (A*scertaining *I*dentity *R*esources*)* is designed to establish which social identities employees perceive to be relevant to their work-related activity and to map their contours within the organization. Here, employees are typically asked to indicate their most important work-related social identities in an organization-wide questionnaire (as in O'Brien et al.'s [2004] hospital study alluded to above).

Second, *Sub-Casing (Sub-*group *Ca*ucus*ing)* is designed to encourage employees to develop a shared understanding of the meaning of these social identities and of the collective goals with which they are associated. Here employees are provided with opportunities to interact and communicate on the basis of those work-relevant identities that they consider important, and to engage in dialogue with other subgroup members in order to identify and agree upon their shared work-related goals. In this, sub-casing groups serve as an alternative to ever-popular focus groups (Eggins, O'Brien, Reynolds, Haslam, & Crocker, 2008). Significantly, though, where the 'focus' for standard focus groups is typically provided by managers, in sub-casing groups it is provided by employees themselves. Accordingly, sub-casing provides a basis for those groups to establish a sense of authentic collective voice which—by engendering a sense of trust and respect—promotes engagement both with the group itself and with the organization as a whole.

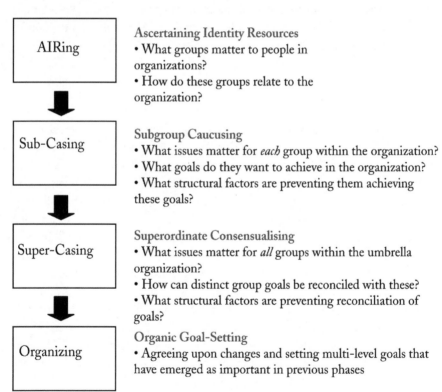

Figure 1: The ASPIRe Model (Haslam et al., 2003)

After this, *Super-Casing* (*Super*ordinate *C*onsensua*lising*) is designed to bring subgroups together under the umbrella of a superordinate organizational identity. In this phase—which can take the form of an internal conference, workshop, or forum—multiple representatives of the various subgroups are tasked first to present and discuss the outcomes from the sub-casing phase and, then, to use this as a basis for identifying points of common ground as well as structural impediments to mutual goal satisfaction. Finally, in a fourth *Organizing* (*Organic* goal-*setting*) phase, these representatives identify and agree upon shared organizational-level goals designed to overcome these impediments.

The activity in these last two phases is intended to promote the development of a consensual, but complex, organizational identity that recognizes and builds upon the distinct contributions and concerns of various sub-groups. Rather than the monolithic, mechanical, and imposed identity envisioned by a strategy of subordination, this identity should be internally differentiated, organic and authentic. In this it should also (help to) harmonize the asymmetrical identities that are characteristic of contemporary organizational life and stand a greater chance of being internalized by employees as a basis not only for mutually beneficial communication but also for coordinated organizational activity.

Conclusion

Organizational leaders have always had to balance the tension between the organizational differentiation that allows sub-groups of employees to focus on tasks that lie within their particular area of expertise and the simultaneous need for these sub-groups to coordinate their efforts in pursuit of the organization's goals. As we emphasized in this chapter, a key task for leaders seeking to achieve this balance is the effective management of the organizational identities that act as communication silos—facilitating communication within sub-groups and inhibiting it between them. The organizational literature has largely focused on two different approaches to this task. While the first seeks to break down communication barriers by promoting an inclusive identity that envelops all members of the organization (i.e., building a bigger silo), the second seeks to break down communication barriers by encouraging employees to interact as individuals (i.e., removing silos altogether). As we have discovered, while each has some intuitive appeal, they are likely to have limited utility because they ignore the centrality of meaningful, distinct and asymmetric social identities to contemporary organizational life.

An approach that can recognize and work with this complexity is especially important in the rapidly changing, globalized environment that today's organizations inhabit. Here, organizations that are flexible and responsive to market forces are likely to succeed. In other words, organizations whose employees can effectively coordinate their efforts in the pursuit of (changing) organizational goals. However, while the changing environment makes the management of identities especially important, it also makes it especially difficult. With changing organizational structures, communication technologies and workforce diversity comes complex and asymmetrical social identities, making it more likely that employees will actively resist the top-down imposition of inclusive organizational identities. This means that organizational leaders need to move beyond traditional approaches and to recognize and work with employees' existing identities in order to build a shared superordinate organizational identity. In the latter part of the chapter, we outlined a set of structured communication activities that are designed to facilitate this process and allow leaders to transform an organization's communication silos from insurmountable obstacles into the starting point for collaborative solutions and organizational success.

CHAPTER NINETEEN

Social Identity and Health Contexts

Melinda M. Villagrán & Lisa Sparks

Patients diagnosed with a chronic or terminal disease gain membership in a group of people who share a common set of symptoms, side effects, and challenges in dealing with providers. The intersection of intergroup communication and health communication was initially revealed with the pioneering work of Jake Harwood and the second author in their applications of social identity to health and cancer communication contexts (see also Dryden & Giles, 1987). It is through communicating with others that patients diagnosed with an illness often see themselves differently and start to recognize that others may view them differently as well (see Harwood & Sparks, 2003; Sparks, 2003; Sparks & Harwood, 2008). Shifts in social identity and health can also have particular effects on medical decision-making in the doctor-patient relationship (see Hajek, Villagran, & Wittenberg-Lyles, 2007; Villagran, Fox, & O'Hair, 2007; Wright, Sparks, & O'Hair, 2008). Barriers faced by groups of patients who deal with similar physical and psychological issues can have a major impact on the self-concept (Williams, 2008). For example, after a negative diagnosis some patients immediately begin to question their own identity with thoughts of biological degradation ("How could my body do this to me?"), to destiny ("Will I possibly be able to get through this?"), to transformations in self ("Losing my breast to cancer makes me feel that I'm no longer a woman"). Although illness is never a positive development in a person's life, the way illness is experienced is based on the patient's pre-diagnosis identity.

Health care communication ranges from explicit and relatively well-known disease conditions affecting our population such as heart disease and cancer but also permeates our society in more subtle and less obvious ways via less visible illnesses such as ALS, multiple sclerosis, celiac disease, and even mental illness. The asymmetrical nature of communication in health care contexts requires a coordinated negotiation of social identity for patients and providers. Providers use instrumental talk to give and receive information and maintain their ingroup identity status. Patients enter the interaction with an existing social identity that may be transformed by a diagnosis of illness. Shifts in social identity and health can have particular effects on medical decision-making in the doctor-patent relationship. Through communicating with others, patients diagnosed with an illness often see themselves differently and start to recognize that others may view them differently as well. Awareness of potential identity shifts as individuals experience a change in their health status is a coordinated effort involving all interactants within and outside of the health care environment.

The purpose of this chapter is to take an intergroup communication perspective as applicable to health care contexts. This chapter will first outline the major tenets of social identity for patients and providers in health care contexts, provide a typology of the role of illness on identity and communication in health care, followed by a brief application of a case study of social identity and mental health to shed light on the function of important intergroup communication theoretical constructs existing in health care communication contexts.

Social Identity Theory and Illness

Social identity theory (SIT: Tajfel & Turner, 1986; see Chapters 1 & 21) explains our responses to difficult situations such as illness based on group memberships. From a broad socio-psychological standpoint, SIT illuminates the complex structure and function of intergroup relations and generally centers on identification with large social groups such as age, culture, sexuality, etc. Smaller and more specialized groups are also relevent to SIT, including such relationships as an organizational group, a family, or even a particular disease condition (see also, Chapters 2, 8, 9, & 13). The tenets of SIT are also germane to understand the potential for shifts in identity such as those experienced by some ill patients and their families.

Patients may experience identity shifts to take on a more active role in their own care by focusing on the goals of treatment as a process. Other patients might try to avoid dealing with illness through denial or by refusing to follow their doctor's advice. Some patients even become depressed and therefore lose the ability to be fully involved in the care process in an assertive manner. If a patient does not want to be labeled with illness, then a shift toward denial is more likely to occur. A young person for example, who gets diagnosed with asthma, might choose to deny her diagnosis because accepting it would mean she would be labeled as "sick" or "chronically ill" for the rest of her life. If, instead, the patient chooses to attribute her symptoms to seasonal dust in her environment or a cold, she can avoid the permanent change in her identity and avoid group membership among asthmatic patients.

Table 1: Social Identity and Group Affiliations*

Level of Communication	Types of Group Identities
Intrapersonal Aspects of Identity	Personality traits Emotional needs Behavioral responses Self-concept
Interpersonal Aspects of Identity	Family relationships Intimate relationships Friendships Co-worker relationships Computer-mediated support groups Impression management
Socio/cultural Aspects of Identity	Gender Ethnicity Age Sexuality Ability Social status Education level

*Adapted from Villagran, Fox, and O'Hair (2007)

The reality for most doctors and patients is that the fear, dread, and terror that accompany certain diagnoses require a greater emphasis on communication processes to combat negative assessments of self as well as understandable conceptions about the finitude or exit of self greatly affecting an individual's cognitive and emotional capacity in ways never before experienced. Open, honest communication with providers can be a valuable weapon against the assault on self-identity that is perpetuated by a negative diagnosis. Communication becomes more important as cognitive, affective, and behavioral responses to illness combine with biological problems that the patient must overcome (see also Chapter 1).

SIT helps illustrate how some people are motivated to maintain a positive view of themselves by identifying with groups they perceive to be desirable and then comparing themselves and other ingroup members to another set of people who are perceived to be outgroup members. For example, a person might view himself as young, or a member of the younger generation, and would then perceive the young generation as the ingroup. Being a member of the younger generation would be viewed as more desirable than being a member of the older generation, or "old people," who are perceived to be an outgroup (see Chapter 4). Table 1 lists some of the most common social groups that contribute to social identities on a variety of levels of communication.

Social identity is directly related to the patient-provider relationships, because we use our social identity to help us deal with difficult situations such as illness. On the other hand, negative social identity can emerge when a patient perceives her group membership to be threatened or less desirable than other group memberships. An African American patient for example, may have a perception that her ethnic identity puts her in jeopardy of receiving substandard care because of discrimination by her provider. The patient views her ability to interact with a provider and receive high quality health care based on the groups to which she belongs. Ethnic identity, level of education, age, and identification with a whole host of other social groups may have a positive or negative impact on health interactions because we choose whether or how to communicate with our providers based on the perceived significance of the groups to which we identify.

SIT has utility for all communication related to illness because of the potential damage illness causes to the identity of ill individuals. Even illnesses such as arthritis or diabetes that may be invisible to the unknowing outsider have the ability to threaten the established identity of people of all ages (Kundrat & Nussbaum, 2003). Illness often disrupts and threatens the order and meaning by which people make sense out of their lives. The overwhelming, uncontrollable, and unpredictable feeling that follows diagnosis of illness often paralyzes a person's ability to act and manage their life based on pre-diagnosis norms (Sparks, 2003). Further, responses to illness that affect social identity may impact decisions made by patients and providers. For instance, when a patient sees herself as intelligent and educated, it is arguably through her agency identity that she is more likely to engage in shared decision-making with her provider (Villagran et al. 2007). Thus, illness can then be a threat to our ability to plan for the future, and to our sense of control over the activities of daily life.

Emotions caused by illness, language choices, and perceptions of physical abilities of an ill person are also impacted by a sense of choice in the negotiation of social and personal relationships. In other words, the extent to which our social identity undergoes a shift after a diagnosis, and the nature of our identity shift, is in part a choice we make based on our perceptions of the negative and positive aspects of our condition as well as the ways by which others orient to our condition via communication. We simultaneously adapt our self-concept to align with our view of the illness and make choices about how to communicate with others because of our new outlook on life. For instance, a couple facing infertility may feel isolated, stressed, or cheated by their lack of ability to have a child. They may feel left out of their social group of friends if they are the only ones without children. The infertile couple may choose to take on a new identity as the "best babysitters," or they may choose to find a new group of friends who do not have children based on the stigma associated with not having children among their peer group. Decisions about whether to pursue infertility treatments can also have a negative stigma for some people, but the reward of having a child may make that stigma more bearable. Whatever the decision, by communicating with each other and their health care provider about their concerns, the couple will be more able to play an active role in the impact of infertility on their identities.

Primary, Secondary, and Tertiary Identities

Three levels of identity typically exist in the health care context. At the primary level, individuals identify with large-scale social groups, and those identifications influence their susceptibility and ability to cope with illness. For instance, highly identified women might, under some circumstances, be more likely to engage in appropriate prevention strategies for their overall health related to a proper and healthy diet, exercise, or relationships. Women who view their gender as a major part of "who they are" may also be more likely take part in activities such as the Susan B. Komen Race for the Cure because it is an event that focuses on women's health issues. Highly identified women feel that their gender is one of their most important, defining characteristics. Women who do not strongly identify with their gender identity are still women, but the details of what it means to engage in the social and cultural roles of women may be less important or less common.

At the secondary level, identifications with particular behaviors influence health communication processes. Secondary-level identification might mean a patient is less concerned with being recognized as a member of a particular social group, but more likely to feel the need to engage in certain behaviors over time. For example, even if a person does not see himself as a first-rate athlete, he may still feel a strong need to exercise on a regular basis. His identity is shaped more by what he does than who he is as a person. Secondary identity is different from primary identity in that a behavior such as exercise may be central to a person's identity at one phase of life but may become less important as time goes on. Another example of secondary identity is that of "a smoker." Smokers who choose to quit engaging in the behavior typically lose membership with the social group of smokers, so that may mean going from being viewed as socially desirable to being viewed as socially undesirable or vice versa. If smoking is seen as a way to identify with the cool people, then stopping the behavior means losing group membership. If, on the other hand, smoking is viewed with a negative stigma, quitting can enable a person to move from the outgroup of smokers to the ingroup of non-smokers and ex-smokers.

Identification with health-specific identities becomes more important at the tertiary level. At this level the major factor is how a person views his or her social identity as it relates to the symptoms and prognosis of a particular disease. If a patient views himself as a fighter, he will view serious illness differently than if he sees himself as weak or defenseless. At this level it is less about who we are or what we do and more about how we choose to frame our behaviors in difficult situations. Harwood and Sparks' previous research on social identity and health dealt largely with the independent effects of different types of identity as well as follow-up elaboration on their interdependence and the ways by which social identity in health care interactions can be considered somewhat unique in that it is often invisible and commonly stigmatized.

Coping with a Stigmatized Identity

A diagnosis of illness often comes with a negative social stigma. Throughout our lives we are exposed to negative information about certain illnesses, so we have preconceived ideas about the stereotypes people face when they are diagnosed with a disease (Sparks, 2003). When a person perceives his or her identity is threatened or devalued based on some change in health status, the natural tendency is to find a way to deal with the threat. A heart disease patient who previously identified as a healthy person (primary identity), ate a healthy diet (secondary identity), and was a tough patient (tertiary identity) experiences shifts in social identity via interaction with others that supports the notion that immortality is not realistic and even healthy people get sick. Identities associated with broader cultural or social collectivist groups are perpetuated by discrimination, stereotyping, and awareness. These negative consequences add to the burden of patients dealing with the biological problems associated with their condition, and can cultivate unnecessary stress for patients and their caregivers.

Outgroup membership is often related to the stigma attached to the type of illness and the view of the illness in society. Patients with a sexually transmitted disease for example, are members of a stigmatized outgroup that can negatively impact their social identity. Certain less visible health issues create a hidden stigma because the patient's social group members cannot see signs of illness, so it may be difficult for them to understand the impact on the patient. Sometimes, health problems that start as very vague cues may be misdiagnosed for months, years, or in many cases, decades before a proper diagnosis is made. By this time the illness has often had an impact on a patient's interactions, relationships, and overall behaviors. For instance, a friend was diagnosed with celiac disease in later life after decades of problems and issues that were viewed by many doctors as "psychosocial" issues. After years of hearing things like, "it is in your head" or "you are fine . . . get over it," the lack of diagnosis related to the symptoms really had taken a toll on the patient's mental as well as physical health. In this case, not belonging to the stigmatized group of ill patients can also create a negative self-concept and a high level of uncertainty about confusing symptoms.

Insight and Identity

The term insight refers to the capacity of a patient to recognize that he or she has an illness in need of treatment (Williams, 2008). Insight involves awareness, acceptance, and willingness to adhere to treatment for illness, and these factors are typically shaped by the perceived stigma associated with a particular disease. Recent research suggests that insight occurs as a cognitive process that is independent of the patient's views of the usefulness of medical treatment (Linden & Godemann, 2007) and should be thought of as a transformative development of social identity. Through social interactions, patients see themselves in a different light and begin to understand that others may view them differently as well. Linking insight to social identity changes a patient's outlook on illness from a purely biomedical perspective to a more holistic experience. Insight has mainly been cited in relation to issues of mental health; however, it has informative properties for examining illness and identity in a variety of health care contexts.

Insights among patients can have differing effects on identity. Williams' (2008) typology of post-diagnosis identity for schizophrenics outlines identity shifts that occur based on cognitive and behavioral experiences of patients. In this chapter, we build on this research to propose a typology that includes a more prominent focus on the role of identity in communication with health care providers. Our approach centers around the notion that patients not only experience illness biologically, cognitively, emotionally, and behaviorally, but they also view illness and its relative importance to their existing identity based on experiences within the clinical setting. The usefulness of medical treatment is not in question, but rather the impact of information sharing in medical encounters is the most important aspect of treatment on social identity. Perceived social stigma is created and reinforced by the information presented by providers and by the way illness is explained and framed. Patients who identify as empowered will be more likely to actively participate in health care interactions, while resistant and detached patients are more likely to exhibit poor communication with providers, including a lack of listening, cognitive processing, and active decision-making. Table 2 outlines a typology of the role of illness on identity and communication for patients in health care.

Engulfed identities are when the patient identity is prominent and includes diminished self-esteem and negative stereotypes of self. These patients may find comfort inside the healthcare system because it creates support and structure from providers and access to social support among other patients. Illness becomes a priority in this patient's life and identity is transformed by the characteristics of disease. In provider-patient interactions, engulfed patients actively seek information and share in health care decisions. Providers may view engulfed patients as overly dependent on caregivers or as too eager to surrender all of their pre-diagnosis identity. Doctors may try to encourage engulfed patients to carry on with certain aspects of their pre-diagnosis life to limit negative identity shifts.

Resistant identities also include negative stereotypes of self, but self-esteem is protected by resistance to, or denial of, illness. Resistant patients maintain a sense of control over their identity by limiting dialogue about their condition with their providers and even by deceiving providers about the severity of symptoms. Resistant patients cannot avoid feeling symptoms of illness, but they can limit their communication on the nature and meaning of those symptoms. For these patients, admitting illness means accepting a diminished self-concept, so resistant patients will use communication as a barrier to dealing with illness. This patient will also resist ingroup affiliation with other patients with the same condition, in part, because of the perceived validity of negative stereotypes of the disease. Acceptance of group membership as a sick person is to accept a stigmatized negative identity. Resistant patients could alternatively be choosing to protect their loved ones from emotional stress and worry instead of protecting themselves.

Empowered identities are when the patient's illness is taken on with full force and a sense of pride, and negative stereotypes of illness are rejected. Empowered patients feel a low internalized stigma, so their communication with others is not framed to combat stigmatized ideals. As a result, empowered patients may be more likely to join social support networks of patients with the same condition and may be advocates for others as well. Communication with providers is active and generally positive because the illness is reframed in both negative and positive terms.

The patient may have lost certain pre-diagnosis views of self but will have also gained a new community membership among those diagnosed with the same condition.

Table 2: Typology of the Roles of Identity and Stigma in Patient-Provider Communication*

	High Level of Perceived Stigma	Low Level of Perceived Stigma
Abundant Identity-based Communication with Provider	**Engulfed Patient Identity** Negative stereotypes applied to self Self-esteem diminished by negative perceptions Patient identity is a primary social identity/Other social identities are seen as more important Communication about illness with provider is lengthy, consistent, negative	**Empowered Patient Identity** Negative stereotypes not applied to self Self-esteem protected by pride Patient identity is a primary social identity/Other social identities are seen as more important Communication about illness with provider is consistent, active, positive
Minimal Identity-based Communication with Provider	**Resistant Patient Identity** Negative stereotypes applied to self Self-esteem protected by denial, resistance to illness Patient identity is not a primary social identity/Other social identities are seen as more important Communication about treatment with provider is sporadic, negative, or combative	**Detached Patient Identity** Negative stereotypes not applied to self Self-esteem protected by detachment, indifference Patient identity is a not primary social identity/Other social identities are seen as more important Communication about illness with provider is sporadic, vague, passive

*Adapted from Williams (2008)

Detached identities are when the patient rejects or denies illness and maintains his or her previous identity without regard to the reality of the situation. This approach not only rejects the characterization of illness but also rejects any social stigma asso-

ciated with disease. Detachment comes from low insight into the nature of the illness, and, therefore communication with providers is not active or well informed.
Detached patients may not even seek treatment from providers at all because of the
need to isolate themselves from reality and maintain their pre-diagnosis identity.
Providers may be viewed as a threat to identity maintenance because open discussion of the illness eliminated the possibility of denying social stigma that may
come up in the conversation. For this reason detached patients' communication with
providers may be vague, sporadic, or passive.

Coping with Negative Patient Identities

SIT further suggests that when a person perceives that an identity is devalued or
does not provide rewards, three potential coping mechanisms are available. The stress
associated with negative patient identities requires the use of these coping strategies to minimize or eliminate association with the undesirable group. The choice
among these coping strategies is grounded in the level of identification an individual has with the group, the degree to which boundaries between the group and other
groups are open or closed, and the degree to which the power structure is viewed
as legitimate and stable (see Shinnar, 2008; see also Chapter 1).

In situations of low identification and open boundaries, an individual may
choose to leave a stigmatized or unrewarding group. This may take the form of physically or psychologically leaving the group, which is known as social mobility. In
terms of a patient's identity, actually leaving the undesirable social group of their illness may not be entirely possible until the illness is eliminated. Social mobility could
occur when there is a desire for a patient to move towards health and in so doing
to leave their ill identity behind. In the long term, regaining one's health and getting rid of an illness is a form of social mobility. When mobility is not viable, individuals typically engage in social creativity or social competition.

Social creativity is typically utilized as a coping mechanism involves using
cognitive restructuring to reframe the nature of what it means to be ill. Patients may
alter the perceptions of illness by finding creative ways to make ingroup or outgroup
comparisons. Such individuals may seek out some dimension on which their group
is valued, regardless of low status. Patients may redefine their values to allow for a
positive assessment of ingroup characteristics. Social creativity might be used as a
strategy to target alternative outgroups, which may occur when lower status ingroup
members attempt to achieve positive identities. For instance, sick patients may actually consider themselves fortunate in comparison to patients with more aggressive
or visible illnesses such as ALS, which is also known as Lou Gehrig's disease (see
also Coupland, Coupland, & Giles, 1991; Coupland, Coupland, Giles, & Henwood,

1988;).

At the level of social competition, people are publicly seeking a change in the status quo in an effort to gain more status and resources for their group. A visible health campaign to raise awareness is the pink ribbon campaign for breast cancer. Such campaigns are interesting in that the primary goal is not to achieve more respect or status for people currently in the group but rather to raise the status of group membership as an issue.

Application: Social Identity and Mental Health Issues

A central concept in this chapter is that communication plays a fundamental role in the way we experience health-related identity shifts. Illnesses accompanied by both subtle and overt symptoms carry with them internal manifestations that greatly impact our insights and all three levels of our identities. Highly stigmatized and less visible conditions such as depression or bipolar disease exacerbate the need for effective communication and also highlight the potential threats to social identity in health care contexts. There are several reasons why mental illness highlights the unique interplay between social identity and communication in health contexts. For example, unlike an illness that manifests itself as a lump or bruise, mental illness is not typically self-diagnosed. It is only through interaction with others that conditions such as these become apparent to the patient and/or their family and friends. Our communication with others is the key to diagnosis of mental health issues, and the impact of the disease is socially constructed from the moment it is detected.

All illnesses cannot be diagnosed entirely with a brain scan or a blood test. Mental health care providers must draw on perceptions of verbal and nonverbal cues to determine to what extent a patient is healthy or sick. Therapy sessions seek to explore the nature of the illness based on lived experiences, and our ability to convey information about symptoms is essential for a proper diagnosis. Social identity shapes the way we see ourselves, and therefore shapes the way symptoms of conditions such as depression will be viewed and conveyed.

Therapeutic approaches to mental health are also rooted in continued communication between the patient and a health care professional, and social identity is central to such discussions. For example, adherence to medication can be heavily reliant on information about the side effects and long-term safety of the treatment protocol. Ongoing communication about adherence to medication relies in part on the social identity of the patient because group affiliations impact conceptions of the stigma associated with taking medication. Such stigma creates barriers to open communication about mental illness with family members and other traditional sources of social support, making patient-provider interactions especially important. Physicians may also miss the symptoms of less visible illnesses because of a patient's obvious or perceived group memberships. If a physician views a patient's behavior based on group-level attributions, certain cues of illness might be missed or misattributed. Negative stereotypes about the patient's social identity may also become barriers to proper diagnosis and care from providers, and such barriers may only be overcome through consistent and competent communication.

Diagnosis and treatment of mental health issues may be the result of symptoms manifested in actions and deeds, as well as feelings of illness. Mental health problems often become apparent to family, friends, and social support networks long before the patient gets to a doctor's office. The history of interactions that emerge before diagnosis can irreversibly damage our relationships and our social identities across the life span. It is only through communication that such damage can be repaired.

Conclusion

Health care communication ranges from explicit and relatively well-known disease conditions affecting our population such as heart disease and cancer but also permeates our society in more subtle ways via less visible illnesses such as ALS, multiple sclerosis, celiac disease, and mental illness. The asymmetrical nature of communication in health care contexts requires a coordinated negotiation of social identity for patients and providers. Providers use instrumental talk to give and receive information and maintain their identity and their ingroup identity status. Patients enter the interaction with an existing social identity that may be transformed by a diagnosis of illness. Shifts in social identity and health can have particular effects on medical decision-making in the doctor-patient relationship. Through communicating with others, patients diagnosed with an illness often see themselves differently and start to recognize that others may view them differently as well. Awareness of potential identity shifts as individuals experience a change in their health status is a coordinated effort involving all interactants within and outside of the health care environment.

The future empirical agenda for an intergroup approach to health contexts needs to explore the role of group-level affiliations in specific contexts. All health care settings are not alike, so it is important for example to explore differences in in-patient, out-patient, and long-term care facilities. We need to conduct empirical studies targeted toward health care providers of all levels and skill sets to include formal and informal providers and their patients and family members. In particular, future research should focus on unique health contexts involving invisible illnesses such as mental health. As discussed, since mental health issues are often hidden and stigmatized, intergroup approaches could shed interesting light on the complexities of group-level stigmatization and its influence on communication about mental health. Health status is a coordinated effort involving all interactants within and outside of the health care environment.

CHAPTER TWENTY

Rival Sports Fans and Intergroup Communication

PAUL M. HARIDAKIS

It is hard to fathom a social setting in which intergroup communication is more dynamic than sport settings. The viewing of sports with others provides a group context that is uniquely and implicitly social. It has been estimated that perhaps fewer than 2% of people attend sporting events alone (Gantz, Wilson, Lee, & Fingerhut, in Hugenberg, Haridakis, & Earnheardt, 2008). Sports bring friends, family, and other fans together in an atmosphere that is conducive to interaction. Whether it is in stadiums and arenas, around a TV in homes or bars, or via online forums such as social network sites, blogs, and websites, fans participate together, plan together, and help each other interpret and relive the sports-viewing experience through the media and face-to-face interaction.

In this chapter, sports viewing is examined as a unique form of intergroup communication through which people connect with some sports fans and teams and distance themselves from rival fans and teams. I also consider the value of applying assumptions of social identity theory for assessing sport as a site for social connection and intergroup communication. Although a chapter of this length can only be representative of a large body of literature on sports communication, my hope is that it will provide the interested reader with at least a flavor of the importance of intergroup communication to sports consumers' social identities and, ultimately, their social and psychological health.

The chapter is organized as follows. First, is a brief discussion of some of the assumptions of social identity theory that have been applied to the study of sports viewing. Second, is a representative review of literature pertaining to fan identification with sports teams, other fans, or groups with whom fans watch sports. Third, is a discussion of motives people have for viewing sports, particularly social motives. Fourth, is a discussion of some activities (or consequences) related to sports viewing and reactions to it, particularly those associated with identification with teams and/or other groups. Finally, how some fans are using online forums to enrich and transform their intergroup sports-related communication activities is considered.

Social Identity and Sports

Social identity theory posits one's identity and sense of self are influenced not only by one's individual characteristics but also by one's experiences with groups to which one belongs (see Chapter 1). Driven by basic needs (e.g., for belongingness, affiliation, self-esteem), people see themselves through the prism of their group memberships. To achieve and maintain positive self- and social-identities, people seek and maintain relationships with favorable groups, which, in turn, advance their overall self-concept and self-esteem (Hogg & Abrams, 1990).

Originally articulated as a way to explain intergroup bias, one assumption of social identity theory (SIT) is that people have strategies for maintaining positive social identities and, by extension, positive self-esteem and self-concept. These strategies are reflected in ingroup bias, outgroup derogation, and various forms of intergroup behavior. In addition, the motivation to use such strategies to make favorable comparisons between one's group and other groups increases under conditions of threat to social identification.

Application of assumptions of SIT has been valuable in advancing understanding of fans' connection to sports, their favorite teams, and groups with which they watch sports. Researchers also have explored motives for watching sports, including motives related to social identification. In addition, researchers have found that social identification and motives are associated with various communication activities that serve to maintain positive social identities. Representative examples of this research are reviewed below.

Identification

Identities are tied to group membership, and people can have a different social identity for each group to which they belong. This makes understanding the connection between sports fans' social identity and communication activities surrounding sports complex, because there are different social identities associated with sports.

Sports fans often identify with a team. However, connection to a team may be through connection to other reference groups with whom fans watch sports and share a connection (Boyle & Magnusson, 2007). The connection to a team also may be through a connection to a larger community such as a university, city, or other geographic locale represented by a team. Even national identity can become a type of attachment to a team or sport. Each of these types of connections is a different "point of attachment"—that is, there are group attachments in the context of sports besides attachment to a team itself (p. 501).

Team identification. Nonetheless, allegiance to sports teams is one of the most visible types of social identification (or point of attachment) portrayed by the media and studied by sports researchers. Team identification has been referred to as "a psychological connection to a team" (Dietz-Uhler & Lanter, in Hugenberg et al., 2008, p. 104). The extent of that connection, or commitment, is a crucial determinant of identification. Therefore, much research has focused on fans' level of identification with a team and sought to distinguish between fans and spectators or between die-hard fans and more fair weather fans. It has been asserted that identification with a team is what separates a fan from a spectator (e.g., Zillmann & Paulus, 1993). Those who identify with a team tend to remain committed to the team during the course of the season (Dietz-Uhler & Murrell, 1999). They attend more games and purchase more team-related products. Interestingly, highly identified fans tend to exhibit these attributes and remain loyal even to poor-performing teams (see Boyle & Magnusson, 2007; Dietz-Uhler, End, Demakakos, Dickirson, & Grantz, 2002).

One who identifies with a team can see it as a reflection of himself/herself (Dietz-Uhler et al., 2002). Therefore, membership with a successful team can enhance one's social identity. By the same token, those who identify with a team tend to see a team loss as a personal loss. This, in turn, can adversely affect how they feel about themselves (Dietz-Uhler & Murrell, 1999).

Although much of the sports research dealing with social identification has focused on fan identification with a team, identification with a team is only one type of social identification among sports fans. Often, team identification is secondary to connection to other reference groups, and a sports event, at times, may merely serve as a means to connect with other important reference groups in one's life (Boyle & Magnusson, 2007). Below are a few of these other types of attachment that have been studied in the context of sports.

Nationalism/national identity. Some sporting contests such as Olympic competitions are particularly conducive to inducing attachment of fans to their nation's teams. The waving of national flags and other nationalistic symbols also are rampant at World Cup soccer matches during which national teams compete against the teams of other nations. But, examples of banal nationalism are prevalent in virtually all sports contests. For example, NASCAR races in the U.S. are routinely preceded by nationalistic symbols such as flyovers by military aircraft, the appearance of military color guards carrying the U.S. flag, and the like. The singing of the national anthem precedes most professional sports contests in the U.S. And, before boxing matches involving boxers from different nations, the singing of the national anthems of their respective countries often precedes the fight.

Not surprisingly, research has suggested that national identity often is salient in sports contexts. For example, Branscombe and Wann (1992) found that after viewing a movie clip between an American boxer and a Russian fighter, outgroup derogation and physiological arousal were greater among participants who highly identified with America. Hughson (1998) found that after the ruling body of soccer in Australia required Australian premier league teams to drop "ethnic" names and insignia, some fans refused to comply. They continued to bring national flags and symbols to games and staked out areas in the stands to sit with others sharing their ethnic identity.

Such displays of nationalistic fervor and research findings suggest that although sports contests themselves are important to fans, their national identity can at times be more important.

Geography/community. Fans also often use team sports to connect with a particular community. Several studies have focused on university students. For example, Dietz-Uhler and Murrell (1999) found that those with a stronger university identity tended to rate a university sports team more favorably than those with a weaker university identity. Boyle and Magnusson (2007) argued that identification with college teams provides "social-interaction opportunities" for peer groups (e.g., other students and alumni) (p. 504). Similarly, Melnick (1993) suggested that sports spectating is a social setting that can provide urban dwellers an opportunity to feel connected to their respective city and other residents.

Other fans. Fans of the same team generally share a connection with each other. One ritual that highlights this connection is the tailgating that often occurs before games. During such pre-game festivities, fans often play games with each other, barbecue, and engage in other activities (Melnick, 1993). Fans often arrive at football games hours before the games to enjoy such interaction with other fans. Before NASCAR races, some fans spend up to a week camping and visiting with each other prior to a weekend of races.

This connection to other fans is obvious during games as well. Charleston (2008) found that feeling connected with other fans was an important determinant of home atmosphere in English football. She speculated that factors such as crowd noise and size increase a sense of belongingness because fans "see themselves as part of one voice, the 12th man, which positively reinforces that aspect of their identity associated with the football club" (p. 321).

Family/friends. On a more intimate level, fans often attend sports or watch them on television with their friends and family. Particularly for marginal fans, a game may provide a place to connect not so much with the team or a sport but with friends. It has long been acknowledged that interest in sports and identification with teams and sports are influenced by friends and family (e.g., Gantz et al., in Hugenberg et al., 2008). As socializing agents, parents, in particular, play a vital role in a person's interest in and identification with sports and teams. Much research suggests that the opportunity to go to games with family and friends is one of the primary motives for watching and attending games (see Chapter 15). Thus, sometimes sport viewing does not necessarily reflect identification with a sport or a team. Rather, the sport-viewing situation simply may serve as a backdrop for intrafamilial and interpersonal/network dynamics.

Motives

It has been suggested that basic needs and desires provide the motivational drive for the development of social identities. These include needs for belongingness and for group affiliation (Gantz et al., in Hugenberg et al., 2008), the need to enhance one's self-concept and self-esteem (Hogg & Abrams, 1990), and the desire for collective involvement and sociability (Melnick, 1993). Research guided by theories such as uses and gratifications suggests that needs and desires are manifested in motives to use media and other communication channels to satisfy them (e.g., Earnheardt & Haridakis, in Hugenberg et al., 2008; see Chapter 16). Thus, if people have needs that SIT researchers have suggested provide a motivational drive for social identification, it is logical to assume that they are manifested in communication motives, including motives for watching sports.

In fact, various motives that have been identified for watching and attending sports reflect the desire to satisfy such underlying needs and to connect with sport teams and other fans. For example, three of the eight motives reflected in Wann's (1995) Sports Fan Motivation Scale include seeking self-esteem, group affiliation, and family connection (e.g., to be with one's spouse or family). The Trail and James (2001) Motivation Scale for Sports Consumption includes family-, social- (e.g., "Interacting with other fans is a very important part of being at games"), and achievement-related (e.g., "I feel like I have won when the team wins") reasons for watching sports. In short, all sports-viewing motives scales commonly used in sports communication research today include items reflecting attachment to the contest and various groups, identification with winning, and self-expressive and self-defining experiences that are consistent with assumptions of SIT (for a review, see Earnheardt & Haridakis, in Hugenberg et al., 2008). This has been the case in qualitative research as well. For example, Hugenberg and Hugenberg (in Hugenberg et al., 2008) found specific social identification motives expressed in narratives of NASCAR fans. They concluded that "identification with their family, friends, or driver emerged as three of the dominant motives of NASCAR fans" (p. 184).

Such intergroup motives seem to be important even in the playing of fantasy sports. Spinda and Haridakis (in Hugenberg et al., 2008) found that people played fantasy sports, in part, for achievement/self esteem (e.g., "I feel a personal sense of achievement when my fantasy team does well"; "winning at fantasy games improves my self-esteem"), socialization (e.g., "Because most of my friends are sports fans"), and bragging rights (e.g., "I love to 'trash talk' and tell other owners how much better my team is"). Serazio (in Hugenberg et al., 2008) found that fantasy sports gave players a chance to maintain networks with family and friends with whom they play and to create new affiliations. These motives, suggest that for some fans, the motivation to connect and socialize with similar others may be more important than the identification with sports or teams. Together, the studies indicate that people attend games and watch sports on television to build self-esteem and for a sense of achievement. But, they also do so to be with friends, family, and other fans.

The research suggests that these motives may be differentially related to one's level of identification. For example, those who strongly identify with a team tend to be more motivated for self-esteem whereas those who identify less strongly often watch for other social reasons or to be with others who are watching. While underlying needs may influence motives for watching sports and different motives may be differentially related to social identification, as communication theory and research would suggest, underlying needs, communication motives, and the extent to which one identifies with teams or groups with which they watch sports are reflected in communication-related activities.

Activities and Consequences of Social Identification

There are various emotional, cognitive, and behavioral responses to sports-related social identification (e.g., Dietz-Uhler & Lanter, in Hugenberg et al., 2008). Some of these activities are prosocial and reflect strategies for maintaining positive social identities (e.g., social comparison, celebrating team wins and distancing oneself from losing teams, coping). Some of these activities are more antisocial, such as violence, hooliganism, aggression, and derogating or "blasting" other fans.

Regardless of the specific attitudinal or behavioral manifestation of social identification, research has shown that reactions of fans who identify with other fan groups or teams are more intense than reactions of those who do not strongly identify with these groups. They exhibit more ingroup bias, judge disloyal ingroup members more harshly, engage in outgroup derogation, have more intense reactions to both wins and losses, and are more likely to carry their sports communication-related behavior online. Here, I focus on a few of these responses that have received considerable attention from sport researchers.

Threat and ingroup bias. As referenced above, some of these activities reflect strategies for maintaining positive social identities. These include exhibiting ingroup bias and outgroup derogation (Wann & Grieve, 2005). The motivation for such responses tends to be greater under conditions of threat to social identity.

A common research finding is that fans exhibit ingroup bias in support of their team (Wann & Grieve, 2005). For example, highly identified fans of a losing team may feel that the winning team played dirtier and benefited from bad officiating (see Dietz-Uhler & Murrell, 1999, for a review of studies). They also may have biased interpretations of media coverage of the team with which they identify (sometimes referred to as a "hostile media effect") (Arpan & Raney, 2003). Generally, they evaluate fellow group members favorably simply because they are members of the same group. But, if an ingroup member does something bad that threatens social identity, other fans may evaluate them more harshly than an outgroup member. Dietz-Uhler et al. (2002) referred to this as a "blacksheep effect" (p. 162).

Outgroup derogation is closely tied to ingroup bias. Simply put, people favor their ingroup (e.g., their favorite team; other supporters) over outgroups (e.g., rival teams and rival fans). Research suggests that in addition to identification, national and cultural differences also can affect derogation of members of outgroups. Halberstadt, O'Shea, and Forgas (2006) identified national differences in outgroup derogation among Australian and New Zealand sport fans. They found that New Zealanders were less likely than Australians to recategorize the teams of the rival nation as an ingroup when their own national team was not competing. Bernache-Assollant, Lacassagne, and Braddock (2007) found cultural differences may also influence the likelihood of outgroup derogation. In their study of fans' comments in soccer fanzines, they found that members of one cultural subgroup of fans were more explicit in their negative comments about outgroup fans after their team lost than was another fan subgroup of the same team.

Ingroup bias and outgroup derogation are mechanisms for maintaining positive social identity. Accordingly, ingroup bias and outgroup derogation tend to be greater as the threats to social identity become greater. In the context of sports, two obvious threats that have been studied are team performance and game location.

Research suggests that home games may be perceived as particularly threatening to social identity. There appears to be heightened intensity when a sporting event occurs at the home field/arena/stadium of a team with which one identifies. The importance of home atmosphere and a home advantage is well recognized among sports fans. It is reflected in phrases such as "our house" to describe home arenas, and descriptions of fans as the 12th player on the field. Feeling connected to other supporters is an aspect of home atmosphere, too (Charleston, 2008). Wann and

Grieve (2005) suggested that visitors may be regarded as intruders and that ingroup bias may be more intense during a home game, where fans may feel their "space" is threatened.

In addition to home games, research also suggests that poor team performance or the mere possibility of a loss is a significant threat to fans' social identity. But, researchers have not found consistent fan reactions to the threat. For example, Bernache-Assollant et al. (2007) found that one group of fans tended to engage in more explicit outgroup derogation after their team lost than after it won. However, in a study of sports message boards, End (2001) found that fans of winning teams tended to post more messages "blasting" (derogating) the opposition than did fans of losing teams.

It should be stressed that even the mere possibility of poor performance can elicit coping mechanisms to deal with the threat, such as pessimism about a favorite team's prior or future performance (Wann & Grieve, in Hugenberg et al., 2008). Thus, findings regarding fans' biases and outgroup derogation, though inconsistent, do suggest that both the nature of the threat and the level of team or group identity are both important factors to consider. And, as Wann and Grieve (2005) suggested, these mechanisms may be used at times as ways of coping for highly identified fans.

Behavioral Consequences

Bias and reactions to threat are reflected in behaviors. Basking in reflective glory (BIRGing) and cutting off reflective failure (CORFing) are two post-sport contest identity management behaviors that have received considerable attention in sports team identification research (e.g., Boen, Vanbeselaere, & Feys, 2002; Cialdini et al., 1976). BIRGing is celebratory behavior that reflects reveling in one's association with a winning team. CORFing reflects efforts to distance oneself from a losing or poor-performing team. According to Cialdini et al. (1976), BIRGing is a way in which fans use their association with sports teams to manage self-presentation. BIRGing is one way they publicize their association with successful teams and is reflected in language such as the use of terms like "we" to describe "our" team when it wins. It also is reflected in wearing the apparel of successful teams and an array of other creative ways fans visibly celebrate the victories of successful teams with which they identify (e.g., driving down main street in a university town and blowing the horn after the local team wins, putting team banners and signs in front lawns and bumper stickers on cars). Relishing such visible expression of one's identification with successful teams arguably enhances one's self-image.

Whereas BIRGing can be characterized as an image enhancement technique, CORFing is an image-protection technique. It reflects affirmative steps to distance oneself from a losing team or unsuccessful others. It can be evidenced in language, such as referring to a losing team in third-person language (e.g., "they lost" or "the team lost"). It also can be reflected in other displays designed to reduce association with "a loser" (e.g., refusal to wear team apparel, taking down team banners, etc.).

Connection between these behaviors and team identification is complex and not always easy to understand. For example, it appears that fans who identify highly with a team may be more likely to BIRG than are low identifiers. However, they may be less likely to CORF than lower identifiers. It may be that those who identify with a team have to find alternative ways to maintain a positive social identity after a team loss. One such alternative image-protection technique has been referred to as COFFing (cutting off future failure). This may involve decreasing identification before a competition. It also has been suggested that those associated with a winning team may actually refrain from BIRGing and other celebratory behavior to protect their ego in the event of a future loss or other poor performance (Dietz-Uhler & Lanter, in Hugenberg et al., 2008). Thus the likelihood of engaging in any of these behaviors can be influenced by the expectation of wins or losses in addition to one's level of identification (Boen et al., 2002).

In recent years, researchers have found that these image enhancement or image protective techniques are reflected in online behavior. For example, Boen et al. (2002) found that the number of visits to soccer teams' websites were greater after the teams won than after losses. End (2001) found that fans used their homepages to publicly express their association with their favorite NFL teams by including links to their favorite teams' page. End also found that fans used these online fora to BIRG and to "blast" (e.g., derogate) opposing teams and their fans. Similarly, Bernache-Assollant et al. (2007) found that fans used fanzines to BIRG but were less likely to use them to blast.

Newer Media and Intergroup Sports Communication

These later studies provide evidence of fans' growing use of newer media such as the Internet to express their association with their favorite teams and other fans, to manage their social identities, and, in some instances, to transform their intergroup situation (see Chapter 17). Of course, sports fans have always used media to accomplish these goals. Most people watch sports on television more often than they attend games or other sporting events. Viewing sports on TV and sharing the experience with co-viewers in the home or in public places like bars and pubs (e.g., Eastman & Land, 1997) help create meaning for the viewer and connection to co-viewers.

But newer media enable fans to play a more direct role in affecting the context of the experience, because they put greater control in the hands of fans. Sports fans are utilizing the on-demand nature of the Internet to immerse themselves in their association with their favorite teams and to connect and identify with other geographically dispersed fans. In one case study, Watts (in Hugenberg et al., 2008) focused on Internet discussion boards pertaining to the Flordia Gator Nation. Watts claimed that gatorcountry.com, a popular gathering place for Florida Gator fans, "had over 90,000 unique users per month and 28,000 visits per day in 2005" (p. 243). Such sites give fans "the opportunity to build community with one another as well as report and even create news about their team, which empowers fans to gain agency and a sense of involvement in regard to their chosen team" (p. 243).

This latter attribute of the Internet—empowerment—is particularly salient in online intergroup sports communication. Fans are using new technologies to transform their intergroup situation. For example, Lavelle (in Hugenberg et al., 2008) asserted that one way identification is expressed is through popular culture. In online environments, fans can connect cultural artifacts to their own experience by changing them. Referred to as "fan poaching" (p. 116), fans do not just experience sports, they change the texts through online debate and discussion, sharing of videos and the like. By doing this, fans have found new ways to seize control of their identity management. It may be that such behavior, as End (2001) suggested, is more likely in the deindividuated environment of the web. In an intergroup environment where people can use avatars, screen names, and the like to express their fanship and connection to a team and other fans while concealing their actual identity, self-presentational inhibitions in managing one's identity may be lacking and creativity fostered.

Related Issues

The above discussion has focused generally on the active maintenance of group identity and intergroup communication by sport fans. There are a couple of related issues that should be acknowledged in the assessment of intergroup communication and the comparison between and connections among sport fans groups.

Fan aggression and violence. Not all fan behavior visible during and after sports contests is prosocial. There are antisocial manifestations of behavior associated with sports and identification with teams. Well-publicized examples include hooliganism and violence during and after games. Some fans who engage in such antisocial behavior may identify with teams or with others with whom they engage in violent behavior. For example, hooligans tend to have very well organized associations of fans, referred to as "firms," with whom they engage in violent acts. Hughson (1998) suggested that hooliganism is a type of social resistance among young men who are socially marginalized—a subculture with which they can identify (see Chapter 5). This suggests that these spectators may share a social identity tangentially related to the games. This could support the suggestion that antisocial behavior of sport fans such as aggression, drinking, berating officials and the like are due more to individual characteristics of the fan than of social identification (e.g., Wakefield & Wann, 2006).

Role of the media. It also should be stressed that the media are not silent in their portrayals of fans and fan groups. Their coverage may influence group perceptions. Research has suggested that national, ethnic, gender, and racial biases are common in media coverage and commentary. In a study of the 2000 Olympics, for example, Billings and Eastman (2002) found some of these biased portrayals present in media coverage of the games. They found that male athletes tended to be portrayed as more committed and athletic than were female athletes. Males also received more airtime. White athletes tended to be applauded for their commitment, whereas Black athletes tended to be applauded because of their skills and physical superiority. In addition, U.S. athletes were mentioned disproportionately more often in sportscaster commentary.

Such discriminatory coverage is not just a recent phenomenon. In an historical analysis of European newspaper coverage of a fight among Brazilian and Hungarian players after a 1954 Football World Cup match, Lippe and MacLean (2008) found that national and racial stereotypes were prevalent. Although the newspapers criticized players from both teams, the Brazilian players seemed to be blamed most often. They tended to be described in racist terms. In addition, the media sometimes cast them as a threat to the game of football.

The point of this discussion is not to lambast the media for discriminatory coverage. It simply suggests that if researchers consider why certain groups or subgroups come together or see each other in a certain light (e.g., as socially marginalized), they should at least account for how such groups are portrayed in the media.

Conclusion

The media may provide unbalanced or stereotypical coverage of teams, athletes and different groups. Some fans may become hostile after games and engage in antisocial behaviors such as aggression and violence. But, the focus on such negative issues should not detract from the positive ways in which the vast majority of sports fans and spectators use sports to connect with each other and use intergroup communication to satisfy their basic human needs for affiliation, belongingness, and self-esteem.

If, as SIT posits, satisfaction of these basic needs drives social identification, then satisfaction of these needs via social identification should link with social and psychological health. This would be consistent not only with assumptions of SIT but also with tenets of other social psychology theories (such as self-determination theory) and mass communication theories (such as uses and gratifications). In fact, for sports fans and spectators, team identification has been linked with social and psychological health. For example, it has been linked with reduced levels of alienation and loneliness, higher levels of self-esteem, social life satisfaction, and psychological well-being (see Wann & Grieve, in Hugenberg et al., 2008, for a review of studies).

In short, fans who identify highly with a team or other sports fans and spectators with whom they share a connection do tend to interpret events in a biased way. But, it is to protect themselves and to support their fellow fans and favorite teams. They may distance themselves from rival fans and even derogate them. But, it is usually is in good spirit—linked more to "trash talk" than outright hostility. Thus, the dynamics of intergroup communication surrounding our sports-viewing experiences helps us satisfy what is basic in all of us: the need to socialize and be associated with others in ways that bolster us and them. It is in good clean fun. More importantly, it is healthy.

The critical research agenda now is to devote more attention to how each intergroup situation is being transformed by sports fans who are finding new ways to enrich their sports-related social identities in a changing globalizing world. We must explore how people are using evolving social media such as social networking and video sharing sites to connect with each other and satisfy their needs for relatedness and sociability. If we truly want to understand better the role of communication in people's lives and their social and psychological health, prior research tells us that the intersection of sports viewing and intergroup communication is an important place to focus.

Part Four

Future Directions

CHAPTER TWENTY-ONE

Towards Theoretical Diversity in Intergroup Communication

DONALD M. TAYLOR, MICHAEL KING &
ESTHER USBORNE

It was 1972. The place, the University of Bristol. The social identity theory group (including Henri Tajfel, John Turner, Rupert Brown, Mick Billig, Michael Hogg, and Howard Giles) was in full production mode, albeit completely off the radar from the point of view of mainstream North American social psychology. This distinguished group pursued its theory and research with more than intelligence and commitment: It was a collective passion. Their mission generally was to carve a place for intergroup relations as a respected and central psychological field of study. Their mission was articulated in the form of crafting a novel theory to be built on a set of novel assumptions: social identity theory. And even in those early stages, communication was very much a central theme for key members of the Bristol group (see Chapter 1).

Fast-forward thirty-seven years and the positioning of communication and intergroup relations could not be more central and may even be poised to make a move to the highest level as an academic discipline. So, where exactly are we in the year 2009, how did we get here, and where are we headed?

In this chapter, we offer some thoughts on these questions. We will describe how social identity theory (Tajfel & Turner, 1986) has grown from relative obscurity in the early 1970s to its current domination of the field of intergroup relations generally, and the discipline of intergroup communication more specifically. In fact, we will argue that social identity theory has gone beyond domination to the point that other theoretical contenders are rarely considered. To address this uncontested domination, we offer two very important developments in mainstream social psychology as a challenge to the field of intergroup communication to expand its theoretical repertoire. The first development is the advent of system justification theory. We discuss system justification theory because, first, it is the most recent manifestation of an array of theories that point to justice as a central concept for understanding human behavior and, second, because this theory arose initially out of what was judged to be a weakness in social identity theory. The second development is more of a movement and focuses on the emerging appreciation for unconscious, automatic, uncontrolled attitudes in social psychology generally but with profound implications for intergroup relations and communication.

The Ascendance of Social Identity Theory

In the early 1970s, social psychology as a field was thriving, attribution theory was dominating, and students filled the classrooms. During this period, intergroup relations was conspicuous by its absence in any of the glossy competing social psychology textbooks. There likely was a chapter on prejudice but no stand-alone chapter on intergroup relations. Equally interesting was the status accorded to the seminal, realistic, conflict theory inspired, camp experiments conducted by Sherif. The experiments were dramatic in terms of the ease with which they were able to generate intergroup conflict and then resolve the conflict by introducing superordinate goals. Thus, the camp experiments joined the Zimbardo prison experiments, the Asch conformity experiments and the Milgram authority experiments as classics in social psychology. Naturally, every textbook described the Sherif experiments, but there was no convenient chapter on intergroup relations in which to place them.

It is in this context that social identity theory was spawned in Europe, in the UK, at the University of Bristol. The social identity group's theorizing was a direct attack on North American social psychology. The Asch, Milgrim, Sherif and Zimbardo experiments were viewed as North American anomalies, and what the social identity group rejected completely was the more pervasive North American focus on the individual who was assumed to be well-meaning and rational. The social identity group countered this mainstream narrative with a view of individuals whose group membership was central to their lived experience in the context of people who are largely irrational and far from well-meaning.

Indeed, it was precisely the North American "rational person" view that made realistic conflict theory and the camp experiments such anomalies. As dramatic as these experiments were, they did not generate an avalanche of research in their wake. This can be accounted for, in our view, by the essential shortcoming of realistic conflict theory: it is devoid of psychology. That is, the core cause of conflict was argued to be real competition for scarce resources. Psychology only came later, as a fallout from the realistic competition. Intergroup attitudes, stereotypes, attribution and ingroup bias were not the root "causes" of conflict, they were merely predictable consequences. Quite simply, the field of intergroup relations was in desperate need of a genuine psychological theory of intergroup relations. And along came social identity theory.

Social identity theory began with the concept of social categorization, introduced social identity to theorizing about the self-concept, illuminated the process of intergroup comparisons, and came to the seminal conclusion that people strive for *distinctiveness along positively valued dimensions*. This fundamental axiom was more than an abstract declaration; social identity theorists lived their own axiom. Early in its development, social identity theorists strove to be distinctive as a group themselves by eschewing everything American. They promoted their ideas throughout Europe with the passion of a minority group adopting "minority influence" strategies to convert anyone and everyone.

It was not long before America began to take notice. The theory was innovative, the minimal group experiments challenging and, unlike realistic conflict theory, social identity theory was a genuine, group-level, full-blown psychological theory. A European theory had now penetrated American-based, mainstream social psychology and, indeed, social identity theory quickly became a mainstream theory itself.

During this process of widespread acceptance, new interpretations of social identity theory evolved (see Rubin & Hewstone, 2004). These developments are now collectively referred to as the social identity "approach." In addition to these variations, several related yet separate theories have been born out of social identity theory, all the while keeping strong familial ties with their parent. Some have emphasized social-cognitive factors, as in self-categorization theory (Turner, Hogg, Oakes, Reicher, & Wetherell, 1987) or offer developmental stages for group conflict, such as the five-stage model (Taylor & McKirnan, 1984). Other influential offspring have focused on specific identity motives, such as optimal distinctiveness theory (Brewer, 1991), and Stürmer and Simon's (2004) dual pathway of collective action. As its theoretical influence continues to spread, many elements of social identity theory are used to explain social psychological processes, such as prejudice, stereotyping, nationalism, patriotism, reactions to group criticism, adherence to group norms, leadership, collective guilt, and perceptions of group homogeneity. This pervasiveness has awarded social identity theory the mantle of "metatheory." Certainly, this theoretical hegemony is well established in the field of intergroup communication (Harwood & Giles, 2005).

Having achieved not only mainstream, but indeed, global dominance, the original promoters would not entertain the possibility that their theory (approach or metatheory) could not explain every and all phenomena in intergroup relations and intergroup communication. When a theory tries to absorb too much, it becomes more a framework than a specific, hypothesis-generating theory. But let us make our argument clear. Social identity theory's domination of the social psychology of intergroup relations and communication is both deserved and understandable. It was the first, theoretically complete, genuine psychological theory. It was also the first theory with an explicit intergroup focus rather than the usual practice of merely taking an interpersonal theory and extrapolating it to the group level. Social identity theory also shifted the field towards an important yet understudied intergroup format. Rather than focus on groups of relatively equal status, which dominated theorizing during the "cold war" era, social identity theory turned its attention to the current reality, relations between groups of unequal status with a special emphasis on the relatively disadvantaged. This is clearly reflected in the topics of the current book, with its focus on communication involving gender, generational, police, religious, and ethnic groups, and indeed, the now salient topic of terrorism.

The dominance of social identity theory is thus richly deserved. However, in our view, there is a pressing need for competing theories. New theories bring new orientations, new questions, new hypotheses, and hopefully, new insights. It is not that social identity theory has lost its importance. But when a theory goes uncontested for too long, there is a danger that researchers come to believe it can explain anything and everything. Because everybody is using the same framework, nobody is keeping the theory honest by challenging its predictions.

Calling for new theories is no easy task, since nothing will be gained by forcing novelty with weak or narrowly defined competitors. We need theories that are broadly based, that are group based and that bring a fresh perspective. Fortunately, there are, in our view, two theories, or more accurately, movements that show such promise: system justification theory and implicit intergroup attitudes. We turn our attention to these important alternatives with the aim of challenging current contributors to the science of intergroup communication.

System Justification Theory as a Reaction to Social Identity Theory

The dominant status of social identity theory does not imply that other theories of intergroup relations were never available as potential alternatives. For example, relative deprivation theory has also been found to predict intergroup strategies (Mummendey, Kessler, Klink, & Mielke, 1999) and continues to generate a large and interesting corpus of research. A further development involves the incorporation of affect in researching intergroup relations, which resulted in the emergence of intergroup emotion theory. However, no theory to date has been able to rival the influence of social identity theory.

Boundaries of Social Identity Theory

For all that social identity theory can explain, certain intergroup situations continue to be challenging to it. To fully appreciate the counter-intuitive nature of these situations, the basic tenets of social identity theory need to be reiterated. The main postulation is that people are motivated to seek, or maintain, a positive and distinct social identity which, in turn, supplies group members with self-esteem. Not only are these identity-related motivations thought to be driving intergroup conflict, but they are also thought to generate a variety of related psychological phenomena: preference for members of their own group, facilitated outgroup stereotyping, and conformity to group norms.

However, many real-world situations exist where people appear to betray these identity motives. The classic study of Clark and Clark (1947), which showed that young Black children preferred white dolls over Black dolls, is a prime example. Also problematic are the instances of negative self-stereotyping and outgroup preference that have been observed among a variety of disadvantaged minority groups across the globe.

In all these situations, it seems as though people have surrendered their desire for a positive social identity and may even have internalized a negative social identity. These psychological reactions to negative status are seemingly not part of the classic repertoire of social identity management strategies, nor do they conform to the theoretical assumption that people are motivated to gain or at least maintain a high intergroup status (Rubin & Hewstone, 2004; Tajfel & Turner, 1986). In some circumstances, disadvantaged group members not only seem to relinquish status to other groups dispassionately but even support the very illegitimate system that perpetuates these status differences.

System Justification Theory

To explain the psychology behind these counter-intuitive phenomena, Jost has developed system justification theory (Jost & Banaji, 1994). This theory posits that certain groups complacently accept a lower group-status in a societal hierarchy because they are motivated by a need to view the hierarchy in a positive light. This theoretical framework does not deny the motivations highlighted by social identity theory, which describes people as motivated by group distinctiveness and esteem. Rather, system justification theory builds upon social identity theory (Rubin &

Hewstone, 2004), and adds another important source of motivation, one related to the "system." Here, the system encompasses the concept of the societal order with all its attributes, such as meritocracy and capitalism in the West. Jost proposes that people must not only manage the personal and group motivations described by social identity theory but also the system level motivations (Jost & Banaji, 1994). In some situations, motivations regarding the system will prevail, resulting in a system justifying stance, possibly to the detriment of personal and group interests. Hence, because people are motivated to positively skew their perception of the legitimacy of the social order, disadvantaged group members may refrain from challenging the status quo and actively support the very system that creates their disadvantage.

In our view, it is not that system justification theory is, in and of itself, the ultimate challenge to social identity. It is that system justification theory is the latest manifestation of psychology's long preoccupation with justice. From social exchange theory to equity theory, to just-world theory, it would seem that people strive for justice in all their relationships. Justice motives, like identity motives, would seem to be deeply rooted. In certain cases, motivations to believe in justice may conflict with motivations for a positive and distinct identity.

In support of system justification theory, Jost and his colleagues have reported robust correlations between low social status and positive attitudes towards the existing social order (e.g., Jost & Kay, 2005). In these studies, low status group members endorsed meritocratic ideology and the heightened power of system leaders, two markers of approval for the prevailing system. Additionally, low status group members reported outgroup favoritism and ingroup ambivalence, results which are at odds with the basic tenets of social identity theory.

The inherent motivation of people to uphold the status quo is also a theme in another related intergroup relations theory: social dominance theory (Sidanius & Pratto, 1999). This theory begins with the premise that group hierarchies are natural, resulting from social adaptation to evolutionary forces. Indeed, a clear societal hierarchy minimizes intergroup conflict. For this hierarchy to remain stable, members of society must adopt hierarchy-legitimizing myths, which dictate how resources should be allocated. For example, sexist beliefs, such as "women have less skills than men," would help maintain the over-representation of men in positions of power.

In addition to providing insights of its own, social dominance theory also offers support for the basic tenets of system justification theory. The hierarchy-legitimizing myths identified by social dominance orientation can be equated to system justifying stereotypes that are central to Jost's theorizing (Jost & Banaji, 1994). Furthermore, as social dominance has been found to be a measurable personality trait, it lends support to system justification theorists' claim that people have an innate motivation to justify the system.

Competition Can Only Make Social Identity Theory Better

Together, the data collected in studies on system justification and social dominance theories, where people derogate themselves or legitimize the social system that disadvantages their own group, are seemingly incompatible with basic assumptions of the social identity approach. And although system justification theorists initially claimed to build upon existing theories of social identity, the accumulation of data supporting their theory eventually led to more explicit criticisms of social identity theory (see Jost, Banaji, & Nosek, 2004).

Not surprisingly, and possibly following the predictions of their own theory, social identity theorists have attempted to maintain their status by criticizing system justification theory. Without contesting its findings, Turner (2006) issued a warning about the harmful framework propagated by system justification theory, as it reinforces the notion that people are simply prisoners of their own psychological biases. In addition, Turner urges researchers to guard against the illusion that system justification research is somehow helping the disadvantaged by identifying the factors leading to the support of the status quo. He bases his warning on the lack of evidence that social change is the absence of status quo or that social change is the inverse of status quo.

At the very least, then, system justification theory has emerged as a credible theory for explaining certain intergroup relations situations. Indeed, the very spirited reaction from social identity theorists is surely a measure of system justification's status. As expected, being the most influential theory of intergroup relations, social identity theory has been, and will continue to be, questioned. Several well-known criticisms have already targeted the theory's concept of social identity (Huddy, 2001) and its assumption of self-esteem as a motivator (Vignoles, Regalia, Manzi, Golledge, & Scabini, 2006). However, amongst these criticisms, explaining why people stifle their desire to gain a more positive intergroup status has been the most difficult. In explaining this, system justification should, and will, attract the attention of researchers in the fields of language and social identity. At the same time, social identity theorists will be asked to clarify their concepts and sharpen their hypotheses. Indeed, self-categorization theory (Turner et. al., 1987) has emerged as the most important theory to arise out of the social identity tradition. Its growing influence may well be the result of a tightened and more focused set of propositions that offer new insights. Competition from system justification theory may well motivate new social identity spin-offs.

Implications for Intergroup Communication

It is somewhat surprising that system justification theory has not yet penetrated the field of intergroup communication. The method by which all members of society arrive at a consensus about the legitimacy of the social hierarchy is particularly pertinent to the social psychology of language. Here, we are referring to the widespread diffusion and espousal of group stereotypes, which act as legitimizing myths about social inequalities. All members of society jointly legitimize the system by holding positive stereotypes about members of advantaged groups and maintaining negative stereotypes about members of disadvantaged groups. This societal consensus in the form of group stereotypes is the scaffold upon which the status quo of the system is built. For example, the stereotype that people in advantaged groups are more competent and hard-working is believed by all members of society, including members of disadvantaged groups. Conversely, the stereotype that people in disadvantaged groups are less competent and, perhaps lazy, is endorsed by all members of society, including members of disadvantaged groups.

A study of benevolent sexism by Jost and Kay (2005) is a prototypical example of the implications of language on system justification. In a series of studies, female participants were exposed to complementary stereotypes about women (e.g., warm and nurturing but not competent), statements of benevolent sexism, and favorable stereotypes about women. As predicted, women who were exposed to complementary stereotypes and statements of benevolent sexism were found to justify the system. Interestingly, this latter group showed higher degrees of support for the system than participants exposed to favorable stereotypes about women. Amongst these results, one finding is of particular pertinence to intergroup communications. Throughout these studies, it was *exposure* to the stereotypes, and not explicit *endorsement* of these stereotypes, that predicted system justification. The implications are that the communication of a stereotype, even if the recipient disagrees with the stereotype, can have a significant impact on people (see Chapters 8 & 9).

More generally, the field of communication is strategically positioned to address the competing hypotheses of social identity and system justification theories. To date the focus has been on how communication, in all its forms, supports the need for disadvantaged group members to arrive at a distinctive and positive social identity. The way is now paved to address the issue of when and how communication contributes to keeping disadvantaged group members in their lower status. We place emphasis on "when" and "how" because it is clear that neither theory is always correct: the real challenge is to understand the conditions that lead disadvantaged group members to challenge the status quo as opposed to supporting it, to their own identity detriment. Theorists, we hope, will continue to pursue gender, age, ethnic, gay and lesbian, authority roles, the media, and terrorism, but with a new lens: one that provides insights into the communication processes that help maintain and regulate the status quo. The important vehicle for communicating status quo myths on the one hand, or fanning the flames of protest on the other, is mass communication. And, now that the internet and text messaging have evolved as important mass communication platforms, the field of intergroup communication is poised to make an important contribution (see Chapter 16).

The Social Cognitive Revolution: Intergroup Attitudes

When the cognitive revolution invaded social psychology, many of us were less than enthusiastic. Intergroup theorists focus most often on socially destructive processes that seem driven far more by emotion than reason. Social cognition with its "information processing" focus on "cold" cognitions seemed to be the wrong direction. Surely we needed research with greater external validity, not less. Furthermore, it was difficult to believe that reaction-time experiments measured in nanoseconds, or seemingly innocuous primes, could be relevant to core processes related to prejudice, discrimination, stereotyping, hatred, and conflict.

But social cognition is here to stay, and it has made a major contribution to intergroup relations. The seemingly innocuous primes have revealed surprisingly powerful intergroup effects: who would have thought that merely placing a small national flag in the corner of a room could have such an effect on cultural identity? What social cognition brought to the study of intergroup relations is an appreciation for unconscious, automatic, uncontrolled cognitions and how they impact intergroup processes. Of all the cognitive processes, we have chosen to focus on implicit attitudes, since intergroup attitudes have the longest history in social psychology and because attitudes are the most emotionally charged of the cognitions.

Attitudes were one of social psychology's first concerns and historically considered to be one of the field's most distinctive and indispensable concepts. Attitudes, defined as favorable or unfavorable evaluative reactions towards a social target, were a major building block of modern social psychology, likely because of their evaluative or emotional essence: the first "hot" cognition in social psychology. They were discovered to be an efficient mechanism through which individuals sized up the world and reacted to social and environmental stimuli. The social psychology of intergroup relations in particular continues to have attitudes as one of its primary concerns. In the context of intergroup relations, an individual's attitude is considered to be the gauge of his or her feelings towards members of another group. Of particular interest are the antecedents and consequences of negative intergroup attitudes. Specifically, intergroup researchers focus on phenomena such as prejudice and discrimination, their prevalence, contributing factors, impact, and the methods by which they can be reduced.

Intimately linked to the study of negative intergroup attitudes, and an important contributor to our understanding of these attitudes, is the study of intergroup communication. Indeed, negative intergroup attitudes and even serious intergroup conflict are often perpetuated through various methods of communication. Negative labeling of the outgroup, speaking more slowly to those in a particular group, ridiculing a group's accent, or even choosing to speak with a particular accent are all examples of instances where communication is used as a vehicle through which negative intergroup attitudes and intergroup conflict are propagated.

In what follows, we trace the evolution of the study of intergroup attitudes, and consider parallel contributions and advances from the field of intergroup communication. From our review of intergroup attitudes we propose a new direction to which the field of intergroup communication might now turn.

The Evolution of Intergroup Attitudes

Originally thought to be simple behavioral guides, the complexity of attitudes and their varied influence on behavior have emerged over many years of study. Much of the historical focus on attitudes operated under the assumption that they existed solely in an explicit, conscious mode. The widespread use of direct or self-report measures to gauge individuals' attitudes is evidence for a once pervasive belief in conscious attitude operation. Researchers initially assumed that a person's attitude could easily be detected merely by asking how he or she felt about a particular target. In the more specific context of intergroup attitudes, researchers sought to detect negative attitudes towards members of a particular social category simply by having participants report their own feelings about a category member in a survey or other direct, explicit measure. Researchers examining intergroup communication advanced the field by exploring overt expressions of prejudice and discrimination, propagated through negative labeling and derogatory language (see Chapter 8).

The study of explicit attitudes spawned a methodological industry. Originally, measuring explicit attitudes was challenging enough, given that attitudes are mental predispositions and not visible behaviors. This challenge of measuring a mental process that is invisible was met by people such as Thurstone and Likert, who developed direct self-report measures involving attitude statements, questions, or ratings. Indeed, these developments gave the entire field of social psychology scientific credibility since even researchers from the "hard" sciences were convinced of the objective quality of these measures of attitude. But attitudes were emotionally charged, "hot" cognitions that posed a serious problem: how to cope with social desirability. For the field of intergroup relations and communication this was, and is, a major issue since attitudes in these domains are extremely sensitive and, thus, especially prone to social desirability.

The issue of social desirability and the overt expression of negative intergroup attitudes has now become an especially challenging issue given the present climate of political and social correctness. This has meant that direct self-report or survey research methods are no longer capable of detecting individuals' attitudes in a way that is thought to be accurate. Indeed, a continued reliance on direct attitude measures would yield results indicating that negative intergroup attitudes have all but disappeared. In order to avoid the social desirability constraints of direct measures, a substantial number of research programs turned to the use of indirect measures of detecting stereotyping and prejudice, such as disguising the true purpose of an attitudinal investigation. These more indirect measures often revealed that anti-Bblack sentiments, for example, were much more prevalent among White Americans than the survey data might lead one to expect. It was shown that prejudiced attitudes surfaced when people could hide behind the screen of some other motive. The study of subtle or modern racism such as exaggerating ethnic differences, feeling less admiration and affection for immigrant minorities, or rejecting them for supposedly non-racial reasons began to replace the study of blatant prejudice. Modern discrimination and prejudice could similarly be revealed and examined by intergroup communication researchers through a careful analysis of the language people used in intergroup contexts. More subtle linguistic cues, such as the speed and volume of one's speech (Giles, Fox, & Smith, 1993), illustrated how modern discrimination could be detected and understood through language.

The idea of subtle or modern discrimination was a precursor to the notion that a person's explicit, conscious attitudes towards a group might be quite different from their automatic/unconscious attitudes towards that same group. Although outwardly expressing a positive intergroup attitude, an individual might, nevertheless hold a very negative unconscious, automatic, uncontrolled attitude. A revolution in intergroup attitude research and in detecting intergroup attitudes in particular, came from the advent of implicit social cognition (Greenwald & Banaji, 1995). No longer were attitudes thought to operate purely in a conscious mode. Instead, implicit attitudes, defined as "introspectively unidentified traces of past experience that mediate favorable or unfavorable feeling, thought, or action toward social objects" (p. 8), were argued to exist and to exert influence on an individual. The evidence for the existence of such unconscious, implicit attitudes came from a vast array of research documenting people's performance on sequential priming tasks where an automatically activated stereotype was shown to increase later discriminatory behavior, and on response latency measures such as the Implicit Association Test (IAT). The IAT requires rapid categorizations of various targets, and results are interpreted such that easier (faster) categorizations are considered to be more strongly associated in memory than more difficult (slower) categorizations. By pairing pleasant or unpleasant words with an attitude object, the IAT is able to measure the positive or negative associations that an individual has with a particular object without the person having to bring this association to conscious awareness and thus modify it depending on social desirability constraints. For example, an individual who has a negative implicit attitude towards African Americans might take longer to categorize a picture of a black face into the category "black and pleasant" than they would to categorize the picture of a black face into the category "black and unpleasant." Using such techniques, researchers believed that they were able to gain access to people's underlying 'true' and often socially unacceptable attitudes towards sensitive issues such as race, gender, and other contentious concerns. This novel revelation has greatly influenced the field of attitudes, intergroup relations and even social psychology as a whole by opening up an entirely new avenue of exploration pertaining to social cognitive processes occurring outside of one's conscious awareness.

The distinction between automatic, unconscious processes and controlled, conscious processes has also provided unexpected findings with considerable applied implications. For example, in her examination of the automatic and controlled processes involved in prejudice, Devine (1989) found that both high- and low-prejudice individuals actually experienced the same automatic activation of a cultural stereotype when in the presence of a member of the stereotyped group. However, only low-prejudiced individuals consciously inhibited the automatically activated stereotype and replaced it with thoughts negating the stereotype. The implications of this research for prejudice reduction were significant: instead of trying to eliminate stereotypes, prejudice may be more effectively reduced by training people to suppress their use. Such groundbreaking research was inspired by a growing acceptance and understanding of the distinction between unconscious and conscious processing. The field of intergroup communication might be similarly expanded to incorporate a new focus on implicit, unconscious processes (see Chapter 4).

Implicit Processes and Intergroup Communication

In fact, issues of communication are already very much embedded in many of the key research questions being addressed by those exploring implicit processes, and in the methodologies that they employ. Many of the experiments that involve unconscious priming, for example, use words as the primes themselves. Thus words, or language, form the very basis for these experiments and are integral to the interpretation of their results. Other research programs examine the implicit meaning that individuals ascribe to labels and descriptions of outgroup members. Because communication plays a mechanistic role in the intergroup phenomena under investigation, intergroup communication specialists are well positioned to unpack the phenomena that have been uncovered by the new research focus on implicit processes.

Some researchers have already taken up this challenge and have examined implicit processes in the context of intergroup communication. For example, Carnaghi and Maass (2007) extended the IAT and asked if derogatory group labels of homosexuals activated less positive associations than neutral labels. They explored participants' associations with the language of the labels themselves. They found that for heterosexual participants, the derogatory words carried less positive associations than neutral category words. However, a counter-intuitive and interesting finding was that the people thought to be most negatively impacted by derogatory labels, homosexual participants, did not experience such negative associations. In this way, the words themselves were shown to be important, as the authors suggest that minority group members may have in fact embraced the derogatory labels and reclaimed their meaning. Here, the exploration of implicit reactions to intergroup communication yields unexpected and interesting results.

Communication researchers are nicely positioned to address the key issues confronting the study of unconscious intergroup attitudes. The parsimonious interpretation is that unconscious attitudes are "true" attitudes because, unlike conscious attitudes, they are not influenced by social desirability. But, unfortunately, it is not that simple. To begin with, different unconscious measures are sometimes not correlated, suggesting that the methods may well be assessing different phenomena or different aspects of the same phenomenon. Similarly, there is not always a correlation between implicit and explicit measures, even when the explicit measures are immune to social desirability constraints. Explicit and implicit measures have also been shown to predict behavior in different ways and to respond to attitude change differently, suggesting that implicit and explicit attitudes might be independent of each other. Moreover, there is controversy with respect to whether or not unconscious measures of intergroup attitudes are in fact measuring attitudes or merely societal norms. An innovative investigation of implicit intergroup attitudes by communications researchers might offer important insights into these key issues.

Conclusion

A cursory glance at the chapters in the present volume leaves no doubt that social identity theory, and its second generation offerings in the form of social categorization theory remain dominant. We have argued for the need to expand the theoretical base of intergroup communication, not as a replacement for social identity but rather to broaden the field and generate new insights.

Suggesting alternative theories, however, is not good enough. The chosen theories must be serious contenders with depth and breadth, and they must be theories that have the potential to add new perspectives (see also Chapter 22). We believe that system justification theory, and justice motives generally and the broad movement towards an appreciation of unconscious, automatic and uncontrolled cognitive processes are leading candidates. Can social neuroscience be far behind?

We are suggesting that the field of intergroup communication needs to consider these alternative theories. In so doing, we believe it will not only add new insights, it will motivate the new generation of social identity theorists to sharpen their concepts and processes.

CHAPTER TWENTY-TWO

An Evolutionary Perspective on Social Identity and Intergroup Communication

SCOTT A. REID, JINGUANG ZHANG, HOWARD GILES & JAKE HARWOOD

The study of communication has relied heavily upon social psychological theories, and this has been particularly true for those who study communication and intergroup relations. In this, the social identity perspective (most notably social identity, ethnolinguistic vitality, communication accommodation, and self-categorization theories) has become pre-eminent in the field. It all began with social identity theory (Tajfel & Turner, 1979), but it has since blossomed into a general social identity perspective on group processes and intergroup relations. Indeed, this book is a testament to the growing influence of the social identity perspective on the study of communication. We have elaborations and extensions that include communicative dimensions of family relationships, terrorism, age, civilian-police relations, disability, media, sport, democracy, religion, stereotyping, social cognition, and stigma. There can be little doubt that social identity and closely allied theories will continue to explain further phenomena and expand into other disciplines. Linguistics, sociology, and political science have sustained limited sorties and should expect more; anthropology, religious and women's studies are obvious candidates for exploration.

The power of the social identity perspective is that it provides a sound metatheory (see Chapter 21). This "theory of theories" tells us that social psychological outcomes (e.g., language use, attitudes, stereotypes, non-verbals) result from an interaction between individual psychological processes and the social environment (Tajfel, 1969). Individual psychological processes (e.g., the motivation to self-enhance and the search for clarity) are worthy of investigation in their own right, but when it comes to explanation it must be recognized that these psychological processes are socially contingent. People communicate and construct shared social realities, and they do so in ways that satisfy these psychological processes. Discrimination, for example, is typically identity enhancing ("we are better than they are and deserve the spoils"), but people communicate and establish norms of discrimination that reflect group status striving in the context of intergroup relations. A theory of discrimination that misses the shared and communicatively constructed reality of prejudice is missing a substantial part of the phenomenon.

The continued success of the social identity approach suggests something important: It must be essentially correct. Striving for positive social identity, coordinating the pursuit of shared goals with ingroup members, developing and clarifying features that distinguish ingroup from outgroup members, and the process of sense-making that produces stereotyping, conformity, persuasion, group cohesion, and so on, are all group processes that hinge upon shared social identity as a group member. While there certainly is and will continue to be debate about processes, explanations for phenomena, as well as theoretical developments, the fundamental insights of the social identity approach are shared across researchers and very likely to persist. Future developments will have to absorb and expand upon the insights of the social identity approach, just as the social identity approach absorbed and expanded upon Festinger's social comparison theory and Sherif's realistic group conflict model. If we are right about this, then we can make some specific predictions about the future direction of research on communication and intergroup relations. This would be a laudable goal for an epilogue, but we believe that the time is ripe for asking a much more important question: How can we further our understanding of social identity, communication, and intergroup relations? Clearly, valuable and novel connections for the study of language and communication could be pursued —as illustrated in the previous chapter—such as with theories of intergroup emotion (Giner-Sorolla, Mackie, & Smith, 2007), modes of identity commitment (Roccas, Sagiv, Schwartz, Halevy, & Eidelson, 2008), and multiple-group membership complexities (Roccas & Brewer, 2002). However, rather than introduce a potpourri of these theoretical linkages, we will focus instead on proposing a major new theoretical direction for exploring processes of intergroup communication.

Toward that end, we believe that evolutionary theorizing will provide the broad theoretical framework for expanding our understanding of social identity. Evolutionary thinking is set to revolutionize the study of psychology. In fact, the last decade has witnessed the emergence and proliferation of evolutionary hypotheses and models in all major areas of psychology. These models have yielded highly provocative findings in the best scientific journals. The rapid expansion and success of the evolutionary perspective in psychology can be attributed to its unique synthetic appeal. It achieves this power by pursing functional questions. Instead of asking '*how* does it happen?' evolutionarily-minded researchers ask a more fundamental question first: '*why* does this happen at all?' By doing so, social psychologists have attempted to discover the evolutionary underpinnings of prejudice, social motivation, altruism, and many other phenomena (see Schaller, Simpson, & Kenrick, 2006). It is becoming apparent that this new evolutionary psychology, which eschews the crude biologism of the past in favor of deeper, functional processes, will take our understanding of social identity further.

To date, relatively little attention has been paid to the evolutionary basis for intergroup communication. Why, for example, do people shift their language in sometimes accommodating and yet, other times, diverging ways? Why do people gossip? Why do questionable conspiracy theories take hold? What is it about the rhetoric of leaders that followers find appealing? In this chapter, we will address the first two of these questions in depth and allude to the others from both an evolutionary and social identity perspective. In doing so, it will be our aim to present some evolutionary speculations and hypotheses and show how the evolutionary framework meshes with the social identity perspective and can carry it to a higher level.

Darwin's Theory of Evolution by Natural Selection

Evolution by natural selection is a very simple yet immensely powerful idea. Individual variation in a population means that some characteristics—be they anatomical, physiological, perceptual, cognitive, or emotional—are more likely than others to persist because they increase the odds of their carriers' survival and reproduction (Darwin, 1859). Those who best fit their social environment, who eke more resources from it and out-compete their conspecifics, are those most likely to survive and reproduce. Over generations, those who possess a characteristic that confers a reproductive advantage will become more frequent in the population, and those who do not possess the characteristic, or a less beneficial version, will become less frequent and eventually extinct. This simple insight—trait variation and trait selection leading to differential reproduction—explains the mass of biological diversity on our planet. Just as natural selection accounts for variation in animal morphology and behavior, it should ultimately provide a functional account of human psychology.

The characteristics that are selected for by natural selection are adaptations. Evolutionary psychology assumes, as does all of biology, that adaptations are functional solutions to environmental problems. The more pressing the environmental problem, the more likely that we will find an adaptation. Particularly strong pressures can be found in evolutionary arms races, such as between predator and prey, and host and parasite. Further to this, just as an arctic fox possesses camouflage (a white coat in winter and a grey-brown coat in summer) that is adaptive for hunting and survival in the seasonally variable arctic environment, humans possess adaptations that have enabled them to solve problems in their ancestral environment. Relatively ancient adaptations would include fear of snakes and yawning to communicate a sense of safety (both of which humans share with other species, and presumably a common ancestor), and relatively recent adaptations would possibly include language and almost certainly the life-long ability to metabolize milk that is found in most European and some African populations.

The focus of evolutionary psychology is neural adaptations. It is hypothesized that the human brain houses a great number of relatively independent modules that address specific environmental challenges faced by humans in their ancestral environment (Tooby & Cosmides, 2005). This massive modularity hypothesis, which borrows the computer metaphor from cognitive psychology, posits that like computers, human brains (hardware) possess neural structures that execute algorithms (software programs) and that these algorithms have been selected and honed by natural selection. Among many others, there is evidence for modules that detect animals in dense foliage (i.e., food and predators), cheater detection (i.e., people who would swindle us in social exchange), and the location of food—evolution engineers solutions to domain-specific challenges. However, domain-general challenges, such as avoiding death, are generally thought too complex for evolution to solve. We should therefore expect most if not all psychological adaptations are domain specific. In brief, our ancestors who possessed neural characteristics that lent them an average survival and reproductive advantage in response to specific environmental challenges have bequeathed the psychology we possess today.

The Social Identity Perspective in an Evolutionary Light

As noted, we are at an early stage in thinking about evolutionary explanations for social identity processes. Further to this, identifying adaptations is not easy. We cannot observe the developmental trajectory of psychological adaptations, we can merely consider present observations in light of what appears most likely to have shaped evolution in the past. Nonetheless, reverse engineering works. For this reason, we will begin with a discussion of extant arguments and present some speculations of our own. In doing so, we will take seriously the idea that the processes identified in the social identity approach are an important part of understanding group processes and intergroup relations and that can inform our evolutionary arguments and speculations.

It is worthwhile to first consider Mayr's (1961) distinction between ultimate and proximate causation. Ultimate causation is evolutionary—it answers the question of *why* we have a particular psychological adaptation. Proximate causation is represented by the explanation of *how* an evolved mechanism works. For example, there is evidence that xenophobic attitudes are driven in part by the salience of the threat of contamination by disease (Faulkner, Schaller, Park, & Duncan, 1999). Presumably, our ancestors who did not avoid people with disease were less likely to survive and reproduce. This evolutionary model predicts the content of what should differentiate between groups (e.g., health indicators), what constitutes a threat (i.e., disease), and why (i.e., disease puts a damper on survival and reproduction). On the other hand, a proximal social identity model would tell us *how* people respond to the threat: through heightened ingroup identification, intergroup differentiation, and the maintenance of distance from outgroup members. As can be seen, the ultimate evolutionary and proximal social identity mechanisms are satisfyingly complementary and provide a deeper explanation for xenophobia than either approach alone. Indeed, evolutionary and proximal social identity mechanisms should be consistent if we have correctly identified the relevant processes. However, it is possible that an evolutionary model that does not take account of proximal findings is incomplete or incorrect. Proximal modeling and evolutionary theorizing are mutually informative.

For example, one hypothesis is that social categorization affects intergroup discrimination because we have evolved the ability to track social and political coalitions (Kurzban, Tooby, & Cosmides, 2001). According to this view, a common feature of social life is the formation of internally cooperative, externally competitive, and fluid political coalitions. Members of coalitions cooperate to increase the status of the coalition, and by extension, coalition members. We are wired by evolution to pursue status because status confers resources (food, shelter, possessions), and resources confer differential survival and reproduction. Kurzban et al. reason that people would, therefore, have developed neural machinery for the detection of fluid coalitions. This neural machinery would enable people to easily track coalitions and to switch allegiances when beneficial.

This evolutionary story is largely consistent with self-categorization theory (see Chapter 1), which predicts that people's social identities are context dependent and fluid. As a social context changes (e.g., coalition hierarchies become unstable), different identities get activated, and the content of those identities shifts to reflect the new intergroup terrain. However, the evolutionary model yields predictions that self-categorization theory does not. According to the coalitional hypothesis, categories like sex and age should be automatically activated in personal perception because they are invariant characteristics of people that would have been socially relevant for much of our evolutionary history (see Chapters 3, 4, & 21). On the other hand, race is not something that would have been apparent in our ancestral social environment. We would have rarely travelled so far as to encounter people who looked different from us. Our ability to attend to and track race should therefore be driven by some other adaptation. Kurzban et al. propose and demonstrate that racial categories are activated when they make sense of coalitional differences between groups and that their salience is easily mitigated. Gender, however, being a stable aspect of people and our social past, that does not require tracking, is resistant to contextual change. People automatically categorize by gender, even when gender has no meaningful relationship to coalition membership.

But there are other possibilities. According to self-categorization theory, the proximal mechanism that tracks all human categories is contextual fit, a core part of which is meta-contrast (Campbell, 1958). When we categorize objects we automatically extract features that are shared in one category but distinct from those in others. Formally, meta-contrast is a cognitive mechanism that categorizes stimuli by maximizing the ratio of shared within-category similarities to inter-category differences. We have no conscious or motivational control over this process—our brains unconsciously and slavishly pursue meta-contrast. Take, for instance, a grey square set against a black background—the grey square will appear to be of a relatively light shade of grey. The same grey square set against a white background, however, appears to be darker. Further, when we switch our attention back and forth between the grey square set in black versus white backgrounds, we notice the brightness subtly shifting up or down as our brains re-calculate meta-contrast. This also happens with rainbows (bands of color are seen as uniform and distinct from neighboring bands, whereas in reality there are no categories), people (e.g., "they all look alike," the outgroup homogeneity effect), inanimate objects, sounds, and, indeed, probably anything subject to human categorization.

Human beings are pattern-seeking animals. The meta-contrast process is a fact of categorization that extracts meaning by placing objects into categories. Meta-contrast goes beyond reality, but only insofar that doing so renders patterns meaningful. A meta-contrast that did too much violence to the facts of arrangements of stimuli would not evolve if the owners of that perception were, for example, unable to spot a hungry leopard in the grass. Given that meta-contrast is an omnipresent feature of our psychology, we would think that it is a candidate for being an adaptation and likely that it is (at least part of) the cognitive machinery responsible for the coalition tracking module posited by Kurzban et al. (2001).

But what led us to evolve meta-contrast? The most obvious answer is that it is a survival mechanism rooted in the identification and demarcation of edible from poisonous foods and the detection of well-camouflaged edible or predatory animals. The ability to determine whether something is nutritious versus poisonous would represent a strong selection pressure. We all are the direct descendants of people who were able to figure out what foods they could eat. Indeed, many plants, animals, and possibly fungi (which should all evolve adaptations against being eaten) have evolved a morphology that is most similar to their poisonous counterparts, rendering them difficult to distinguish. For example, the tasty and nutritious scarlet king snake has evolved to mimic the poisonous coral snake. While the contrast between nutritious versus poisonous plants and animals makes for a vivid story about how this adaptation could evolve, even more subtle differences would produce the same result. A plant that merely makes an animal sick for a few hours would produce the same effect, as would a plant that is edible but that contains few useful calories.

The detection of food and predators is a problem faced by our non-hominid ancestors. We would, therefore, expect the meta-contrast process to be a very old adaptation. We would certainly expect other apes to categorize stimuli following meta-contrast. Experiments could easily be designed to test whether this is the case. One could teach a chimp to discriminate lighter from darker hued cards by providing edible rewards for correct choices. Once this is learned, we could test the same process by keeping the hue of a card constant but varying the background color. If chimps employ meta-contrast, they will choose what they perceive to be a lighter hue when it is, in fact, constant. This same experiment could be repeated on other species. If our adaptation story is correct, we should find that non-social species—that have faced the problem of food detection but not coalition tracking—possess meta-contrast. This would be consistent with our meta-contrast hypothesis but inconsistent with the coalition tracking hypothesis that places this adaptation in more recent, and social, hunter-gatherer environments.

Another hypothesis is that humans have developed intergroup differentiation as a pathogen avoidance mechanism. Fincher and colleagues (e.g., Faulkner et al., 1999; Fincher & Thornhill, 2008; Fincher, Thornhill, Murray, & Schaller, 2008) have shown that the greater the number of pathogenic diseases in an environment, the more collectivism (i.e., valuing group goals over individual goals), ethnocentrism (i.e., ingroup preference and wariness of outgroups), languages, and religions. Their argument is that people and pathogens co-evolve in a Red Queen process. Members of the host group continually evolve counter measures against the pathogen that continually evolves new measures against the host. Over time, a group develops an equilibrium state where the pathogen is held at bay. This means that our reproductive fitness will be decreased by mating with members of other groups that do not possess the pathogen defense. Proximally, we can aid our survival by finding ways to maintain social distance from other groups and to find ways of reliably distinguishing ingroup from outgroup.

The anti-pathogen defense hypothesis readily generates follow-up predictions. Groups that are subject to environmental pathogens will quickly develop and communicate norms, justifications in the form of stereotypes, and conspiracy theories about the evils of outgroups. These would rapidly diffuse through groups with this common fate and would function to maintain group cohesion and distinctiveness in face of the pathogen threat. In fact, it may be that our ancestors who pursued group-bonding/outgroup avoidance fictions in pathogenic hard times were more likely to survive than their more "rational" counterparts. We may, therefore, find cultural differences in the ease with which such collective images can be transmitted. For example, people from relatively pathogen-free environments may be less likely to use health based indicators to distinguish between groups than those from more pathogen-laden environments.

In sum, and as the foregoing hopefully shows, we do not fully understand the set of evolutionary pressures that have rendered social identity a core component of human psychology. Nonetheless, we can expect consensus to emerge on the importance of status pursuit through shared social identity, the kinds of threats that motivate us, and further still, the scope conditions of social identity processes. In what follows, we consider these evolutionary mechanisms with reference to communication phenomena.

Communication Accommodation and Divergence

People manage social distance by varying their linguistic (e.g., lexical-diversity), paralinguistic (e.g., accent), and non-verbal (e.g., gaze while speaking) communication. Sometimes people move towards others by matching features of their communication; at other times people maintain or increase social distance by emphasizing distinctiveness. These tactics are known as communication convergence and maintenance/divergence, respectively. Communication accommodation theory (CAT; e.g., Gallois, Ogay, & Giles, 2005) was designed to provide a theoretical account of why people communicatively converge or diverge (see Chapters 3, 4, 5, 10, & 15). Convergence is thought to be motivated by a desire to show similarity and attraction, whereas maintenance and divergence are thought to be motivated by a desire for a positively distinct social identity. Since its inception, CAT has been very successful at explaining intercultural variation in linguistic shifts (such as code-switching and patterns of bilingualism), patterns of doctor-patient communication, forms of discriminatory communication like elderspeak, and police-civilian relations (see relevant chapters in this volume).

Communicative shifts have been observed in many societies and are likely to have an adaptive function. One is the pathogen defense function that Fincher and Thornhill (2008) have identified. These authors argue that, in a region with many parasites, evolution should favor ingroup breeding and keeping close to one's tribe. These strategies foster group separation which, in turn, produce cultural diversity, including dialects and ultimately language. Language, then, serves as an important group-marker to facilitate pathogen avoidance. If this is true, a simple prediction is that when cues activate the disease avoidance mechanism, people will communicatively diverge from outgroup members. More interestingly, we can expect that, even when boundaries between low- and high-status groups are highly open, members of a low-status group may not converge towards the high-status group as CAT would predict so long as pathogen avoidance is primed.

The pathogen avoidance hypothesis suggests a number of group differences. Pathogen resistance varies across ethnic groups but not across gender or age groups. This suggests that a pathogen prime will successfully produce ethnolinguistic differentiation but not age or gender differentiation. Further, we may find that ethnolinguistic differentiation is stronger for some groups than others. Women, for example, make greater parental investment than men and are thus more likely to suffer reproductively from pathogens. This suggests that women will diverge from ethnic outgroups more readily than men in response to pathogenic risks. Similarly, elderly people often have more compromised immune systems than younger people, so we may find that they, too, are particularly likely to respond to a pathogen prime with ethnolinguistic differentiation. Indeed, this may also account, in part, for the increase in political conservatism with age (Eaves et al., 1997).

But linguistic diversity cannot be fully explained by anti-pathogen defense. There are many examples of groups that have developed linguistic distinctiveness absent differences in pathogens. For example, the relatively pathogen free and homogenous Britain was, until quite recently, replete with linguistic diversity. Another evolutionary pressure on linguistic divergence and accommodation is suggested by Nettle and Dunbar (1997). These researchers propose that shifts in languages and dialects evolved to manage resources by providing a heuristic cue to trustworthiness. We trust people who share our language or accent more than those who do not, because ingroup members in the evolutionary past were more likely to be kin and to reciprocate our generosity in the future ("I'll scratch your back if you scratch mine"). The reason that language and dialect are such strong cues to trust can be found in the simple fact that it is difficult to replicate other people's languages and accents with native efficiency. Indeed, Nettle and Dunbar's computer simulations showed that cheating as a resource-gaining tactic quickly disappeared in a population when dialect was introduced as a marker of group identity. If this resource allocation hypothesis is right, then we might find that countries with a history of resource scarcity and intergroup conflict but pathogen homogenous environments possess different accents but not languages.

Indeed, there are many examples of pronunciation being used to determine group membership. Shibboleths provide an interesting case. For example, pronunciation of the Dutch city, Scheveningen, was said to be used during WWII to detect

German spies because it contains sounds that are exceedingly difficult to pronounce correctly, even for seasoned bilinguals. But how do shibboleths work? One possibility is that they are sounds located at the extremes of our vocal apparatus and that are likely to be non-prototypical in most other languages (in fact, probably more distinct from neighboring languages than more distant ones). It may be that languages contain these environmentally distinctive sounds as an implicit barrier to true group membership. Of course, this explains what kinds of sounds are likely to be used but not why they are difficult to replicate. One might think that the answer to replication difficulty is simply learning and experience, but this is not likely, as motivated bilinguals would eventually pick up the correct sounds to pass as bona fide ingroup members.

An alternative possibility is that shibboleths are explained by meta-contrast. Meta-contrast functions not just by differentiating between one sound and another, it also assimilates closely related sounds to the prototype. For example, some instances of the vowel /i/ (as in *peep*) sound more prototypical (i.e., typical and representative) than other versions of the same vowel. Interestingly, prototypical sounds act like a magnet that attracts and assimilates closely related sounds. In fact, Kuhl (1991) identified this prototype magnet effect when she gave participants a simple discrimination task using prototypical and non-prototypical versions of /i/ as a reference. People were less able to accurately discriminate between the reference and other examples of /i/ when the reference was prototypical. In other words, the prototype distorted and assimilated closely related versions of /i/ that the non-prototypical instance did not. People literally could not perceive some sounds as distinctive entities because they were assimilated to the prototype.

Thus, shibboleths should be made up of sounds that are environmentally rare but distinctive features of languages or dialects. People from the outgroup cannot perceive, let alone replicate the correct sounds, partly because of learning and experience, but particularly because that sound does not exist as a distinction in their language, and it is therefore assimilated to a different prototype that does exist in their language. Indeed, there are many cases of sounds that are difficult for speakers of certain languages. English, for example, is one of the few languages with the /th/ sound, as in *th*ree, which is very difficult for non-native speakers to replicate.

It may be that groups develop sounds that are difficult to replicate, and/or make fine grained distinctions between some sounds *because* this makes it particularly difficult for non-native speakers to learn their language with native efficiency. We might therefore find areas of intense and ongoing international trade or resource conflict are those that are most likely to have shibboleth sounds in their language. On the one hand, these groups would want to have a language that is largely accessible to members of other groups to make trade possible, but at the same time they would want to reserve certain linguistic features for the task of group differentiation and, thus, costly trust signaling.

Further still, these sounds, which remain difficult to replicate even for long-time immigrants, may be a particularly effective linguistic marker of deviance. People who cannot replicate the prototypical sounds with native efficiency will be seen as marginal or deviant group members, will garner less trust from native speakers, and will be kept in a low-status position. Groups that have easier to replicate languages should therefore be more likely to use other means of maintaining intergroup distinctiveness for regulating their status hierarchies. Features such as ethnophaulisms (e.g., *Italian perfume* for garlic in the United States; *coconut* for Samoan in New Zealand) and hostile intergroup attitudes may be more prevalent in these cultures.

In the above, we discussed the possible evolutionary mechanisms that underpin communication accommodation. While social attraction, liking, and positive distinctiveness are certainly important motivations, it is likely that people communicatively converge to or diverge away from others for more fundamental evolutionary reasons, namely survival and reproduction. How people talk (at the lexical, phonetic, and phonological levels) in an intergroup context might have, among other functions, helped them keep away from pathogen-carrying outgroup members and facilitate social exchange in the evolutionary past. Yet in addition to why they talk differently (i.e., forms of communication), an evolutionary perspective should also suggest what people talk about (i.e., the content of communication). In the following, we will discuss one type of seemingly mundane informal communication that may bear important evolutionary significance.

Gossip

People have an inordinate fondness for gossip. Research suggests that approximately two thirds of our conversations focus on social topics (Dunbar, 1996; Emler, 2001). Barkow (1992) points out that from an evolutionary perspective, people should be interested in political dealings, people's reliability in social exchange, health and physical conditions, births and deaths, and information about sexual rivals. In this, people are particularly interested in hearing about and passing along positive information about friends and allies, and negative information about competitors and enemies (McAndrew, Bell, & Garcia, 2007). In essence, gossip is about the management of status because status confers differential survival and reproduction. Indeed, this remains largely true in contemporary democracies—people with high socio-economic status access more resources and suffer considerably less from stress and disease (Sapolsky, 2004). Further, the centrality of status to gossip further suggests that gossip has evolved, at least in part, to regulate membership in coalitions. People in coalitions can cooperate with one another to increase their status, but this can only happen successfully if free-riders and cheats are identified and sanctioned. Wilson, Wilczynski, Wells, and Weiser (2000) propose that gossip has, therefore, evolved to enforce social norms.

Where evolutionary considerations suggest much about the content of gossip, social identity theory provides detailed predictions about the degree to which gossip will be pernicious, to whom it is directed, when, and why. As a starting point, consider that many if not most of our social relationships are structured around our group memberships, which we use to further our interests. Take a typical middle-class existence: People spend much of their time working in hierarchical environments where different organizational sub-groups compete with one another and where people within those groups compete with one another individually. Gossip is rife, but who gossips about whom, about what, and when? If we assume, as social identity theory does, that people are motivated for social status, we can see that there are two general ways in which people can pursue status. People who are socially mobile (people who are individually motivated to dispense with their low-status group and join a high-status group) are people who: 1) lack commitment to their low-status group; 2) view boundaries between groups as permeable; and 3) perceive the intergroup status distinction as relatively stable and legitimate. We would predict that socially mobile people will direct their gossip strategically with the aim of increasing status by joining the higher-status group. Given that people within high-status groups are the arbiters of group membership (they control group boundary permeability and its attendant rewards—e.g., salary and promotions), it is likely that such people will attempt to curry favor with powerful members of the high-status group, when they talk with these people they will gossip unfavorably about their competitors in the low-status ingroup, and they will do so in ways that enable them to form a bond with that high-status member (i.e., gossip will be accompanied by ingratiation and accommodation to the high-status person). In terms of content, we can expect socially mobile people to focus on competency as a group member. They will manage self-enhancing impressions of themselves to make themselves appear to be good (i.e., prototypical) group members who work hard. Any information that suggests otherwise will be concealed, justified, or downplayed ("I was sick that week").

At the same time, members of high-status groups will be driven to maintain or extend their high-status position, and will do so by cultivating relationships with some members of the low-status group. Members of high-status groups that have modestly permeable boundaries will gossip with one another about members of the low-status group, and their gossip will center around the competency of those members. High-status group members will select low-status group members that can help to extend their personal status within the high-status group. Low-status group members whose behavior undermines the position of a high-status group member will lead to gossip designed to undermine the reputation of that member to prevent their further status ambitions.

But it is obviously also true that there are group status distinctions within organizations that are socially competitive. It is possible to be a member of a work group where one is committed to group membership and sees little or no possibility of promotion. Group boundary permeability is low, and ingroup commitment is high. If this is accompanied with beliefs that the high-status outgroup has illegitimate high status, then we can expect members of this low-status group to gossip with fellow ingroup members (cementing ingroup bonds), that the gossip will be directed at members of the high-status group, and it will likely be designed to undermine those persons standing in their group.

Conclusion

Tajfel (1969) argued for the role of rationality in intergroup relations, and he did so in reaction, in part, to crude pseudo-evolutionary reasoning that purported to explain patterns of intergroup relations from unreasoning blood-and-guts motives:

> The prevailing model of Man as a creature trying to find his way in his social environment seems to have nothing in common with the ideas of exploration, of meaning, of understanding, of rational consistency. We have the rational model for natural phenomena; we seem to have nothing but a blood-and-guts model for social phenomena. In this new blood-and-guts romanticism so fashionable at present in some science and semi-science, Man's attitudes and beliefs concerning the social environment are seen mainly as a by-product of tendencies that are buried deeply in his evolutionary past or just as deeply in his unconscious. (p. 80)

Since then, evolutionary modeling has pursued functional questions. Contemporary evolutionary considerations suggest, as Tajfel proposed, that humans possess functional, rational, and reflexive adaptations to social situations. The current evolutionary reasoning is therefore consistent with the underpinning functional logic of social categorization, assimilation, and the search for coherence that Tajfel described.

While this is true, in this chapter we have argued that evolutionary social psychology has yet to take seriously Tajfel's point that these processes (biological or otherwise) need to be placed in social context. We hope that our speculations in this chapter demonstrate at least some ways in which biological processes can interact with and operate through social identity, communication, and social context. Indeed, in addition to communication accommodation and intergroup gossip transmission, leadership is another topic suitable for a combined proximate- and ultimate-analyses. Existing work points to the importance of language use in leadership emergence and maintenance as a social identity process (e.g., Reid & Ng, 2003). Future work may explore how such evolutionarily significant individual difference factors as basal testosterone level interact with contextual variables (e.g., salient ingroup norms) to affect leader-follower language use (e.g., competitive vs. relational) and communication (e.g., proactive versus reactive). Also, in the area of language use and social influence, it will be interesting to see how linguistic cues related to such evolutionarily significant contexts as intra-sexual competition and inter-sexual attraction (e.g., speech assertiveness, voice pitch) may constrain or amplify the effect of self-categorization on conformity and attitude change.

Ultimately, we believe that an evolutionary basis for understanding social identity in general, and language and intergroup relations in particular, will lead our field into a new era of scientific advance. This will be a highly interdisciplinary enterprise. In this small chapter alone, we have considered evidence for evolutionary processes using research in communication, social psychology, anthropology, genetics, sociology, biology, operant conditioning, and of course, evolutionary psychology. The field of social psychology and communication is set for a new and exciting era of paradigm change.

Bibliography

Abrams, D., & Hogg, M. A. (1988). Comments on the motivational status of self-esteem in social identity and intergroup discrimination. *European Journal of Social Psychology, 18*, 317–334.

Abrams, J. R., & Giles, H. (2004). An intergroup approach to communicating stigma: Gays and lesbians. In Ng, S.H., Candlin, C.N., & Chiu, C.Y. (Eds.), *Language matters: Communication, identity, and culture* (pp. 27–61). Hong Kong: City University of Hong Kong Press.

Abrams, J. R., & Giles, H. (2007). Ethnic identity gratifications selection and avoidance by African Americans: A group vitality and social identity perspective. *Media Psychology, 9*, 115–134.

Abrams, J. R., Eveland, W., & Giles, H. (2003). The effects of television on group vitality: Can television empower nondominant groups? In P. Kalbfleisch (Ed.), *Communication yearbook 27* (pp. 193–219). Mahwah, NJ: Erlbaum.

Adorno, T. W., Frenkel-Brunswik, E., Levinson, D. J., & Sanford, R. N. (1950). *The authoritarian personality.* New York: Harper and Row.

Alimi, E. Y. (2006). Contextualizing political terrorism: A collective action perspective for understanding the Tanzim. *Studies in Conflict and Terrorism, 29*, 263–283.

Allen, I. L. (1983). *The language of ethnic conflict: Social organization and lexical culture.* New York: Columbia University Press.

Allport, G. W. (1954). *The nature of prejudice.* Cambridge, MA: Addison-Wesley.

Amichai-Hamburger, Y., & McKenna, K. Y. A. (2006). The contact hypothesis reconsidered: Interacting via the Internet. *Journal of Computer-Mediated Communication, 11*(3), article 7. Retrieved June 1, 2007 from http://jcmc.indiana.edu/vol11/issue3/amichai-hamburger.html

Anderson, B. (1983). *Imagined communities: Reflections on the origin and spread of nationalism*. London: Verso.

Angelino, A. F., & Treisman, G. J. (2001). Management of psychiatric disorders in patients infected with human immunodeficiency virus. *Clinical Infectious Diseases, 33*, 847–856.

Arendt, H. (1963). *Eichmann in Jerusalem: A report on the banality of evil*. New York: Penguin.

Arpan, L. M., & Raney, A. A. (2003). An experimental investigation of news source and the hostile media effect. *Journalism and Mass Communication Quarterly, 80*, 265–281.

Banchoff, T. (2007). Introduction. In T. Banchoff (Ed.), *Democracy and the new religious pluralism* (pp. 3–16). Oxford, UK: Oxford University Press.

Banker, B. S., & Gaertner, S. L. (1998). Achieving stepfamily harmony: An intergroup-relations approach. *Journal of Family Psychology, 12*, 310–325.

Barker, V., Giles, H., Hajek, C., Ota, H., Noels, K., Lim, T-S., & Somera, L. (2008). Police civilian interaction, compliance, accommodation, and trust in an intergroup context: International data. *Journal of International and Intercultural Communication, 1*, 93–112.

Barkow, J. H. (1992). Beneath new culture is old psychology: Gossip and social stratification. In J. H. Barkow, L. Cosmides, & J. Tooby (Eds.), *The adapted mind* (pp. 627–637). Oxford, England: Oxford University Press.

Bar-On, D. (2000). *Bridging the gap: Storytelling as a way to work through political and collective hostilities*. Hamburg, Germany: Kober-Stiftung.

Baumeister, R. F., & Leary, M. R. (1995). The need to belong: Desire for interpersonal attachments as a fundamental human motivation. *Psychological Bulletin, 117*, 497–529.

Bazarova, N. N., & Walther, J. B. (2009). Attributions in virtual groups: Distances and behavioral variations in computer-mediated discussions. *Small Group Research, 40*, 138–162.

Belanger, E., & Verkuyten, M. (in press). Hyphenated identities and acculturation: Second generation Chinese of Canada and the Netherlands. *Identity: An International Journal of Theory and Research*.

Bell, A. (1984). Good copy—bad news: The syntax and semantics of news editing. In P. Trudgill (Ed.), *Applied sociolinguistics* (pp. 73–118). London: Academic Press.

Bem, S. L. (1981). Gender schema theory: A cognitive account of sex typing. *Psychological Review, 88*, 354–364.

Benedict, H. (2009). The nation: The plight of women soldiers. NPR Partner content from: The nation. http://www.npr.org/templates/story/story.php?storyID=10384570&sc=emaf accessed May 19, 2009.

Berger, P. L. (1996/1997). Secularism in retreat. *The National Interest, 46*, 3–12.

Berger, P. L. (2007). Pluralism, Protestantization, and the voluntary principle. In T. Banchoff (Ed.), *Democracy and the new religious pluralism* (pp. 19–29). Oxford, UK: Oxford University Press.

Berkowitz, L. (1962). *Aggression: A social psychological analysis*. New York: McGraw-Hill.

Bernache-Assollant, I., Lacassagne, M-F., & Braddock, J. H., II (2007). Basking in reflected glory and blasting: Differences in identity-management strategies between two groups of highly identified soccer fans. *Journal of Language and Social Psychology, 26*, 381–388.

Billings, A. C., & Eastman, S. T. (2002). Selective representation of gender, ethnicity, and nationality in American television coverage of the 2000 Summer Olympics. *International Review for the Sociology of Sport, 37*, 351–370.

Boen, F., Vanbeselaere, N., & Feys, J. (2002). Behavioral consequences of fluctuating group success: An internet study of soccer-team fans. *Journal of Social Psychology, 142,* 769–781.

Bohman, J. (2007). Political communication and the epistemic value of diversity: Deliberation and legitimation in media societies. *Communication Theory, 17,* 348–355.

Bourhis, R. Y., el-Geledi, S., & Sachdev, I. (2007). Language, ethnicity and intergroup relations. In A. Weatherall, B. M. Watson, & C. Gallois (Eds.), *Language, discourse and social psychology* (pp. 15–50). New York: Palgrave.

Bourhis, R. Y., Giles, H., Leyens, J-P., & Tajfel, H. (1979). Psycholinguistic distinctiveness: Language divergence in Belgium. In H. Giles & R. N. St. Clair (Eds.), *Language and social psychology* (pp. 158–85). Oxford: Basil Blackwell.

Bourhis, R.Y., Giles, H., & Tajfel, H. (1973). Language as a determinant of Welsh identity. *European Journal of Social Psychology, 3,* 447–460.

Boyle, B. A., & Magnusson, P. (2007). Social identity and brand equity formation: A comparative study of collegiate sports fans. *Journal of Sport Management, 21,* 497–520.

Braithwaite, D. O., Olson, L., Golish, T., Soukup, C., & Turman, P. (2001). "Becoming a family": Developmental processes represented in blended family discourse. *Journal of Applied Communication Research, 29,* 221–247.

Branscombe, N. R., & Wann, D. L. (1992). Physiological arousal and reactions to outgroup members during competitions that implicate an important social identity. *Aggressive Behavior, 18,* 85–93.

Brashers, D. E., Haas, S. M., Neidig, J. L., & Rintamaki, L. S. (2002). Social activism, self-advocacy, and coping with HIV illness. *Journal of Social and Personal Relationships, 19,* 113–134.

Brewer, M. B. (1991). The social self: On being the same and different at the same time. *Personality and Social Psychology Bulletin, 17,* 475–482.

Broermann, M. (2008). Language attitudes among minority youth in Finland and Germany. *International Journal of the Sociology of Language, 187/188,* 129–160.

Brown, L. M. (1998). *Raising their voices: The politics of girls' anger.* Cambridge, MA: Harvard University Press.

Brown, L., Macintyre, K., & Trujillo, L. (2003). Interventions to reduce HIV/AIDS stigma: What have we learned? *AIDS Education and Prevention, 15,* 49–69.

Brown, R., & Hewstone, M. (2005). An integrative theory of intergroup contact. In M. P. Zanna (Ed.), *Advances in experimental social psychology* (Vol. 37, pp. 255–343). San Diego, CA: Elsevier.

Browning, C. (1992). *Ordinary men: Reserve Police Batallion 101 and the final solution in Poland.* London: Penguin Books

Buijs, F., & Rath, J. (2002). *Muslims in Europe: The state of research.* New York: Russell Sage.

Burkhalter, S., Gastil, J., & Kelshaw. T. (2002). A conceptual definition and theoretical model of public deliberation in small face-to-face groups. *Communication Theory. 12,* 398–422.

Campbell, D. T. (1958). Common fate, similarity and other indices of the status of aggregates of persons as social entities. *Behavioral Science, 3,* 14–25.

Carnaghi, A., & Maass, A. (2007). In-group and out-group perspectives in the use of derogatory group label: *gay* vs. *fag. Journal of Language and Social Psychology, 26,* 142–156.

Carnaghi, A., & Maass, A. (2008). Derogatory language use in intergroup contexts: Are "gay" and "fag" synonymous? In Y. Kashima, K. Fiedler, & P. Freytag (Eds.), Stereotype dynamics: Language-based approaches to stereotype formation, maintenance, and transformation (pp. 117–134). New York: Erlbaum.

Carr, P. J., Napolitano, L., & Keating, J. (2007). We never call the cops and here is why: A qualitative examination of legal cynicism in three Philadelphia neighborhoods. Criminology, 45, 445–480.

Carter, D. T. (1995) The politics of rage. Baton Rouge: Louisiana State University Press.

Casanova, J. (1994). Public religions in the modern world. Chicago: University of Chicago Press.

Catan, L., Dennison, C., & Coleman, J. (1996). Getting through: Effective communication in the teenage years. London: BT Forum/Trust for the Study of Adolescence.

Cesarani, D. (2004). Eichmann: His life and crimes. London: Heinemann.

Chang, I. (1998) The rape of Nanking. Harmonsworth: Penguin

Charleston, S. (2008). Determinants of home atmosphere in English football: A committed supporter perspective. Journal of Sport Behavior, 31, 312–328.

Cialdini, R. B., Borden, R. J., Thorne, A., Walker, M. R. Freeman, S., & Sloan, L. R. (1976). Basking in reflected glory: Three (football) field studies. Journal of Personality and Social Psychology, 34, 366–375.

Clark, A. E., & Kashima, Y. (2007). Stereotypes help people connect with others in the community: A situated functional analysis of stereotype consistency bias in communication. Journal of Personality and Social Psychology, 93, 1028–1039.

Clark, H. H. (1996a). Communities, commonalities, and communication. In J. J. Gumperz & S. C. Levinson (Eds.), Rethinking linguistic relativity (pp. 324–355). Cambridge, UK: Cambridge University Press.

Clark, H. H. (1996b). Using language. Cambridge, UK: Cambridge University Press.

Clark, K. B., & Clark, M. P. (1947). Radical identification and preference in Negro preschool children. In T. M. Newcomb & E. L. Hartley (Eds.), Readings in social psychology (pp. 169–178). New York: Holt.

Clay, A. (2003). Keepin' it real: Black youth, hip hop culture, and Black identity. American Behavioral Scientist, 46, 1346–1358.

Clément, R. (1980). Ethnicity, contact and communicative competence in a second language. In H. Giles, W. P. Robinson, & P. M. Smith (Eds.), Language: Social psychological perspectives (pp. 147–154). Oxford, UK: Pergamon.

Clément, R. (Ed.) (1996). The social psychology of intergroup communication. Journal of Language and Social Psychology, 15 (4).

Clément, R. (Ed.) (2007). Communication, language, and discrimination. Journal of Language and Social Psychology, 26 (2).

Coleman, J. C., & Hendry, L. (1999). The nature of adolescence (3rd ed.). London: Routledge.

Coleman, P. T. (2003). Characteristics of protracted, intractable conflict: Towards the development of a meta-framework-I. Peace and Conflict, 9, 1–37.

Coover, G. (2001). Television and social identity: Race representation as "White" accommodation. Journal of Broadcasting and Electronic Media, 45, 413–431.

Correll, J., Park, B., Judd, C. M., & Wittenbrink, B. (2002). The police officer's dilemma: Using ethnicity to disambiguate potentially threatening individuals. *Journal of Personality and Social Psychology, 83*, 1314–1329.

Correll, S. J., & Ridgeway, C. (2003). Expectation states theory. In J. Delamater (Ed.), *The handbook of social psychology* (pp. 29–51). New York: Kluwer-Plenum Press.

Cottrell, C. A., & Neuberg, S. L. (2005). Different emotional reactions to different groups: A sociofunctional threat-based approach to "prejudice." *Journal of Personality and Social Psychology, 88*, 770–789.

Coupland, N., Coupland, J., & Giles, H. (1991). Telling age in later life: Identity and face implications. *Text, 9*, 129–151.

Coupland, N., Coupland, J., Giles, H., & Henwood, K. (1988). Accommodating the elderly: Invoking and extending the theory. *Language in Society, 17*, 1–41.

Coupland, N., Coupland, J., Giles, H., Henwood, K., & Wiemann, J. M. (1988). Elderly self-disclosure: Interactional and intergroup issues. *Language and Communication, 8*, 109–131.

Crandall, C. S., & Coleman, R. (1992). AIDS-related stigmatization and the disruption of social relationships. *Journal of Social and Personal Relationships, 9*, 163–177.

Crocker, J., & Major, B. (1989). Social stigma and self-esteem: The self-protective properties of stigma. *Psychological Review, 96*, 608–630.

Crocker, J., Major, B., & Steele, C. (1998). Social stigma. In D. T. Gilbert & S. T. Fiske (Eds.), *The handbook of social psychology* (4th ed., Vol. 2, pp. 504–553). New York: McGraw-Hill.

Cronin, P., & Reicher, S. (2009). Accountability processes and group dynamics: A SIDE perspective on the policing of an anti-capitalist riot. *European Journal of Social Psychology, 39*, 237–254.

Crum, R. M., Brown, C., Liang, K.-Y., & Eaton, W. W. (2001). The association of depression and problem drinking: Analyses from the Baltimore ECA follow-up study. *Addictive Behaviors, 26*, 765–773.

Dahl, R. A. (1998). *On democracy.* New Haven, CT: Yale University Press.

Dailey, R., Reid, S. A., Anderson, M. C., & Giles, H. (2006). Community review of police conduct: An intergroup perspective. *Social Psychological Review, 8*, 20–34.

Dallaire, C. (2003). "Not just Francophones": The hybridity of minority Francophone youths in Canada. *International Journal of Canadian Studies, 28*, 163–199.

Darwin, C. R. (1859). *The origin of species.* London, UK: John Murray.

Dennison, C., & Drury, J. (1998). *Professionals' perceptions of communication with teenagers.* Unpublished Manuscript: Trust for the Study of Adolescence.

Derlega, V. J., Lovejoy, D., & Winstead, B. A. (1998). Personal accounts on disclosing and concealing HIV-positive test results: Weighing the benefits and risks. In V. J. Derlega & A. P. Barbee (Eds.), *HIV and social interaction* (pp. 147–164). Thousand Oaks, CA: Sage.

Devine, P. (1989). Stereotypes and prejudice: Their automatic and controlled components. *Journal of Personality and Social Psychology, 56*, 5–18.

Dietz-Uhler, B., End, C., Demakakos, N., Dickirson, A., & Grantz, A. (2002). Fans' reactions to law-breaking athletes. *International Sports Journal, 6*, 160–170.

Dietz-Uhler, B., & Murrell, A. (1999). Examining fan reactions to game outcomes: A longitudinal study of social identity. *Journal of Sport Behavior, 22*, 15–27.

Dixon, J., & Durrheim, K. (2003). Contact and the ecology of racial division: Some varieties of informal segregation. *British Journal of Social Psychology, 42,* 1–23.

Dixon, T. L., Schell, T., Giles, H., & Drogos, K. (2008). The influence of race in police-civilian interactions: A content analysis of videotaped interactions taken during Cincinnati police traffic stops. *Journal of Communication, 58,* 530–549.

Douglas, K. M., & Sutton, R. M. (2006). When what you say about others says something about you: Language abstraction and inferences about describers' attitudes and goals. *Journal of Experimental Social Psychology, 42,* 500–508.

Douglas, K. M., & Sutton, R. M. (2008). Could you mind your language? An investigation of communicators' ability to inhibit linguistic bias. *Journal of Language and Social Psychology, 27,* 123–129.

Drury, J., & Dennison, C. (1999) Individual responsibility versus social category problems: Benefit officers' perceptions of communication with teenagers. *Journal of Youth Studies, 2,* 171–192.

Drury, J., & Dennison, C. (2000). Representations of teenagers among police officers: Some implications for their communication with young people. *Youth and Policy, 66,* 62–87.

Drury, J., Catan, L., Dennison, C., & Brody, R. (1998). Exploring teenagers' accounts of bad communication: A new basis for intervention. *Journal of Adolescence, 21,* 177–196.

Dryden, C., & Giles, H. (1987). Language, social identity, and health. In H. Beloff & A. Colman (Eds.), *Psychology Survey 6* (pp. 115–139). Leicester: British Psychological Society.

Dunbar, R. (1996). *Gossip, grooming, and the evolution of language.* Cambridge, MA: Harvard University Press.

Durkheim, E. (1912/2001). *The elementary forms of religious life.* Oxford, UK: Oxford University Press.

Eagly, A. H., & Karau, S. J. (2002). Role congruity theory of prejudice toward female leaders. *Psychological Review, 109,* 573–598.

Eastman, S. T., & Land, A. M. (1997). The best of both worlds: Sports fans find good seats at the bar. *Journal of Sport and Social Issues, 21,* 156–178.

Eaves, L., Martin, N., Heath, A., Schieken, R., Meyer, J., Silberg, J., Neale, M., & Corey, L. (1997). Age changes in the causes of individual differences in conservatism. *Behavior Genetics, 27,* 121–124.

Eggins, R. A., O'Brien, A. T., Reynolds, K. J., Haslam, S. A., & Crocker, A. S. (2008). Refocusing the focus group: AIRing as a basis for effective workplace planning. *British Journal of Management, 19,* 277–293.

Eisenlohr, P. (2004). Register levels of ethno-national purity: The ethnicization of language and community in Mauritius. *Language in Society, 33,* 59–80.

Ellis, D. G. (2005). Intercultural communication in intractable ethnopolitical conflicts. In W. J. Starosta & G. Chen (Eds.), *International and intercultural communication annual* (pp. 45–69). Washington, DC: National Communication Association.

Ellis, D. G., & Maoz, I. (2002). Cross-cultural argument interactions between Israeli-Jews and Palestinians. *Journal of Applied Communication Research, 30,* 181–194.

Ellis, D. G., & Moaz, I. (2007). Online argument between Israeli Jews and Palestinians. *Human Communication Research, 33,* 291–309.

Emler, N. (2001). Gossiping. In W. P. Robinson & H. Giles (Eds.), *The new handbook of language and social psychology* (pp. 317–338). Chichester, UK: John Wiley & Sons.

Emler, N., & Reicher, S. (1995). *Adolescence and delinquency: The collective management of reputation.* Oxford, UK: Blackwell.

End, C. M. (2001). An examination of NFL fans' computer mediated BIRGing. *Journal of Sport Behavior, 24,* 162–181.

Eriksen, H. (1994). Nationalism, Mauritian style: Cultural unity and ethnic diversity. *Comparative Studies in Society and History, 36,* 549–574.

Erikson, E. H. (1963). *Childhood and society* (2nd ed.). Harmondsworth, UK: Penguin.

Erjavec, K., & Volcic, Z. (2007). The Kosovo battle: Media's recontextualization of the Serbian nationalistic discourses. *The Harvard International Journal of Press/Politics, 12,* 67–86.

Esposito, J. L. (2002). *Unholy war: Terror in the name of Islam.* Oxford, UK: Oxford University Press.

Faulkner, J., Schaller, M., Park, J. H., & Duncan, L. A. (1999). Evolved disease-avoidance mechanisms and contemporary xenophobic reactions. *Group Processes and Intergroup Relations, 7,* 333–353.

Fiedler, K. (Ed.). (2007). *Social communication.* New York: Psychology Press.

Fiedler, K. (2008). Language: A toolbox for sharing and influencing social reality. *Perspectives on Psychological Science, 3,* 38–47.

Fielding, N. (1995). *Community policing.* Oxford, UK: Clarendon.

Fincher, C. L., & Thornhill, R. (2008). A parasite-driven wedge: Infectious diseases may explain languages and other biodiversity. *Oikos, 117,* 1289–1297.

Fincher, C. L., Thornhill, R., Murray, D. R., & Schaller, M. (2008). Pathogen prevalence predicts human cross-cultural variability in individualism/collectivism. *Proceedings of the Royal Society, Biology, 275,* 1279–1285.

Fiske, S. T., & Neuberg, S. L. (1990). A continuum of impression formation, from category-based to individuating processes: Influences of information and motivation on attention and interpretation. In M. P. Zanna (Ed.), *Advances in experimental social psychology* (Vol. 23, pp. 1–74). New York: Academic Press.

Fiske, S. T., & Taylor, S. E. (1984). *Social cognition.* New York: Random House.

Forbes, H. D. (2004). Ethnic conflict and the contact hypothesis. In Y. T. Lee, C. McCauley, F. Moghaddam, & S. Worchel (Eds.), *The psychology of ethnic and cultural conflict* (pp. 69–88). Westport, CT: Praeger.

Fortman, J. (2003). Adolescent language and communication from an intergroup perspective. *Journal of Language and Social Psychology, 22,* 104–111

Fox, J. (2006). World separation of religion and state in the 21st century. *Comparative Political Studies, 39,* 537–569.

Frable, D. E., Blackstone, T., & Scherbaum, C. (1990). Marginal and mindful: Deviants in social interactions. *Journal of Personality and Social Psychology, 59,* 140–149.

Fromkin, D. (1975). The strategy of terror. *Foreign Affairs, 53,* 638–698.

Fryberg, S. (2003). *Really? You don't look like an American Indian: Social representations and social group identities.* Retrieved May 13, 2009, from Proquest Dissertations and Theses. (AAT 3085287)

Fujioka, Y. (2005a). Emotional TV viewing and minority audience: How Mexican Americans process and evaluate TV news about in-group members. *Communication Research, 32*, 566–593.

Fujioka, Y. (2005b). Black media images as a perceived threat to African American ethnic identity: Coping responses, perceived public perception, and attitudes toward affirmative action. *Journal of Broadcasting and Electronic Media, 49*, 450–476.

Gaertner, S. L., & Dovidio, J. F. (2000). *Reducing intergroup bias: The common ingroup identity model.* Philadelphia: Psychology Press.

Gaertner, S. L., Dovidio, J. F., Nier, J. A., Banker, B. S., Ward, C. M., Houlette, M., & Loux, S. (2000). The common ingroup identity model for reducing intergroup bias. In D. Capozza & R. Brown (Eds.), *Social identity processes: Trends in theory and research* (pp. 133–148). London: Sage.

Gallois, C., Ogay, T., & Giles, H. (2005). Communication accommodation theory: A look back and a look ahead. In W. B. Gudykunst (Ed.), *Theorizing about communication and culture* (pp. 121–148). Thousand Oaks, CA: Sage.

Galvin, K. M. (2003). International and transracial adoption: A communication research agenda. *Journal of Family Communication, 3*, 237–253.

Galvin, K. M. (2006). Diversity's impact on defining the family: Discourse-dependence and identity. In L. H. Turner & R. West (Eds.), *The family communication sourcebook* (pp. 3–20). Thousand Oaks, CA: Sage.

Gans, H. J. (1979). Symbolic ethnicity: The future of ethnic groups and culture in America. *Ethnic and Racial Studies, 2*, 1–20.

Gardner, R. C., & Lambert, W. E. (1972). *Attitudes and motivation in second-language learning.* Rowley, MA: Newbury House.

Garstka, T. A., Hummert, M. L., & Branscombe, N. R. (2005). Perceiving age discrimination in response to intergenerational inequity. *Journal of Social Issues, 61*, 321–342.

Gaudet, S., & Clément, R. (in press). Forging an identity as a linguistic minority: Intra- and intergroup aspects of language, communication and identity in Western Canada. *International Journal of Intercultural Relations.*

Genesee, F., & Bourhis, R. Y. (1988). Evaluative reactions to language choice strategies: The role of sociostructural factors. *Language and Communication, 8*, 229–50.

Germain, A., & Rose, D. (2000). Language, ethnic groups and the shaping of social space. In A. Germain & D. Rose (Eds.), *Montréal: The quest for a metropolis* (pp. 213–253). Toronto, ON: John Wiley & Sons.

Getty, J.A. & Naumov, O.V. (2002) *The road to terror.* New Haven: Yale University Press.

Giles, H. (1978). Linguistic differentiation between ethnic groups. In H. Tajfel (Ed.), *Differentiation between social groups* (pp. 361-393). London: Academic Press.

Giles, H. (1979). Ethnicity markers in speech. In K. R. Scherer and H. Giles (Eds.), *Social markers in speech* (pp. 251–289). Cambridge, UK: Cambridge University Press.

Giles, H. (Ed.). (2002). *Law enforcement, communication, and the community.* Amsterdam: John Benjamins.

Giles, H., Bourhis, R. Y., & Taylor, D. M. (1977). Towards a theory of language in ethnic group relations. In H. Giles (Ed.), *Language, ethnicity and intergroup relations* (pp. 307–348). New York: Academic Press.

Giles, H., Coupland, N., & Coupland, J. (1991). Accommodation theory: Communication, context, and consequence. In H. Giles, J. Coupland, & N. Coupland, (Eds.), *Contexts of accommodation: Developments in applied linguistics* (pp. 1–68). Cambridge, UK: Cambridge University Press.

Giles, H., Denes, A., Hamilton, D. L., & Hajda, J. M. (2009). Striking a chord: A prelude to music and intergroup relations research. *Group Processes and Intergroup Relations, 12*, 291–301.

Giles, H., Fortman, J., Dailey, R. M., Barker, V., Hajek, C., Anderson, M. C., & Rule, N. O. (2006). Communication accommodation: Law enforcement and the public. In R. M. Dailey & B. A. Le Poire (Eds.), *Applied communication matters: Family, health, and community relations* (pp. 241–269). New York: Peter Lang.

Giles, H., Fox, S., & Smith, E. (1993). Patronizing the elderly: Intergenerational evaluations. *Research on Language and Social Interaction, 26*, 129–149.

Giles, H., Hajda, J. M., & Hamilton, D. L. (Eds.). (2009). Harmony and discord: The music of intergroup relations. *Group Processes and Intergroup Relations, 12* (3).

Giles, H., & Johnson, P. (1981). The role of language in ethnic group relations. In J. C. Turner & H. Giles (Eds.), *Intergroup behavior* (pp. 199–243). Oxford, UK: Blackwell.

Giles, H., & Johnson, P. (1987). Ethnolinguistic identity theory: A social psychological approach to language maintenance. *International Journal of the Sociology of Language, 68*, 256–269.

Giles, H., & Watson, B. (2008) Intergroup and intercultural parameters of communication. In W. Donsbach (Ed.), *International Encyclopedia of Communication* (Vol. VI, pp. 2337–2348). Oxford, UK: Blackwell.

Giles, H., Willemyns, M., Gallois, C., & Anderson, M. C. (2007). Accommodating a new frontier: The context of law enforcement. In K. Fiedler (Ed.), *Social communication* (pp. 129–162). New York: Psychology Press.

Giner-Sorolla, R., Mackie, D. M., & Smith, E. R. (Eds.) (2007). Intergroup emotions. *Group Processes and Intergroup Relations, 10* (1).

Goffman, E. (1959). *The presentation of self in everyday life*. New York: Doubleday.

Goffman, E. (1963). *Stigma: Notes on the management of spoiled identity*. Englewood Cliffs, NJ: Prentice-Hall.

Goldhagen, D. J. (1996). *Hitler's willing executioners: Ordinary Germans and the Holocaust*. London: Little, Brown & Company.

Gómez, A., Dovidio, J. F., Huici, C., Gaertner, S. L., & Cuadrado, L. (2008). The other side of we: When outgroup members express common identity. *Personality and Social Psychology Bulletin, 34*, 1613–1626.

Gorham, B. (2006). News media's relationship with stereotyping: The linguistic intergroup bias in response to crime news. *Journal of Communication, 56*, 289–308.

Greenwald, A. G., & Banaji, M. R. (1995). Implicit social cognition: Attitudes, self-esteem, and stereotypes. *Psychological Review, 102*, 4–27.

Greenwald, A. G., McGhee, D. E., & Schwartz, J. L. K. (1998). Measuring individual differences in implicit cognition: The implicit association test. *Journal of Personality and Social Psychology, 74*, 1464–1480.

Griffin, C. (1993). *Representations of youth: The study of adolescence in Britain and America*. Cambridge, UK: Polity.

Griffin, C. (1997). Representations of the young. In J. Roche & S. Tucker (Eds.), *Youth in society: Contemporary theory, policy and practice* (pp. 17–25). London: Sage.

Gudykunst, W. B. (Ed.). (1986). *Intergroup communication*. London: Edward Arnold.

Gutmann, A., & Thompson, D. (1996). *Democracy and disagreement*. Cambridge, MA: Harvard University Press.

Gutmann, A., & Thompson, D. (2004). *Why deliberative democracy?* Princeton, NJ: Princeton University Press.

Habermas, J. (1984). *The theory of communicative action: Vol. 1. Reason and rationalization of society* (T. McCarthy, Trans.). Boston: Beacon.

Hajek, C., Abrams, J. R., & Murachver, T. (2005). Female, straight, male, gay, and worlds betwixt and between: An intergroup approach to sexual and gender identities. In J. Harwood & H. Giles (Eds.). *Intergroup communication: Multiple perspectives* (pp. 43–64). New York: Peter Lang.

Hajek, C., Villagran, M., & Wittenberg-Lyles, E. (2007). The relationships among perceived physician accommodation, perceived outgroup typicality, and patient inclinations toward compliance. *Communication Research Reports, 24*, 293–302.

Halberstadt, J., O'Shea, R. P., & Forgas, J. (2006). Outgroup fanship in Australia and New Zealand. *Australian Journal of Psychology, 58*, 159–165.

Hamers, J. F., & Blanc, M. H. A. (2000). *Bilinguality and bilingualism* (2nd ed.). Cambridge, UK: Cambridge University Press.

Hann, C. (1997). Ethnicity, language, and politics in North-east Turkey. In C. Govers & H. Vermeulen (Eds.), *The politics of ethnic consciousness* (pp. 121–156). London: Macmillan.

Hargie, O., Dickson, D., Mallett, J., & Stringer, M. (2008). Communicating social identity: A study of Catholics and Protestants in Northern Ireland. *Communication Research, 35*, 792–821.

Harwood, J. (1999a). Age identification, social identity gratifications, and television viewing. *Journal of Broadcasting and Electronic Media, 43*, 123–136.

Harwood, J. (1999b). Age identity and television viewing preferences. *Communication Reports, 12*, 85–90.

Harwood, J., & Anderson, K. (2002). The presence and portrayal of social groups on prime-time television. *Communication Reports, 15*, 81–97.

Harwood, J., & Giles, H. (Eds.).(2005). *Intergroup communication: Multiple perspectives*. New York: Peter Lang.

Harwood, J., Giles, H., & Palomares, N. A. (2005). Intergroup theory and communication processes. In J. Harwood & H. Giles (Eds.), *Intergroup communication: Multiple perspectives* (pp. 1–20). New York: Peter Lang.

Harwood, J., Giles, H., & Ryan, E. B. (1995). Aging, communication, and intergroup theory: Social identity and intergenerational communication. In J. F. Nussbaum & J. Coupland (Eds.), *Handbook of communication and aging research* (pp. 133–159). Hillsdale, NJ: Erlbaum.

Harwood, J., Hewstone, M., Paolini, S., & Voci, A. (2005). Grandparent-grandchild contact and attitudes towards older adults: Moderator and mediator effects. *Personality and Social Psychology Bulletin, 31*, 393–406.

Harwood, J., Raman, P., & Hewstone, M. (2006). Communicative predictors of group salience in the intergenerational setting. *Journal of Family Communication, 6,* 181–200.

Harwood, J., & Roy, A. (2005). Social identity theory and mass communication research. In J. Harwood & H. Giles (Eds.), *Intergroup Communication: Multiple Perspectives* (pp. 189–211) New York: Peter Lang.

Harwood, J., & Sparks, L. (2003). Social identity and health: An intergroup communication approach to cancer. *Health Communication, 15,* 145–160.

Harwood, J., Soliz, J., & Lin, M. C. (2006). Communication accommodation theory. In D. O. Braithwaite & L. A. Baxter (Eds.), *Engaging theories of family communication* (pp. 19–34). Thousand Oaks, CA: Sage.

Haslam, S. A. (2001). *Psychology in organizations: The social identity approach.* Thousand Oaks, CA: Sage.

Haslam, S. A., Eggins, R. A., & Reynolds, K. J. (2003). The ASPIRe model: Actualizing social and personal identity resources to enhance organizational outcomes. *Journal of Organizational and Occupational Psychology, 76,* 83–113.

Haslam, S. A., Turner, J. C., Oakes, P. J., McGarty, C., & Hayes, B. K. (1992). Context-dependent variation in social stereotyping I: The effects of intergroup relations as mediated by social change and frame of reference. *European Journal of Social Psychology, 22,* 3–20.

Hausmann, L. R. M., Levine, J. M., & Higgins, E. T. (2008). Communication and group perception: Extending the 'saying is believing' effect. *Group Processes and Intergroup Relations, 11,* 539–554.

Herek, G. M. (1999). AIDS and stigma. *American Behavioral Scientist, 42,* 1106–1116.

Herman, N. J. (1993). Return to sender: Reintegrative stigma-management strategies of ex-psychiatric patients. *Journal of Contemporary Ethnography, 22,* 295–330.

Hertz-Lazarowitz, R., & Eden, D. (2002). Israel: Empowering Arab and Jew–School Leadership in Acre. In G. Salomon & B. Nevo (Eds.), *Peace education* (pp. 209–216). Mahwah, NJ: Erlbaum.

Hewstone, M., & Brown, R. J. (1986). Contact is not enough: An intergroup perspective on the "contact hypothesis." In M. Hewstone & R. J. Brown (Eds.), *Contact and conflict in intergroup encounters* (pp. 1–44). Oxford, UK: Blackwell.

Hewstone, M., Cairns, E., Voci, A., Hamberger, J., & Niens, U. (2006). Intergroup contact, forgiveness, and experience of "The Troubles" in Northern Ireland. *Journal of Social Issues, 62,* 99–120.

Hewstone, M., Hopkins, N., & Routh, D. A. (1992). Cognitive models of stereotype change. I: Generalization and subtyping in young people's views of the police. *European Journal of Social Psychology, 22,* 219–234.

Hitler, A. (1980 ed.). *Mein Kampf.* London: Hutchinson.

Hobsbawn, E. (1995). *The age of extremes: The short Twentieth Century, 1914-1992.* London: Abacus.

Hogg, M. A., & Abrams, D. (1990). Social motivation, self-esteem, and social identity. In D. Abrams & M. A. Hogg (Eds.), *Social identity theory: Constructive and critical advances* (pp. 28–47). New York: Harvester Wheatsheaf.

Hogg, M. A., & Reid, S. A. (2006). Social identity, self-categorization, and the communication of group norms. *Communication Theory, 16,* 7–30.

Holtgraves, T. M., & Kashima, Y. (2008). Language, meaning, and social cognition. *Personality and Social Psychology Review, 12,* 73–94.

Hopkins, N. (1994). School pupils' perceptions of the police that visit schools: Not all police are 'pigs'. *Journal of Community and Applied Social Psychology, 4,* 189–207.

Hornsey, M. J. (2005). Why being right is not enough: Predicting defensiveness in the face of group criticism. *European Review of Social Psychology, 16,* 301–334.

Hornsey M. J., & Hogg, M. A. (2000). Assimilation and diversity: An integrative model of sub-group relations. *Personality and Social Psychology Review, 4,* 143–156.

Hornsey, M. J., & Imani, A. (2004). Criticizing groups from the inside and the outside: An identity perspective on the intergroup sensitivity effect. *Personality and Social Psychology Bulletin, 30,* 365–383.

Hornsey, M. J., Trembath, M., & Gunthorpe, S. (2004). You can criticize because you care: identity attachment, constructiveness, and the intergroup sensitivity effect. *European Journal of Social Psychology, 34,* 499–518.

Howard, J. A. (2000). Social psychology of identities. *Annual Review of Sociology, 26,* 367–393.

Huda, Q. (2006). Conflict prevention and peace-building efforts by American Muslim organizations following September 11. *Journal of Muslim Minority Affairs, 26,* 187–203.

Huddy, L. (2001). From social to political identity: A critical examination of social identity theory. *Political Psychology, 22,* 127–156.

Hugenberg, L. W., Haridakis, P. M., & Earnheardt, A. C. (Eds.). (2008). *Sports mania: Essays on fandom and the media in the 21ᵗ century.* Jefferson, NC: McFarland & Company, Inc.

Hughes, P. C., & Dickson, F. C. (2005). Communication, marital satisfaction, and religious orientation in interfaith marriages. *Journal of Family Communication, 5,* 25–41.

Hughson, J. (1998). Soccer support and social identity: Finding the 'thirdspace'. *International Review for the Sociology of Sport, 33,* 403–409.

Human Rights Watch Backgrounder (2003). *Incarcerated America.* Retrieved April 17, 2009, from http://www.hrw.org/legacy/backgrounder/usa/incarceration/

Hummert, M. L., Garstka, T. A., & Shaner, J. (1997). Stereotyping of older adults: The role of target facial cues and perceiver characteristics. *Psychology and Aging, 12,* 107–114.

Hummert, M. L., Garstka, T. A., O'Brien, L. T., Greenwald, A. G., & Mellott, D. S. (2002). Using the Implicit Association Test to measure age differences in implicit social cognitions. *Psychology and Aging, 17,* 482–495.

Hummert, M. L., Garstka, T. A., Ryan, E. B., & Bonnesen, J. L. (2004). The role of age stereotypes in interpersonal communication. In J. F. Nussbaum & J. Coupland (Eds.), *The handbook of communication and aging,* (2nd ed., pp. 91–114). Mahwah, NJ: Erlbaum.

Hummert, M. L., Garstka, T. A., Shaner, J. L., & Strahm, S. (1994). Stereotypes of the elderly held by young, middle-aged and elderly adults. *Journal of Gerontology: Psychological Sciences, 49,* P240-P249.

Hummert, M. L., Shaner, J. L., Garstka, T. A., & Henry, C. (1998). Communication with older adults: The influence of age stereotypes, context, and communicator age. *Human Communication Research, 25,* 125–152.

Hurwitz, J., & Peffley, M. (2005). Playing the race card in the post Willie Horton era: The impact of racialized code words on support for punitive crime policy. *Public Opinion Quarterly, 69,*

99–112.

Jones, E. E., Farina, A., Hastorf, A. H., Markus, H., Miler, D. T., & Scott, R. A. (1984). *Social stigma: The psychology of marked relationships*. New York: Freeman.

Jost, J. T., & Banaji, M. R. (1994). The role of stereotyping in system justification and the production of false consciousness. *British Journal of Social Psychology, 33*, 1–27.

Jost, J. T., Banaji, M. R., & Nosek, B. A. (2004). A decade of system justification theory: Accumulated evidence of conscious and unconscious bolstering of the status quo. *Political Psychology, 25*, 881–919.

Jost, J. T., & Kay, A. C. (2005). Exposure to benevolent sexism and complementary gender stereotypes: Consequences for specific and diffuse forms of system justification. *Journal of Personality and Social Psychology, 88*, 498–509.

Kahneman, D., & Tversky, A. (1973). On the psychology of prediction. *Psychological Review, 80*, 237–251.

Kashima, Y. (2001). Culture and social cognition: Toward a social psychology of cultural dynamics. In D. Matsumoto (Ed.), *The handbook of culture and psychology* (pp. 325–360). New York: Oxford University Press.

Kashima, Y., Fiedler, K., & Freytag, P. (Eds.), (2008). *Stereotype dynamics: Language-based approaches to the formation, maintenance, and transformation of stereotypes*. Mahwah, NJ: Erlbaum.

Katz, D., & Braly, K. (1933). Racial stereotypes of one hundred college students. *Journal of Abnormal and Social Psychology, 28*, 280–290.

Kaufman, G. (1996). *The psychology of shame: Theory and treatment of shame-based syndromes* (2nd ed.). New York, NY: Springer Publishing Co.

Kidwell, M. (2009). What happened? An epistemics of before and after in "at-the-scene" police questioning. *Research on Language and Social Interaction, 42*, 20–41.

Kite, M. E., & Wagner, L. S. (2002). Attitudes toward older adults. In T. D. Nelson (Ed.), *Ageism: Stereotyping and prejudice towards older persons* (pp. 129–161). Cambridge, MA: MIT Press.

Klein, O., Spears, R., & Reicher, S. (2007). Social identity performance: Extending the strategic side of SIDE. *Personality and Social Psychology Review, 11*, 28–45.

Koonz, C. (2003) *The Nazi conscience*. Cambridge, MA: Belknap Press.

Kopec, D. (2006). *Environmental psychology for design*. New York: Fairchild.

Krejci, J., & Velimsky (1981). *Ethnic and political nations in Europe*. London: Croom Helm.

Kuhl, P. K. (1991). Human adults and human infants show a "perceptual magnet effect" for the prototypes of speech categories, monkeys do not. *Perception and Psychophysics, 50*, 93–107.

Kunda, Z. (1999). *Social cognition: Making sense of people*. Cambridge, MA: MIT Press.

Kundrat, A. L., & Nussbaum, J. F. (2003). The impact of invisible illness on identity and contextual age across the life span. *Health Communication, 15*, 331–347.

Kuroiwa, Y., & Verkuyten, M. (2008). Narratives and the constitution of a common identity: The Karen in Burma. *Identities: Global Studies in Culture and Power, 15*, 391–412.

Kurzban, R., Tooby, J., & Cosmides, L. (2001). Can race be erased? Coalitional computation and social categorization. *Proceedings of the National Academy of Sciences, 98*, 15387–15392.

Lambert, W. E. (1978). Cognitive and socio-cultural consequences of bilingualism. *Canadian Modern Language Review, 34*, 537–547.

Laponce, J. (2001). Politics and the law of Babel. *Social Science Information, 40,* 179–194.

Le Bon, G. (1895, trans 1947). *The Crowd: A study of the popular mind.* London: Ernest Benn.

Lea, M., Spears, R., & de Groot, D. (2001). Knowing me, knowing you: Anonymity effects on group polarization in CMC within groups. *Personality and Social Psychology Bulletin, 27,* 526–537.

Leader, T., Mullen, B., & Rice, D. (2009). Complexity and valence in ethnophaulisms and exclusion of ethnic out-groups: What puts the "hate" into hate speech? *Journal of Personality and Social Psychology, 96,* 170-182.

Lee, E-J. (2006). When and how does depersonalization increase conformity to group norms in computer-mediated communication? *Communication Research, 33,* 423–447.

Leets, L., & Giles, H. (1997). Words as weapons: When do they wound? *Human Communication Research, 24,* 260–301.

LePoire, B. A. (1994). Attraction toward and nonverbal stigmatization of gay males and persons with AIDS: Evidence of symbolic over instrumental attitudinal structures. *Human Communication Research, 21,* 241–279.

Levine, M., Prosser, A., Evans, D., & Reicher, S.D. (2005) Identity and emergency intervention: How social group membership and inclusiveness of group boundaries shapes helping behavior. *Personality and Social Psychology Bulletin, 31,* 443–453.

Levy, B. R. (2003). Mind matters: Cognitive and physical effects of aging self-stereotypes. *Journal of Gerontology: Psychological Sciences, 58B,* P203-P211.

Lewis, A. C., & Sherman, S. J. (2003). Hiring you makes me look bad: Social-identity based reversals of the ingroup favoritism effect. *Organizational Behavior and Human Decision Processes, 90,* 262–276.

Linden, M., & Godemann, F. (2007). The difference between lack of insight and dysfunctional health beliefs in schizophrenia. *Psychopathology, 40,* 236–241.

Link, B. G., & Phelan, J. C. (2001). Conceptualizing stigma. *Annual Review of Sociology, 27,* 363–385.

Lippe, G., von der, & MacLean, M. (2008). Brawling in Berne: Mediated transnational moral panics in the 1954 Football World Cup. *International Review for the Sociology of Sport, 43,* 71–90.

Lippmann, W. (1922). *Public opinion.* New York: Macmillan.

Little, D. (Ed.). (2007). *Peacemakers in action: Profiles of religion in conflict resolution.* Cambridge, UK: Cambridge University Press.

Loader, I. (1996). *Youth, policing and democracy,* Basingstoke: Macmillan.

Lundman, R. J., & Kaufman, R. L. (2003). Driving while Black: Effects of race, ethnicity, and gender on citizen self-reports of traffic stops and police actions. *Criminology, 41,* 195–220.

Lyons, A., & Kashima, Y. (2003). How are stereotypes maintained through communication? The influence of stereotype sharedness. *Journal of Personality and Social Psychology, 85,* 989–1005.

Maass, A. (1999). Linguistic intergroup bias: Stereotype perpetuation through language. *Advances in Experimental Social Psychology, 31,* 79-121.

Maass, A., Ceccarelli, R., & Rudin, S. (1996). The linguistic intergroup bias: Evidence for ingroup-protective motivation. *Journal of Personality and Social Psychology, 71,* 512–526.

Maass, A., Corvino, G., & Arcuri, L. (1994). Linguistic intergroup bias and the mass media. *Revue de Psychologie Sociale, 1,* 31–43.

Maass, A., Milesi, A., Zabbini, S., & Stahlberg, D. (1995). The linguistic intergroup bias: Differential expectancies or ingroup protection. *Journal of Personality and Social Psychology, 68,* 116–126.

Maass, A., Salvi, D., Arcuri, L., & Semin, G. R. (1989). Language use in intergroup contexts: The linguistic intergroup bias. *Journal of Personality and Social Psychology, 57,* 981–993.

Mackie, D. M., Worth, L. T., & Asuncion, A. G. (1990). Processing of persuasive in-group messages. *Journal of Personality and Social Psychology, 58,* 812–822.

Manin, B. (1987). One legitimacy and political deliberation. *Political Theory, 15,* 338–368.

Mann, M. (2005) *The dark side of democracy.* Cambridge: Cambridge University Press.

Maoz, I., & Ellis, D. G. (2008). Intergroup communication as a predictor of Jewish-Israeli agreement with integrative solutions to the Israeli-Palestinian conflict: The mediating effects of out-group trust and guilt. *Journal of Communication, 58,* 490–507.

Marranci, G. (2007). Faith, language and identity: Muslim migrants in Scotland and Northern Ireland. In M. N. Craith (Ed.), *Language, power, and identity politics* (pp. 167–178). New York: Palgrave.

Mastro, D. (2003). A social identity approach to understanding the impact of television messages. *Communication Monographs, 70,* 98–113.

Mastro, D. (2009). Effects of racial and ethnic stereotyping. In J. Bryant & M. B. Oliver (Eds.), *Media effects: Advances in theory and research* (3rd ed., pp. 325–341). Mahwah, NJ: Erlbaum.

Mastro, D., Behm-Morawitz, E., & Kopacz, M. (2008). Exposure to TV portrayals of Latinos: The implications of aversive racism and social identity theory. *Human Communication Research, 34,* 1–27.

Mastro, D., Behm-Morawitz, E., & Ortiz, M. (2007). The cultivation of social perceptions of Latinos: A mental models approach. *Media Psychology, 9,* 1-19.

Mastro, D., Tamborini, R., & Hullett, C. (2005). Linking media to prototype activation and subsequent celebrity attraction: An application of self-categorization theory. *Communication Research, 32,* 323–348.

Mayr, E. (1961). Cause and effect in biology. *Science, 134,* 1501–1506.

McAndrew, F. T., Bell, E. K., & Garcia, C. M. (2007). Who do we tell and whom do we tell on? Gossip as a strategy for status enhancement. *Journal of Applied Social Psychology, 37,* 1562–1577.

McCormick, K. (2002). Code choices in the family, the neighborhood, the workplace. In K. McCormick (Ed.), *Language in Cape Town's District Six* (pp. 111–133). New York: Oxford University Press.

Melnick, M. J. (1993). Searching for sociability in the stands: A theory of sports spectating. *Journal of Sport Management, 7,* 44–60.

Merriam-Webster Dictionary (2008). Retrieved January 16, 2009 from http://www.merriam-webster.com/dictionary/bilingualism

Millward, L., Haslam, S. A., & Postmes, T. (2007). Putting employees in their place: The impact of hot desking on organizational and team identification. *Organization Science, 18,* 547–559.

Moghaddam, F. M. (2005). *Great ideas in psychology.* Oxford, UK: Oneworld.

Moghaddam, F. M. (2008). *Multiculturalism and intergroup relations.* Washington, DC: American

Psychological Association.

Moghaddam, F. M., Harré, R., & Lee, N. (2008), Positioning and conflict. In F. M. Moghaddam, R. Harré, & N. Lee (Eds.), *Global conflict resolution through positioning analysis* (pp. 3–20). New York: Springer.

Mojzes, P. (1994). *Yugoslavian inferno: Ethnoreligious warfare in the Balkans.* New York: Continuum.

Mojzes, P. (1998). The camouflaged role of religion in the war in Bosnia and Herzegovina. In P. Mojzes (Ed.), *Religion and the War in Bosnia* (pp. 74–98). Atlanta, GA: Scholars Press.

Molloy, J., & Giles, H. (2002). Communication, language, and law enforcement: An intergroup communication approach. In P. Glenn, C. LeBaron, & J. Mandelbaum (Eds.), *Studies in language and social interaction* (pp. 327–340). Mahwah, NJ: Erlbaum.

Morash, M., & Ford, J. K. (Eds.). (2002). *The move to community policing: Making change happen.* Thousand Oaks, CA: Sage.

Morr-Serewicz, M. C., Hosmer, R., Ballard, R. L. & Griffin, R. L. (2008). Disclosure from in-laws and the quality of in-law and marital relationships. *Communication Quarterly, 56,* 427–444.

Mortensen, M., & Hinds, P. J. (2001). Conflict and shared identity in geographically distributed teams. *The International Journal of Conflict Management, 12,* 212–238.

Mulac, A. (2006). The gender-linked language effect: Do language differences really make a difference? In K. Dinda & D. J. Canary (Eds.), *Sex differences and similarities in communication* (2nd ed., pp. 219–230). Mahwah, NJ: Lawrence Erlbaum.

Mulac, A., Bradac, J. J., & Gibbons, P. (2001). Empirical support for the gender-as-culture hypothesis: An intercultural analysis of male/female language differences. *Human Communication Research, 27,* 121–152.

Mullen, B. (2001). Ethnophaulisms for ethnic immigrant groups. *Journal of Social Issues, 57,* 457–475.

Mullen, B., Calogero, R. M., & Leader, T. I. (2007). A social psychological study of ethnonyms: Cognitive representation of the in-group and intergroup hostility. *Journal of Personality and Social Psychology, 92,* 612–630.

Mummendey, A., Kessler, T., Klink, A., & Mielke, R. (1999). Strategies to cope with negative social identity: Predictions by social identity theory and relative deprivation theory. *Journal of Personality and Social Psychology, 76,* 229–245.

Mummendey, A., & Wenzel, M. (1999). Social discrimination and tolerance in intergroup relations: Reactions to intergroup difference. *Personality and Social Psychology Review, 3,* 158–74.

Murray, R. K. (1955) *Red scare.* Minneapolis: University of Minnesota Press.

Myers, P., Giles, H., Reid, S. A., & Nabi, R. (2008). Law enforcement encounters: The effects of officer accommodativeness and crime severity on interpersonal attributions are mediated by intergroup sensitivity. *Communication Studies, 59,* 1–15.

Neisser, P. T. (2006). Political polarization as disagreement failure. *Journal of Public Deliberation, 2* (1), article 9. Retrieved May 12, 2009, from http://services.bepress.com/jpd/vol2/iss1/art9

Nettle, D., & Dunbar, R. I. M. (1997). Social markers and the evolution of reciprocal exchange. *Current Anthropology, 38,* 93–99.

Neuberg, S. L., Smith, D. M., & Asher, T. (2000). Why people stigmatize: Toward a biocultural framework. In T. F. Heatherton, R. E. Kleck, M. R. Hebl, & J. G. Hull (Eds.), *The social psychology of stigma* (pp. 31–61). New York: Guilford Press.

Ng, S. H. (1990). Androcentric coding of man and his in memory by language users. *Journal of Experimental Social Psychology, 26,* 455–464.

Noels, K. A., & Clément, R. (1996). Communicating across cultures: Social determinants and acculturative consequences, *Canadian Journal of Behavioral Science, 28,* 214–228.

Nortier, J., & Dorleijn, M. (2008). A Moroccan accent in Dutch: A sociocultural style restricted to the Moroccan community? *International Journal of Bilingualism, 12,* 125–142.

O'Brien, A. T., Haslam S. A., Jetten, J., Humphrey, L., O'Sullivan, L., Postmes, T., Eggins, R. A., & Reynolds, K. J. (2004). Cynicism and disengagement among devalued employee groups: The need to ASPIRe. *Career Development International, 9,* 28–44.

O'Brien, L., & Hummert, M. L. (2006). Age self-stereotyping, stereotype threat, and memory performance in late middle-aged adults. *Social Cognition, 24,* 338–358.

O'Duffy, B. (2008). Radical atmosphere: Explaining Jihadist radicalization in the UK. *PS: Political Science and Politics, 41,* 37–42.

Oakes, P. J. (1987). The salience of social categories. In J. C. Turner, M. A. Hogg, P. J. Oakes, S. D. Reicher, & M. S. Wetherell (Eds.), *Rediscovering the social group: A self-categorization theory* (pp. 117–141). Oxford, UK: Blackwell.

Oakes, P. J., Haslam, S. A., & Turner, J. C. (1994). *Stereotyping and social reality.* Oxford, UK: Blackwell.

Oberle, A. (2004). Coalition bring positive image to CA law enforcement. *PORAC Law Enforcement News, 36,* 26–27.

Ogbu, J. U. (1993). Differences in cultural frame of reference. *International Journal of Behavioral Development, 16,* 483–506.

Ortiz, M. & Harwood, J. (2007). A social cognitive theory approach to the effects of mediated intergroup contact on intergroup attitudes. *Journal of Broadcasting and Electronic Media, 51,* 615–631.

Overy, R. (2004) *The dictators.* London: Allen Lane.

Palomares, N. A. (2004). Gender schematicity, gender identity, salience, and gender-linked language use. *Human Communication Research, 30,* 556–588.

Palomares, N. A. (2008). Explaining gender-based language use: Effects of gender identity salience on references to emotion and tentative language in intra-and intergroup contexts. *Human Communication Research, 34,* 263–286.

Palomares, N. A. (2009). Women are sort of more tentative than men, aren't they? *Communication Research OnlineFirst,* published on April 15, 2009 as dol:10.1177/0093650209333034, accessed April 22, 2009.

Palomares, N. A. (in press). Gender-based language use: Understanding when, how, and why men and women communicate similarly and differently. In M. Hinner (Ed.), *The interrelationship of business and communication.* Frankfurt am Main, Germany: Peter Lang.

Palomares, N. A., & Lee, E (in press) Virtual gender identity: The linguistic assimilation to gendered avatars in computer-mediated communication. *Journal of Language and Social Psychology.*

Palomares, N. A., Reid, S. A., & Bradac, J. J. (2004). A self-categorization perspective on gender and communication: Reconciling the gender-as-culture and dominance explanations. In S. H. Ng, C. N. Candlin, & C. Y. Chiu (Eds.) *Language matters: Communication, identity, and culture* (pp. 85–109). Hong Kong: City University of Hong Kong Press.

Peal, E., & Lambert, W. E. (1962). The relation of bilingualism to intelligence. *Psychological Monographs, 76*, 1–23.

Peplau, L. A., & Beals, K. P. (2004). The family lives of lesbians and gay men. In A. Vangelisti (Ed.), *The handbook of family communication* (pp. 233–248). Mahwah, NJ: Erlbaum.

Perlmutter, D. (2000). *Policing the media.* Thousand Oaks, CA: Sage.

Pettigrew, T. (1998). Intergroup contact theory. *Annual Review of Psychology, 49*, 65–85.

Pettigrew, T. (2008). Future directions for intergroup contact theory and research. *International Journal of Intercultural Relations, 32*, 187–199.

Peukert, D. J. K. (1988) *Inside Nazi Germany: Conformity, opposition and racism in everyday life.* Harmondsworth: Penguin.

Pinizzotto, A. J., Davis, E. F., & Miller, C. E. (1997). *In the line of fire: A study of selected felonious assaults on law enforcement officers.* Washington, DC: US Dept. of Justice, Federal Bureau of Investigation: National Institute of Justice.

Polzer, J. T., Crisp, C. B., Jarvenpaa, S. L., & Kim, J. W. (2006). Extending the faultline model to geographically dispersed teams: How collocated subgroups can impair group functioning. *Academy of Management Journal, 49*, 679–692.

Postmes, T., & Spears, R. (2002). Behavior online: Does anonymous computer communication reduce gender inequality? *Personality and Social Psychology Bulletin, 28*, 1073–1083.

Postmes, T., Spears, R., & Lea, M. (1998). Breaching or building social boundaries? SIDE-effects of computer-mediated communication. *Communication Research, 25*, 689–715.

Postmes, T., Spears, R., & Lea, M. (2000). The formation of group norms in computer-mediated communication. *Human Communication Research, 26*, 341–371.

Postmes, T., Spears, R., & Lea, M. (2002). Inter-group differentiation in computer-mediated communication: Effects of depersonalization. *Group Dynamics, 6*, 3–16.

Pyszczynski, T., Solomon, S., & Greenberg, J. (2004). *In the wake of 9/11: The psychology of terror.* Washington, DC: American Psychological Association.

Ramakrishna, K. (2005). Deligitimizing global Jihadi ideology in Southeast Asia. *Contemporary Southeast Asia, 27*, 343–369.

Rees, L. (2005). *Auschwitz: The Nazis and the 'Final Solution'.* London: BBC Books.

Reicher, S. D. (1996a). Social identity and social change: Rethinking the context of social psychology. In W. P. Robinson (Ed.), *Social groups and identities: Developing the legacy of Henri Tajfel* (pp. 317–336). London: Butterworth.

Reicher, S. D. (1996b). 'The Battle of Westminster': Developing the social identity model of crowd behaviour in order to explain the initiation and development of collective conflict. *European Journal of Social Psychology, 26*, 115–34.

Reicher, S. D., & Haslam, S.A. (2006). Rethinking the psychology of tyranny: The BBC Prison Study. *British Journal of Social Psychology, 45*, 1–40.

Reicher, S.D., & Haslam, S.A. (in press). Beyond help: A social psychology of social solidarity and social cohesion. In M. Snyder & S. Sturmer (Eds.) *The psychology of helping.* Oxford, UK: Blackwell.

Reicher, S. D., & Hopkins, N. (2001). *Self and nation*. London: Sage.

Reicher, S. D., Hopkins, N., Levine, M., & Rath, R. (2006) Entrepreneurs of hate and entrepreneurs of solidarity: Social identity as a basis for mass communication. *International Review of the Red Cross, 87,* 621–637.

Reicher, S. D., Spears, R. & Haslam, S. A. (2009) The social identity approach in social psychology. In M. Wetherell & C. T. Mohanty (Eds.) *The Sage handbook of identities*. London: Sage.

Reicher, S. D., Spears, R., & Postmes, T. (1995). A social identity model of deindividuation phenomena. In W. Stroebe & M. Hewstone (Eds.), *European review of social psychology* (Vol. 6, pp. 161–198). Chichester, UK: Wiley & Sons.

Reid, S., & Giles, H. (Eds.). (2005). Intergroup relations: Its linguistic and communicative parameters. *Group Processes and Intergroup Relations, 8* (3).

Reid, S. A., Giles, H., & Abrams, J. R. (2004). A social identity model of media usage and effects. *Zeitschrift für Medienpsychologie, 16,* 17–25.

Reid, S. A., Keerie, N., & Palomares, N. A. (2003). Language, gender salience and social influence. *Journal of Language and Social Psychology, 22,* 210–233.

Reid, S. A., & Ng, S. H. (1999). Language, power, and intergroup relations. *Journal of Social Issues, 55,* 119–139.

Reid, S. A., & Ng. S. H. (2003). Identity, power, and strategic social categorizations: Theorizing the language of leadership. In D. van Knippenberg & M. A. Hogg (Eds.), *Leadership and power: Identity processes in groups and organizations* (pp. 210–223). New York: Psychology Press.

Reid, S. A., Palomares, N. A., Anderson, G. L., & Bondad-Brown, B. (in press). Gender, language, and social influence: A test of expectation states, role congruity, and self-categorization theories. *Human Communication Research*.

Richardson, J. (2005). Switching social identities: The influence of editorial framing on reader attitudes toward affirmative action and African Americans. *Communication Research, 32,* 503–528.

Richey, J. A. (2003). *Women in Alaska constructing the recovered self: A narrative approach to understanding long-term recovery from alcohol dependence and/or abuse*. Retrieved May 13, 2009, from Proquest Dissertations and Theses. (AAT 3108306)

Rittenour, C. E., & Soliz, J. (2009). Communicative and relational dimensions of shared family identity and relational intentions in mother-in-law/daughter-in-law relationships: Developing a conceptual model for mother-in-law/daughter-in-law research. *Western Journal of Communication, 73,* 67–90.

Robinson, W.P., & Giles, H. (Eds.). (2001). *The new handbook of language and social psychology*. Chichester and New York: Wiley & Sons.

Roccas, S., & Brewer, M. B. (2002). Social identity complexity. *Personality and Social Psychology Review, 6,* 88–106.

Roccas, S., Sagiv, L., Schwartz, S., Halevy, N., & Eidelson, R. (2008). Toward a unifying model of identification with groups: Integrating theoretical perspectives. *Personality and Social Psychology Review, 12,* 280–306.

Ronjat, J. (1913). *Le développement du langage observé chez un enfant bilingue*. [Language development in a bilingual child] Paris: Librairie Ancienne H. Champion.

Roosens, E. (1989). *Creating ethnicity*. London: Sage.

Rubenfeld, S., Clément, R., Vinograd, J., Lussier, D., Amireault, V., Lebrun, M., & Auger, R. (2007). Becoming a cultural intermediary: A further social corollary of second language mastery. *Journal of Language and Social Psychology, 26*, 182–203.

Rubin, M., & Hewstone, M. (2004). Social identity, system justification, and social dominance: Commentary on Reicher, Jost et al., and Sidanius et al. *Political Psychology, 25*, 823–844.

Ruscher, J. B. (2001). *Prejudiced communication*. New York: Guilford Press.

Russill, C. (2006). For a pragmatists perspective on publics: Advancing Carey's cultural studies through John Dewey . . . and Michel Foucault? In J. Packer & C. Robertson (Eds.), *Thinking with James Carey: Essays on communications, transportation, history* (pp. 57–78). New York: Peter Lang.

Ryan, E. B., & Capadano, H. L. (1978). Age perceptions and evaluative reactions toward adult speakers. *Journal of Gerontology, 33*, 98–102.

Ryan, E. B., Giles, H., Bartolucci, G., & Henwood, K. (1986). Psycholinguistic and social psychological components of communication by and with the elderly. *Language and Communication, 6*, 1–24.

Rymes, B. (1995). The construction of moral agency in the narratives of high-school drop-outs. *Discourse and Society, 6*, 495–516.

Sachdev, I., & Bourhis, R. Y. (2001). Multilingual communication. In W. P. Robinson & H. Giles (Eds.), *The new handbook of language and social psychology* (pp. 407–428). Chichester, UK: Wiley & Sons.

Sachdev, I., & Giles, H. (2004). Bilingual accommodation. In T. K. Bathia & W. Ritchie (Eds.), *Handbook of Bilingualism* (pp. 353–378). Oxford, UK: Blackwell.

Saguy, T., Dovidio, J.F., & Pratto, F. (2008). Beyond contact: Intergroup contact in the context of power relations. *Personality and Social Psychology Bulletin, 34*, 432-445.

Sapolsky, R. M. (2004). Social status and health in humans and other animals. *Annual Review of Anthropology, 33*, 393–418.

Sassenberg, K. (2002). Common bond and common identity groups on the Internet: Attachment and normative behavior in on-topic and off-topic chats. *Group Dynamics: Theory, Research, and Practice, 6*, 27–37.

Schaller, M., Simpson, J. A., & Kenrick, D. T. (Eds.). (2006). *Evolution and social psychology*. New York: Psychology Press.

Schbley, A. (2004). Religious terrorism, the media, and international Islamization terrorism: Justifying the unjustifiable. *Studies in Conflict and Terrorism, 27*, 207–233.

Scheepers, D., Spears, R., Doosje, B., & Manstead, A. S. R. (2003). Two functions of verbal intergroup discrimination: Identity and instrumental motives as a result of group identification and threat. *Personality and Social Psychology Bulletin, 29*, 568–577.

Schiappa, E., Gregg, P. B., & Hewes, D. E. (2005). The parasocial contact hypothesis. *Communication Monographs, 72*, 92–115.

Schmid, A. P. (2009). Handbook of terrorism research. London: Routledge.

Schuck, A. M., Rosenbaum, D. P., & Hawkins, D. F. (2008). The influence of race/ethnicity, social class, and neighborhood context on residents' attitudes toward the police. *Police Quarterly, 11*, 496–519.

Schulz, H. L. (2000). Identity conflicts and their resolution: The Oslo agreement and Palestinian national identities. In H. Wiberg & C. P. Scherrer (Eds.), *Ethnicity and intra-state conflict: Types, causes and peace strategies* (pp. 229–248). Aldershot, UK: Ashgate.

Scurr, R. (2006) *Fatal Purity*. London: Chatto & Windus.

Semin, G. R. (2008). Language puzzles: A prospective retrospective on the Linguistic Category Model. *Journal of Language and Social Psychology*, 27, 197–209.

Semin, G. R., & Fiedler, K. (1988). The cognitive functions of linguistic categories in describing persons: Social cognition and language. *Journal of Personality and Social Psychology*, 54, 558–568.

Sherif, M. (1966). *Group conflict and cooperation*. London: Routledge Kegan Paul.

Shinnar, R. (2008). Coping with negative social identity: The case of Mexican immigrants. *The Journal of Social Psychology, 148*, 553–575.

Shrum, L. J. (2002). Media consumption and perceptions of social reality: Effects and underlying processes. In J. Bryant & D. Zillmann (Eds.), *Media effects: Advances in theory and research* (2nd ed., pp. 69–96). Mahwah, New Jersey: Lawrence Erlbaum.

Shulman, J. L., & Clément, R. (2008). Expressing prejudice through the linguistic intergroup bias: Second language confidence and identity among minority group members. *Diversité Urbaine, 8*, 109–130.

Sidanius, J., & Pratto, F. (1999). *Social dominance: An intergroup theory of social hierarchy and oppression*. New York: Cambridge University Press.

Simon, H. (1983). *Models of bounded rationality*. Cambridge, MA: MIT Press.

Skutnabb-Kangas, T., & Phillipson, R. (2008). A human rights perspective on language ecology. In A. Creese, P. Martin, & N. H. Hornberger (Eds.) *Encyclopedia of language and education*, Vol. 9 (2nd ed., pp. 3–14). New York: Springer.

Smith, A. G. (2004). From words to action: Exploring the relationship between a group's value references and its likelihood of engaging in terrorism. *Studies in Conflict and Terrorism, 27*, 409–437.

Smith, A. G. (2008). The implicit motives of terrorist groups: How the needs for affiliation and power translate into death and destruction. *Political Psychology, 29*, 55–75.

Smith, T. W. (1987). That which we call welfare by any other name would smell sweeter: An analysis of the impact of question wording on response patterns. *Public Opinion Quarterly, 51*, 75–-83.

Soliz, J. (2008). Interethnic relationships in families. In W. Donsbach (Ed.), *International Encyclopedia of Communication* (Vol. 6, pp. 2358–2362). Oxford, UK: Wiley-Blackwell.

Soliz, J., & Harwood, J. (2006). Shared family identity, age salience, and intergroup contact: Investigation of the grandparent-grandchild relationship. *Communication Monographs, 73*, 87–107.

Soliz, J., Ribarsky, E., Harrigan, M., & Tye-Williams, S. (in press). Family communication with gay and lesbian family members: Implications for relational satisfaction and outgroup attitudes. *Communication Quarterly*.

Soliz, J., Thorson, A., & Rittenour, C. E. (2009). Communicative correlates of satisfaction, family identity, and group salience in multiracial/ethnic families. *Journal of Marriage and Family, 71*, 819-832.

Sontag, S. (2005). Introduction. In J. Hatzfeld (Ed.), *Machete season* (pp. vii-viii). New York: Picador.

Southgate, P. (1986). *Police-public encounters*. Home Office Research Study 90, London: Her Majesty's Stationery Office (HMSO).

Sparks, L. (Ed.). (2003). Cancer communication and aging. *Health Communication, 15*(2).

Sparks, L. (2005). Social identity and perceptions of terrorist groups: How others see them and how they see themselves. In H. D. O'Hair, R. L. Heath, & G. R Ledlow (Eds.), *Community preparedness and response to terrorism: Communication and terrorism* (pp. 13–28). Westport, CT: Praeger.

Sparks, L., & Harwood, J. (2008). Cancer, aging, and social identity: Development of an integrated model of social identity theory and health communication. In L. Sparks, H. D. O'Hair, & G. L. Kreps, (Eds.), *Cancer communication and aging* (pp. 77–95). Cresskill, NJ: Hampton.

Spears, R., & Lea, M. (1992). Social influence and the influence of the "social" in computer-mediated communication. In M. Lea (Ed.), *Contexts of computer-mediated communication* (pp. 30–65). London: Harvester-Wheatsheaf.

Stapel, D. A., & Semin, G. R. (2007). The magic spell of language: Linguistic categories and their perceptual consequences. *Journal of Personality and Social Psychology, 93*, 23–33.

Starace, F., & Sherr, L. (1998). Suicidal behaviors, euthanasia and AIDS. *AIDS, 12*, 339–347.

Steele, C. M., & Aronson, J. (1995). Stereotype threat and the intellectual test performance of African Americans. *Journal of Personality and Social Psychology, 69*, 797–811.

Stohl, M. (2006). The state as terrorist: Insights and implications. *Democracy and Security, 2*, 1–25.

Struch, N., & Schwartz, S. H. (1989). Intergroup aggression: Its predictors and distinctness from ingroup bias. *Journal of Personality and Social Psychology, 56*, 364–373.

Stürmer, S., & Simon, B. (2004). Collective action: Towards a dual-pathway model. *European Review of Social Psychology, 15*, 59–99.

Sunstein, C. (1999). Agreement without theory. In S. Macedo (Ed.), *Deliberative politics* (pp. 123–150). New York: Oxford University Press.

Sunstein, C. (2004). *Group judgments: Deliberation, statistical means, and information markets*. U Chicago Law & Economics, Olin Working Paper No. 219; U Chicago Public Law Working Paper No. 72. Retrieved July 7, 2008, from http://ssrn.com/abstract=578301

Sutton, R. M., Douglas, K. M. (2008). Celebrating two decades of linguistic bias research. *Journal of Language and Social Psychology, 27*, 2.

Sutton, R. M., & Farrall, S. D. (2008). Untangling the web: Deceptive responding in fear of crime research. In M. Lee & S. D. Farrall (Eds.), *Fear of crime: Critical voices in an age of anxiety* (pp. 108–124). London: Routledge.

Sutton, R. M., Douglas, K. M., Elder, T. J., & Tarrant, M. (2008). Social identity and social convention in responses to criticisms of groups. In Y. Kashima, K. Fiedler & P. Freytag (Eds.), *Stereotype dynamics: Language-based approaches to stereotype formation, maintenance, and transformation* (pp. 345–372). New York: Erlbaum.

Sutton, R. M., Elder, T. J., & Douglas, K. M. (2006). Reactions to internal and external criticism of outgroups: Social convention in the Intergroup Sensitivity Effect. *Personality and Social Psychology Bulletin, 32*, 563–575.

Syrkin, M. (Ed.). (1973). *Golda Meir speaks out*. London: Weidenfeld & Nicolson.

Tajfel, H. (Ed.). (1978), *Differentiation between social groups*. London: Academic Press.

Tajfel, H. (1969). Cognitive aspects of prejudice. *Journal of Social Issues, 25*, 79–97.

Tajfel, H. (1981). Social stereotypes and social groups. In J. C. Turner & H. Giles (Eds.), *Intergroup behavior* (pp. 144–167). Oxford, UK: Blackwell.

Tajfel, H., Billig, M. G., Bundy, R. P., & Flament, C. (1971). Social categorization and intergroup behavior. *European Journal of Social Psychology, 1*, 149–177.

Tajfel, H., & Turner, J. C. (1979). An integrative theory of intergroup conflict. In W. G. Austin & S. Worchel (Eds.), *The social psychology of intergroup relations* (pp. 33–47). Monterey, CA: Brooks/Cole.

Tajfel, H., & Turner, J. C. (1986). The social identity theory of intergroup behavior. In S. Worchel & G. Austin (Eds.), *Psychology of intergroup relations* (pp. 7–24). Chicago: Nelson-Hall.

Tam, T., Hewstone, M., Kenworthy, J., & Cairns, E. (2009). Intergroup trust in Northern Ireland. *Personality and Social Psychology Bulletin, 35*, 45–59.

Taylor, D. M., & McKirnan, D. J. (1984). A five stage model of intergroup relations. *British Journal of Social Psychology, 23*, 291–300.

Taylor, F. W. (1911). *Principles of scientific management.* New York: Harper.

Taylor, T., Turner, K., Esbensen, F., & Winfree, L. (2001). Coppin' an attitude: Attitudinal differences among juveniles toward police. *Journal of Criminal Justice, 29*, 295–305.

Terry, D. J., & O'Brien, A. T. (2001). Status, legitimacy and ingroup bias in the context of an organizational merger. *Group Processes and Intergroup Relations, 4*, 271–289.

Thompson, G. J. (1983). *Verbal judo: Words for street survival.* Springfield, IL: Charles C. Thomas.

Thurlow, C. (2005). Deconstructing adolescent communication. In A. Williams & C. Thurlow (Eds.), *Talking adolescence: Perspectives on communication in the teenage years* (pp. 1–20). New York: Peter Lang.

Todorov, T. (2004) *Hope and memory.* London: Atlantic Books.

Tooby, J., & Cosmides, L. (2005). Conceptual foundations of evolutionary psychology. In D. M. Buss (Ed.), *The handbook of evolutionary psychology* (pp. 5–67). Hoboken, NJ: John Wiley & Sons.

Trail, G. T., & James, J. D. (2001). The motivation scale for sport consumptions: Assessment of the scale's psychometric properties. *Journal of Sport Behavior, 24*, 108–127.

Turner, J. C. (1982). Towards a cognitive redefinition of the social group. In H. Tajfel (Ed.), *Social identity and intergroup relations* (pp. 15–40). Cambridge, UK: Cambridge University Press.

Turner, J. C. (1991). *Social influence.* Milton Keynes, UK: Open University Press.

Turner, J. C. (2006). Tyranny, freedom and social structure: Escaping our theoretical prisons. *British Journal of Social Psychology, 45*, 41–46.

Turner, J. C., Hogg, M. A., Oakes, P. J., Reicher, S. D., & Wetherell, M. S. (1987). *Rediscovering the social group: A self-categorisation theory.* Oxford, UK: Blackwell.

Tyler, T. R., & Huo, Y. (2002). *Trust in the law.* New York: Russell Sage.

Veenstra, K., Haslam, S. A., & Reynolds, K. J. (2004). The psychology of casualization: Evidence for the mediating roles of security, status and social identification. *British Journal of Social Psychology, 43*, 499–514.

Verkuyten, M. (2005). *The social psychology of ethnic identity.* Hove, UK: Psychology Press.

Verkuyten, M., & Zaremba, K. (2005). Interethnic relations in a changing political context. *Social*

Psychology Quarterly, 68, 375–386.

Vignoles, V. L., Regalia, C., Manzi, C., Golledge, J., & Scabini, E. (2006). Beyond self-esteem: Influence of multiple motives on identity construction. *Journal of Personality and Social Psychology, 90,* 308–333.

Villagrán, M. M., Fox, L., & O'Hair, H. D. (2007). Patient communication processes: An agency-identity model for cancer care. In D. O'Hair, G. L. Kreps, & L. Sparks (Eds.), *Handbook of communication and cancer care* (pp. 127–143). Cresskill, NJ: Hampton.

Wakefield, K. L., & Wann, D. L. (2006). An examination of dysfunctional sport fans: Method of classification and relationships with problem behaviors. *Journal of Leisure Research, 38,* 168–186.

Walter, E. V. (1969). *Terror and resistance.* Oxford, UK: Oxford University Press.

Walther, J. B. (1996). Computer-mediated communication: Impersonal, interpersonal, and hyperpersonal interaction. *Communication Research, 23,* 3–43.

Walther, J. B. (1997). Group and interpersonal effects in international computer-mediated collaboration. *Human Communication Research, 23,* 342–369.

Walther, J. B. (in press). Computer-mediated communication and virtual groups: Applications to interethnic conflict. *Journal of Applied Communication Research.*

Wang, Z., Walther, J. B., & Hancock, J. T. (2009). Social identification and interpersonal communication in computer-mediated communication: What you do versus who you are in virtual groups. *Human Communication Research, 35,* 59–85.

Wang, Z., Walther, J. B., Pingree, S., & Hawkins, R. (2008). Health information, credibility, homophily, and influence via the Internet: Web sites versus discussion groups. *Health Communication, 23,* 358–368.

Wann, D. L. (1995). Preliminary validation of the sport fan motivation scale. *Journal of Sport and Social Issues, 19,* 377–396.

Wann, D. L., & Grieve, F. G. (2005). Biased evaluations of in-group and out-group spectator behavior at sporting events: The importance of team identification and threats to social identity. *Journal of Social Psychology, 145,* 531–545.

White, M. P., Cohrs, J. C., & Göritz, A. S. (2008). The police officer's terrorist dilemma: Trust resilience following fatal errors. *European Journal of Social Psychology, 38,* 947–964.

White, W. J. (2008). The interlocutor's dilemma: The place of strategy in dialogic theory. *Communication Theory, 18,* 5–26.

Wigboldus, D., & Douglas, K. M. (2007). Language, stereotypes, and intergroup relations. In K. Fiedler (Ed.), *Social communication* (pp 79–106). New York: Psychology Press.

Williams, A., & Garrett, P. (2005). Intergroup perspectives on communication, age and intergenerational communication. In J. Harwood & H. Giles (Eds.), *Intergroup communication: Multiple perspectives* (pp. 93–115). New York: Peter Lang.

Williams, A., & Harwood, J. (2004). Intergenerational communication: Intergroup, accommodation, and family perspectives. In J. F. Nussbaum & J. Coupland (Eds.), *Handbook of communication and aging research* (pp.139–166). Mahwah, NJ: Erlbaum.

Williams, A., & Nussbaum, J. F. (2001). *Intergenerational communication across the life span.* Mahwah, NJ: Erlbaum.

Williams, C. C. (2008). Insight, stigma, and post-diagnosis identities in schizophrenia. *Psychiatry,*

71, 246–255.

Williams, J., & Giles, H. (1978). The changing status of women in society: An intergroup perspective. In H. Tajel (Ed.). *Differentiation between social groups* (pp. 431–446). London: Academic Press.

Williams, K. N., Herman, R., Gajewski, B., & Wilson, K. (2009). Elderspeak communication: Impact on dementia care. *American Journal of Alzheimer's Disease and Other Dementias, 24*, 11–20.

Wilson, D. S., Wilczynski, C., Wells, A., & Weiser, L. (2000). Gossip and other aspects of language as group-level adaptations. In C. Heyes & L. Huber (Eds.), *Cognition and evolution* (pp. 347–365). Cambridge, MA: MIT Press.

Wittes, T. C. (2005). Conclusion: Culture as an intervening variable. In T. C. Wittes (Ed.), *How Israelis and Palestinians negotiate* (pp. 133–148). Washington, DC: United States Institute of Peace.

Wohl, M. J. A., & Branscombe, N. R. (2008). Remembering historical victimization: Collective guilt for current ingroup transgressions. *Journal of Personality and Social Psychology, 94*, 988–1006.

Wolfsfeld, G. (1997). *Media and political conflict: News from the Middle East.* Cambridge, UK: Cambridge University Press.

Womack, M. M., & Finley, H. H. (1986). *Communication: A unique significance for law enforcement.* Springfield, IL: Charles C. Thomas.

Wright, K. B., Sparks, L., & O'Hair, H. D. (2008). *Health communication in the 21st century.* Oxford, UK: Blackwell.

Wyer, R. S., & Srull, T. K. (Eds.). (1984). *Handbook of social cognition* (Vols. 1–3). Hillsdale, NJ: Erlbaum.

Zillmann, D., & Paulus, P. (1993). Spectators: Reactions to sports events and effects on athletic competition. In R. Singer, M. Murphey, & L. Tennant (Eds.), *Handbook of research on sports psychology* (pp. 600–619). New York: Macmillan.

Contributors

Grace L. Anderson is currently a doctoral student in the Department of Communication at the University of California, Santa Barbara. Her research interests are indirect aggression, social identity, and intergroup relations.

Dale E. Brashers is David L. Swanson Professorial Scholar and Head of Communication at the University of Illinois, Urbana-Champaign. His research has been funded by the National Institutes of Health, including the National Institute of Nursing Research (NINR) and the National Institute of Mental Health. One recently completed NINR-funded study tested an uncertainty management intervention for people living with HIV. He is vice-chair of the Health Communication Division of the International Communication Association (ICA) and received the Golden Anniversary Monograph Award and the Health Communication Division Outstanding Article Awards from the National Communication Association, and the ICA Young Scholar Award.

Caleb T. Carr is a doctoral student in the Department of Telecommunication, Information Studies & Media at Michigan State University. His research interests include the intersections of organizational and interpersonal communication, implications of new media for self-presentation and impression formation, and how technologies facilitate interactions. His current research focuses on the use of Internet systems in employment screening and job seeking, intergroup cueing in social network systems, and how individuals exploit web-based information to support interpersonal conversations online. He has taught courses in organizational communication, public and presentational speaking, international business, and the history and economics of telecommunication.

Charles W. Choi is a doctoral student in the Department of Communication at University of California, Santa Barbara, and he received his master's degree from Louisiana State University. Prior to this, he earned a Bachelor's degree from Biola University in public relations and worked for several years in sales management and marketing. Currently his research focus is on the formation of ethnic identity among second-generation individuals born into immigrant families. Other areas of interest include intergroup contexts such as police-civilian dynamics and various facets of intercultural communication.

Richard Clément is Professor of Psychology at the University of Ottawa. His current research interests include issues related to bilingualism, second language acquisition and identity change and adjustment in the acculturative process, topics on which he has published in both French and English. In 2001, he was awarded the Otto Klineberg Intercultural and International Relations Prize by the Society for the Psychological Study of Social Issues. He is a Fellow of both the Canadian and the American Psychological Associations and was elected Fellow of the Royal Society of Canada in 2008.

Travis L. Dixon is Associate Professor of Communication at the University of Illinois at Urbana-Champaign. He is a media effects scholar dedicated to investigating the prevalence of stereotypes in the mass media and the impact of stereotypical imagery on audience members. Much of his work has been focused on racial stereotyping in television news. His most recent investigations examine the content and effects of stereotypes and counter-stereotypes in major news events, online news, and musical contexts.

John Drury is Senior Lecturer in Social Psychology at the University of Sussex. His main research interests focus on crowd behavior and dynamics—in particular, psychological change, as well the role of social identity in situations of mass emergency and crowding. He also studies power and ideology using critical discourse analysis. He has published over 40 papers and chapters in a range of international outlets. He serves on the editorial boards of the *British Journal of Social Psychology* and the *European Journal of Social Psychology*.

Donald G. Ellis is Professor of Communication in the School of Communication at the University of Hartford. His Ph.D. is from the University of Utah. He is the author of numerous books and articles including *Transforming Conflict: Communication and Ethnopolitical Conflict* published by Rowman and Littlefield. His work focuses on communication approaches to conflict resolution for ethnopolitical conflicts. These include dialogical and deliberative theories of decision making. Dr. Ellis has held various fellowships and was a Fulbright Scholar in Israel during the 2004–2005 academic year.

Howard Giles is Professor of Communication at the University of California, Santa Barbara and previously Professor of Social Psychology as well as Head of Psychology at the University of Bristol, England. He is current and Founding Editor and Co-Editor of the *Journal of Language & Social Psychology* and the *Journal of Asian Pacific Communication* as well as past President of the International Communication Association and the International Association of Language and Social Psychology. His research explores very different areas of applied intergroup communication research and theory, with a focus on intergenerational communication and aging across cultures and, more recently, police-civilian relations.

Paul M. Haridakis is Associate Professor in the School of Communication Studies at Kent State University. His research interests include media use and effects, new communication technologies, freedom of speech, sports communication, and media history. He is a co-author of *Communication Research: Strategies and Sources* (7th ed.). (Wadsworth Cengage Learning). He is co-editor of *Sports Mania: Essays on Fandom and the Media in the 21st Century*. McFarland & Co., Inc.

Jake Harwood is Professor of Communication at the University of Arizona. He is author of *Understanding Communication and Aging* (Sage, 2007) and co-editor of *Intergroup Communication: Multiple Perspectives* (Peter Lang, 2005). His recent publications have appeared in *Personality and Social Psychology Bulletin, Journal of Communication*, and *Communication Monographs*. He was editor of *Human Communication Research* from 2006–2009. In 2004, he was the recipient of the National Communication Association's Giles/Nussbaum Distinguished Scholar Award for outstanding teaching, scholarship, and service to the field of communication and aging.

S. Alexander Haslam is Professor of Social and Organizational Psychology at the University of Exeter. He is former Editor of the *European Journal of Social Psychology*, and currently on the editorial board of 10 international journals including *Scientific American Mind*. His work with colleagues focuses on the study of social identity in social and organizational contexts, illustrated by his most recent book *Psychology in Organizations: The Social Identity Approach* (2nd Ed., Sage, 2004). He is a Fellow of the Canadian Institute of Advanced Research and a former recipient of EASP's Kurt Lewin award.

Mary Lee Hummert is Vice Provost for Faculty Development and Professor of Communication Studies at the University of Kansas. She studies the social cognitive processes linking age stereotypes and communication. Her research has been supported with funding from the National Institute on Aging/NIH. She has published extensively in communication, psychology, and gerontology journals, and is the co-editor of two books on aging, communication, and health. Professor Hummert is a Fellow of the Gerontological Society of America and a Giles-Nussbaum Distinguished Scholar in Communication and Aging.

Pamela Kalbfleisch is Professor of Communication and of Psychology at the University of North Dakota. She is an American Council on Education Fellow. Her research examines issues of trust and distrust and includes the study of communication in mentoring relationships and health care environments as well as the study of deceptive communication, gender, and culture. She is the co-editor of *Gender, Power, and Communication in Human Relationships* with Michael Cody, and the author of *Interpersonal Communication; Evolving Interpersonal Relationships* both published by Lawrence Erlbaum Associates. She is the founding editor of the *Journal of Native Aging and Health* and the editor of three volumes in the *Communication Yearbook* series.

Jason Klocek received his B.A. in Psychology from the University of Notre Dame in 2003 and his M.A. in Conflict Resolution from Georgetown University in 2009. He is presently a Ph.D. candidate in the Department of Political Science at the University of California, Berkeley. His primary research interests focus on the role of religion in global politics, specifically the role of religious actors in the politics of transitional justice.

Michael King is a doctoral student in the Psychology Department at McGill University, Montreal. His research focuses on intergroup conflict and terrorism. In particular, he is looking to identify the factors that contribute to the psychological legitimization of violence. In the laboratory, he conducts controlled role-playing scenarios manipulating variables that are thought to justify violence. In the field, he collects the narratives of people who engage in terrorism, and their families, in hopes of understanding the social influences involved. His recent field work is done in collaboration with Demos, a British think-tank, investigating the links between violent and non-violent extremism.

Dana Mastro is Associate Professor and the Director of Graduate Studies in the Department of Communication at the University of Arizona. She received her Ph.D. in Communication from Michigan State University, her M.A. in Communication-Urban Studies from Michigan State, and her B.A. in History from UCLA. Her research investigates the role of the media in processes of stereotype formation and application. More specifically, her work documents depictions of Latinos on English- and Spanish-language television and assesses the extent to which exposure to these images influences stereotyping and racial/ethnic cognitions as well as a variety of intergroup and identity-based outcomes.

Fathali M. Moghaddam is Professor, Department of Psychology, and Director of the Conflict Resolution Program, Department of Government, Georgetown University, and Senior Fellow at the Center on Policy, Education and Research on Terrorism. Dr. Moghaddam's most recent books include *Multiculturalism and Intergroup Relations* (2008, APA Press) and *How Globalization Spurs Terrorism* (2008, Praeger); his forthcoming book is *The New Global Security* (2010).

Thomas Morton is Senior Lecturer in Social Psychology at the University of Exeter. His research interests include group processes and intergroup relations, prejudice and stereotyping, stigma and minority identity, language and communication. His work is published in leading social psychology and communication journals, including *Journal of Personality and Social Psychology*, *Personality and Social Psychology Bulletin*, and *Communication Research*. He also serves on the editorial boards of the *British Journal of Social Psychology*, *European Journal of Social Psychology*, and Social *Psychological and Personality Science*.

Paul D. Myers is a doctoral candidate at the University of California, Santa Barbara. Paul's research focuses on persuasion and attitudinal change, specifically as it relates to counter-terrorism and law-enforcement, and has been published in academic and professional journals. He previously served as a police constable with London's Metropolitan Police Service where he worked on IRA counter-terrorism patrols with Operation Rainbow. Paul is currently a subject matter expert for government and private sector groups and he advises law enforcement on counter-terrorism strategies.

Cristina Novoa received her bachelor's degree in Psychology from Yale University in 2006. She is currently a doctoral candidate in Georgetown University's Human Development and Public Policy program. Her research focuses on diversity in intergroup relations from perspectives in psychology and policy-making.

Kim Peters is a Research Fellow in Social and Organizational Psychology at the University of Exeter. Her research focuses on the social structural implications (including identity formation, leadership and collective action) of communication and emotion processes in social and organizational settings. Her work has been published in leading social psychological journals, including *Journal of Personality and Social Psychology* and *European Journal of Social Psychology* and she serves on the editorial board of the *European Journal of Social Psychology*.

Stephen Reicher is Professor of Psychology at the University of St Andrews. He is a Fellow of the Royal Society of Edinburgh, a past Editor of the *British Journal of Social Psychology* and a Scientific Advisor to *Scientific American Mind*. His interest lies in the relationship between social identity and collective action, and he has studied such topics as crowd behavior, political rhetoric and mass social influence, national identity and, latterly, the psychology of tyranny.

Scott Reid is Associate Professor in the Department of Communication at the University of California, Santa Barbara. His research interests are in social identity and intergroup relations.

Lance S. Rintamaki is Assistant Professor in the Departments of Communication and Health Behavior at the State University of New York at Buffalo. He received his Ph.D. from the University of Illinois at Urbana-Champaign and completed a post-doctoral fellowship in general internal medicine through the

Feinberg School of Medicine at Northwestern University. His current research examines stigma in the context of provider-patient communication as well as the role of stigma management in patient health behavior outcomes.

Sara Rubenfeld recently completed her Ph.D. at the University of Ottawa under the supervision of Dr. Richard Clément. Her dissertation investigated the role of second language learning in the use of anti-discriminatory behaviours. Prior to this, Sara completed a Bachelor of Arts (Honours) at the University of Winnipeg. Her research interests are integration, intercultural mediation, second language learning, and intercultural communication.

Jessica Shulman is a doctoral student in psychology at the University of Ottawa. She has been a member of the Cross-Cultural Communication Laboratory since 2005. Her research interests are grounded in language and social psychology. Her doctoral research investigates the extent to which subtle linguistic bias is communicated within a bilingual (i.e., Francophone-Anglophone) context and examines the role of ethnolinguistic and identity factors in influencing either the maintenance or mitigation of linguistic prejudice.

Jordan Soliz is Assistant Professor in the Department of Communication Studies at the University of Nebraska-Lincoln. His research focuses on communication and intergroup processes in family and personal relationships, with an emphasis on grandparent-grandchild relationships, multiethnic families, and step-family relationships. His work has appeared in edited volumes and has been published in journals such as *Communication Monographs, Journal of Applied Communication Research, Journal of Family Communication, Journal of Marriage and Family,* and *Western Journal of Communication.* He has served or currently serves on the editorial boards of *Communication Reports, Communication Research Reports,* and *Communication Quarterly.*

Lisa Sparks is Professor and Presidential Research Fellow of Health and Risk Communication at Chapman University in Orange, California, where she serves as Director of Graduate Studies, a Full Member of the Chao Family/NCI Designated Comprehensive Cancer Center, and Adjunct Professor at University of California, Irvine. Dr. Sparks is a teacher-scholar whose published work spans more than 100 research articles and scholarly book chapters and is the author and editor of more than ten books in the areas of communication, health, and aging with a distinct focus on cancer communication science.

Michael Stohl is Professor of the Department of Communication at the University of California, Santa Barbara. His research and teaching focus on political and organizational communication and global relations with special reference to political violence, terrorism, and human rights. He was a member of the Search for Common Ground sponsored United States-Soviet Union Task Force on International Terrorism which met in Moscow and Santa Monica in January and

September 1989. In 2005, he was an invited expert at the Club of Madrid International Summit on Democracy, Terrorism and Security. In 2008, his article, co-authored with Cynthia Stohl, "Networks of Terror," published in *Communication Theory* in May 2007 was awarded Outstanding Article of the Year by the International Communication Association.

Robbie M. Sutton is Senior Lecturer in Psychology at the University of Kent. He is a social psychologist with interests in strategic and normative aspects of communication and social cognition. He has published in leading social psychological journals, including *Journal of Personality and Social Psychology, Journal of Experimental Social Psychology, Personality and Social Psychology Bulletin, British Journal of Social Psychology, European Journal of Social Psychology*, and *Journal of Language and Social Psychology*. He serves on the editorial boards of the latter three journals.

Donald M. Taylor is Professor of Psychology at McGill University, Montreal. He has published both scientific articles, and books arising from projects in a variety of cultural settings including South Africa, Indonesia, the Philippines, India and the United States. By far his longest-term research and teaching commitment has been with Aboriginal peoples with a special focus on the Inuit of Arctic Quebec (Nunavik). His most recent book is entitled *The Quest for Identity* and is published by Praeger.

Esther Usborne is a senior doctoral student in the Department of Psychology at McGill University, Montreal. Her doctoral research explores the importance of cultural identity clarity for the self and for psychological well-being. Esther is also involved in ongoing research projects focusing on the importance of heritage language instruction for Inuit children in Northern Canada and on parental involvement in schools in Inuit communities. Among her scientific papers are recent articles addressing the motivation and well-being of Montreal street youth, and the transfer of language skills from Inuktitut to English or French among Inuit students.

Melinda M. Villagrán is Associate Professor of Communication and Director of the MA in Communication at George Mason University, Fairfax, VA. Her research investigates the interplay between cognition and communication in health care contexts. She earned her Ph.D. from the University of Oklahoma and was previously on faculty at the University of Texas Health Science Center Medical School, where she was part of a NCI-funded project on cancer communication among Latinos. Currently, she is conducting funded research on medication adherence. She has authored dozens of books, journal articles, and instructional materials on communication topics.

Maykel Verkuyten is a Professor in the Department of Interdisciplinary Social Science at Utrecht University in the Netherlands. He is also the academic director of the European Research Centre on Migration and Ethnic Relations (ERCOM-

ER) at the same university. By training he is a social psychologist and an anthropologist. His research interest is in ethnic identity and interethnic relations and he has published several books and many articles in a variety of social scientific journals. His most recent book is entitled *The Social Psychology of Ethnic Identity* (Psychology Press, 2005).

Joseph B. Walther is a Professor in the Department of Communication and the Department of Telecommunication, Information Studies & Media at Michigan State University. He has previously held appointments in Psychology, Information Technology, and Education and Social Policy at universities in the US and England. His research focuses on the social dynamics of Internet communication in personal relationships, virtual groups, and social support, and in educational and organizational settings. He has been chair of the Organizational Communication and Information Systems division of the Academy of Management, and the Communication and Technology division of the International Communication Association.

Jinguang Zhang is currently a doctoral student in the Department of Communication at the University of California, Santa Barbara. He is interested in human communicative behaviors and various kinds of social perceptions in media environments from an intergroup perspective.

Index

About the Authors

Howard Giles is Professor of Communication at the University of California, Santa Barbara and was previously Professor of Social Psychology as well as Head of Psychology at the University of Bristol, England. He is current and founding Editor and Co-Editor of the *Journal of Language & Social Psychology* and the *Journal of Asian Pacific Communication* as well as past President of the International Communication Association and the International Association of Language and Social Psychology. His research explores very different areas of applied intergroup communication research and theory, with a focus on intergenerational communication and aging across cultures and, more recently, police-civilian relations.

Scott Reid is Associate Professor in the Department of Communication at the University of California, Santa Barbara. His research interests are in social identity, group processes, and intergroup relations. He has published empirical and theoretical work on leadership, status hierarchy formation in small groups, power, media uses and perceptions, and social influence.

Jake Harwood is Professor of Communication at the University of Arizona. He is author of *Understanding Communication and Aging* (2007) and co-editor of *Intergroup Communication: Multiple Perspectives* (Peter Lang, 2005). His recent publications have appeared in *Personality and Social Psychology Bulletin, Journal of Communication,* and *Communication Monographs.* He was editor of *Human Communication Research from 2006–2009.* In 2004, he was the recipient of the National Communication Association's Giles/Nussbaum Distinguished Scholar Award for outstanding teaching, scholarship, and service to the field of communication and aging.

Language as SOCIAL ACTION ▶

Howard Giles,
GENERAL EDITOR

This series explores new and exciting advances in the ways in which language both reflects and fashions social reality—and thereby constitutes critical means of social action. As well as these being central foci in face-to-face interactions across different cultures, they also assume significance in the ways that language functions in the mass media, new technologies, organizations, and social institutions. Language as Social Action does not uphold apartheid against any particular methodological and/or ideological position, but, rather, promotes (wherever possible) cross-fertilization of ideas and empirical data across the many, all-too-contrastive, social scientific approaches to language and communication. Contributors to the series will also accord due attention to the historical, political, and economic forces that contextually bound the ways in which language patterns are analyzed, produced, and received. The series will also provide an important platform for theory-driven works that have profound, and often times provocative, implications for social policy.

For further information about the series and submitting manuscripts, please contact:

Howard Giles
Dept of Communication
University of California at Santa Barbara
Santa Barbara, CA 93106-4020
HowieGiles@aol.com

To order other books in this series, please contact our Customer Service Department at:

(800) 770-LANG (within the U.S.)
(212) 647-7706 (outside the U.S.)
(212) 647-7707 FAX

Or browse online by series at:

www.peterlang.com